E   Studies in English Literature

The Theory and Analysis of Drama

Manfred Pfister's book is the first to provide a coherent and comprehensive framework for the analysis of plays in all their dramatic and theatrical dimensions. The material on which his analysis is based covers all genres and periods of drama, from Greek tragedy and comedy to the contemporary theatre, with the plays of Shakespeare providing a special focus. His approach is not historical but systematic, combining more abstract categorisations with detailed and concrete interpretations of specific sample texts. An extensive international bibliography of relevant theatre and drama studies further enhances the practical value of the book.

Since its first German publication this volume has established itself in German-speaking countries as a standard work of dramatic theory. Dr John Halliday's translation, based on the fifth and latest edition, makes Professor Pfister's research available for the first time in English.

European Studies in English Literature

SERIES EDITORS
Ulrich Broich, Professor of English, University of Munich
Herbert Grabes, Professor of English, University of Giessen
Dieter Mehl, Professor of English, University of Bonn

Roger Asselineau, Professor Emeritus of American Literature, University of
    Paris-Sorbonne
Paul-Gabriel Boucé, Professor of English, University of Sorbonne-Nouvelle
Robert Ellrodt, Professor of English, University of Sorbonne-Nouvelle
Sylvère Monod, Professor Emeritus of English, University of Sorbonne-Nouvelle

This series is devoted to publishing translations into English of the best works
written in European languages on English and American literature. These may be
first-rate books recently published in their original versions, or they may be classic
studies which have influenced the course of scholarship in their field while never
having been available in English before.

To begin with, the series has concentrated on works translated from the German; but its range will expand to cover other languages.

TRANSLATIONS PUBLISHED
Walter Pater: The Aesthetic Moment by Wolfgang Iser
*The Symbolist Tradition in English Literature: A Study of Pre-Raphaelitism and
    'Fin de Siècle'* by Lothar Hönnighausen
The Theory and Analysis of Drama by Manfred Pfister
Oscar Wilde: The Works of a Conformist Rebel by Norbert Kohl
The Fall of Women in Early English Narrative Verse by Götz Schmitz
The Rise of the English Street Ballad 1550–1650 by Natascha Würzbach
The Eighteenth-Century Mock Heroic Poem by Ulrich Broich
Romantic Verse Narrative: The History of a Genre by Hermann Fischer
The Middle English Mystery Play: A Study in Dramatic Speech and Form by
    Hans-Jürgen Diller
*Shakespeare's Festive World: Elizabethan Seasonal Entertainment and the
    Professional Stage* by François Laroque

UNDER CONTRACT FOR TRANSLATION
L'Etre et l'avoir dans les romans de Charles Dickens by Anny Sadrin

The Theory and Analysis of Drama

Manfred Pfister
Professor of English, University of Passau

translated from the German by John Halliday

CAMBRIDGE
UNIVERSITY PRESS

Published by the Press Syndicate of the University of Cambridge
The Pitt Building, Trumpington Street, Cambridge CB2 1RP
40 West 20th Street, New York, NY 10011–4211, USA
10 Stamford Road, Oakleigh, Melbourne 3166, Australia

Originally published in German as *Das Drama*
by Wilhelm Fink Verlag, Munich 1977
and © Wilhelm Fink Verlag
First published in English by Cambridge University Press 1988 as
The Theory and Analysis of Drama

English translation © Cambridge University Press 1988
Reprinted 1991
First paperback edition 1991
Reprinted 1993

British Library cataloguing in publication data
Pfister, Manfred
The theory and analysis of drama. – (European
studies in English literature).
1. Drama – History and criticism
I. Title   II. Series   III. Das Drama. *English*
809.2   PN1721

Library of Congress cataloguing in publication data
Pfister, Manfred
[Drama, English]
The theory and analysis of drama / Manfred Pfister: translated
from the German by John Halliday.
p.   cm. – (European studies in English literature)
Translation of: Das Drama. 5th ed. 1982.
Bibliography.
Includes index.
ISBN 0 521 32060 7
1. Drama.   I. Title.   II. Series.
PN1631.P513   1988
801'.952 – dc 19   87–33396   CIP

ISBN 0 521 32060 7 hardback
ISBN 0 521 42383 X paperback

Transferred to digital printing 2000

FP

Wenn man nur endlich aufhören wollte,
vom Drama im allgemeinen zu sprechen.

(If only people would at last refrain
from speaking of drama in general terms.)

Contents

Preface

In one sense, the quotation from Hugo von Hofmannsthal's *Unterhaltung über den 'Tasso' von Goethe*[1] that I have chosen as a motto for the beginning of this book can be interpreted as a critical attack on it. For cannot the objection raised by the 'poet' in the *Unterhaltung*, that any attempts to talk about drama in general terms are bound to fail miserably in the face of specific plays by dramatists such as Goethe or Shakespeare, also be levelled against this book, whose title states quite categorically that it is supposed to be a general theory of drama? In its defence, though, it is fair to say that Hofmannsthal was directing his ire not at those who like to discuss drama in more general terms but at those who make unashamedly sweeping statements as to what drama should be. In this sense, then, I do not feel that this objection can apply to the present study because, although my intention has been to establish a systematic general theory, I have tried to avoid falling into the trap of making normative and prescriptive value judgements. Furthermore, my interest has not been in drawing up a comprehensive definition of drama as a whole but in putting together a detailed and sophisticated description of its structures and textualisation processes.

The underlying aim of this introductory study is therefore not, in the first instance, to be scientifically or theoretically innovative but rather to integrate what is already known into some sort of comprehensive system and to make it more accessible to readers by inserting bibliographical references at the appropriate places. At the same time, though, I hope that the considerable influence exerted by communication theory and structuralist ideas on this system will also stimulate the specialist into renewed reflection on a systematic poetics of drama. Nonetheless, my plan to write this book with a particular readership in mind and to provide an introduction to practical analysis meant that I was obliged to abandon the idea of substantiating my own efforts methodologically or theoretically and of situating them within the context of the unabating methodological debate. In the context of this book I consider it to be far more important to develop the most coherent, systematic and workable sort of metalanguage possible for analysing and describing dramatic texts rather than indulging in the construction of various metatheories.

Since this book is intended to be a more general introduction, I also felt I had to exclude a systematic analysis of the specific problems associated with tragedy, comedy and tragi-comedy, and also the historical approach to drama together with its various genres and subgenres, in favour of a study of the universal structures and textualisation processes in the dramatic mode. An introduction to the analysis of drama cannot also be a history of drama, but it can prepare the ground for such a history if its descriptive models are accessible to the literary historian in such a way that he or she is then able to grasp and describe the diachronic relations that link the various structures and functions in a dramatic text. Of course, this does not mean that I have not tried to integrate specific historical texts or structural transformations into this analysis, but when I did so I was hoping to demonstrate their exemplary quality as structural models rather than just provide a number of unconnected historical analyses of individual plays. The wide typological and historical variety of the dramatic texts that form the basis of the present study was intended both to demonstrate the universal applicability of the theoretical models I have employed and also to illustrate the breadth of variation in the ways the individual structures and textualisation processes are realised. However, this variability is predominantly described from a typological and systematic rather than from a historical and diachronic perspective.

One further limitation is the fact that it has been possible to do no more than outline the problems associated with the communicative functions of drama in society as a whole – these begin with the questions as to the anthropological origins of drama and its connections with ritual,[2] but they are also a dominant feature of the contemporary discussion of the role and place of theatre in society – either in its systematic context or its historical development (see below, 2.4.). This is because I felt I should concentrate on the structures that exist *within* a dramatic text. And even here I was obliged to exclude a number of aspects that are not specific to dramatic texts, such as the analysis of stylistic texture, metrical and rhythmic form and the deep structure of the 'story' presented. Instead, I decided to concentrate on the structures of stage-design associated with particular plays (chapter 2), the multimedial transmission of information (chapter 3), the presentation of figure and story (chapters 5 and 6), monological and dialogical communication (chapter 4) and the structures of time and space (chapter 7). However, within the framework of our introductory study, much of this has had to remain sketchy and, because of the state of current research, rather tentative.

The primary texts that I selected as specific illustrations of the various structural types were chosen from the corpus of all existing dramatic texts, but the criteria affecting their selection did not always seem entirely consistent. I was concerned, on the one hand, to assemble a supranational sample with the broadest possible historical and typological base – stretching from the tragedies of ancient Greece to the experiments of the contemporary avant-garde – and in doing so I tried to restrict myself to the most representative works. On the other hand, my freedom of choice was hampered by the extent of my by no means encyclopaedic familiarity with world dramatic literature. If I have repeatedly had to have recourse to the works of Shakespeare, then this does not merely reflect my own interests but is also determined by the hope that these are the plays most likely to be familiar to a wide circle of readers.

The detailed and analytical table of contents – a close-knit framework for dividing up the various sections according to their positions in the structural hierarchy – and the index of names are intended to assist the reader and to make it easier for him or her to look things up later on. This is also the reason for the numerous cross-references integrated into the text which, together with the analytical table of contents, rendered a subject-index unnecessary.

After all these preliminaries, I should now like to express my thanks to those who not only made it possible for me to work on this book but also positively encouraged me to do so. My most profound gratitude must go to my much-respected teacher, Professor Wolfgang Clemen, in whose seminars on Shakespeare I first learnt how dramas should be read. I should also like to thank the students who participated in my own seminars on drama and with whom I tested, discussed and developed many of the ideas that ended up in this book. Their constructive criticism enabled me to correct those aspects of it that were too vague, ambiguous, or one-sided. To name them all is impossible, but those concerned will no doubt recognise the passages I am referring to.

Last, but by no means least, Professor Ernest Schanzer, a close friend and highly esteemed philologist who dedicated the last ounces of his working energy to criticising and improving this book, and who can no longer receive my thanks. It is therefore to his memory that I should like to dedicate this book.

Translator's note

Unless otherwise indicated, the translations of passages from works by non-anglophone authors are my own. Source-editions for English translations other than my own are given in section II of the bibliography.

A note on the English edition

This book was first published in Germany more than a decade ago. At that time, in 1977, it was a pioneering work in its attempt to bridge the gap between drama and theatre studies and to devise a model for a coordinated analysis of the various levels of verbal and non-verbal communication in a dramatic text performed on stage. It soon became a standard work on the subject in university courses all over Germany, where its impact has been felt in almost all relevant studies published since then. Its continued success in German-speaking countries – the English translation coincides with the fifth edition of the German original – and the positive response from many colleagues and students encouraged me to prepare this version for a wider readership abroad.

This new readership has prompted several changes. Many passages which draw upon rather remote samples of German drama have had to be discarded or, more often than not, to be replaced by more accessible English examples, and many references to less important or by now out-dated German academic studies have had to be omitted. On the other hand, the new upsurge in theatre semiotics both in- and outside Germany over the last decade has changed the critical climate so decisively that some of my original points have had to be reconsidered or at least rephrased. The most important contributions to this exciting and stimulating, even if at times technically cluttered, discipline have been included in the updated bibliography and integrated into the footnotes; a full-scale semiotic revision of my book, on the other hand, would have made it too unwieldy for the average reader looking for practical analysis rather than self-conscious theorising. I am still happy for it only to be generally sympathetic towards a semiotic approach, rather than going the whole technical way.

Finally, the translation of this book did not just involve translating from German into English, but meant the reworking of a Continental structuralist discourse into the terminologically less standardised idiom of English criticism. This is an extremely difficult and unrewarding task, and I am deeply grateful to my friend and translator Dr John Halliday for having undertaken it. He has grappled bravely with my knotty prose and has gone a long way towards de-teutonising it. Next to him, my gratitude is due to Iris Hunter, who has copy-edited the book with painstaking precision and admirable perseverance.

1. Drama and the dramatic

1.1. A critical summary of existing theories

1.1.1. The continuing influence of normative and deductive theories of drama

Our efforts to put forward a descriptive and communicative poetics for a historically and typologically extremely diverse corpus of dramatic texts have not been greatly assisted by previous theoretical discussions of the dramatic genre, which all tend to elevate a historically specific form to an absolute norm, thereby narrowing the concept of 'drama' in a most decisive way.[1] This was already true of Aristotle's theory of drama. Although he derived his theoretical categories epagogically from the text corpus of Greek tragedies and although it was not his intention to establish a norm, his description of drama as the 'imitation of an action' in speech, involving closed structures of time and space and a particular set of characters, not to mention his concepts of catharsis and hamartia, have, since the Renaissance at least, been considered as the norm for dramatic texts.[2] The same is true of the dramatic theories of the nineteenth and early twentieth centuries, which, based on the classical tragedy, European Renaissance drama and the plays of German and French classicism, identified conflict as the essence of the dramatic (G. W. F. Hegel, F. Brunetière, W. Archer *et alii*). Others used Hegel's subject–object dialectic as a point of departure to define drama as a synthesis of epic objectivity and lyric subjectivity (G. W. F. Hegel, F. W. Schelling, F. Th. Vischer *et alii*) and allocated to it the temporal dimension of future (Jean Paul, F. Th. Vischer, G. Freytag *et alii*) or the distinctive quality of suspense (E. Staiger).

This deductive and historically one-sided way of thinking in triadic generic systems continues to exert considerable influence on academic teaching and research. The epigonic and normative poetic theories of drama that have resulted from this have been undermined by a number of influential dramaturgical experiments in the course of the twentieth century (such as the Bauhaus notion of abstract theatre, Antonin Artaud's 'theatre of cruelty', Brecht's epic theatre, the 'theatre of the absurd', the multifarious forms of street-theatre and happenings, the experimental dramas of Peter Handke or Robert Wilson) and by the increased interest in

1

historically varied and even non-European theatrical traditions[3] to such an extent that they can only be taken seriously if one chooses to ignore these phenomena.

1.1.2. The structuralist deficit

The continuing influence of this normative and deductive tradition on contemporary research is all the more detrimental in that it has only recently been compensated for by a few initial attempts to put forward a descriptive, structuralist theory of dramatic texts, such as those that have already been applied to narrative and lyric texts. The reasons for this are both scholastic and methodological.

First, the multimedial unity of the dramatic text was disrupted by the institutionalised separation of research into literary and theatre studies. The consequence of this was a strong bias towards either the printed page or its presentation on stage. Secondly, important new developments in literary analysis, such as Russian formalism and New Criticism, with their preoccupation with language theory, have neglected a genre whose expressive qualities are not exclusively verbal – namely drama.[4]

There has been decisive progress in two other areas, however: first, in historical poetics, which has counteracted the prevailing tendency to define particular historical forms as normative absolutes, and secondly, in semiotic analysis, which interprets the dramatic text as a complex verbal, visual and acoustic supersign activating various sociocultural codes.[5] We have attempted, therefore, to integrate the results reached in these areas into the present study.

1.2. Dramatic speech situation and dialogue

1.2.1. Narrative versus dramatic speech

Of the qualities that enable us to distinguish narrative from dramatic texts, one of the historically most consistent may be defined on the level of the 'speech situation'[6] as the communicative relationship between author and receiver. The beginnings of a text typology of this kind may be found in the third book of Plato's *Republic*, which draws a distinction between 'report' and 'representation' according to whether the poet is speaking himself, or whether it is the characters who are allowed to speak. From this 'speech criterion' he is then able to propose the following method of classification, namely,

that there is one kind of poetry and tale-telling which works wholly through imitation, . . . tragedy and comedy; and another which employs the recital of the

poet himself, best exemplified . . . in the dithyramb; and there is again that which
employs both, in epic poetry . . . .[7]

Thus, dramatic texts may be distinguished from epic or narrative texts
in that they are consistently restricted to the representative mode, the poet
never allowing himself to speak directly. Of course, in the light of recent
narrative theory, one might object that even in narrative texts it is not the
author himself who is speaking, but a fictional narrator created by him.
Nonetheless, this objection does not detract from the fundamental importance of this categorical distinction. For, whilst the receiver of a dramatic
text feels directly confronted with the characters represented, in narrative
texts they are mediated by a more or less concrete narrator figure.

1.2.2. A communication model for narrative and dramatic texts

The diagrams of the communication models for dramatic and narrative
texts included in this section should help to clarify this distinction.
a) Narrative texts:

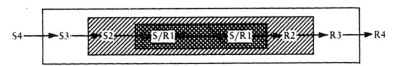

This model classifies the sender and receiver positions according to the
various superimposed semiotic levels. S4 stands for the actual author in his
socio-literary role as the producer of the work, S3 for the 'ideal' author
implied in the text as the subject of the whole work, S2 for the fictional
narrator whose role in the work is formulated as the narrative medium,
S/R1 for the fictional characters communicating with each other through
dialogue, R2 for the fictional addressee of S2, R3 for the implied 'ideal'
receiver of the whole work, and R4 for the actual reader – that is, not only
the reader envisaged by the author, but also other, later ones.[8] The
dark-coloured area represents the 'internal communication system' (L1 =
level 1) of the text, the light-coloured area the 'mediating communication
system' (L2) and the superimposed levels L3 and L4 the 'external communication system', first in idealised form, then in its real form. Depending on the particular 'narrative situation' (F. Stanzel), 'authorial narrative'
requires that positions S2 and R2 be occupied by fully independent characters, 'I-narrative' requires that S2 should be occupied by one of the characters that function on L1, and 'personal narrative' that positions S2 and R2
should fade out into a transparent, disembodied medium of narration. In
this respect there is a certain similarity between personal narrative and the
dramatic communication model.[9]

b) Dramatic texts:

The difference between the two models[10] may be seen in the fact that, in dramatic texts, positions S2 and R2 are left vacant, thereby eliminating the mediating communication system. This 'loss' of communicative potential in comparison to narrative texts is compensated for in two ways, however. First, dramatic texts have access to non-verbal codes and channels which are able, in part, to take on the communicative functions of S2 and R2, and secondly, aspects of the narrative function may be transferred to the internal communication system – for example by means of the type of questions and answers from S/R1 designed to inform the audience more than the protagonists do themselves. Having already established (in our historical analysis of the narrative communication model) that the modern form of personal narrative reflects a reduction of the mediating communication system and thus an approximation of narrative to drama we must now, in a similar way, qualify the dramatic model in the face of drama's tendency to produce 'epic' structures (see below, 3.6.). These include, for example, the chorus in classical tragedy, the allegorical characters in medieval morality plays interpreting their own roles to the audience with homiletic directness, the explanatory and interpretative functions of 'para-texts' (R. Ingarden) in the form of introductions, prefaces or extended stage-directions, and, finally, the introduction of commentator or producer figures in modern 'epic dramas'. Nonetheless, the creation of a mediating communication system in drama is always interpreted as a deviation from the normal model of dramatic presentation. As a fundamental principle, then, this model retains its validity and heuristic value.

1.2.3. The absolute nature of dramatic texts

The absence of a mediating communication system – resulting in the unmediated overlapping of the internal and external communication systems – is what conditions the 'absolute nature' of the dramatic text with regard to both author and audience, and it has been manifested on stage most accurately in the realist convention of the so-called 'fourth wall' (see below, 2.2.1.).

It is only as a whole that a drama belongs to the author and this link is not an essential component of its existence as a dramatic work. A drama exhibits the same absolute quality with regard to the spectator. A dramatic utterance is not addressed to the spectator any more than it is a statement by the author.[11]

The absolute autonomy of drama that Szondi talks about does, of course, not really exist. It is fictional, and may therefore be broken at various times – by an aside, a monologue *ad spectatores* or by commentary from the chorus, for example – causing alienation and the awareness of its fictionality. Here, too, it is the disruption of the communication model by this kind of apparent 'short-circuit' of levels L1 and L3/4 which underlines the model's significance.

1.2.4. The time–space structures of narrative and dramatic texts

In the absence of the mediating, fictional narrator (S2) from dramatic texts, the time–space continuum associated with it – i.e. the one which, in narrative texts, spans the time–space continuum of the world presented in the narrative – does not apply. In narrative texts, the variability of these two deictic systems of reference allows all sorts of arbitrary rearrangements of time–space relationships to be made, especially in the chronology of the narrative, topographical juxtapositions, the stretching and shrinking of narrative time, and the extension or restriction of locale. Dramatic texts, on the other hand, lack the fictional narrator as an overriding point of orientation. Here, it is therefore the time–space continuum of the plot alone that determines the progress of the text within the individual scenic units. Seen from the perspective of the implied author (S3), it is only the act of choosing the various scenic units with their respective time–space proportions and relationships towards the plot as a whole that is of intentional and communicative relevance – whereas the invariable continuity and homogeneity of time and space within the chosen scenic unit is a condition of the medium of drama, and thus, finally, of the dramatic communication model (see below, ch. 7).

At the same time, the elimination of the mediating communication system in dramatic texts creates a sense of immediacy in the action on stage in the way it enables both the dramatic text and its reception process to take place simultaneously. Conversely, in narrative texts the time-scale of the narrative is eclipsed by the time-scale of the narration process, thus distancing the narrative into the past. This temporal immediacy of dramatic presentation is *one* of the prerequisites for its physical enactment on stage.

1.2.5. Dialogue in dramatic and narrative texts

Whilst the narrator's discourse and that of the fictional characters quoted by the narrator overlap in narrative texts, the verbal utterances produced in the course of the multimedial enactment of a dramatic text are reduced to the mono- or dialogical speeches of the dramatic figures. This limitation is the second key precondition that is indispensable for the enactment of drama on stage. In other words, the characters are allowed to present themselves directly in their role as speakers. It is therefore the figures' speech, and, above all, their dialogical speech, which constitutes the predominant verbal matrix used in dramatic texts – something that was scarcely even acknowledged in Aristotle's essentially plot-orientated poetics, and that was all but ignored until the dramatic theories of A. W. Schlegel and Hegel gave it the recognition it deserved. In 'lyric' and narrative texts, dialogue is but one of a number of optional formal elements. In drama it is the fundamental mode of presentation.[12] In it, the relationship between plot and dialogue is a dialectical one, since the dramatic dialogue is, in Pirandello's words, an *azione parlata* or spoken action.[13] Since dramatic dialogue is spoken action, each individual dramatic utterance does not just consist in its propositional expressive content alone, but also in the way it is itself the execution of an act – whether in the form of a promise, a threat or an act of persuasion etc. Therefore, the performative aspect described by speech-act theory is always present in dramatic dialogue. Even at the most general level this condition of the performative aspect always applies:

There is something which is at the moment of uttering being done by the person uttering.[14]

As a speech-act, the dramatic speech constitutes its own particular speech situation. This is in contrast to dialogue in narrative texts, in which the fictional speech situation can be constituted by the narrator's report; and unlike philosophical dialogue, for example, dramatic speech is bound to that particular situation. This has been pointed out emphatically by the dramatist Friedrich Dürrenmatt:

If dialogue has to arise out of a situation, it has to lead to a situation, to another one, certainly. Dramatic dialogue occasions forms of action and endurance, a new situation, out of which a new dialogue arises, etc.[15]

1.3. Drama as a multimedial form of presentation

1.3.1. The dramatic text as a scenically enacted text

The criteria outlined in the previous sections, namely the omission of the mediating communication system and performative speech, are indispensable, though in themselves still rather inadequate preconditions for a model of dramatic communication. Taken on their own, these criteria would force us to identify as dramatic texts such historical forms as, for example, the Victorian 'dramatic monologue' of Tennyson and Browning[16] or novels written entirely in dialogue form. There is, however, one criterion which enables us to distinguish between such literary forms and drama: the multimedial nature of dramatic text presentation. As a 'performed' text, drama, in contrast to purely literary texts, makes use not only of verbal, but also of acoustic and visual codes. It is a synaesthetic text.[17] This important criterion provides the starting point for any semiotic analysis of drama. Similarly, S. Jansen distinguishes between the *plan textuel* and the *plan scénique* and M. Pagnini between *complesso scritturale* and *complesso operativo*.[18] Both definitions correctly regard the dramatic text as the scenically enacted text, one of whose components is the verbally manifested text. These two levels may be distinguished by their differing degrees of stability and/or variability, for whilst the verbally manifested text is normally fixed orthographically, and thus remains historically more or less stable, the scenic component of the stage enactment is variable − a fact clearly demonstrated in modern productions of the classics, even in those that do not alter the written text in any significant way.

The scenic level itself may be divided into two components by implementing the same criterion of stability versus variability. First, there are those elements of the stage enactment which are either explicitly demanded by the literary text, or at least clearly implied by it, and secondly, there are those which are the 'ingredients' added by the production. Such ingredients are always present, even in the most 'authentic' productions, since the very physical presence of the multimedial text always adds a surplus of information to the literary text. This dual-layered aspect of dramatic texts has resulted in two often strongly diverging types of interpretation: the purely literary interpretations of the verbally fixed text substrata, and the various productions and enactments of the texts on stage.

1.3.2. The repertoire of codes and channels

Dramatic texts have the potential to activate all channels of the human senses. Over the centuries, of course, dramatic productions have been restricted almost exclusively to texts employing acoustic and visual codes alone. Exceptions to this are more recent developments such as happenings or ritualist theatre, which also experiment with haptic (physical contact between actors and audience), olfactory and even gustatory effects.[19]

The dominant acoustic sign system is usually language, but this may be accompanied or replaced by non-verbal acoustic codes such as realistic noises, conventionalised sound effects (bells, thunder etc.) and music. Similarly, the visual component of the supersign 'dramatic text' presents itself as a structured complex of individual visual codes. The most impor-

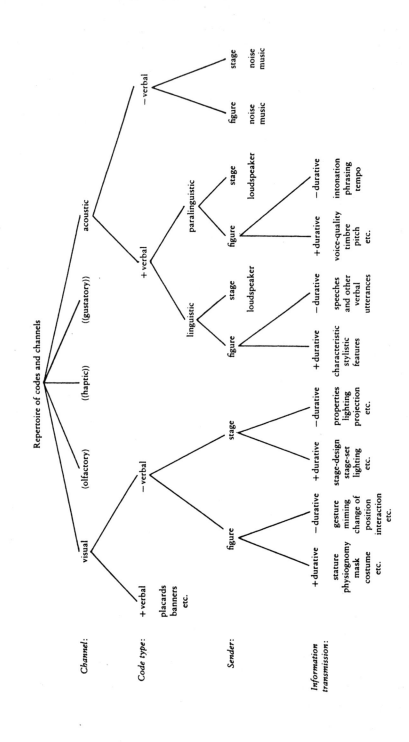

Repertoire of codes and channels

tant of these are the stature and physiognomy of the actors, choreography and the grouping of characters, mime and gesture, mask, costume and properties, the size and form of the stage itself, the set and, finally, lighting.[20] This set of components is integrated into the dramatic text as a system of interdependent structural elements. The relationships that exist between these various components will be the subject of the following paragraphs.

We have presented, in the form of a diagram, the repertoire of the codes and channels that are employed in dramatic texts (see diagram, p. 8). Our first classification criterion has been derived from the structure of human sensual perception – that is, from the five senses as channels for conveying information. As we remarked above, the vast majority of dramatic texts has exhibited a clear preference for the visual and acoustic channels, whilst the remaining senses of smell, touch and taste have been activated extremely sporadically, and then almost exclusively in the modern theatre of the avant-garde. An example of the use of touch was given in *Paradise Now* (1968) by the 'living theatre' of Julian and Judith Beck, in which the audience was invited to join the actors for the great love-scene and then to be carried into the street on the actors' shoulders. Since these channels are activated so rarely, however, they have been placed in brackets in the diagram, and further classification of information mediated by them has been omitted.

The second classification criterion is the type of code used. Of particular semiotic relevance in this context is the distinction between verbal and non-verbal codes and the further subdivision of the verbal codes into linguistic and paralinguistic codes. Generally speaking, the linguistic code is a 'symbolic code', whose signs are based on an arbitrary set of conventions. This means that the relationship between the sign and the signified object is unmotivated. At the same time, however, the majority of signs belonging to the paralinguistic and non-verbal codes are either 'indices' that are related to the signified object physically or contiguously or 'icons' which represent the signified object by being similar to it.[21]

Thus, within the supersign of the dramatic text, codes of varying degrees of standardisation operate together. Whilst the linguistic code represents a strictly standardised system of rules that guarantees a relatively high level of explicitness in the decoding process, the non-verbal indices and icons are much more ambiguous. As a result, this frequently leads to marked differences of interpretation.[22]

In the external communication system, however, this horizontal juxtaposition of the various code-types is transformed into a vertically arranged hierarchy. The text appears as an iconic supersign, within which even the transmission of symbolic and indexical signs has been iconicised into a fictional model of real communication. This iconic supersign is itself determined by comprehensive secondary codes – i.e. the numerous literary and dramatic conventions and genres – and is transmitted by the distributive channels open to dramatic texts. It has not been possible to show this process directly on our diagram, simply because it takes place on a more comprehensive plane.

The third classification criterion derives from the fictional sender of information. Put rather simply, we distinguish between character and non-character – i.e. the stage. Thus, costume is related to character as the properties are to the stage, for example. However, shifts in these relationships may occur, as a result of which a property might be so strongly associated with a particular character that it becomes a part of his or her costume, or, conversely – as in a masquerade or travesty – a character might become so far removed from his or her costume that it becomes a property.[23]

Our final classification criterion refers to the characteristics that apply to the various ways of transmitting information. In this context, we distinguish between durative and non-durative elements, according to whether the same single piece of information is being transmitted over an extended period of time or whether new pieces of information are continually being transmitted. The difference is merely relative, however, and the decision to allocate a particular sign to one or another of these categories depends on the length of the observation period. Thus, the transmission of information by the set within a closed scenic context is generally durative, whereas in the course of the text as a whole, with set-changes between scenes and/or acts, it is generally non-durative. The structuring of this part of our diagram was therefore based on relative values and general tendencies alone and would have to be revised before it could apply to certain individual texts or historical text-types. In a large number of modern texts, for example, developments in stage technology have made it possible for the set, lighting and even stage-design to change from durative to non-durative.

Listing these criteria has underlined and clarified our thesis that the multimedial dramatic text contains more information than the literary text. Not even the purely verbal component of the supersign 'dramatic text' can be determined from the orthographically fixed text alone, since there are a number of unpredictable, paralinguistic variables of both a durative – such as the voice-quality of the particular actor – and non-durative kind – such as intonation, tempo and the use of pauses etc. – which are introduced into the oral enactment of the text by the actor. As far as non-verbal, acoustic and visual codes are concerned, this information differential is generally even greater, for even the most detailed description of a dramatic figure, his actions and sphere of action must, of necessity, be subordinate to the physical presence, mimetic skills and gestures of each individual actor, and the physical presence of each individual set.

1.3.3. The collective nature of production and reception

Our analysis of the components that make up the dramatic text as a supersign points towards a further quality specific to dramatic texts – indeed, one that derives from its very multimediality: the collective nature of production. The extreme division of labour that operates in the modern theatre, which distinguishes quite clearly between the various functions of production, such as author, producer, theatre administrator, actor, costume and mask designers, set designers and lighting engineers, should not be understood as the historical norm (see below, 2.4.3. and 2.4.4.). Nonetheless, the stage-enactment of the literary text always presupposes collaboration in the production collective of a kind that does not generally exist for purely literary texts. In the normal course of events, this collective nature of production corresponds to a collective form of reception in the audience, which, at the present time, is again the exception as far as purely literary texts are concerned. As we shall see, both elements – the collective nature of production and reception – directly influence the structure of dramatic texts.[24]

1.4. Drama in the context of public performance activities

Structurally speaking, the features associated with dramatic texts that we analysed in the preceding sections (the overlapping of internal and external communication systems, relative autonomy, multimediality and the collective nature of production and reception) are all qualities that also apply to non-literary performance activities. Indeed, if 'performance' can be described as 'the doing of an activity by an individual or group largely for the pleasure of another individual or group',[25] then drama clearly belongs to this category as much as games with fixed rules, sporting competition, ritual and unstructured forms of 'play'. What all of these share is the indirect nature of their relationship with the real world. In all cases, this has been brought about by embedding the internal communication system in the external system (which, in drama, provides the specific link between 'fictionality' and reality), by clearly distinguishing between performers and spectators, by emphasising the differences between drama and more specifically economic forms of productivity, by suspending the temporal and spatial relationships of ordinary everyday life, and, finally, by implementing special rules and conventions.

These structurally related performance activities are partly connected to each other as progressive steps in the context of a general process of development. Thus, unstructured play may serve as the ontogenetic source of all the other activities in the development of the individual, and, historically speaking, ritual may be interpreted as a phylogenetic precursor of drama. The weakest structural affinity exists between drama and unstructured play, since the latter is not necessarily public, does not require an audience and is not preprogrammed with fixed rules. More recent developments, such as those in the sphere of the happening, have nonetheless often come close to unstructured play in so far as the distinction between performers and spectators tends to disappear, and the execution of the text is not completely determined in advance.

2. Drama and the theatre

2.1. Literary text and stage-enactment

2.1.1. Literary versus theatrical reception

The literary historian is not always quite as sharply aware of the importance of non-verbal codes for the dramatic text as the dramatist. Poring
over his printed texts, the former tends to neglect the multimedial aspect of
theatrical performance, whereas the latter regards this as a crucial component of the literary text. For, in the words of Max Frisch:

> Whoever appears on the stage and does not make proper use of the stage will find it
> working against him. Making use of the stage means: not being just *on* it, but *with*
> it.[1]

Like Frisch, Ionesco is another to emphasise the unity of the multimedial
dramatic text, maintaining that to strip it down to the bare minimum
would be an inexcusable aberration and abbreviation:

> . . . mon texte n'est pas seulement un dialogue mais il est aussi 'indications
> scéniques'. Ces indications scéniques sont à respecter aussi bien que le texte, elles
> sont nécessaires.[2]

Statements such as these seem particularly important at a time when, for
various socio-cultural reasons, plays — at least the non-trivial ones — are
more often read than seen in the theatre. They apply particularly to the
institutionalised study of dramatic texts at schools and universities, where
they are frequently stripped of their theatrical qualities. Dr Johnson's
neoclassical dictum: 'A play read affects the mind like a play acted',[3] can
only be true of the reader who is able to bring the numerous explicit and
implicit signs and signals inherent in the literary text to life in his
imagination.[4]

2.1.2. Primary and secondary text

The printed text generally distinguishes more or less clearly between two
layers of text. This distinction is often expressed typographically. One
layer comprises the spoken dialogue that takes place between the dramatic
figures, whilst the other refers to the verbal text segments that are not

13

reproduced on stage in spoken form. This second category would therefore include the title of the play, the inscriptions, dedications and prefaces,
the dramatis personae, announcements of act and scene, stage-directions,
whether applicable to scenery or action, and the identification of the
speaker of a particular speech. Ingarden's concepts of 'main' or 'primary'
and 'side' or 'secondary' text have been adopted as the accepted labels for
these different layers of text, and his definition of what constituted a
secondary text was based on the extent to which it could be translated by
the production into a physical presence on stage.[5] We, too, would like to
adopt Ingarden's terminology, but not without remarking that the quantitative and qualitative relationships between these two layers suggested
by the terms 'primary' and 'secondary' cannot be taken as universal
norms. For texts such as Samuel Beckett's *Acte sans paroles I* and *II*, or
Peter Handke's *Das Mündel will Vormund sein*, neither of which contain
spoken dialogue, and thus have no primary text, the use of the term
'secondary text' to describe the entire printed text would be highly misleading.

In both historical and typological terms, then, the qualitative and quantitative relationships between primary and secondary texts have been
extremely variable. Inscriptions, dedications, and prefaces were absent
from the majority of printed dramatic texts of the Shakespearean period,
since drama had not yet been accorded the social status of 'serious'
literature. It was only the works of 'serious' literature that were deemed
worthy enough to include such editorial paraphernalia. Even the stage-
directions were kept to a minimum, since the printed text had virtually no
autonomous value, and was essentially limited to its function as a reminder of the performance. When Ben Jonson published his own dramas
under the imposing title *Works* in 1616 and included a Latin inscription,
dedications, prologues and stage-directions, he was making a programma-
tically innovative gesture.

At the other end of this historical spectrum there are printed dramatic
texts, such as those of George Bernard Shaw, in which the primary text is
almost overwhelmed by the secondary text. The play *Androcles and the
Lion* (1916), for example, opens with a preface that is more than twice the
length of the actual text, and whose connection with it is rather tenuous.
Similarly, *Man and Superman* (1903) contains stage-directions that are up
to four pages long and which can only be partially translated into physical
action on stage. Such practices reveal a highly developed distrust of the
stage, and of producers and actors, and, by implication, elevate the printed
text to an autonomous entity in itself:

... the fact that a skilfully written play is infinitely more adaptable to all sorts of
acting than available acting is to all sorts of plays ... finally drives the author to the

conclusion that his own view of his work can only be conveyed by himself. And since he could not act the play single-handed even if he were a trained actor, he must fall back on his powers of literary expression, as other poets and fictionists do.[6]

The intention here is no longer to invoke the multimediality of a text – at least under the existing theatrical circumstances – and, by overemphasising the explanatory, descriptive and narrative functions of the secondary text, Shaw has established what amounts to a mediating communication system in its own right. In doing so, he has undermined the criteria essential for differentiating between dramatic and narrative texts. That Shaw was aware of this transgression himself is clearly shown when he compares his own technique with that of a 'fictionist' or literary narrator.

2.1.3. Stage-directions in the secondary text

From a functional point of view, the first step in classifying the stage-directions in secondary texts is to analyse to what extent they reappear in the stage-enactment – that is, to examine the extent to which they can be translated into paralinguistic and non-verbal codes, or, if a purely literary reception is expected, their literary value. Thus, the theatrical stage-directions refer to either the actor or the visual and acoustic context within which he performs. Those that refer to the actor can be divided in turn into the different kinds of instructions governing the manner and timing of entrances and exits, stature and physiognomy, mask and costume, gestures and mime, the paralinguistic elements of speech and, finally, the grouping and interaction of the characters. The contextual stage-directions, on the other hand, give instructions governing the set, the properties, lighting, music and sound, special effects such as artificial fog or the use of stage machinery, and, finally, changes of scene or act – including 'transformations' on open stage. Of course, this system of subdividing stage-directions into those that refer to the actor and those that refer to the context could never pretend to be complete. It may be expanded at any time by the application of technological innovations – such as film projection. For this reason, it might be regarded as no more than a non-systematic, accumulative catalogue.

2.1.4. Implicit stage-directions in the primary text

Stage-directions are not restricted to the secondary text, however; they may also be found, implicitly, in the primary text – as the following extract from Chekhov's *Cherry Orchard* demonstrates:

LOPAKHIN: What's the matter, Dooniasha?
DOONIASHA: My hands are trembling. I feel as if I'm going to faint.
LOPAKHIN: You're too refined and sensitive, Dooniasha. You dress
yourself up like a lady, and you do your hair like one too.[7]

The performative nature of dramatic speech (see above, 1.2.5.) ensures
that the dramatic situation is constituted in the speech-act, and this then
sends out a number of implicit signals to the audience that help to make the
dramatic situation more concrete. Purists of theatrical form such as Hugo
von Hofmannsthal have expounded this into a normative absolute in its
own right:

The more powerful the dramatic dialogue, the more it will convey of the suspense,
tension and atmosphere, and the less it will entrust to the stage-directions.[8]

Thus, it is possible to construct a large part of the stage-action in classical
drama, or in the plays of the Shakespearean period, from the speeches of
the dramatic figures, in so far as the speech implies an action carried out by
either the speaker himself or one of the other figures (see below, 3.3.).

Of course, implicit stage-directions in the primary text may also refer to
the visual and acoustic context. However, this should be distinguished
from 'word-scenery', the technique of evoking the locale when there is no
actual scenery on stage (see below, 7.3.3.1.). This technique is particularly
important for such theatrical conventions as the Elizabethan, which employed virtually no scenery, or indeed any other visual means of representation, to define the locale in any precise way. In this, then, we are not
dealing with stage-directions as such, but with a technique of verbal
compensation for the slow development — or the consciously stylised
reduction — of non-verbal codes.

2.1.5. Variability in the relationship between the enacted text and the literary text substratum

The variability of the quantitative and qualitative relationships between
primary and secondary text results in a variable relationship between the
literary text substratum and the enacted text.[9] That is, in its stage-
enactment, the literary text may either allow the production to choose
from a large number of scenic interpretations, or it may strictly determine
the way the events on stage are performed. One extreme in this spectrum of
possible relationships would be a text in which every gesture and action is
both bound up with and demanded by a particular speech. This ideal form
is approached most closely in the plays of Racine. Within the given
theatrical and performing conventions, it is the speeches of the dramatic
figures that determine every important action. Actions and events only
occur as variants of the spoken word, and not as autonomous and equally

important channels for the transmission of signs. It was therefore possible to exclude virtually all the stage-directions in the secondary text that refer to the action since they had been fully integrated into the dialogue.[10] At the other end of the scale there are plays by dramatists such as Chekhov, in which there is no longer a clearly definable direct or even necessary connection between words and actions. Instead, the producer and actor have to work out their own paralinguistic, mimetic and gestural interpretation of the speeches.

As both our examples show, the exact relationship between the literary text and its enactment is not only determined by the structure of the text, but also by the degree to which theatrical practice has been conventionalised. As a rule, dramatic texts that are produced at a time when performance and means of expression are extremely codified (as in Greek, French or German classicism, for example) are determined by their particular literary substratum to a far greater extent than those conceived within a more experimental form of theatrical practice.

2.1.6. The interrelationship of the sign systems

The relationships linking the various sign systems or codes that constitute a dramatic text are no less variable than the relationships outlined in the two previous sections. Thus, in certain historical periods, the visual means of presentation that we take for granted, such as lighting or set, are almost completely absent, with the result that the verbal element gains in importance – quantitatively at least. However, even the mimetic and gestural codes, which are, after all, not a particularly recent development, are related to the verbal code historically and typologically in an extremely varied number of ways.

The complete absence of non-verbal codes in plays intended for reading alone (closet-dramas), such as Shelley's *Prometheus Unbound*, marks one end of the scale. Such plays are conceived from the outset without a performance in mind, either because the author is sceptical towards the current theatrical situation or because his imaginative constructions are simply unstageable. The other end of the spectrum is represented by mime and ballet, which are characterised, of course, by the complete absence of verbal codes. Between these two poles, a complete spectrum of possible relationships between verbal and non-verbal sign systems may be observed. In the classical tragedies of Seneca and his Renaissance imitators in France, Germany and England, for example, the verbal code dominates so strongly that the action is hardly ever presented on stage, but is verbalised in rhetorically structured recitatives voiced by speakers acting within the bounds of a particular style. In naturalist drama and the modern theatre of the absurd, on the other hand, it is frequently the mimetic and gestural elements which dominate, since the notion that the dramatic figure is an individual with a reduced sense of awareness leads towards a reduction in the means of verbal expression in favour of mute acting.

This kind of subordination of the verbal code may also be found – albeit with a different function – in such theatrical offerings as masques and operas, both of which are primarily concerned with spectacle and sensual fascination. And it has been in the modernist age above all that the leading theoreticians and practitioners of drama such as Adolphe Appia, E. Gordon Craig, V. E. Meyerhold or Antonin Artaud have pleaded for a deliterisation process resulting in the domination of non-verbal codes.[11]

The examples cited above show quite clearly that a purely quantitative description of these relationships is not sufficient and must be complemented by one of a qualitative or functional kind. The fundamental question that must be asked at this point is whether the verbal and non-verbal codes are transmitted simultaneously, or whether one precedes the other. If the first is true, then we have 'behaviour that accompanies the word', and if the second is true, we have an alternating sequence of verbal sign transmission and 'wordless behaviour'.[12] This sequence may occur in larger blocks, as, for example, in a succession of spoken scenes in which the visual information is only durative, or in the 'dumb shows' inserted into early Elizabethan tragedies in the Senecan tradition, in which the mimetic additions clarify or generalise allegorically the moral content of the spoken scenes.[13] In realist drama, however, mimetic elements generally no longer take the form of block-like insertions. Instead, they are closely bound up with the preceding and succeeding phases of behaviour that accompany the word. In such cases, the non-verbal elements do not clarify what is said, but rather function as an unconscious manifestation of a psychic condition or reflect a need for silence in the face of verbal impotence.

However, even on the occasions that verbal and non-verbal codes are transmitted simultaneously, varying degrees of interdependence may be found. Ideally speaking, it is possible to distinguish between analytical and synthetic relationships.[14] In analytical relationships – they predominate in classical drama – mimetic and gestural action clarifies what is said; that is, it explains and comments directly on the spoken word. In synthetic relationships on the other hand – they predominate in realist drama – the mimetic and gestural elements either transcend, relativise or even contradict what is said.

To conclude, the types of relationships between the non-durative, verbal and non-durative, non-verbal channels can be represented graphically in the following way:

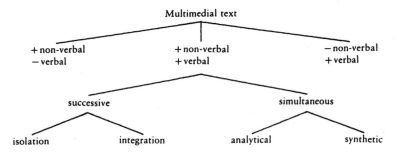

2.2. Dramatic text and theatre design

2.2.1. The relationship between stage and auditorium

As multimedial texts, dramatic texts are conditioned structurally by the spatial dimensions and technical sophistication of the stage they are performed on. A dramatic text is conceived with a particular type of stage in mind, and this becomes clear when a text is performed on a stage whose dimensions and technical sophistication are different. Examples of this are virtually all productions of dramatic texts written before 1800 on the standard modern type of stage, the so-called proscenium arch or 'picture-stage'. The problems engendered by nineteenth- and twentieth-century productions of Shakespeare are a case in point. Texts that were intended for a relatively neutral stage-area with little décor have been subjected to the conditions of illusionist theatre, in which the verbally evoked locales are actually recreated visually by means of illusion, and the original flexibility in the distance between the actors and the audience is destroyed.

This is not the place for a detailed historical analysis of the technical aspects of theatre architecture or stage-design.[15] Nonetheless, by isolating a number of strongly schematised models, we should like to sketch the historical variations and developments in the spatial relationship between stage and auditorium.[16] In the diagram on page 20, the stage is represented by the darker area.

1. Classical Greek comedies and tragedies were performed in the open air for the entire free male population of a city state on religious holidays. The religious context underlines the importance of such performances for the social community and reflects the cult-like and ritual origins of drama. As far as the intended audience was concerned, the amphitheatres of ancient Greece were of spatial proportions that are more comparable to a modern sports stadium than a modern theatre. The amphitheatre at Epidaurus held an audience of fourteen thousand and that at Ephesus one of twenty-four thousand. The audience was grouped around the stage-area in

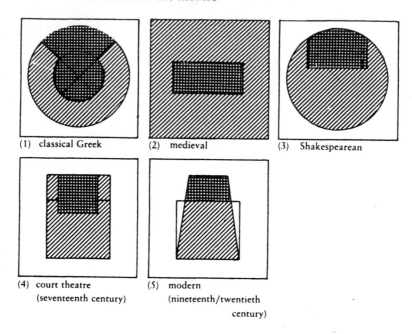

(1) classical Greek

(2) medieval

(3) Shakespearean

(4) court theatre
     (seventeenth century)

(5) modern
     (nineteenth/twentieth
     century)

the form of an extended semicircle, thus making the use of an illusionist set impossible. The backdrop to the stage-area consisted of the neutral wall of the *skene* and the countryside behind. Understandably, this kind of stage did not permit a realist style of acting. In view of the distances between the spectators and the actors, subtleties of mime or gesture, or a more realistically performed conversational tone, would have been simply imperceptible. Thus, this particular theatre design tended to encourage stylisation. Verbal performance was characterised by declamation and choral commentary, the delineation of character by the use of masks and symbolic costumes, and the acting itself by the use of exaggerated gestures.

2. Traces of the origins of theatre in religion and cult were still present even in medieval drama. The English 'mystery plays' portrayed nothing less than the history of the Salvation from the Creation to the Day of Judgement in a number of episodes. These performances also took place on religious holidays – and also in the open air – but this time in the form of pageants or on primitive, static platform stages which were surrounded by the street audience on all sides. This spatially close contact between the actors and the audience was thus significantly different from the classical Greek stage and it conditioned a theatrical style which contrasted ritualist elements of liturgical origin with burlesque and crudely realistic elements that reflected the tastes and everyday reality of the spectators. The dividing-line separating the audience from the stage was very flexible and

occasionally broken by the actors. Under such circumstances, then, a realist or illusionist type of theatre was neither possible nor intended.

3. Elizabethan plays of the Shakespearean period were no longer performed in the street, but in purpose-built theatres, and troupes of amateur actors gave way to professional companies. Since the audience surrounded the stage on three sides, close contact between the actors and spectators remained an influential feature. This proximity demanded sophisticated forms of verbal, mimetic and gestural impersonation from the actors. At the same time, it meant they were unable to ignore the presence of the audience in the same way that they can do on the modern picture-stage. By employing epic techniques such as asides or monologues *ad spectatores*, the actors repeatedly established direct contact with the audience, thus undermining the dramatic illusion. This was especially true of the action taking place on the forestage, which, being closest to the audience, made illusion very difficult. The action upstage took place within something like a closed communication system. The paucity of set and décor and the need for daylight performances presupposed an ability on the part of the spectators to recreate the 'verbal décor' in their respective imaginations, and enabled simple and quick scene-changes to take place. It would therefore have been extremely unnatural for this type of theatre to preserve the classical unities of time and space.

4. The English Restoration theatre, which we have selected as an example of the European court theatre of the seventeenth and eighteenth centuries, was designed to cater for a considerably smaller audience than its Elizabethan predecessor. Whilst Shakespeare's Globe could hold an audience of two thousand, the Restoration theatres generally seated no more than five hundred. In addition, the audience was much more socially homogeneous than before, and this was reflected in the greater ideological unity and bias of the dramatic texts. Theatrical performances were now regarded as social events, taking place within an enclosed space and using artificial light. An extended forestage apart, the audience was separated from the stage by a richly decorated proscenium arch. There was still no proscenium curtain, however. This did not appear in England until the late eighteenth century. Scene-changes took place on the open stage and the background scenery had a decorative rather than an illusionist function. Despite the greater distances involved, the audience had by no means been completely separated from the stage. Indeed, the intention was not to produce a realistic imitation or illusion of reality, but rather a stylised ideal image of the audience's world. Stage-design, the set, the grouping of characters, their movements and gestures, and the structure of the dialogue were all determined by the desire for symmetry and formalisation.

5. In turning our attention to the modern stage of the nineteenth and

twentieth centuries, we should like to concentrate on its most common and familiar form, the proscenium arch or picture-stage – though not without acknowledging the numerous and multifarious experiments with new stage-designs or the reactivation of older ones.

The proscenium-arch stage represents a decisive step towards the complete separation of audience and stage, and towards the notion of the 'absolute autonomy' of dramatic fiction. The illuminated stage is separated from the darkened auditorium by the proscenium arch and the footlights, thus creating the illusion of an enclosed image. Set, costumes, properties, the manner of acting and use of language are conceived as a faithful imitation of society, and this illusion is preserved during scene-changes by the use of the proscenium curtain. The audience looks into a room, one of whose walls is missing – apparently without the actors within that room being aware of this. All forms of addressing the audience directly are thus ruled out since, in its capacity as an inviolable dividing-line, the front of the stage is the scenic manifestation of the absence of a mediating communication system.

This particular type of stage and the stage–audience relationship associated with it were influential in determining a particular dramatic form, namely the realist, illusionist theatre of Ibsen and Chekhov. One need not fully endorse Brecht's polemics against this particular stage-form to recognise its limitations. As a theatrical medium it is simply inadequate for the dramas of classical antiquity, the works of Shakespeare and Molière, the modern verse-dramas of Eliot, and Brecht's own 'epic theatre'. Experiments with technically more variable forms of theatre architecture such as arenas, neutral stage-platforms or street theatre have emphasised the inadequacies of this theatre form.

2.2.2. Stage-area and fictional locale

In the previous section, priority was given to the spatial aspects of the relationship between the audience and the stage. There is, however, a second aspect that is equally important, namely the relationship between the physical stage-area and the various fictional locales. The producer of a dramatic text is always faced with the fundamental question as to whether the stage should be consciously preserved as a stage (anti-illusionist) or whether it should be presented as something that it is not (illusionist). Between these two extremes – from Brecht's ideal of an epic stage stripped of all illusionistic effects to the perfect illusions created by naturalist conventions – there is a complete spectrum of possible relations. In these, there is an element of qualitative and functional tension that is always 'weighted' differently towards either the physical stage-area or the fictional locale. Nonetheless, there are a few special cases in which the two elements appear to be identical. An example of this is a play about a play, such as Pirandello's *Six Characters in Search of an Author*, in which the physical stage-area and the fictional locale appear to coincide – and this 'identity' is emphatically marked as a deviation from the norm of 'non-identity' (see below, 7.1.).

2.2.3. Actor and fictional figure

An analogous scale of relationships may also be observed in those existing between the actor as an actual human being and the fictional figure he represents. Thus, Brecht attacked the obliteration of the actor's own personality in naturalist drama and his 'total submersion' in the fictional figure ('He didn't play Lear; he *was* Lear'), and demanded instead a style of acting that clarified this relationship in a more deliberate way:

This principle – that the actor actually appears on stage in a double role, as Laughton and as Galileo; that the showman Laughton does not disappear in the Galileo whom he is showing . . . – comes to mean simply that the tangible, matter-of-fact process is no longer hidden behind a veil; that Laughton is actually there, standing on the stage and showing us what he imagines Galileo to have been.[17]

Here, too, it is possible to imagine special cases where the actor and the figure he represents are apparently identical. In Molière's *L'impromptu de Versailles* (1663), for example, the actors in his company appear as themselves.

The question of identification versus distance is merely *one* aspect of the relationship between actor and figure, but, because of the influence of Brecht's theoretical reflections, it has established itself as the focal point of twentieth-century critical attention.[18] The degree of theatrical illusion is also determined by the style of acting employed – that is, to what extent the behaviour of the fictional figure is rounded off by the actor with realistic details, or, conversely, reduced to characteristic behavioural archetypes. This perspective would make it possible to establish a further scale of relationships, stretching from the gestural and mimetic conventions of Greek tragedy or baroque opera, to the naturalist style of acting employed by the Stanislavsky school.

2.3. Drama and film: some observations

Subsequent to our historical survey of the ways theatre-design might influence the dramatic text, we feel it would be useful to discuss the relationship between drama, the theatre and film, since film, in its initial phases at least, was considered primarily a technological innovation that enabled theatre to be preserved photographically, and thus made accessible to a wider public. In this view, film appeared to be no more than the technological reproduction of a multimedial dramatic text, in which the three-dimensional immediacy of live presentation was replaced by a two-dimensional image. Apologists of the theatre, irritated by the success – including the financial success – of the new rival medium, differentiated between film and drama by pointing out the inevitable time-lag between the production and reception of a film. This eliminated the constant interchange between the audience and the actors which makes each live performance in the theatre such a unique and gripping occasion.

This view need not prevent us from regarding drama and film as structurally closely related variants of the same authorial method. Their shared characteristics – multimediality and the collective nature of production and reception – distinguish them from narrative texts. Nonetheless, there are a number of features specific to film texts that are reminiscent of narrative texts in certain areas and clearly distinguish them from dramatic texts.

In dramatic texts, the plot of a single, closed scenic unit is presented within a time–space continuum (see above, 1.2.4.), whereas in film it may be – and generally is – dissolved into a sequence of non-continuous perspectives. It is in the nature of drama as a medium that it preserves time–space continuity and homogeneity within a particular scene. A film, on the other hand, affects the way a scene is perceived by the continual variation of focus and perspective, by cutting and editing, by the use of fade-ins and fade-outs, lighting and camera movement. The result of this is that the audience in the theatre perceives the action from a constant distance and perspective, whereas in a film, this perspective may be subjected to considerable variations as a result of alterations in the camera position and focus. By employing the montage technique, a scene that has been conceived as a time–space continuum and which, in the theatre, must be performed as such, may be divided up into individual elements of differing spatial perspective and temporal discontinuity. Similarly, a time–space continuum may be interrupted by the insertions of settings taken from different temporal and spatial perspectives.

The flexibility and mobility of the camera makes it possible to disrupt the chronology of the story (as in the flashback technique), to stretch or concentrate time, to introduce topographical superimposition and to change the perspective of the presentation. All these are features familiar to us from narrative texts. For, unlike dramatic texts, both film and narrative texts possess a 'mediating communication system' – which is what makes such manipulations of time and space possible in the first place. Thus, the flexible and mobile camera functions as a mediating communication system, fulfilling a narrative function that corresponds to the fictional narrator (position S2) in narrative texts.[19] The film audience, like the readers of a narrative text, is not confronted directly with the material presented, as is the audience in the theatre, but indirectly, via the selective, accentuating and structuring medium of the camera or narrator. This structural similarity between film and narrative texts may also be demonstrated by the fact that, in addition to the optical narrative function of the camera, film frequently inserts elements of verbal narrative (such as the use of titles and the voice-over), and that, unlike drama, it can also present space 'descriptively' without the use of characters. In plays that include extended periods when the stage is empty, as occurs between scenes 14 and 15 of Act IV in Chekhov's *The Cherry Orchard*, for example, the result is not simply a descriptive section inserted for its own sake – as is true of landscape shots in films – because all that this emptiness emphasises is the absence of people. As such, this emphasis is reinforced by the very fact that it violates the dramatic norm that requires the stage to be populated.

Film, then, has shown itself to be a form which combines structural features of both narrative and dramatic texts. The former is reflected in the existence of a mediating communication system, the latter in its multi-mediality and the collective nature of its production and reception. To regard this mixture as an aesthetic defect is to adhere to the classical fundamentalist belief in the strict separation and purity of literary genres. To the film-maker it is no more than a welcome expansion of the repertoire of codes, channels and structuring processes available to him.

2.4. Theatre as a social institution

2.4.1. The public character of dramatic communication

As a form of public communication, literature may be regarded essentially as a social institution since – like all forms of communication – it presupposes a system of generally accepted norms and conventions and, in addition, requires a complex organisational base for its production, distribution and reception. Although this applies to all literary genres, it is particularly true of dramatic texts, the performance of which depends on an institutionalised theatre business as an organisational basis. As such, the theatre as an institution manifests itself more clearly in the receiver's mind than the publishing business does as the institutional medium for purely literary texts. The collective nature of their reception makes the dependence of the theatre and dramatic texts on particular social groups much more obvious than is the case for other kinds of texts. Furthermore, dramatic texts – particularly those of the modern period – have an organisational basis that is twice the size of that of other literary texts, simply because they are not only produced as dramatic texts in the theatre, but also as literary texts by the publishers.

G. Gurvitch has perceived an 'affinité frappante entre la société et le théâtre'.[20] This affinity is reflected in the metaphor describing the world as a stage, a view that is not confined to literature alone, but which is widespread in folk and popular culture.[21] Petronius' classic formulation, 'Totus mundus agit histrionem', has become an infinitely variable topos, in which the original transcendental perspective (God as dramatist and audience, mankind as actors or puppets) was retracted in the early modern period in favour of a purely mundane perspective in which the theatre metaphor points towards the role-playing component in conventional modes of behaviour and towards the pretensions and hypocrisy of social life. This tradition is also connected with a branch of modern sociology known as role theory, which has turned the theatre into an analytical model for the description of social phenomena and processes, and, in doing so, has even borrowed its terminology from the technical language of the theatre. (Apart from 'role' they also use 'enactment', 'mask', 'scenario', 'frame', 'scenery', 'improvisation' and 'repertoire', amongst others.)[22] In the most recent dialectical version of this tradition, role theory sociologists have applied their analytical machinery to the theatre and its conventions, taking the view that theatre and society share certain common propensities for role-play and spectacular display, and that the theatre is a reflection of actual human interaction.[23]

From our arguments it is clear that the most important kind of socioliterary analysis is one which examines the pragmatic environment of a text's external communication system and which identifies the correspondences between aspects of both the external and internal communication systems. This introduction is not the place for a systematic sociological analysis of drama – and, given the state of current research and theoretical analysis, this would scarcely be possible anyway.[24] Instead, we should like to take Roman Jakobson's communication model as a point of departure,[25] and go on to outline systematically the types of sociological questions that apply to drama, thereby creating a useful procedure for identifying the relevant aspects in the interdependent relationship between drama and society.

2.4.2. A model for the external communication system of dramatic texts

The model that enabled us to distinguish between narrative and dramatic texts (see above, 1.2.2.) was a 'flow diagram' designed to clarify the various inlaid levels of sender/receiver positions. The other factors influencing the communication process were therefore not considered in that particular context. In view of the altered perspective, however, we should now like both to simplify and develop this model – simplify it in so far as we can now largely ignore the relationships within the internal communication system and develop it by taking the other communicative factors into consideration. For the establishment of a communication process does not depend on the existence of a *sender* and *receiver* alone, but also on a *channel* that forms a physical and psychological link between sender and receiver, a *message*, which is transmitted as a complex of signs along the channel, and a *code*, which enables sender and receiver to en- or decode the message respectively, thus revealing the *content* (reference to the context). It should also be noted that the sender and receiver codes are only identical in an ideal context. In the real world they overlap to a greater or lesser degree. The content decoded by the receiver is therefore not identical to that encoded by the sender, and the message itself is distorted by the channel's own noise.

Bearing these factors in mind, we should like to propose the following model for the external communication system of dramatic texts:

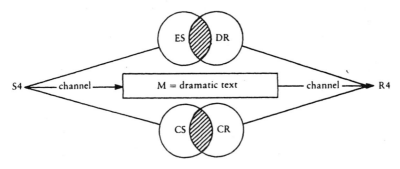

ES stands for the encoding code of the sender, and DR for the decoding code of the receiver. CS stands for the content as encoded by the sender, and CR for the content decoded by the receiver. This model reflects the external relationships of a dramatic text and so may serve as a method for identifying its socio-literary implications.

2.4.3. The sociology of authorship

The sociology of authorship is concerned with the relationship between the dramatic text and the empirical author in his role as a producer of dramas (S4). It is not our intention to propose some sort of biographical analysis which attempts to explain a work in terms of the 'genetic' and 'psychological' make-up of a particular author. Of course, the biographical aspect is an important mediator between literature and society, but it is by no means the only one. For even if one does not espouse a radically materialist world-view, in which the individual appears to be conditioned completely by the effects of his environment, there is little doubt that his thoughts and actions are shaped by the social norms he has internalised in the course of his development. Even the act of revolt against such norms – as in the case of Brecht, for example – is itself a sociological phenomenon, since it presupposes the existence of such norms. Thus, the individual's social sphere of reference determines his potential and represents the conditions that affect this potential.

An extreme version of this view has been argued by Lucien Goldmann, a representative of the structural–geneticist school of socio-literary analysis. In his study of Racine, he presents the playwright's relationship towards the various Jansenist movements and also to Jansenism as a whole in the overall context of the economic, political and social antagonisms that characterised the social classes of the seventeenth century.[26] In his view, the 'subject of cultural creation' is, ultimately, the social group to which the author belongs, with the author himself, as the 'creative individual', having no more than a mediating function:

That is why, although it is not completely absurd to imagine that if the individual Racine had received a different education or lived in a different environment, he might have been able to write plays like those of Corneille or Molière, it is, on the other hand, absolutely inconceivable that the seventeenth-century *noblesse de robe* should have developed an Epicurean or radically optimistic ideology.[27]

One might not endorse such a drastic reduction and minimalisation of the role of the creative individual. Nonetheless, it is possible to demonstrate to what extent the structure of a dramatic text is dependent on the author's social background, his education, and his social sphere of reference.

By producing a literary text, and this is particularly true of the dramatist, the author is making a public statement. For this very reason, his role as a producer of literature is not the result of a freely taken decision or the manifestation of an autonomous identity, but is orientated towards the given social norms for this public role – in so far as he either conforms to them or breaks them.

Such norms or authorial stereotypes are historically extremely variable, and it is often possible to find several rival stereotypes from different sociological backgrounds existing simultaneously. These can see the dramatist variously as the interpreter of a people's religious and political myths, the homiletic promulgator of unquestioned religious behavioural norms, the idealising apologist of a class-bound world-view, the socially appointed entertainer, the satirical critic of social failings, the actively committed spokesman for socially underprivileged groups, the propagandist of revolutionary ideas, a moral authority, and an experimentor and planner of communicative processes – to name but a few.

In addition, these authorial stereotypes contain various implications that help the reader to determine the social function of the dramatic author. These functions may be boiled down to two basic types: first, there is an expressive function, in which the dramatist affirmatively articulates an already existing social consensus, and, secondly, there is an instrumental function in which the consensus must first either be established or changed.[28]

As far as dramatic texts are concerned, the sociology of authorship becomes even more complicated in view of the multiplicity of productive functions. That is, the author of the printed and literary text substratum is no more than one of the several 'authors' of the multimedial, enacted text. This raises the question of the nature of the institutionalised relationship between the literary author and the various productive functions in the theatre (such as director, actor, set-designer etc.). This clear separation of literary and theatrical productive functions – the norm in the modern theatre – should not be understood as the norm historically. Shakespeare and Molière are exemplary illustrations of the way the functions of dramatist, actor and theatre entrepreneur could be united in one person. Given the present institutionalised separation of literary and theatrical functions, there is the inherent danger of literary texts becoming too far removed from the theatre, since, in such circumstances, the author has scant opportunity to test and improve the multimedial effectiveness of his texts. This can also lead to the literary text being overshadowed by the production, relegating the former to relative insignificance. Such negative tendencies have stimulated the numerous recent attempts to reunite literary and theatrical productive functions (such as the 'playwright in residence' schemes).

The productive functions within the theatre itself have also been subjected to historical change, and this has been reflected structurally in the form of the texts performed. Modern theatre organisation, with its extreme division of labour, is a relatively recent phenomenon. Indeed, it was not until the nineteenth century that the role of the director came to assume a central, coordinating function.[29] A further decisive element in the structure of a performance is whether it is enacted by an established company with a well thought out and consistent style of presentation or whether the actors are a group of individual actors brought together *ad hoc* for the performance. Other influential factors are whether the same play is performed on successive evenings or whether it is part of a repertoire and is thus seen in the context of an overall seasonal programme. As alternative approaches to the organisation of theatrical productions they all coexist in the contemporary theatre and are therefore not merely of historical interest. They condition the structure of the multimedial text and are conditioned, in turn, by the economic structure of the theatre involved. The latter is dependent on the socially determined function accorded to the theatre that is prevalent at a particular time.

2.4.4. The sociology of mediating channels

This is concerned with the conditioning features of the mediating channels and their influence on the structure of the dramatic text. They consist of a complex collection of individual, interdependent aspects. In general terms, these may be identified as the technological aspect, which covers the technological means available for the stage-enactment of the multimedial dramatic text, the economic aspect, covering the production costs and the financing thereof, the legal and political aspect, which includes the extent of state control – either by censorship or advancement – the organisational aspect, which examines the relationship between the functions of production and mediation, and, finally, the socio-political aspect, which covers the institutionalised channels of mediation, such as public education and critical journalism.

In this section we shall restrict ourselves to the economic and political aspects, but even in these areas, lack of space prevents us from offering more than a sketchy outline of the important problems.

In the course of its historical development, the specifically public nature of communication via dramatic texts has meant that the theatre has repeatedly been regarded as a political matter. Viewed by the authorities with considerable suspicion, it has been controlled either by the imposition of a set of religious, moral or political restrictions by the official censorship authorities,[30] or by the granting of financial subsidies, thereby ensuring a certain level of dependence on the state and political conformity. Of course, one might also argue that the costs involved in building and maintaining a theatre are normally so high that a purely commercial, self-financing theatre is only able to flourish in sociologically particularly happy circumstances – although even then the economic interest may threaten to influence the aesthetic standards of the dramatic production in a negative way. Historically, then, theatres have repeatedly been obliged to rely on various kinds of private or public patronage – whether from a feudal desire for self-aggrandisement and the determination to spread ideological propaganda and political influence or from humanist efforts to encourage education and culture as unquestioned aims in their own right. The contemporary situation is characterised by the increasing importance of state- or council-operated theatres which, in Germany at least, have developed out of the feudal court theatres. The few remaining private theatres are only able to continue with the help of public subsidies. Purely commercial theatres are still to be found in the industrial centres and conurbations, but even in Great Britain, the traditional homeland of the private, commercial theatre, a network of council- or state-subsidised theatres has grown up since the Second World War.[31]

A second crucial sociological question concerns the position and respect enjoyed by the theatre within the cultural and intellectual channels of a particular society. Here, too, there have been far-reaching historical and structural changes – something that becomes clear when a comparison is made between, for example, the differing theatrical contexts of the Renaissance and the late twentieth century. In the Shakespearean period, drama – along with other often purely verbal forms such as the sermon or street-ballad – was the sole medium of mass communication. In the twentieth century, by contrast, drama in its original form (i.e. as a non-technologically reproducible form) has been forced into a peripheral position in the modern system of communication media. Indeed, even within the subsystem of literary communication, drama has lost its importance in favour of narrative texts.

2.4.5. The sociology of reception

The sociology of reception analyses the relationship between the dramatic text and its audience or readers.[32] In this, it is the audience as intended by the author that is of primary relevance since it is the direct addressee of his text. The author must take the audience's predilections and intellectual background into consideration in the production of his text if he is at all concerned to achieve either a successful form of aesthetic communication or financial reward – or both.

This 'intended audience' may represent an extremely variegated segment of society as a whole. However, one extreme situation is created by the complete absence of an intended contemporary audience. In such cases, the dramatic text undermines the horizon of expectation of the contemporary audience or readers by implementing formal and/or ideological innovations in such a radical way that its stage-enactment becomes impossible – for either economic or legal reasons – thereby leading the dramatist to look to an audience of the future as the potential receivers of his or her texts.

The opposite extreme occurs when the intended audience corresponds exactly to society as a whole – that is, when the audience forms a representative cross-section of that society. The closest an audience has come to approaching this ideal was in Elizabethan popular theatre, in which all social classes of the urban population were represented, from the apprentices to the nobility – albeit with the exception of the strictly puritan section of the middle-classes.[33] This particular audience structure, itself conditioned by the overall balance of conflicting interests and tensions between the court, the aristocracy and the middle-classes of the semi-feudal nation-state under Queen Elizabeth, was a conditioning element of considerable influence on the structure of Shakespeare's dramas and was manifested in the overlapping of various stylistic levels and perspectives, the contrasting strands of plot, and the mixture of plebeian, middle-class and courtly figures that are so characteristic of them.

This causal connection between the social structure of the intended audience and the dramatic texts written for it becomes even clearer when the situation in the Elizabethan theatre is compared to the Restoration theatre of the late seventeenth century. In the latter, the intended audience is no longer society as a whole, but a narrow segment of it, namely the court and the urban upper middle-classes that associated with it. This restriction of the intended audience was reflected in the radical decline in the number of theatres in London and in the reduction in the size of the auditorium (see above, 2.2.1.). The tragedies and comedies of the Restoration period also reflected this social selectiveness and bias in their own particular ways: tragedies by the pathos-ridden idealisation of conservative and heroic behavioural norms, comedies by their realistically veiled idealisation of the fashionable, hedonistic norms of elegance, cynical wit and a refined enjoyment of life. Such tension between the genres of tragedy and comedy was a reflection of the ideological tensions within the intended audience. However, at the same time, any social perspective that deviated from these norms was either totally excluded or dismissed satirically. Plays thus lost that multifaceted interplay of perspectives and tensions that had characterised the plays of Shakespeare and many of his contemporaries, and which over the centuries has made it possible for them to be performed meaningfully in new and sociologically varied reception contexts.

It is perhaps surprising that, at least as far as technologically non-reproducible – i.e. live – drama is concerned, the relative one-sidedness and social unity of the Restoration audience has also become a feature of the audiences in modern pluralist democracies. Of course, dramatic texts reach a socially more widespread audience through the media of film and television, on the one hand, because access in these areas is not impeded by the existence of social barriers, and, on the other, because commercial motives often preclude formal and/or ideological innovations and encourage the trivialisation of texts in order to reach a mass audience.[34]

2.4.6. The sociology of content

If a sociological analysis of dramatic content is to do justice to its subject matter then it cannot afford to isolate the social content of a text from the social context outside it, but should concern itself with the very relationship between these two aspects. The overriding purpose in this context should be to discover how selective the fictional model of the world created by the dramatic text is when compared to social reality, and in what way the author's specific selectivity is itself socially conditioned.

In his study of the way reality was portrayed in French seventeenth-century drama,[35] Erich Auerbach was able to demonstrate that even in the comedies of Molière, of which it could hardly be said that they shied away from caricaturing figures of the educated classes such as the 'marquis ridicule', the 'common people' only appear as 'personnages ridicules', standing apart from 'la cour et la ville'. It is therefore impossible to speak of a realistic presentation of the lives of statistically the largest social class. The hierarchical structure of the existing feudal society was accepted unquestioningly as a universal truth, and every profession, trade or occupation, whether peasant, merchant or doctor, was either excluded or dismissed satirically in favour of the social ideal of the universally educated 'honnête homme'.

An even more selective process may be observed in the contemporary form of high tragedy epitomised by Racine, in whose plays the populace is referred to in little more than general terms, and neither practical, everyday activities, such as the desire for economic reward, nor other more natural forms of human behaviour are presented on stage at all. Such exemplary abstractions into the ideal were a reflection of the over-inflated position of the aristocracy under the absolutist rule of Louis XIV, and it was to these leading social classes that French classical drama addressed itself.

In 'content analysis', a method of establishing an 'objective, systematic and quantitative description of the manifest content of communication' (B. Berelson), empirical social research has established a method that can be applied fruitfully to a sociological analysis of dramatic texts. So far, it has only been applied to trivial drama,[36] since it has proved difficult to introduce quantitative arguments into the analysis of serious literature in the face of the hermeneutic and interpretative types of analysis procedure. On the basis of precisely formulated hypotheses, content analysis examines a particular corpus of texts for their relevant features. These then have to be defined operationally in order to guarantee intersubjective verifiability. By restricting oneself to the 'manifest contents' it is possible to increase the likelihood of objectivity. However, the 'latent contents' are also accessible – in principle at least – assuming that their features can be defined operationally.

J. S. R. Goodlad has used this methodological apparatus to examine the social content of popular television drama and London West End plays from 1955 to 1965, measuring 'popularity' in terms of audience statistics and viewing figures.[37] He analysed this corpus of dramatic texts by isolating the five crucial aspects of the dominant themes, dramatic genres used, the aims and motives of the fictional characters, the social milieu of the plot and the endings. In each case he developed an operationally defined classification system. Not surprisingly, perhaps, the results of his statistical analysis show (1) that the clearly predominant themes were those of love and morality and thus the problems created when people deviate from socially accepted moral norms, (2) that compared to the class structure in the real world a socially elevated milieu was over-represented, (3) that the most common motivation in the positive heroes was love, whilst the negative heroes sought power and social advancement, and (4) that the overwhelming majority of endings were of the 'happy' variety, thereby affirming the socially sanctioned moral norms. Goodlad concluded that these results vindicated his hypotheses that the public goes to see popular drama in order to have its experiences of society, particularly with regard to socially accepted behaviour, structured and affirmed (expressive function) and that this kind of drama is instrumental in the dissemination and definition of the moral values and norms upon which the predominant social structure is based.

2.4.7. The sociology of symbolic forms

Under the heading 'sociology of symbolic forms' (P. Bourdieu), we should like to summarise the remaining dimensions of the Jakobson model – namely the metalinguistic dimension of the code, and the self-reflective, poetic dimension of the message itself.

In its very conception a code has something supra-individual about it, since communication is not possible without at least some degree of partial overlap of the sender- and receiver-codes. As a result, the verbal and non-verbal codes are to varying degrees strongly normative systems of rules which reflect the interests and needs of a particular society or social stratum. Examples of this are the behavioural norms associated with fashion or other such social conventions.

An individual's command of the aesthetic codes of a particular period signifies the extent of his or her ability to distinguish between aesthetic and non-aesthetic texts and to recognise the fictionality of aesthetic texts and their special relationship to the real world. Of course, this is not generally formulated explicitly, but rather remains implicit as a tacit social agreement between author and receiver. That it was not possible to assume that this competence existed in all the social strata of late sixteenth- and early seventeenth-century England, for example, is shown not only by contemporary reports on the intervention by members of an audience in dramatic situations they had understood as real, but was reproduced explicitly in the behaviour of the workmen in Shakespeare's *A Midsummer Night's Dream* towards their own play, and the naïve interventions of a fictional audience of workmen in the romanesque action in Beaumont and Fletcher's *The Knight of the Burning Pestle*. A contrasting phenomenon may be observed in modern theatre, particularly in happenings and documentary theatre, both of which strive, from the producer's perspective, to abolish the socially accepted consensus on the categorical distinction between real and fictional dramatic situations. By subverting the audience's expectations, they attempt to make it aware of – and adopt a critical attitude towards – fictionality as a conventional coding procedure.

An important part of the aesthetic codes are the inherited patterns of form and genre. As supra-individual 'institutions' they represent the sum of the existing aesthetic structures that are both available to the dramatist and comprehensible to the audience, and which have been conditioned in this capacity by social interests and needs. The dramatist Friedrich Dürrenmatt has emphasised this fact with reference to tragedy and comedy:

Tragedy and comedy are concepts of form, dramaturgical manners of behaviour, fictional figures of aesthetics which have the capacity to describe the same sort of thing. Only the conditions among which they arise are different, and these conditions only come within the ambit of art to a minor extent.

Tragedy assumes guilt, trouble, moderation, range of vision, responsibility. In the routine muddle of our century, in this last dance of the white race, there are no longer any guilty people, nor any responsible ones either. . . . Only comedy can still get at us.[38]

Dürrenmatt presumably had the tragedies of French and German classicism in mind here, whose social premises consisted in the belief in an individual that is autonomous in his or her actions and rational in his or her thought, and in a fixed and coherent philosophical system. Since the nineteenth century it has become impossible to apply these premises to modern drama. The modern individual is regarded as a biologically and psychologically determined being, bound by social influences and constraints. The old unified view of the world has given way to a whole range of rival social viewpoints. This has also affected the structure of the tragic mode as a part of the aesthetic code. Since the plays of Büchner and naturalist drama, tragedy has lost its central position in the system of dramatic genres and been replaced by comedy, the modern form of tragicomedy, the problem play, the 'theatre of the absurd' and other recent developments. An important formal aspect of the structural change in the genre of tragedy is the replacement of the tectonic or closed form by atectonic or open forms (see above, 6.4.3.). Although this development occurred in the field of tragedy, it can also be understood as a paradigm for a more general affinity between strictly hierarchical social structures and formal unity or standardisation in the field of aesthetics.

The exploratory questions sketched out here do not amount to a complete repertoire for describing the pragmatic elements of dramatic texts. This introductory analysis never pretended to provide a complete answer. Instead, the intention underlying this sketch was to arrange these initial questions into some sort of systematic order, so as to clarify the various communicative dimensions and their structural interdependence.

2.5. The dramatic text and the audience

2.5.1. Collective reception and the transmission of information

In the preceding section we concentrated our attention on the sociological make-up of the audience and in doing so identified a number of historical structural types. The collective nature of the reception of dramatic texts, however, is itself a historical and sociological constant – that is, apart from a few pathological exceptions such as Ludwig II of Bavaria, the king who arranged private performances of Wagner operas with himself as an audience of one. The intended collective reception of a dramatic text has considerable bearing on its internal structure. A. W. Schlegel emphasised this in his *Lectures on Dramatic Art and Literature*, when he identified the theatrical component of dramatic texts as their capacity to 'have an effect on a crowd of people, to focus their attention, and to stimulate their participation', thus demanding of a dramatic text the qualities of a popular speech, namely 'clarity, speed, and vigour'.[39] In nineteenth-century France, too, Francisque Sarcey emphasised this reception-orientated aesthetic perspective by declaring that the audience should be the subject of the first and most important chapter of every dramaturgical treatise, and defining the art of drama provocatively as the art of keeping an audience in the theatre.[40] Despite this, twentieth-century theoretical studies of drama have largely continued to disregard the collective nature of reception and its influence on the structure of dramatic texts.[41]

One consequence of the collective reception of dramatic texts is that the individual receiver is unable to vary the tempo of the reception process, nor can he usually interrupt it at will or have sections repeated if he has failed to understand the text. The reader of a novel, on the other hand, can determine his own reading speed, abandon or take up the text when he wishes, or even simply leaf through it forwards or backwards as his whim takes him. This embedding of individual reception into collective reception even conditions the length of dramatic texts. For whilst it is impossible to set upper or lower limits for the length of a narrative text – they may vary from an anecdote of a few lines to a baroque novel of several thousand pages – the length of a dramatic text generally falls between two relatively narrow parameters. The upper limit is defined by the physiological needs and endurance of the audience, with the result that a text lasting longer than around five hours is only possible by the insertion of correspondingly long intervals. A lower limit is set by determining an appropriate relationship between the personal and organisational effort put into a production, the level of audience attendance and the quantity of text. Samuel Beckett's *Breath*, which lasts less than a minute and yet is performed on its own, clearly transgresses this lower limit, but in doing so it serves to make the audience critically aware of these normative conventions.

If its collective reception means that the performance of a dramatic text is irreversible, then the clarity and comprehensibility with which the information is transmitted becomes an important focus of dramaturgical attention. In order to ensure successful communication in the theatre certain degrees of codal complexity on both the macrostructural level of figure conception and plot, and the microstructural level of verbal and stylistic texture should not be exceeded.

This degree of complexity is, of course, historically variable depending on the level of education in the audience and the reception conventions of the time. In the Restoration period in England, for example, in which going to the theatre had a markedly social function and the reception of the text was interrupted and accompanied by social intercourse, the degree of complexity of the dramatic texts was necessarily lower than it is in the modern 'high-brow' theatre, in which, thanks to a greater appreciation of the value of art, it is possible to reckon with a greater level of concentrated attention on the part of the audience. Beyond this, however, there are fundamental limitations to the degree of complexity, and this is shown by the number of relatively ahistorical strategies that are employed to reduce or clarify the information transmitted in dramatic texts. These include concentration on the central situation and conditions, transparency of the macrostructure, the use of redundancy created by the multiple transmission of the same information in both verbal *and* non-verbal codes, and, finally, the repetition of information by, for example, anticipating the events of the next scene and then providing a summary of them later on (see below, 6.2.2.3.).

2.5.2. The social psychology of collective reception

The aspects outlined above give the impression that the influence exerted on dramatic texts by the collective nature of their reception is merely negative and restrictive. However, this may be countered by remembering that the collective aspect actually increases the intensity of the reception. If we read the printed literary text of a comic scene on our own, we are generally less inclined to laugh than when we experience it with others in the theatre. Even if it were possible to trace this difference in intensity back to the difference between a purely verbal and a multimedial text, it would still be necessary to explain why the same scene is received less intensively when the auditorium is half-empty than when it is sold out. Obviously, collective reception sparks off various socio-psychological group-dynamic processes in which the numerous individual reactions reinforce and harmonise with each other to produce a relatively homogeneous group reaction.

2.5.3. Feedback from the audience to the stage

In actors' memoirs, the homogeneity of an audience's reactions is often described in terms of an intuitive, rhythmic form of synchronisation between actor and audience. These memoirs also contain frequent references to the effect of the audience's reactions on the production itself – that is, on the way it 'carries' the actor, improves his performance, stimulates him into spontaneous improvisation, or, conversely, unnerves or inhibits him.[42] This feedback effect also explains why a performance of even the most carefully rehearsed production is different to the one before, depending on the particular audience involved, and why each performance is unique and unrepeatable – in a way that the technically reproducible dramatic texts of films and television- or radio-plays are not.

Of course, this feedback effect could never be described even potentially as a symmetrical two-way communication system with reversible senders and receivers, as is ideally the case in face-to-face communication. Here, the relationship between senders and receivers is asymmetrical, though, of course, this asymmetry is historically and typologically extremely varied. The *commedia dell'arte*, with its freedom to improvise, relied heavily on reactions from the audience, and certain modern theatrical experiments have striven to regain this more spontaneous form of interplay with the audience. By contrast, the feedback effect in serious contemporary theatre is only of marginal significance. The reason for this is that, on the one hand, the modern audience is neither very spontaneous nor does it react in an extrovert way, and on the other, the high standard of professional acting and the care taken over the production mean that the dramatic text is largely fixed on all its levels and is therefore largely reproducible.[43]

In the preceding discussion of the psychology of perception and memory in the reception process, the socio-psychological processes taking place in the audience and the interplay between the actors and the audience, we concentrated our attention on position R4 in the external communication system – that is, on the receivers intended by the author and, in addition, on the total number of actual receivers of a dramatic text. In the following chapters, however, we shall turn our attention to the relationships that exist within the internal system. We shall therefore have to move away from the historical, sociological and psychological contexts of the receivers outside the text in order to argue from the point of view of the idealised receiver implied in the text itself (R3).

3. Sending and receiving information

3.1. Information in the internal and external communication systems

One of the difficulties involved in analysing the ways information is transmitted in dramatic texts results from the embedding of the internal communication system in the external system that we referred to in chapter one. Generally speaking, the informational value of a single verbal or non-verbal signal changes according to whether it is evaluated within the framework of the internal or the external communication system. An example of this would be a particular interior décor presented on stage. Normally, this is of little informational value to the figures acting within it, since it is merely a part of their familiar and automatically perceived environment. For the audience, however, it is often the bearer of important information that reveals something of the characteristics of the fictional protagonists inhabiting it (see below, 5.4.2.3.). Similarly, in the sphere of verbal communication there are speeches that have scarcely any novelty value for the fictional listener on stage, but which serve to clarify certain relationships for the audience. Speeches of this kind are particularly common in the exposition sections, during which the audience has to be informed of the events leading up to the play, although these are already familiar to the fictional characters on stage.

An example of this is Prospero's report on Ariel's past in *The Tempest* (I,ii,250–93); this contains no information that could possibly be unfamiliar to Ariel, but it is new, and thus important, to the audience. In dialogues of this kind it is interesting to observe the techniques the dramatist employs in his efforts to veil the informative intention (see below 3.7.2.) and to make such a psychologically implausible conversation credible within the internal communication system. Thus, in this example, Prospero's internally redundant report is justified as an attempt to make Ariel aware of the extent of his ingratitude.

Naturally, the reverse situation also arises – that is, when a speech is redundant in the external communication system but of great informational importance to one or more of the fictional characters on stage. In such cases, the attention of the already well-informed audience is left free to focus on both the reactions of the as yet uninformed figure or figures and the form and perspective given to the information by the informant involved. An example of this is the letter Macbeth writes to his wife informing her of his meeting with the three witches (I,v,1–11), a scene that the audience had already witnessed in dramatic form two scenes earlier.

Extreme cases of this kind demonstrate that there is always a fundamental divergence in the informational value of a message according to whether it is considered within the context of the internal or external communication system of a dramatic text – even if it does not always take quite such a radical form. An analysis of a dramatic text from the point of view of sending and receiving information must therefore always take this into consideration.

3.2. Advance information and the audience's horizon of expectations

3.2.1. The expectations associated with genre and the titles as advance information

These headings already indicate that, on the basis of socially received knowledge and experience and a certain familiarity with the conventions of dramatic texts, the receivers of a dramatic text bring information to bear on a performance that is inaccessible to the fictional protagonists. On the most general and thus historically the least variable level, this refers to the divergence between the audience's awareness of the fictionality of what is presented on the one hand, and the fictional figures' 'awareness of reality' on the other. This divergence is always present in latent form and may become more explicit if the fictional figures present their own reality as illusory by invoking the image of the theatre.[1]

In this case, the divergence is derived from fictionality, which is the most general of all criteria governing aesthetic texts – though it should not be forgotten that fictionality *per se* can assume various historical forms, the fictionality of a Greek tragedy being rather different from that of a medieval mystery play and different again from that of a drama by Brecht. However, this divergence becomes much sharper when the audience has specific expectations associated with a particular genre, and this may be illustrated by the following simple example.

Part of the horizon of expectation of a knowledgeable Elizabethan theatre-going public was the assumption that, by definition, a comedy had a happy ending, at least for the positive figures. The contemporary receiver of Shakespeare's *Comedy of Errors* knew as early as the first act that Aegeon would escape the death sentence that threatened him and be reunited with his wife Emilia and their twin sons. The conventions of the genre guarantee a non-tragic solution of this kind, thereby enabling the audience to follow the often ominous 'errors' with the distance that is necessary as a precondition of comic effect. The fictional protagonists, by contrast, are simply not aware that they are participating in comic theatre, nor are they aware of the conventions associated with the comic mode. They therefore react to the alarming events with complete existential seriousness.

This is no more than a particularly clear example of how the audience's advance knowledge of generic conventions affects the passage of information in the external communication system. Further examples could be cited at will. Thus, the title of a play, in accordance with the rhetorical convention that demands that it should point forward to a crucial episode in the text, also contains advance information which affects the reception process – whether it refers to the central figure (as in the *Oresteia*, *Hamlet* or *Mother Courage*) or passes some form of moral judgement on him or her (as in Molière's *L'Avare* or Ben Jonson's *Volpone*), whether it anticipates the atmosphere of the play (as in *Twelfth Night*) or points towards a central element in the plot (as in *The Taming of the Shrew*, Beckett's *Waiting for Godot* and Heinrich von Kleist's *The Broken Jug*), or, finally, whether it suggests ways of evaluating the action (as in Calderón's *La vida es sueño* and Marivaux's *Le Jeu de l'amour et du hazard*).

Of course, as with generic expectation, advance information of this kind can be a form of strategic disinformation if the author invokes a convention and the expectations associated with it only to break them. By disappointing the audience's expectations, the dramatist increases both the audience's attention and the informational value of the deviating elements. The discrepancy between what is expected and what actually occurs can be used to create an ironic effect. In this sense, many productions of the 'theatre of the absurd' frequently play around with the expectations associated with the genres of 'farce' and 'comedy'. An older example is Shakespeare's *Measure for Measure*, whose title leads one to expect an Old Testament pattern of value judgements, an expectation that is refuted and transcended in the play itself, rather than fulfilled. Advance information derived from the audience's generic expectations and the interpretation of the title is therefore by no means reliable. Nonetheless, even when it is modified or negated by the text, it still influences the reception of the text through its function as a contrasting background.

3.2.2. Thematic advance information

If the expectations associated with a particular genre presuppose advance information that refers to the form of a dramatic text, the advance information contained in the title is primarily of a thematic nature – so long as it does not actually announce the genre itself, such as the *Comedy of*

Errors, for example. Advance information of this kind is also conveyed in the frequent intertextual references in dramatic texts to mythical or historical events that the dramatist can safely assume are familiar to his or her intended audience.[2] The particular frequency of this referential aspect is probably conditioned by the medium itself. On the one hand, it is a consequence of the special affinity of drama as a collectively produced and received art form with the collective constitution of meaning in myth and history. At the same time, the reliance on collective advance knowledge enables the dramatist to cut the amount of information transmitted (see above 2.5.1.) since it relieves the exposition of the need to relate the events leading up to the play.

Advance knowledge, whether furnished from myth or history, does not only embrace the background events, but also the context of the plot in its totality. In other words, the audience has prior knowledge not only of the events leading up to the play, but also of their further development. An example: the intended audience of Aeschylus' *Choephori*, the second play of the *Oresteia* trilogy, knows as soon as Orestes enters that there will be a recognition scene between himself and Electra, that the two of them will plot revenge against Clytemnestra and Aegisthus, and that Orestes will finally murder the adulterous couple. In view of such detailed advance knowledge, the information given in the play itself is therefore to some extent redundant. However, this redundancy has a twofold function. First, the discrepancy between the ignorance of the fictional protagonists and the awareness of the audience creates dramatic irony (see below, 3.4.3.). Secondly, and more importantly, it releases the attention of the audience to appreciate the particular variant and interpretation of the myth enacted in the play.

This example also serves to illustrate a second point. The episode from the saga of the House of Atreus that was dramatised in this play was adapted again in the same century in the two versions of *Electra* by Sophocles and Euripides. The reception of these plays was therefore determined not only by advance knowledge of the myth, but also by the audience's awareness of the previous dramatic versions of it. This last kind of knowledge has the effect of forming a contrasting intertextual background which emphasises the elements that deviate from the older version, thus enduing those elements with greater informational significance. Sophocles transferred the focus of the presentation away from Orestes' metaphysical inner conflict over the question of action and revenge on to Electra, whose character is given greater depth by her peripeteia from hopelessness to hope after recognising the brother she had believed to be dead, and greater psychological sophistication by contrasting and confronting her dialogically with Clytemnestra and a sister, Chrysothemis, invented by Sophocles for that purpose. In Euripides' version, the myth was changed even more substantially. The locale was moved from the royal palace at Mycenae into the country where Electra had been banished to prevent her avenging the murder of her father. The dramatist explains the reasons for this drastically altered starting-point in a long exposition in the form of a narrative prologue delivered by Electra's husband – again a figure invented by the author. The recognition scene is drawn out over several stages, the revenge on Aegisthus and Clytemnestra expanded into a plot of intrigue conducted on two different levels, and in the final *deus-ex-machina* entrance of Zeus's sons, Castor and Pollux, who discuss the metaphysical import of the events, the myth is turned against itself in order to demonstrate 'the inability of the Olympian Gods to establish a decent moral order on earth'.[3] However, this interpretation is possible only when the play is seen against the background of both the myth as it was handed down and the previous dramatised versions of it, an awareness of which could be assumed by the playwright concerned.

This type of intertextual reference back to previous dramatic versions of mythical or historical material is an extremely common feature of dramatic texts. The reasons for this have already been given. In line with his own theatrical productions, in which the adaptation of existing dramas played a particularly important part, Brecht put forward as early as the 1920s a theory for the adaptation of plays, in which the 'material' stood for the extent of the audience's advance knowledge and the 'new viewpoints' for the innovative informational aspect.[4]

3.3. The interrelationship of verbal and non-verbal information

3.3.1. The matrix of possible relationships

In the previous section on the relationship between the advance information available to the receivers and the transmission of information it was not deemed necessary to decipher the codes and channels used to transmit that information. This will be the aim of the present section, however. In 2.1.6. above we briefly discussed the quantitative variability of this relationship. Now we should like to analyse it more from the point of view of its qualitative and functional variability.

In the simplified model below, we have isolated three possible types of basic relationships, according to whether the information units transmitted through the verbal and non-verbal codes and channels are 'identical' to each other, 'complementary' or 'discrepant'. The matrix on page 45 should clarify what we mean by this.

Entries '+a' and '+b' are not mutually exclusive, whilst '+a' and '−a' are logical contradictions of each other. The heuristic advantage of this model is that it allows us to differentiate between various historical forms accord-

	Identity	Complementarity	Discrepancy
Verbally transmitted information:	+a	+a	+a
Non-verbally transmitted information:	+a	+a + b/+b	−a

ing to the constellation of these three elements prevalent at a particular time. Thus, in a theoretical programme such as Wagner's notion of the *Gesamtkunstwerk*, the predominating elements are identity and complementarity, whilst in the diametrically opposed theoretical model represented by Brecht's strict 'separation of the elements', they are complementarity and discrepancy.[5]

3.3.2. Identity

From the audience's point of view, the existence of 'identity' means that, in the majority of dramatic texts, familiarity with the primary text is sufficient in itself to ensure a reasonable measure of comprehension. The more this relationship predominates, the more redundant non-verbally transmitted information becomes in comparison with the verbal primary text. Information that has already been mediated verbally is merely 'translated' into the medium of mime and gesture, and into the physical immediacy of the stage. Thus, identity always occurs when stage-directions are implicit in the primary text (see above 2.1.4.). Of course, it is rare that identity, this redundant doubling-up of verbal and non-verbal information, occurs in such a pure form as in the following passage from Samuel Beckett's play *Happy Days*:

> WINNIE (Pause. She takes up a mirror): I take up this little glass, I shiver it on a stone – (does so) – I throw it away (does so far behind her) . . .[6]

The virtual identity of primary and secondary text in this passage makes the doubling-up of verbal and non-verbal information clear even from the printed text. This creates the impression that in doing so Beckett was trying to produce a pure and extreme example of one particular dramatic technique in order to draw the audience's attention to that technique and to turn it into an implicit theme in itself. At the same time, however, the predominance of identity is also motivated from within the internal communication system, since on the basis of her equating verbal and non-verbal or mimetic and gestural behaviour, Winnie is identified as a figure with a pathological urge to give verbal expression to the banal. In this example, then, redundancy functions as another way of characterising the speaker.

Identity can also be an important aspect of realist drama. The following extract from Ibsen's *A Doll's House*, reproduced without the stage-directions, is a clear illustration of this:

> HELMER: . . . Nora, what do think I've got here?
> NORA: . . . Money!
> HELMER: There! . . . Good heavens, I know only too well how Christmas runs away with the house-keeping.
> NORA: . . . Ten, twenty, thirty, forty. Oh, thank you, thank you, Torvald! This will see me quite a long way.
> HELMER: Yes, it'll have to.
> NORA: Yes, yes, I'll see that it does. But come over here, I want to show you all the things I've bought. And so cheap! Look, some new clothes for Ivar . . . and a little sword. There's a horse and a trumpet for Bob. And a doll and a doll's cot for Emmy. They are not very grand but she'll have them all broken before long anyway. And I've got some dress material and some handkerchiefs for the maids. Though, really, dear old Anne-Marie should have had something better.
> HELMER: And what's in this parcel here?
> NORA: . . . No, Torvald! You mustn't see that till tonight![7]

A high percentage of the verbally transmitted information is mediated non-verbally at the same time. The questions directed at the dialogue partner, the discovery of the purse, the handing-over of the money, the inspection of the Christmas shopping, Helmer's interest in the parcel and Nora's warding-off gesture are all actions that are clearly implied in the dialogue of the primary text. The frequent deictic references such as 'here' or 'there', and the verbal description of the objects have their information-al correlatives in the physical presence of the set and the properties.

3.3.3. Complementarity

Nevertheless, even in passages such as this one, which is so rich in signals to the producer, the relationship between verbal and non-verbal informa-tion is not restricted to the dimension of identity alone, but is also con-stantly being enriched by the synthetic dimension of complementarity (for the contrast between 'analytical' and 'synthetic' see above, 2.1.6.). Non-verbal information does not just involve repeating or translating informa-tion that has already been transmitted verbally – whether implicitly or explicitly. It will also always complement this to form a closed and concrete continuum of illusion. From a purely verbal point of view, the questions directed towards the dialogue partner in the above extract remain abstract, but with the addition of mime and gesture they become more individual and are given a particular physical interpretation. This establishes the spatial arrangement of the dialogue partners and embeds them firmly in a specific and coherent set – something that is realised verbally only to a partial extent. In their concrete plasticity, the 'new clothes for Ivar' become 'meaningful' properties etc. Thus, in this passage which conforms to the conventions of realist drama the element of complementarity accompanies identity, complementing the verbal transmission of information to a coherent and three-dimensional model of reality. This corresponds to the type: verbal '+a', non-verbal '+a +b'.

Complementarity displays greater independence in type: verbal '+a', non-verbal '+b'. This is especially common in cases where the primary text contains few implicit stage-directions, or where, as in Edward Bond's *Saved*, the verbally transmitted information loses significance, at least in purely quantitative terms, in favour of mime and gesture, frequently leaving the actors to act in silence, or, finally, where sequences of verbal and non-verbal information are transmitted alternately.

Examples of the first are the numerous discussion scenes in Shaw's dramas. In these, the verbal information given is often entirely preoccupied with defining the dialectical positions of an ideological problem, whilst the set and the use of mime and gesture – described in detail in the stage-directions contained in the extensive secondary text – subjectify the ideological positions, give emotional nuances to them and place them in a particular social milieu. The following dialogue from *Major Barbara* contains stage-directions in the secondary text that are not implied in the primary text at all. In fact, they relativise it in a decisive way:

> BARBARA: . . . We want thousands! tens of thousands! hundreds of thousands! I want to convert people, not to be always begging for the Army in a way I'd die sooner than beg for myself.
> UNDERSHAFT: (in profound irony) Genuine unselfishness is capable of anything, my dear.
> BARBARA: (unsuspectingly, as she turns away to take the money from the drum and put it in a cash bag she carries) Yes, isn't it? (Undershaft looks sardonically at Cusins).
> CUSINS: (aside to Undershaft) Mephistopheles! Machiavelli!
> BARBARA: (tears coming into her eyes as she ties the bag and pockets it) How are we to feed them? I can't talk religion to a man with bodily hunger in his eyes. (Almost breaking down) It's frightful.[8]

The alternate transmission of verbal and non-verbal information was discussed in 2.1.6. above. Here, too, it is possible to distinguish between complementarity and identity. Although, for example, the spoken scenes in the Elizabethan dumb shows in the Senecan tradition or those in the German baroque tragedy with its allegorical tableaux[9] were preceded or followed by mimetic or allegorical interpretations of their contents, this did not necessarily mean that the verbally transmitted information had been merely translated or repeated into a non-verbal medium – which is what would have been the case with identity. Instead, the specific situation presented in the spoken scene functions as an example for a more general problem which is then complemented by the allegorical or emblematic abstractions associated with pure mime.

3.3.4. Discrepancy

Whilst identity and complementarity are features of all dramatic texts – albeit in a range of historically and typologically variable combinations – the predominance of discrepancy appears to be a more recent development. By discrepancy we do not just mean any contradiction that may occur between a character's words and his or her actions since these can often be understood psychologically and thus be resolved by the receiver. Situations involving disguise or deception, for example, could therefore be interpreted as extreme cases of complementarity. Instead, we understand it to be a radical and unresolvable discrepancy between verbally and non-verbally transmitted pieces of information. The development of this particular relationship ought therefore to be seen in the context of the innovatory tendencies prevalent in modern drama which have broken the established principles of dramatic textualisation that have traditionally been regarded as axiomatic, namely, the Aristotelian concept of drama as the representation of action, fictionality, the separation of the internal and external communication systems, and the conventional repertoire of codes and channels in dramatic texts. By breaking these conventions, the dramatist makes the audience aware of their very conventionality and axiomatic status. The displacement of identity and complementarity by discrepancy thus represents a violation of the existing fundamental principles of dramatic textualisation. To illustrate this, we should like to cite three short passages from Samuel Beckett's *Waiting for Godot* in which discrepancy occurs, two of which are in a particularly prominent position at the end of an act:

> ESTRAGON: I'm going.
>   (He does not move)
> ESTRAGON: Well, shall we go?
> VLADIMIR: Yes, let's go.
>   (They do not move)
> VLADIMIR: Well? Shall we go?
> ESTRAGON: Yes, let's go.
>   (They do not move)[10]

The discrepancy between the directions implied in the dialogue and the figure's non-verbal behaviour can no longer be explained in purely psychological terms as evidence of Estragon's and Vladimir's indecisiveness or of the incompatibility of their desires and capabilities. The discrepancy that occurs here is the formal equivalent of an ideological position in which the very possibility of intentional action – and thus one of the key precepts of Aristotelian dramatic theory – has become problematic.

Of course, the three aspects that we have discussed in the last three sections never occur in isolation. They always overlap to some degree or other. The variability of the relationships between the three aspects is as common in typologically and historically diverse texts as it is in the course of a single text.

3.4. Levels of awareness in the dramatic figures and the audience

3.4.1. Discrepant awareness

The problems associated with the transmission of information should not be discussed in the context of the external communication system alone. Information is also sent and received within the internal communication system, in which the levels of awareness attained by the individual figures fluctuate constantly. A further aspect that is subject to constant change is the relationship between the levels of awareness of the dramatic figures on the one hand, and that of the audience on the other. In fact, in Friedrich Dürrenmatt's view, it is this discrepancy between audience and figure awareness that contains the very essence of the dramatic:

If I show two people drinking coffee together and talking about the weather, politics or fashion, however cleverly they may be doing this, it is not as yet a dramatic situation or a dramatic dialogue. Something must be added which will make their speech special, dramatic, ambiguous. If, for instance, the audience know that there is poison in one of the coffee-cups, or indeed both, so that what results is a conversation of two poisoners drinking coffee, as a result of this trick a dramatic situation emerges from which and at the basis of which the possibility of dramatic dialogue ensues.[11]

The 'ambiguity' of dramatic dialogue which Dürrenmatt illustrates here is nothing other than the overlapping of the internal and external communication systems that we described in 1.2.2. as just one of the qualities necessary for identifying dramatic communication – but by no means the only one.

In more recent literary criticism in English, the expression 'discrepant awareness' has gained general acceptance as the most appropriate way to describe this phenomenon. It was coined by Bertrand Evans, who studied Shakespeare's comedies with particular emphasis on their 'arrangements of discrepant awarenesses' and the 'dramatist's means and ends in the creation, maintenance and exploitation of differences in the awarenesses of the participants and of differences between participants' awarenesses and ours as audience.'[12]

The concept of 'discrepant awareness' refers to two different relationships. First, there are the differences in the levels of awareness of the various dramatic figures, and, secondly, there are those between the fictional figures and the audience. Thus, the first aspect refers exclusively to the internal communication system, whilst the second refers to the relationship between the internal and external systems. Before going any further, we ought to clarify what we mean by 'awareness', with reference to both the dramatic figures and the audience.

From the events leading up to the play the figures bring a body of background information into it which they then articulate in the course of the dramatic action. All we are interested in is the advance information actually articulated by the dramatic figures; to speculate on a greater degree of prescience is to misunderstand the status of fictional figures. Their advance information is then expanded in the course of the play itself by the information received both from dialogue and from their observations of their respective environments. It is therefore possible to calculate the sum of information held by each dramatic figure at any point in the text which they are able to use as a factual basis to help them assess each particular dramatic situation. However, as a result of their discrepant awareness, the same situation is assessed differently by each figure involved. Dürrenmatt's example serves as an illustration of this: figure *A*, who knows that figure *B*'s coffee is poisoned, assesses the situation differently to the unsuspecting character *B*. Or – to make it symmetrical – if *A* knows that *B*'s coffee is poisoned and *B* knows that *A*'s coffee is poisoned, their respective assessments of the situation will be diametrically opposed. In this, the concept of audience awareness remains relatively abstract since the thematic and formal advance information that we analysed in 3.2. is not brought to bear. The only relevant information at this point is what the audience receives by listening in on the conversations of the dramatic figures, and that received through the non-verbal codes and channels. Here too, then, it is possible to establish the level of audience awareness at every point in the course of the text with which it judges each particular situation.

The discrepant awareness that separates dramatic figures and the audience is the result of two contradictory factors. First, the audience is always present as a group of spectators throughout the action, whereas the individual figures do not generally participate directly in more than a part of it. The audience is therefore in the position of being able to join up and collate the partial 'awarenesses' of the individual figures. At the same time, the advance information held by the figures introduces an element of insecurity for the audience, because it can never know until the end whether or not a figure has articulated his or her advance information in full, or whether important pieces of information have been suppressed.

These two factors work against each other and bring about opposing structures of discrepant awareness. The first is capable of creating a situation where the audience knows more than the individual figures, whereas the second leads to the reverse.

3.4.1.1. Superior audience awareness

In the corpus of existing dramatic texts that stretches from classical antiquity to the present day, the quantitative bias in the discrepant levels of awareness has almost always been in favour of the audience rather than the dramatic figures. This is true of both tragedy and comedy. Indeed, the essence of both the tragic and the comic is frequently to be found in the contrast between the superior awareness of the audience and the inferior awareness of the dramatic figures, a view Lessing clearly supported in Part 48 of his *Hamburg Dramaturgy*:

> It is true, our surprise is greater if we do not discover with complete certainty that Aegisthus is Aegisthus before Merope discovers it herself. But the enjoyment gained from surprise is so thin! And why should a poet need to surprise us? May he surprise his characters as much as he wishes; we for our part know what to take even if we have foreseen the events that will befall them long before they do themselves. Yes, the longer and more reliably we have been to foresee what will happen, the greater our involvement will become. . . . If . . . we are aware of everything concerning the characters then I regard this as a prerequisite for and source of the most moving emotions.[13]

From its position of superior awareness, the audience is able to recognise the discrepancies between the levels of awareness in the individual dramatic figures. It is therefore consciously aware of the ambiguities of every situation, and is thus in a position to judge to what extent the figures' differing assessments of a given situation deviate from the facts. As a contrast to the existential problems of real life, this superior awareness can be very pleasurable. This element in the reception of texts of this type is occasionally condemned as 'escapist', but it is complemented aesthetically and cognitively by the realisation that, potentially, there are always tragic or comic discrepancies between the actual objective circumstances and the subjective interpretation of them, and that a particular view of reality is always dependent on the level of information available.

Let us clarify the patterns of superior awareness by analysing one concrete example: Plautus' *The Brothers Menaechmus* – and, as a point of comparison, the play by Shakespeare that was based on it, *A Comedy of Errors*. We have chosen these particular plays because the patterns of discrepant awareness they display are particularly simple. The dramatic figures are all equally unaware of the crucial secret of the drama, namely the presence of twin brothers in the city. There is no discrepant awareness between the various figures in this respect. However, the audience in both Shakespeare and Plautus are let in on the secret early on in the play. The difference between Plautus' original and its Elizabethan imitation lies in the techniques employed to supply this information. Plautus introduces it in the form of a prologue before the drama proper. Addressing the audience directly, the anonymous speaker – who is not a member of the dramatis personae – relates the story of the twin brothers up to the beginning of the play. This then leads directly into the first scene: the arrival of Menaechmus of Syracuse in Epidamnus in search of his missing twin brother.

Shakespeare's version dramatises this epic narrative by introducing an additional figure to the drama who can be plausibly seen as being informed about the events leading up to the play – namely Aegeon, the twins' father. These events are then presented dramatically in dialogue form in Act I, Scene i. Admittedly, Aegeon is unaware of the most recent events and thus cannot know that his twin sons, together with a pair of twin servants, are in the same city as he is himself. However, this last fact is conveyed to the audience in the next scene by the arrival of Antipholus and Dromio from Syracuse and Dromio from Ephesus. The complex game of mistaken identity and deception that this initiates, and which remains on a constant level of discrepant awareness throughout, is structured to enable two separate strands of plot to become repeatedly intertwined. Each time these strands overlap – that is, each time the figures from Syracuse meet those from Ephesus – the situation is judged by the participants from two complementary perspectives which, by the repeated addition of new and falsely interpreted information, grow further and further apart. The sole witness to each and every one of these encounters is the audience who thus attain a level of awareness that enables it to fuse the various complementary perspectives into a single reception perspective. In fact, this is the source of one of the key ironies in both *A Comedy of Errors* and *The Brothers Menaechmus*. What appears as confused chaos to the protagonists involved is in fact, as far as the audience is concerned, a geometrical pattern of complementary misunderstandings.

3.4.1.2. Inferior audience awareness

As a dominating factor in dramatic texts, inferior audience awareness is far less common than the reverse. In fact, it does not even necessarily predominate in dramas that use an analytical technique. Sophocles' *Oedipus the King*, for example, which Schiller regarded as an ideal model for 'tragic analysis',[14] initiates the audience into the central secret of the events leading up to the play very early on – in addition to any advance knowledge the audience might have of the myth:

The most inspired feature of the structure of this play ... is the fact that the whole truth is revealed briskly right at the outset. Teiresias wishes to remain silent but Oedipus manages to extract the truth from him – namely that he, Oedipus the King, is the murderer now living in an incestuous relationship. ... And then slowly, step by step, the spoken utterances of the first part of the play are imbued with the validity of something that has been recognised as the truth.[15]

Here too, then, by analogy with the pattern of superior awareness, the specific awareness of the audience is contrasted with the ignorance of the central figure who, although he knows the truth, does not accept it as such:

The seeing and yet blind Oedipus constitutes the empty centre of a world that is aware of his fate, a world whose messengers gradually succeed in conquering his innermost being and filling it with the awful truth.[16]

One play in which the pattern of inferior audience awareness does play an important part is a comic version of the Oedipus myth, Heinrich von Kleist's *The Broken Jug*. For the first few scenes of the play the spectator remains unaware of the nocturnal escapades of the village judge, Adam, and is thus in a state of inferior awareness in relation to him. He does not yet see through Adam's excuses and attempts to deceive the other figures. This lack of awareness arouses a sense of suspense in the audience, allowing it the intellectual enjoyment of indulging in hypothesis and speculative detective work. Slowly, however, the hints and clues as to the real situation begin to accumulate until, at the beginning of Scene vii, when Adam delivers one of his few monologues, a short three-line aside, suspicion becomes certainty: 'Surely they won't haul me up before myself?'

By now, at the latest, the pattern of discrepant awareness has been reversed. The gap in the audience's knowledge of the central figure has been filled and it possesses a clear informational advantage over the other figures who, even if they suspect something, have no proof. The audience is thus able to follow both the increasingly desperate and absurd stratagems adopted by Adam and the way the other figures close in on the truth as a process of dramatic development. This combination of two conflicting patterns of discrepant awareness in *The Broken Jug* is clearly a significant factor in its effectiveness on stage.

In Ibsen's dramas, whose structures are determined almost exclusively by their analytical technique,[17] the dramatic present appears as an epiphenomenon of events in the distant past, manifested in dialogue form. Even here, however, inferior awareness cannot be said to be a predominant feature. In *Nora*, for example, it is only in the first half of Act I that the audience has access to considerably less information than the central figure. Nora's secret attempts to save her husband are presented to the audience early on in the dialogue between Nora and Mrs Linde, and the legal complications that arise out of these attempts are the subject of the dialogue between Nora and Krogstadt. This lack of information in the initial phase of the play makes it impossible for the audience to correct Helmer's view of his wife – also conditioned by an informational deficiency – as a superficial, thoughtless and wasteful creature and serves to make Helmer's distorted and superficial judgements credible to the audience.

The lack of information available to the audience is therefore not intended to arouse suspense or bewilderment, but serves an identificatory function. For, although Helmer's view of his wife is later undermined and devalued, it must be made plausible to the audience – at least initially. The price of this effect, however, is a loss of 'ambiguity'. The opening dialogue between Nora and Helmer is full of ironic contradictions between Helmer's view and the true situation which the audience cannot appreciate the first time round – except perhaps retrospectively. The change in the pattern of discrepant awareness from inferior to superior on the audience's part that occurs in Act I takes this circumstance into consideration.

In creating patterns of inferior awareness, the texts we have discussed share a common device, namely the reduction in the communicative possibilities open to a dramatic figure. The information carrier is left opaque and is only presented in dialogues with figures in front of whom it has to suppress important information. In such cases, dramatists tend to avoid conventions such as the soliloquy as far as possible. The need for such restrictions and the subsequent loss of 'ambivalence' in the dramatic situations and dialogues make it easier to understand why there are so few texts that are dominated throughout by patterns of inferior awareness. Most of those that do exist are what are known as trivial dramas, whose intended effect is both generated by and restricted to creating powerful elements of suspense and surprise or encouraging the audience to indulge in intellectual detective work. The classical examples of this genre are the British or American 'whodunnits' and thrillers, in which the audience competes with the fictional detective in the race to decipher the clues and thus to reconstruct the events that happened before the play started. Of course, texts of this kind are only intended to be seen once, since actually knowing 'whodunnit' undermines the whole intended effect. That they nonetheless continue to find an audience is demonstrated emphatically by the popularity of Agatha Christie's *Mousetrap*, a play that has been performed continuously in a London commercial theatre since 1952.

3.4.2. Congruent awareness

In our analysis, the congruent awareness of audience and dramatic figures really represents a borderline case of discrepant awareness in which the element of discrepancy is zero. This perspective – that is, one in which discrepancy is shown to be the norm and congruence a deviating borderline case – is the most appropriate one for dramatic texts. Indeed, Bertrand Evan's intuitive generalisation that defines congruent awareness as 'the most prevalent way for both dramatic and narrative story-tellers past and present', 'the "normal" or standard way' to construct a text,[18] definitely does not apply to dramatic texts. Of course, congruent awareness does occur sporadically in all kinds of historically and typologically varied texts, but then usually only in one particular phase of the text or in the relationship between one particular figure and the audience. There are, however, very few texts that display this pattern throughout.

One such example is Samuel Beckett's *Waiting for Godot*, which we have already cited on a number of occasions as a manifestation of statistically uncommon, deviating structures. What is it that conditions congruent awareness as a predominant pattern in this play? First, it is undoubtedly Beckett's special conception of plot and figure. In the situation presented, the central figures Estragon and Vladimir appear isolated, almost completely divorced from any kind of past that may have existed before the play begins. The dramatic situation is not characterised by the kind of crisis that is demanded by the Aristotelian view of a dynamic dramatic plot, but by a static condition that appears to be without beginning and end, and whose causes are steadfastly ignored in the text. Consequently, there are no previous events conditioning the plot which could give the figures an informational advantage over the audience. The sole prerequisite for the situation presented is the earlier contact between Vladimir, Estragon and Godot, and yet even this contact is as vague and puzzling to the figures as it is to the audience. Did it really take place? If so, in what form?

A second point worth considering refers to the configurational patterns (see below, 5.3.3.) of the figures on stage. Apart from a few brief interludes, Vladimir and Estragon are continuously on stage together. As far as the time-period covered by the play is concerned, it is therefore impossible to speak of any significant form of discrepant awareness, either between the two protagonists or between them and the audience. The concurrence of these various factors in *Waiting for Godot* makes it possible for a condition of congruent awareness to prevail throughout – though perhaps it would be more accurate to describe it as a condition of congruent unawareness!

3.4.3. Dramatic irony

The theory of discrepant awareness forms an appropriate backdrop to an analysis of dramatic irony, the subject of this section. In any discussion of irony, though, it would be wrong to equate dramatic irony with irony in drama since the latter encompasses an extremely broad spectrum of ironic structures. Thus, one of the most famous examples of irony in all drama – Antony's spoken refrain 'Brutus is an honourable man' in his funeral oration for the central figure in Shakespeare's *Julius Caesar* (III, ii) – has nothing to do with dramatic irony in the strict sense since it is a verbal utterance that the speaker intended to be ironic, and whose irony is intended to be, and indeed does become, obvious to the fictional receivers. It is therefore an example of an ironic effect already operating within the internal communication system. Dramatic irony, on the other hand, is created when the internal and external communication systems interfere with each other and overlap.

If our concept of 'dramatic irony' is to retain any degree of clarity, then it must also exclude any theories that refer to irony as an intellectual posture rather than an aesthetic structure. This applies to the theories of R. B. Sharpe, for instance, for whom drama, as a form of 'impersonation' is itself fundamentally ironic since impersonation always implies the 'simultaneous perception of the two concepts "art" and "nature" as at the same time contradictory and harmonious, untrue and true'. It also applies to G. G. Sedgewick's receiver-oriented study, in which dramatic irony is generally felt to stem from the combination of superior knowledge and distanced sympathy. It may also be said to apply to B. O. States's theory which, as a derivation from Kenneth Burke's neo-rhetorical arguments, defines drama as 'the dancing of the ironic-dialectical attitude' and establishes a close connection between dramatic irony and the concept of peripeteia.[19] Finally, an additional obstacle to a clearer definition is the fact that in the jargon made popular by New Criticism, 'irony' and 'drama' are actually defined in identical terms, 'irony' being the conflict between an utterance and its context, and 'drama' being conflict pure and simple. As a result, drama, as a literary genre *per se*, becomes an ironic genre, and it even becomes possible to discover 'dramatic irony' in narrative or lyric texts.

In our own analysis, we shall restrict the term 'dramatic irony' to refer to the ironic contradictions that are created when the internal and external communication systems conflict with each other. This always happens whenever the superior awareness of the audience adds an additional layer of meaning to either the verbal utterance or the non-verbal behaviour of a figure on stage in such a way as to contradict or undermine the meaning intended by that figure. It is thus possible to talk of both verbal and non-verbal dramatic irony.

This definition of dramatic irony largely coincides with the concept of 'Sophoclean irony' that was formulated by nineteenth-century classical philologists to describe the ironic discrepancy between, for example, Oedipus' words and deeds, and the audience's advance knowledge of their consequences.[20] However, whilst the concept of 'Sophoclean irony' was only applied to the analysis of 'tragic irony', our view is that there is a direct structural correspondence between tragic irony and dramatic irony in comedy.

To illustrate this we should like to cite two Shakespeare plays as examples. His *Macbeth* is particularly rich in dramatic irony – to the extent that the individual incidences of it form an iterative pattern. Macbeth's opening words, 'So foul and fair a day I have not seen' (I, iii) are a particularly transparent and frequently cited example. The interpretation of these words as intended by Macbeth refers to the contrast between the appalling weather conditions and the joy felt after his military victory. At the same time, however, his remark reminds the audience of the witches' words in Act I, Scene i, 'Fair is foul, and foul is fair', which give Macbeth's words an ominous layer of additional meaning, of which the speaker himself is unaware. He has thus already subconsciously succumbed to the devilish influence of the witches even before he has actually seen them in the flesh. Dramatic irony is thus created on the syntagmatic level by arranging the dramatic situations in such a way as to make the links between them obvious to the audience but to keep them hidden from the stage-figure itself. On the paradigmatic level it rests in the ambiguity, of which the audience alone is aware, of a verbal or non-verbal utterance made by the dramatic figure.

A comic version of this very same structure may be found in the early Shakespearean comedy *The Two Gentlemen of Verona*, when Julia praises the fidelity of her lover Proteus in the following effusively rhetorical terms:

> His words are bonds, his oaths are oracles;
> His love sincere, his thoughts immaculate;
> His tears pure messengers sent from his heart;
> His heart as far from fraud as heaven from earth.   (II, vii, 75–78)

This speech is delivered to an audience that has just heard Proteus' long soliloquy in the immediately preceding scene, in which he determines, with no less rhetorical effort, to be unfaithful to Julia. As in *Macbeth*, the dramatic irony arises from the discrepancy between the figure's intended meaning and the actual interpretation of it by the audience. This discrepancy is the result of discrepant awareness, which is caused in turn by a particular arrangement of a sequence of scenes. The basic structures are identical. The only difference lies in the emotions that are attached to them.

3.5. The perspective structure of dramatic texts

3.5.1. Figure-perspective versus the reception-perspective intended by the author

The relationship between figure- and audience-awareness that we analysed in the previous section is only one particular dimension of the overall context of perspective structure.[21] For the perspective from which a dramatic figure observes the action and the perspectival nuances he gains from it are only partially conditioned by the level of advance information the figure has had access to. Two additional factors governing figure-perspective are psychological disposition and ideological orientation. As an illustration of this we can take the case of the Antipholus twins from Syracuse and Ephesus in Shakespeare's *Comedy of Errors*. Both figures are equally unaware that the mechanism of mistaken identity is the cause of their experiences. Nonetheless, these experiences, which encourage a sense of self-alienation and loss of identity, are perceived differently by the two men. Right from the start, the perspective associated with Antipholus from Syracuse is characterised by melancholy instability and a tendency to-wards the irrational, whereas that associated with his twin brother from Ephesus is moulded by a cholerical temperament, an underdeveloped imagination and an implicit trust in the rational. Thus, despite their congruent awareness a marked level of perspectival discrepancy is created by their conflicting temperaments and different ideological orientations.

We have not yet defined what we mean by perspective and have been using the word metaphorically rather than in any strict sense of the term. In fact, it is exactly because this concept has been used so imprecisely and in so many contradictory ways in previous dramatic theories[22] that we feel it is necessary to establish a coherent and clear theoretical definition of this term. It is only by doing this that the concept of perspective can become as heuristically fruitful for the analysis of drama as it has already been for some considerable time for the analysis of narrative texts.

On the basis of the model of overlapping external and internal com-munication systems, and by analogy with the distinction between figure- and audience-awareness it is important to distinguish between figure-perspective on the one hand and the reception-perspective intended by the author on the other. If we restrict ourselves initially to an ideal model of dramatic texts in which the external and internal communication systems are kept strictly separate – that is, to a model which fulfils Szondi's call for 'absolute autonomy' (see above, 1.2.3.) then each verbal utterance is associated strictly and in its entirety with the perspective of the figure making it who, in turn, can only articulate what corresponds plausibly to his or her particular dramatic situation and psychological disposition. Of course, the reverse is also true, namely that a figure's speeches constitute his perspective. The various figure-perspectives must be regarded as being independent of the author's personal perspective. Thus, the absolute autonomy of a drama with regard to audience and author implies that every verbal utterance in drama is associated entirely with a particular perspective.

As far as the verbal primary text is concerned, the 'absolute' dramatic text is therefore presented as a pattern of contrasting and corresponding figure-perspectives. On the level of the internal communication system it is 'polyperspectival'. Francis Fergusson has given us an apt description of the pattern of figure-perspectives in *Hamlet*:

The situation, the moral and metaphysical 'scene' of the drama, is presented only as one character after another sees or reflects it; and the action of the drama as a whole is presented only as each character in turn actualises it in his story and according to his lights.[23]

The various figure-perspectives are coordinated on equal terms – that is, they possess the same degree of fictionality and, in principle, have the same degree of validity for the receiver. From the outset, all of the figure-perspectives within the framework of the accepted principle of perspectivity are of equal importance in constituting the authorially intended reception-perspective.

3.5.2. The hierarchical arrangement of figure-perspectives

Of course, as an idealised model, the 'absolute' drama has no normative validity. In fact, there are many periods in the history of drama in which not a single play was written that was characterised by the unmediated superimposition of internal and external communication systems. Instead, playwrights have preferred to integrate some sort of mediating communication system or 'narrative function' (K. Hamburger) into their plays. These can either remain isolated incidents in the form of an informative or commentative aside, or a monologue *ad spectatores*, for example, or they can be integrated into the overall structure of the play. This is sometimes achieved by a particular use of songs or choruses, or by introducing a philosophising figure that can be distanced from the action (see below, 3.6.2.). Traditionally, then, dramatists have tended to create mediating communication systems that activate positions S2 and R2, whether in the guise of the chorus in classical tragedy, the objective self-descriptions of the allegorical figures in the medieval morality plays, the numerous examples of direct contact between stage and audience in plays ancient and modern, or Brecht's epic theatre. All of these examples involve a hierarchical pattern of figure-perspectives, with the perspective of the figure associated with the mediating narrative function situated above those of the other figures. The former, therefore, has a greater degree of validity since it embraces all of the other figure-perspectives. However, this does not mean that this superordinate figure-perspective can be equated with the authorially intended reception-perspective. There is a categorical distinction that must be upheld here, too, for the simple reason that it is possible to introduce an epic, mediating figure into a drama with the same ironic intention often associated with the fictional or 'unreliable' narrator

(W. C. Booth) in narrative texts. Even when there is no irony involved, the superordinate figure-perspective still does not coincide completely with the authorially intended reception-perspective because the subordinate figure-perspectives always have some kind of concrete, qualifying and relativising effect.

One example of the non-ironic application of a superordinate figure-perspective is the 'Singer' in Brecht's *The Caucasian Chalk Circle*, whose function is to provide a narrative transition from one episode to the next and add his own reflective commentary on the parable presented on stage. This figure is placed above the action and the figures that he reports on, and the parable is presented as if it had been produced by him – this is emphasised by the play-within-the-play structure – in order to illustrate the idea he formulates in the exposition, namely, 'That what there is shall belong to those who are good for it . . .'.[24] The 'Singer's' perspective, from which he comments on the events portrayed, is confirmed rather than undermined by the pattern of subordinate figure-perspectives.

The relationships between the various sub- and superordinate perspectives in plays like Thornton Wilder's *Our Town* are less unambiguous, however. Seen from the superordinate perspective of the 'Stage Manager', the events that take place in the small town are felt to be essentially trivial, dull and mundane, whereas from the subordinate perspectives of the inhabitants they are perceived as unique, moving and quite unusual. In this case, then, the contrast between the sub- and superordinate perspectives constitutes an authorially intended reception-perspective in which, to the universal consciousness, everyday events are given cosmic significance.

3.5.3. Techniques used to control and coordinate the perspectives

We should now like to determine how the audience in the external communication system is able to recreate the authorially intended reception-perspective from the range of individual figure-perspectives – or, seen from the production point of view, what channels are used by the author to influence the constitution of this perspective in the receiver. This question is especially pertinent in the case of 'absolute' dramatic texts, in which the author completely dispenses with the mediating figure-perspective. Nevertheless, it may also be asked of texts that have a hierarchical pattern of figure-perspectives since there is ultimately no reason why the superordinate, mediating character-perspective should be accepted as the ultimate authority.

3.5.3.1. A-perspectival information

First it should be remembered that the transmission of information in dramatic texts is not restricted to the verbal primary text alone. It is only a historically variable fraction of the total information transmitted that is mediated to the audience verbally via the perspectival 'awareness' of a particular figure. The rest – what is known as non-verbal information – is transmitted direct to the audience and remains completely independent of the various figure-perspectives. Stature, physiognomy and costume, gesture and mime, the set and props, voice-quality, noises off and music (see above, 1.3.2.) are all elements that fall into this second category. The juxtaposition of a-perspectively transmitted information and information transmitted via a figure-perspective enables the receiver to recognise an utterance as perspectively distorted if it deviates from the non-verbal information and then allows him or her to make allowances for it in the intended reception-perspective. There is a particularly vivid example of this in *A Comedy of Errors*, in the scene where Adriana describes her husband, Antipholus of Ephesus, as

> ... deformed, crooked, old, and sere,
> Ill-faced, worse-bodied, shapeless everywhere;
> Vicious, ungentle, foolish, blunt, unkind;
> Stigmatical in making, worse in mind.   (IV,ii,19–22)

As a characterisation of Antipholus' physical appearance this description is clearly refuted by the visual information conveyed a-perspectively during his earlier appearances in the play. The audience concludes therefore that this description is perspectively extremely distorted. The audience is able to understand the way Adriana's perspective, restricted from the outset by her jealousy and self-righteousness, is influenced by the games of deception and mistaken identity to such an extent that her view of her husband becomes totally distorted. The audience is thus able to contrast Adriana's view with its own more sophisticated and balanced interpretation of Antipholus.

This method of controlling and coordinating the various perspectives is a feature of all dramatic texts and is a consequence of their multimediality. However, there are others that are restricted to certain historical or typological types of text. One particularly clear and explicit example of this is the use of telling names (see below, 5.4.2.4.) as evaluative signals. These have been used by dramatists ever since the comedies of classical antiquity and they represent an evaluative signal employed to influence the orientation of the figure-perspective. In English Restoration comedies this technique was used with remarkable consistency. In fact every single figure in William Congreve's *The Way of the World* (1700) is evaluated authorially by being associated with a telling name. That the two central figures, the lovers Mirabell and Millamant, belong together is signalled by the phonological, morphological and etymological similarity and harmony of their two names. As positive figures they are contrasted with the others, whose names are intended to convey varying degrees of deviation from this positive norm. Thus, the perspectives of Mr and Mrs Fainall are distorted by financial avarice, whilst Witwood and Petulant actually display a genuine lack of wit, for which they attempt to compensate by indulging in rather forced banter. Lady Wishfort's perspective is coloured by a degree of erotic lasciviousness that is not in keeping with either her age or her moral façade whilst that of Mrs Marwood has suffered as a result of her participating in a number of intrigues born of malice and envy. Such names give the audience a clear indication of how the various figure-perspectives are to be integrated into the overall reception-perspective intended by the author.

Of course, in addition to this specific authorial technique used to control the figure- and reception-perspectives, the overall behaviour pattern of a particular figure may help to shed light on his or her perspective. Thus, the behaviour of Tartuffe, to take another vivid example, who has already been condemned by the author in the title of the play as a *hypocrite* and *imposteur* and in the dramatis personae as a *faux dévot,* is enough to discredit the views on religion and virtue he had been expressing verbally and creates a reception-perspective that recognises Tartuffe's own figure-perspective as a gross distortion.

In addition to these essentially figure-oriented techniques there are also those that are associated with the plot, though it is often difficult to keep these two categories apart. One of those associated with the plot is the convention of 'poetic justice' used in connection with the ending of a play. According to this convention, a happy ending for one figure is tantamount to a retrospective affirmation of his or her perspective, whilst conversely, a tragic ending for another will negate his or her perspective. Once again, *Tartuffe* may be cited as an example – this time as a play in which the convention of poetic justice becomes an implicit central theme in itself in the rather unnatural *deus-ex-machina*-type resolution at the end. Moreover, this example clearly shows that the whole notion of perspective should not be regarded as something exclusively static. For, alongside the figure-perspectives of Tartuffe, Cléante and Dorine, which remain constant throughout, there is also that of Orgon, which undergoes a spectacular transformation. The affirmative aspect of the happy ending to this particular play can therefore only be applied to Orgon's 'enlightened' figure-perspective.

3.5.3.2. The selection of figure-perspectives

In the previous section we concentrated on control and coordination techniques that are applied to one individual perspective in isolation. As we have seen, however, the primary text of a drama is usually constructed as a collection of different perspectives. From the way this collection is structured it is possible to deduce an additional implicit control technique that can be used in the constitution of the authorially intended reception-perspective. Following linguistic analytical practice we should now like to examine the structure of this collection of figure-perspectives according to two criteria: the paradigmatic aspect associated with selection and the syntagmatic aspect associated with combination.

The paradigmatic dimension refers to the number and the diversification of the figure-perspectives that are to be considered in the context of the intended reception-perspective. The purely quantitative aspect of number is relevant for the simple reason that, as a rule, it is easier to establish the reception-perspective when there are just two figure-perspectives involved than when there are many. Thus, the greater complexity of the perspective structures in the comedies of Shakespeare and his contemporaries – compared to the Tudor interludes – was conditioned, amongst other things, by a quantitative growth in the number of individual perspectives. At the same time, though, this particular comparison may also be used to illustrate the qualitative aspect of perspective diversification. Whilst the plot structure of the early Tudor interludes and even the early Elizabethan comedies was one- or, at best, two-dimensional, the late Elizabethan dramatists generally developed more complex, three-level plots by integrating classical, popular and Romanesque traditions into their plays.[25] The social contrasts between these various levels resulted in a highly diversified spectrum of figure-perspectives stretching from the heroic and Romanesque to the farcical and clown-like. When we are confronted with the broad and finely-differentiated spectra in Shakespeare's mature comedies, it becomes considerably more difficult to determine the focal point of all these diverging perspectives than it is for texts whose figure-perspectives are much less diverse.

The paradigmatic aspect of selection is also concerned with the degree of 'emphasis' given to each individual figure-perspective. Our model has not yet accounted for this. There is, however, absolutely no doubt that, in dramatic texts, the perspective of a minor figure, who perhaps appears no more than once and only has a few lines, is considered to be less important than that of the central protagonist. We would like to use the term focus, an expression that was introduced into dramatic theory by C. Brooks and R. B. Heilman, to describe the differing degrees of emphasis applied to perspectives. According to Brooks and Heilman, what focus manages to achieve is to direct 'the reader's attention primarily to one character, situation, or concept, and the subordination of other interests to the central one', and they see it as being 'functionally related to the author's attitude – a means of indicating his point of view'.[26]

However, unlike Brooks and Heilman, we would like to restrict our analysis of the concept of focus to the way it highlights the various figure-perspectives. At the same time, though, we would also like to go further than they did and determine more precisely how it contributes as an implicit control technique towards establishing 'the author's attitude' and 'his point of view' – in other words, the reception-perspective intended by the author. It should be remembered, though, that focus is something that really cannot be defined with any degree of precision. For although it is possible to calculate the length and number of utterances allocated to each individual figure, it is neither this nor the audience's tendency to identify most strongly with the quantitatively predominant figure-perspective that ultimately determines the audience's perspective on the contrasting figure-perspectives. The urgency and the poetic quality of the way a particular figure-perspective is articulated are dimensions that are at least as powerful in influencing the audience's attitude. If the intended reception-perspective in *Macbeth* is so strongly conditioned by the perspective of the central figure, then this is because the play focusses so forcefully on his perspective: Macbeth's speeches do not merely constitute a large proportion of the primary text – they are also couched in a highly charged and poetic language. Conversely, if the audience is unsure of what the authorially intended reception-perspective is actually supposed to be – this is true of the plays of Chekhov, for example – then this stems from the fact that the focus is spread out relatively evenly amongst the individual figure-perspectives. Chekhov therefore consciously dispensed with an important implicit control technique.

3.5.3.3. The combination of figure-perspectives

The most important implicit control technique is probably the syntagmatic combination and coordination of figure-perspectives. One aspect of this was analysed in the above discussion of discrepant awareness: the audience's overview of the informational deficiencies in the individual figure-perspectives enables it to collate the contradictory or complementary pieces of information into superior audience awareness. The relationship between figure- and audience-awareness is thus a part of the relationship between the figure-perspective and the intended reception-perspective.

The structured correlation of the figure-perspectives guides the audience towards the intended reception-perspective. Particularly transparent models of this kind of implicit, evaluative ordering of figure-perspectives are 1) the symmetrical grouping of falsely orientated and diametrically opposed figure-perspectives around a central figure-perspective whose orientation coincides with the intended reception-perspective and only needs to be recognised as such by the receiver; 2) the contrasting of a correct figure-perspective and a false one, leaving the receiver to choose between them; 3) the contrasting of two opposite and extreme types of falsely orientated figure-perspectives in such a way as to persuade the audience to choose the 'golden mean' as the intended reception-perspective. Of course, the structure of figure-perspectives in the empirical texts is rarely so simple and clear as these schematic models suggest. However, it is generally possible to reduce it to these basic contrasting or corresponding relationships.

As an illustration of the ways the structured pattern of figure-perspectives may be used implicitly to guide the reception-perspective we would like to cite Shakespeare's comedy *Twelfth Night*. The lack of space prevents us from pursuing the perspectival presentation of more than one thematic aspect and restricts us to an analysis that is really too simplistic to do justice to the complexity of these relationships.[27] The theme of feasting and play associated with Twelfth Night (popular custom used to reserve the period between Christmas and Epiphany for some form of high-spirited masquerade) recurs throughout the play in ever new perspectival combinations. The three perspectives inherent in the holiday motif are 1) the aristocratically refined culture of play in the Renaissance, embodied in the ceremonial poses of Orsino and Olivia, with their love of music and the sophisticated wit of Feste, the fool, and also in Viola's subtle role-playing; 2) the puritanical world of Malvolio and his hatred of all forms of feasting or play; 3) the saturnalian excesses of Sir Toby and his oafish acolyte, Sir Andrew Aguecheek. All three perspectives are interwoven in a finely nuanced tapestry of ethical and aesthetic evaluations. By diametrically opposing the figure-perspectives of Malvolio on the one hand and Sir Toby and his chums on the other, and by qualifying both of these extreme positions through the perspectives of the lovers and the fool, the author is able to imply a reception-perspective that is orientated towards the central group, leaving Malvolio and Sir Toby as one-sided distortions.

3.5.4. Types of perspective structure

An analysis of the relationships between the pattern of figure-perspectives on the one hand and the authorially intended reception-perspective on the other, enables us to construct three idealised models for the perspective structure of dramatic texts. In doing so, our concern is not to equate different historical manifestations of dramatic form – or even individual texts – with these idealised abstractions. Rather, they are intended to serve as heuristic aids to help us grasp the historical and typological transformations of drama.

3.5.4.1. A-perspectival structure

Our insight into the perspectival aspect of every speech in the ideal or 'absolute' drama has given us the tools with which to sketch out the contrasting model of a drama with an a-perspectival structure. What we mean by this is an extreme form of drama in which the principle of absolute autonomy towards both author and audience – and thus also the separation of the external and internal communication systems – is abolished. The result is a text in which the author uses the utterances of the figures to express his own conviction and in which, in turn, the figures serve as mouthpieces for the author by addressing the audience. In terms of verbal communication, the communication model for this kind of text is identical to that for expository texts. The various figure-perspectives all share and reinforce the orientation of the intended reception-perspective. They run 'parallel' to it, show no form of perspectival deviation from it and are absorbed into it. This idealised model of an a-perspectival structure is not merely the product of theoretical speculation and there are a number of historical dramatic forms that go some considerable way in approaching it.

Examples of this were the allegorical morality plays of the late middle ages. Their function was similar to the sermon in so far as they were designed to teach the fundamental and as yet unquestioned Christian ethical truths and belief in salvation. The figures do occasionally develop their own independent perspectives in a number of exemplary episodes within the drama. Nonetheless, they continue to be dominated by the homiletic directness of the communication process that takes place between the author and the audience. The morally didactic content of the play is clear as early as the prologue, and its message is summarised and interpreted once again in the epilogue. The allegorical figures constantly interpret themselves and their own actions in accordance with the intended evaluative schema. Addressing the audience directly was the rule rather than the exception. The figure-perspectives and the authorially intended reception-perspective thus largely coincided. This was particularly true of the personifications of vice who were capable of articulating an objective definition of their depravity and integrating it into the play's structure of value judgements as an affront to virtue. Contrary to all the laws of psychological plausibility and tactical reason, they even went so far as to warn the audience against the vices they represent.

3.5.4.2. Closed perspective structure

Unlike the 'frontal' didaxis in dramas with an a-perspectival structure, in which the intended reception-perspective in the text is formulated explicitly by all the figures, in dramas with a closed perspectival structure the line of convergence linking the various contrasting and corresponding figure-perspectives – i.e. the authorially intended reception-perspective – must be imagined in the receivers themselves. As such, this kind of drama may be distinguished from one with an a-perspectival structure by the way it eschews ready solutions and activates or challenges the receiver's power of moral judgement. Thus, inherent in this structural distinction there is also an implicit functional one: direct didaxis gives way to an indirect mode of mediation which engages the receiver in the process of discovering the truth and in constituting the intended reception-perspective. The shifting perspectives enable the receiver to see the problem from different angles and thus to create a complex, multidimensional image of it.

Even dramas with a closed perspective structure, however, tend to contain a number of implicit or explicit guidelines inserted by the author to manipulate the receiver's perspective. In fact, this type may be divided into two subtypes, depending on the level of explicitness: the first refers to dramas in which the intended reception-perspective is articulated in the text itself, in the form of one of the figure-perspectives – and which must be recognised by the audience as such (examples of this are *Twelfth Night* and the comedies of Molière that contain a *raisonneur* figure – like *Tartuffe* for example). The second refers to the sort of plays that leave the audience to reconstruct the intended reception-perspective for itself from the spectrum of contrasted or similar figure-perspectives.

3.5.4.3. Open perspective structure

Although plays with a closed perspective structure may leave it to the audience to identify the intended reception-perspective, there is no doubt that the latter, though implicit, is usually rendered unambiguous by the structural arrangement of the figure-perspectives or other control techniques that the author cares to implement. In plays with an open perspective structure, on the other hand, there is no single line of convergence that might draw all of these perspectives together. The relationships between the figure-perspectives remain unclear, either because all control signals are omitted or because those that are not contradict one another. The intended reception-perspective thus remains uncertain or ambivalent. The absence of any preprogrammed solutions is therefore complete.

In this context it might also be possible to apply Ingarden and Iser's notion of 'blanks' to a theory of drama. Between the 'schematised viewpoints'

(Roman Ingarden) 'blanks' are created and these open up 'scope for interpretation of the way in which it is possible to relate the aspects imagined in the perspectives to one another'.[28] Faced with a complex and contradictory pattern of figure-perspectives and a number of inadequate or ambiguously coded control signals, the audience does not feel in a position to integrate the individual figure-perspectives into a unified reception-perspective.

Here too, implicit in this structural distinction is one of a more functional kind. The absence of one clearly implied reception-perspective has the effect of challenging the sensibilities and critical faculties of the audience and leaving it to choose between accepting the perspectival ambiguity of the text or creating its own 'unofficial' reception-perspective that has not been sanctioned by the author, in the awareness that its judgement is always going to be relative in perspectival terms. Plays with an open perspective structure therefore simply do not transmit any specific value norms – either directly or indirectly. All that is conveyed to the receiver is the perspectival relativity of all value norms. Thus, this structure cannot function as the mediator of unquestioned norms but serves to deconstruct norms that have become problematic or questionable. The ethos behind this was articulated by Chekhov when he asked, 'Am I not leading the reader up the garden path since I do not know how to answer the most important questions.'[29] George Bernard Shaw was even more sharply aware of this openness. In the 'Epistle dedicatory' in *Man and Superman* he wrote the following about his dramatic figures:

They are right from their several points of view; and their points of view are, for the dramatic moment, mine also. This may puzzle the people who believe that there is such a thing as an absolutely right point of view, usually their own.[30]

To conclude, it is possible to arrange the perspectival types that have been discussed in these sections according to the extent to which they omit all ready-made solutions and their level of polyperspectivity. The following matrix therefore represents a summary of the way mono- and/or polyperspectivity is distributed in the internal and external communication systems:

	a-perspectival structure	closed perspective structure	open perspective structure
internal communication system	monoperspectivity	polyperspectivity	polyperspectivity
external communication system	monoperspectivity	monoperspectivity	polyperspectivity

3.6. Epic communication structures in drama

3.6.1. Epic tendencies in drama

In our discussion of the hierarchical arrangement of figure-perspectives in the previous chapter, we emphasised the fact that the complete lack of mediation between the internal and external communication systems and the absence of a mediating narrative function represent an idealised norm from which dramatic texts have frequently deviated over the centuries. Theoretical discussion of the validity of this norm and the playwright's right to transgress it was stimulated in particular by Bertolt Brecht's designs for an anti-Aristotelian, 'epic theatre'[31] and this has led to a sharper awareness of epic tendencies in all kinds of dramatic texts, from classical antiquity to naturalism. This debate has been partially confused, however, by the existence of diverging concepts of what the term 'epic' actually means. Thus, before applying ourselves to an analysis of epic communication structures, we should like to summarise the three most important features that are associated with the concept of 'epic' in drama. The ambiguity of this term can be explained by examining its historical development for – ever since Plato and Aristotle (see above, 1.2.1.) – the contrast between 'epic' and 'dramatic' has been defined from a number of differing aspects and points of view.

3.6.1.1. The abolition of finality

According to one of the most influential of these definitions, formulated in the correspondence between Goethe and Schiller in 1797, the epic quality of a work rests in the 'independence of its parts', and its dramatic quality in its finality – i.e. the degree to which these parts focus on the ending.[32] According to this view, then, an epic drama is one whose individual scenes remain relatively independent of each other. That is, the individual scenes and the relationships linking them with each other are more important than the relationships between them and the ending. This aspect is undoubtedly a part of Brecht's concept of epic theatre, though, of course, Brecht himself goes much further than this, as we shall see later. In fact, the formulation Brecht uses to express his demand for plays that omit conclusively conducted intrigues in favour of a 'succession of relatively independent events' is reminiscent of Schiller's definition of the epic.[33] In this way, the emphasis on the 'process-orientated' suspense in epic theatre, which contrasts sharply with the hitherto generally accepted dramatic norm of 'result-orientated suspense', is also linked up with Goethe and Schiller's theoretical reflections on the genre.[34] According to this definition, epic theatre is characterised by an episodic structure in which the individual scenes are sharply contrasted with each other. This relativises them in their relationships to one another and creates alienation. As far as the aesthetics of reception is concerned, the primary function of this type of epic theatre is to undermine the suspense to the extent that the spectators are able to distance themselves critically from the action, thus leaving them free to reflect, compare and evaluate. At the same time, Brecht abolishes finality in order to imply a model of reality that views the latter as something variable and open to change.

3.6.1.2. The abolition of concentration

A second definition, in its final version by Hegel, contrasts the breadth and the plethora of detail of the epic with the concentrated forms associated with the dramatic. Seen from this perspective, the epic tendency in drama may be described as the attempt to present reality on stage in its totality, together with all its minuscule details. In the late nineteenth century, for example, the critic Friedrich Spielhagen condemned naturalist theatre – and in particular the dramas of Henrik Ibsen – for exhibiting this tendency to develop epic forms. Spielhagen's extreme generic purism led him to the conviction that such plays attempted to present 'the chaos in the roots of human motivation right down to its smallest and finest ramifications' and strive towards 'an impossible goal, namely the presentation of an epic idea in its totality'. As 'dramatised novels' they were thus 'fundamentally epic'.[35]

A drama that is epic in this sense is to be understood as a detailed picture of reality, the totality of which can be presented either intensively in the form of a representative segment of it, or extensively by introducing panoramic structures of time and place and having a comprehensive range of figures. The function of this epic tendency is to clarify psychological and, in particular, social causal connections. It is also intended as a medium for a critical appraisal of the concrete social and institutional structures that impede human development.

3.6.1.3. The abolition of dramatic autonomy

The third definition of the contrast between epic and dramatic is based on the speech criterion – the contrast between report and representation – that was formulated by Plato and Aristotle. Within the framework of our dramatic communication model (see above, 1.2.2.), we described this speech criterion as the presence of a mediating communication system in narrative texts and its absence in dramatic texts. In contrast to normative theories of genre, we should like to regard this definition as a heuristic rather than a normative model.

If we understand the epic tendencies in drama to be those that encourage the development of a mediating communication system, then they were a recurrent feature of dramatic texts long before Brecht ever thought of them. Nonetheless, it is to Brecht's credit that he defended this tendency against the predominant form of normative generic purism and was consistently able to put it into practice in the productions of his own dramas. Thanks to his systematic use of dramaturgical techniques such as prologues and epilogues, choruses and songs, montage, banners and film projections, *conférencier* figures, asides and the exposure of theatrical machinery to the audience – all of which contribute in some way to the foundation of a mediating communication system – he created a form of drama in which the epic element was not just conceived as an occasional effect, but determined the actual structure of his plays. As far as the aesthetics of reception is concerned, these epic elements have an anti-illusionist function which is intended to counter any identification or empathy on the part of the audience with the figures and situations within the internal communication system, thereby encouraging a posture of critical distance. Furthermore, a mediating communication system of reflection and commentary enables the author to guide the receiver more directly in accordance with his critical and didactic intentions.

3.6.2. Techniques of epic communication

From our survey of the three most fundamental types of epic tendencies in drama it is clear that only the last one is relevant to our present discussion of the epic communication structures in drama. The other two definitions will be examined more closely later on within the structural contexts of plot, time and space. Our next step, then, is to isolate and categorise the various structures and techniques of epic communication in drama. It should also be noted that the role of epic tendencies varies according to the dramatic genre involved and that there is a particularly strong affinity between epic communication structures and comedy. This has been acknowledged by Brecht himself in his essay on 'The literarisation of the theatre (Notes to the *Threepenny Opera*)':

But whenever one comes across materialism, epic forms arise in the drama, and most markedly and frequently in comedy, whose 'tone' is always 'lower' and more materialistic.[36]

3.6.2.1. The author as epic narrator

It seems appropriate to construct our classification according to the various layers of text in which the expressive subject of the epic commentary is situated. An important element within the most external layer of text is the so-called authorial secondary text (see above, 2.1.2.). This should be mentioned because, especially in more recent dramas, it has been considerably expanded to include descriptive and commentative elements which often cannot be completely transposed into the stage-enactment (see above, 2.1.3.). As an example of this we can take one of the stage-directions that precede each act of Chekhov's *Cherry Orchard*:

A room, which used to be the children's bedroom and is still referred to as the 'nursery'. There are several doors: one of them leads into Ania's room. It is early morning: the sun is just coming up. The windows of the room are shut, but through them the cherry trees can be seen in blossom. It is May, but in the orchard there is morning frost.[37]

These are not the kind of stage-directions that simply refer to the lay-out of the stage-area. They are themselves part of a literary construction – a narrative and descriptive text which preimposes an interpretative perspective on the dramatic presentation that follows it. As an element in the mediating communication system, this perspective is superordinate to the figure-perspectives and approaches the authorially intended reception-perspective. Indicative factors are the references to time ('still', 'just') in which the dramatic locale has already been placed. It is exactly because they are left unexplained that they direct the audience's attention along a particular channel. This then highlights the utterances in the ensuing dialogues that seem to answer such questions as: For whom does the nursery still have such past significance? Which period of time is due to expire in May? When and by whom will the windows that still hide the blossoming cherry trees in the morning frost be opened? By drawing attention to essentially external phenomena in this way, the author succeeds in creating a mediating communication system in the secondary text which can guide the receiver's attention in a particular direction and suggest a meaningful interpretation of the internal dramatic level.

On the external level – i.e. that which cannot be directly associated with any of the characters – there are also epic devices such as film, banners and scene headings, etc. Brecht made frequent use of these techniques in his own plays, and also justified them theoretically. Our own example is taken from an English text that was heavily influenced by Brecht and which made particularly frequent use of such techniques: the dramatic revue *Oh! What a Lovely War* (1963) by Joan Littlewood's 'Theatre Workshop'. As the entire cast sings the closing songs dealing with the way the war is transfigured by memory ('And when they ask us' and 'Oh it's a lovely war'), a news board carries the following text:

THE WAR TO END WARS . . . KILLED TEN MILLION . . . WOUNDED TWENTY-ONE MILLION . . . MISSING SEVEN MILLION.

And an oversized projection screen shows pictures such as:

Five Tommies trying to pull a field-gun out of the mud.

Or:

Two weary British officers, both in battledress, one with bandaged head.[38]

The laconic summary of the horrors of the First World War on the news board and the portrayal of its mundane and trivial misery by the use of film both serve to undermine the content of the songs performed on the internal dramatic level and emphasise their bitter irony. In this way, then, the mediating communication system creates a platform from which it is possible to comment on and relativise the action.

A further dramaturgical technique used to establish a mediating communication system which is independent of the dramatic figures is montage. Both the word and the phenomenon are derived from film,[39] and ever since D. W. Griffith's *The Birth of the Nation* (1915) the use of montage techniques in film has directly influenced more recent developments in the theatre. In our short discussion of film (see above, 2.3.), we showed that the technique of dissolving temporal and spatial continuity by the use of flashbacks and the insertion of simultaneous or future events was a technique that was analogous to the function of the authorial narrator in narrative texts. This also applies to montage in stage-dramas. The rearrangements of time and space imply an authority that is able to undertake such rearrangements. This authority comments on and interprets the action presented on stage through the contrasts and correspondences created by these arrangements (see below, 7.2.2.2. and 7.4.2.).

There are particularly clear examples of this in *Oh! What a Lovely War*. The plans and preparations for war made by the Great Powers – Great Britain, France, Germany and Russia – are portrayed in a swift montage of short scenes, and although the events portrayed are supposed to have occurred simultaneously they are set apparently a long way apart.[40] In one of these, Wilhelm II and Moltke discuss their plan to attack Paris on the right flank, on the assumption that Russia would not be ready for war until 1916 at the earliest. In another, this time a monologue, France also argues in favour of a direct attack, since the German armies were pinned down by the Russians in the East. In view of its vast human resources, Russia also arms itself for an offensive war, and then a British admiral and a British general discuss the decisive role to be played by Britain, despite the fact that her position was not even mentioned by the other parties and the naval and army authorities were unable to decide on a common plan. This brief summary of the contents is sufficient in itself to indicate that the disintegration of temporal and spatial continuity appears as a deliberate policy on the part of a dramatic authority which is thus able to comment on the individual scenes by arranging them in such a way that the military plans portrayed in them are seen to cancel each other out *ad absurdum*.

3.6.2.2. The introduction of epic elements by figures outside the action

We can now turn to the epic communication structures that are presented by the figures on stage. It is possible to divide these into two subtypes, depending on whether the figures appear in the mediating communication system alone or whether they appear in this *and* the internal communication system. We shall begin with the first.

This includes the prologues and epilogues that are presented by a figure outside the internal dramatic action, either an anonymous speaker, an allegorical personification or god-figure, or a stylised personification of the author himself. Whether these take the form of apologias for a poetological programme, as the prologues to the six comedies by Terence do, or whether they outline the events leading up to the play or even the plot itself, as is the case in most of Plautus' plays, they nonetheless comment and reflect on the ensuing action through a mediating communication system, thereby placing it in a certain perspective. A particularly striking example of this is the famous epilogue to Brecht's *The Good Woman of Setzuan*, in which one of the actors, speaking out of character, apologises to the audience for the lack of a final dénouement and invites it to find its own solution to the dilemma presented in the play. The action on the internal dramatic level is exposed explicitly as a 'play' and the action that revolves around Shen Te is viewed from a distance as an exemplary model created by the company in order to demonstrate to the audience the impossibility of combining personal goodness and success in a capitalist society.

The chorus also belongs to this first subtype, in so far as it remains a figure-collective outside the internal dramatic system and comments on the dramatic situations without getting involved in them.[41] This view of the chorus' role was defended by Schiller in his treatise *On the Use of the Chorus in Tragedy* with reference to the *Bride of Messina*:

The feature of the chorus that tends to arouse most criticism is the fact that it destroys the dramatic illusion and undermines the power of feeling and emotion, but in fact this is precisely what makes it most commendable: for it is exactly these powerful emotions and the creation of this kind of illusion that the true artist deplores and strives to avoid. For if the blows to the heart with which tragedy affects us are allowed to continue without interruption then all activity would give way to mere suffering. We would ourselves become completely enmeshed in the subject matter and fall from our position above it. By separating the various parts and cooling the inflamed passions with its calming observations the chorus hands back to us our freedom that had been lost in the whirlwind of affects and emotions.[42]

Since it does not participate in the dramatic action, it can also transcend

the level of information in the internal communication system and refer to
'the past and the future, events and peoples distant in time and place'.[43] In
its omniscience and its ability to discuss and pre-empt future events, this
type of chorus is therefore similar to the authorial narrator figure used as a
medium in narrative texts.

Schiller's emphasis on the anti-illusionist, reflective distance created by
this function of the chorus already looks forward to Brecht, though, of
course, the ideological motivation behind their respective interpretations
is very different. One example of a chorus that does not participate in the
action in Brecht is the group of 'Musicians' in the *Caucasian Chalk Circle*
who, together with the 'Singer', compensate for the time omitted from the
action by delivering a narrative report, announce the content of the next
scene and pose ethical questions or comment on the figures' decisions.

The 'Singer' in *The Caucasian Chalk Circle* represents yet another type
of figure that is independent of the figures on the internal dramatic level
and supports a mediating communication system: the producer figure. He
has a similar function to that of the speakers of the prologues and epilogues and the chorus. However, he differs formally from the first two
because he is continuously present on stage and is not restricted to the
beginnings and endings, and from the second because he is an individual
figure rather than a group. Under titles such as 'Singer' or 'Court Crier'
(Brecht: *The Trial of Lucullus*), 'Stage Manager' (Wilder: *Our Town*),
'Explicateur' (Claudel: *Le livre de Christophe Colomb*), this figure serves
as a mediator between the internal dramatic level and the audience.
Transcending the merely explanatory and reflective function of the
chorus, he appears as the fictional authorial subject presenting the internal
dramatic system. Wilder's Stage Manager is thus able to interrupt the
action at any time:

> Thank you, thank you! That'll do. We'll have to interrupt again here.
> Thank you, Mrs Webb; thank you, Emily.

He can invert the chronology of events:

> You see, we want to know how all this began – this wedding, this plan to
> spend a lifetime together. . . . George and Emily are going to show you
> now the conversation they had when they first knew that . . . that . . . as
> the saying goes . . . they were meant for one another.

Or he can make chronological jumps which he bridges by introducing an
informative narrative:

> Now we are going to skip a few hours. But first we want a little more
> information about the town, kind of scientific account, you might say.

He can make the audience aware of the play as a theatrical performance:

> There's some scenery for those who think they have to have scenery.

And he can even draw attention to the principles of his own arrangement of the plot:

> The first Act was called the Daily Life. This act is called Love and Marriage. There's another act coming after this: I reckon you can guess what that's about.

Finally, he can even take on a minor role himself:

> In this wedding I play the minister. That gives me the right to say a few more things about it.

Using these informative narratives and evaluative commentaries to remain in constant contact with the audience, he is able to develop an independent figure-perspective, that is superordinate to and embraces those of all the other figures on the internal dramatic layer (see above, 3.5.2.). His superordinate perspective is demonstrated by the fact that he possesses far more information than the figures of 'his' play. This enables him to disrupt the level of information in the internal communication system at any time and to pre-empt future events:

> Want to tell you about that boy Joe Crowell there. Joe was awful bright – graduated from high school here, the head of his class. So he got a scholarship to Massachusetts Tech. Graduated head of his class there, too. It was all wrote up in the Boston paper at the time. Goin' to be a great engineer, Joe was. But the war broke out and he died in France – All that education for nothing.[44]

Passages of this kind make it clear that – for him, as for the narrator in narrative texts – the events portrayed happened in the past and are already complete. The present tense used in most of the narrative segments is really a 'historical present' designed to bring the events home more emphatically. In short, these observations demonstrate that, as a type, the functions embodied in the producer or stage-manager figures are structurally the closest dramatic texts come to the communication model for narrative texts.

3.6.2.3. The introduction of epic elements by figures inside the action

We now turn to the structures of epic communication in which a mediating communication system is created by figures situated inside rather than outside the dramatic action.

This kind of 'personal union' of dramatic figure and epic mediator can occur in prologues or epilogues, as well as in the chorus and in commentaries by individual figures. In such cases this may often lead to complex and ambiguous transitions if a figure does not step outside the dramatic action and its temporal and spatial *deixis* obviously enough to comment or reflect on it to the audience. This is especially true if this change occurs either gradually as a drawn-out process or if it does not actually culminate in a complete break from the internal dramatic situation.

Prologues declaimed by one of the dramatic figures were already a feature of classical drama – see, for example, Mercury's prologue in Plautus' *Amphitryon*. However, one particularly interesting example is Prospero's epilogue in Shakespeare's *Tempest*, whose ambivalent transitions from dramatic immediacy to epic distance has provoked a broad spectrum of differing interpretations:

> Now my charms are all o'erthrown,
> And what strength I have's mine own,
> Which is most faint. Now, 'tis true,
> I must be here confin'd by you,
> 5 Or sent to Naples. Let me not,
> Since I have my dukedom got,
> And pardon'd the deceiver, dwell
> In this bare island by your spell;
> But release me from my bands
> 10 With the help of your good hands.
> Gentle breath of yours my sails
> Must fill, or else my project fails,
> Which was to please. Now I want
> Spirits to enforce, Art to enchant;
> 15 And my ending is despair,
> Unless I be reliev'd by prayer,
> Which pierces so that it assaults
> Mercy itself, and frees all faults.
> As you from crimes would pardon'd be,
> 20 Let your indulgence set me free.

The fact that the speaker of the epilogue and the banished duke and island magician of the play appear to be identical (this is suggested by means of costume and mask) establishes a clear link with the internal dramatic level. The epilogue also contains a large number of verbal references back to the fictional world of the play. The speaker cites various incidents from the plot – such as the renunciation of his role as magician 1ff., the reconquering of the duchy (6), the pardoning of his opponents (7) and his planned return to Naples (5) – without attempting to emphasise their fictionality in any explicit way. The chronological and spatial context of the fictional island world is preserved (4 and 8) and even the stylistic character of the epilogue is similar to Prospero's earlier speeches in its use of ethical, evaluative abstract nouns, for example. However, this extension of the internal communication system is undermined by the development of a mediating communication system. The new speech situation is signalled by the use of a different metre. The four-footed rhyming couplets contrast with the blank verse that predominates in the play itself. The addressee of the epilogue is no longer a character on the internal dramatic level but the audience, to whom the speaker turns with his *captatio benevolentiae*. In this sense, it is no longer Prospero who is the speaker, but the actor of the part of Prospero. It is he who begs for applause on behalf of the cast, justifying his request by invoking the virtues of 'mercy' and 'indulgence' which had been exemplified in the play. Of course, by 'actor of the part of Prospero' we do not mean the empirical actor who happens to be performing that role at any one time, but rather an additional fictional role (S2) created by the author. This categorical distinction is analogous to the difference between the author and the fictional narrator in narrative texts.

This superimposition of epic and mediating elements on to the internal communication system creates an ambivalent blend of fiction and reality in which the speaker of the epilogue reminisces about both his political career in his role as the Duke of Milan and his theatrical performance as an actor. The author is thus able to introduce an element of ambiguity into an important group of thematically linked concepts. The semantically linked concepts 'charms' (1), 'strength' (2), 'project' (12), 'Spirits' and 'Art' (14) not only refer to Prospero's White Magic but also provide an epic commentary on the performance itself, whose quasi-magic illusionism has now come to an end. However, this ambivalence does not justify the equation of Prospero's magic with the poetics of *The Tempest* as a play – a view that is defended in allegoricising interpretations. Even less defensible is the commonly held view that Prospero and the actor of the part of Prospero should be equated with the author, William Shakespeare, who in the epilogue and in Prospero's renunciation of magic is supposed to have dramatised his own departure from the theatre.

In the history of drama, the external and internal variants have generally been roughly equal in importance as far as the prologues and epilogues are concerned. If we now turn to the chorus, there is no doubt that the internal variant predominates. Indeed, in classical theories of drama this was held to be the absolute norm. For example, Aristotle demanded:

The chorus too must be regarded as one of the actors. It must be part of the whole and share in the action . . . as it does in Sophocles.[45]

Horace expressed this even more clearly:

actoris partis chorus officiumque virile
defendat, neu quid mediosus intercinat
quod non propositi conducat et haereat apte.[46]

A chorus that adhered strictly to these demands would be completely absorbed into the internal action as one of the participating characters, distinguishable from the others only by virtue of its collectivity.

In existing texts, however, Aristotle's demand that the chorus should 'share in the action' is almost always reduced to the function of the chorus as an interested but generally passive observer who is only active in a verbal sense, offering words of advice, warning or prayer. It does therefore participate in the dramatic action, as the dialogues between the chorus and the protagonists clearly demonstrate, but it can just as easily distance itself from it. It is this very ability to distance itself from and reflect upon the dramatic action that enables it to function as an epic mediary.

Thus, the chorus of Theban Elders in *Oedipus the King*, for example, remains closely bound up with the concrete situation in most of its songs. In the introductory song, or *parode*, it begs the tutelary gods of Thebes for help in their fight against the plague that has been afflicting the city. In the first stationary song, or *stasimon*, it wrestles with the doubts and fears provoked by Teiresias, in the third it succumbs to illusory hopes for a change for the better, and, finally, in the fourth it laments Oedipus' fate. Every one of these songs performed by the chorus is characterised by clear thematic references to the events and dialogues taking place around it, out of which it grows and into which it returns.

One song that differs from all the others by virtue of its greater degree of abstraction is the second stationary song (lines 863–910). It refers neither to the preceding dialogue between Oedipus and Jocasta, nor to concrete details of the dramatic situation, but reflects in a personally emotional and yet abstract manner on justice and irreverence, and the gods as guarantors of truth. By virtue of its distance from the dramatic action, this stationary song serves as a reflective commentary on the drama as a whole, and therefore functions as a tentative epic communication system mediating between the dramatic action and the audience. However, despite the degree of abstraction involved, it remains little more than tentative because the illusions created by the internal communication system are not broken, nor does the audience become the direct addressee of the chorus' words. A more radical form of the epic mediating chorus may be found in the Old Comedy of Greece – further evidence of the special affinity between comedy and the epic – in the form of *parabasis*, in which the chorus, stepping outside the plot and breaking the dramatic illusion, addresses its satirical comments directly to the audience. As such, this type may be classified as one of the variants of the chorus discussed above that remains outside the action.

A modern equivalent of the chorus is the song, of the type propagated both in theory and in practice in the dramaturgy of Bertolt Brecht. In contrast to the traditional type of song in drama, Brecht's 'songs' do not remain entirely within the internal system of communication, but break or transcend it by addressing the audience directly. Even Brecht's songs, however, frequently feature an overlapping of the internal and mediating communication systems. Brecht described this phenomenon himself in the poem 'The Songs':

> The actors
> Change into singers. They have
> A new attitude
> As they address themselves to the audience, still
> Characters in the play, but now also undisguisedly
> Accomplices of the playwright.[47]

In so far as they still remain 'characters in the play' their song is part of the internal communication system. However, as 'accomplices of the playwright' they address the audience directly, establishing a mediating communication system that exposes the fictionality of the play and subjects it to a critical and distanced commentary. The extent to which these poles can differ is quite pronounced, even in Brecht's songs, and we should like to illustrate this by briefly comparing the Solomon Songs in *The Threepenny Opera* and *Mother Courage*.

In *The Threepenny Opera*, the scenic context of Jenny's Solomon Song[48] clearly raises it above the internal dramatic level: the lighting is changed, the title of the song is announced on a board, Jenny appears with a hurdy-gurdy before the closed curtain at the front of the stage and when she sings, she addresses herself directly to the audience. In his 'Notes to the Threepenny Opera', Brecht explained his decision to distinguish between the internal dramatic situation and the song as an epic commentary:

When an actor sings he undergoes a change of function. Nothing is more revolting than when the actor pretends not to notice that he has left the level of plain speech and started to sing. The three levels – plain speech, heightened speech and singing – must always remain distant, and in no case should heightened speech represent an intensification of plain speech, or singing of heightened speech. In no case therefore should singing take place where words are prevented by excess of feeling. The actor must not only sing but show a man singing.[49]

The epic mediating function of the song is thus clear from both the scenic context and the manner of delivery. The actor playing the part of the dramatic figure almost completely disappears behind the actor as a singing commentator. The predominance of the mediating function can also be confirmed by examining the relationship between the song and its dramatic context. Since it does not arise out of a preceding dramatic dialogue it remains unmotivated on the internal dramatic level. Jenny does not refer to the dramatic context – the fall of Macheath – until the last of five stanzas, and even then does not mention her decisive role in bringing it about. The song thus remains highly abstract, and as such provides a commentary on the drama as a whole, striving to expose its central theme: bourgeois–capitalist morality. The song lists a whole catalogue of examples of how it is man's positive qualities that bring him down – whether it is Solomon by his wisdom, Cleopatra by her beauty, Caesar by his audacity, Brecht by his thirst for knowledge or Macheath by his sensual desires. The metrical and syntactical similarities between the five stanzas, made even more obvious by the four-line refrain, serve to emphasise the disparate nature of this catalogue and the audience is challenged to use its dialectical acumen to resolve the incongruences and ironies. The fact that the author cites himself as one of the examples shatters the illusion completely and exposes the play as an artifact designed to be performed.

Mother Courage and Her Children was written considerably later. The Solomon Song Brecht rewrote for it omitted a few of the original stanzas but also added a number of new ones and was integrated into the primary dramatic action to a much greater degree.[50] Sung as a begging song by the cook and Mother Courage together, it is motivated, to some extent at least, by its dramatic setting. From a purely dramaturgical point of view, then, it does not break through the internal communication system. Thematically, though, it does, and it achieves this by placing the begging scene in a world-historical context and using it as an example of an unprofitable form of morality. At the same time there is a marked contrast between the ideology of the song and the character of the cook, who can scarcely be said to be a victim of an unprofitable moral system. As a result, the song violates his figure-perspective. By stepping outside his role in this way, the actor, as a mediator, is released from the role portrayed by him and becomes the voice of a mediating communication system. Finally, there is also a conflict between Mother Courage's behaviour as a figure in the internal communication system and her song, since the notion expressed in the latter that all unselfish or high-minded acts are meaningless is immediately contradicted by Courage's decision not to abandon her dumb and disabled daughter. Although the song has been integrated more fully into the internal dramatic system, this does not mean that there are no epic structures whatsoever, but that they have been refined into something more indirect and implicit.

The epic communication structures outlined above all represent separate units that can be clearly distinguished from the dialogues of the internal dramatic level. In addition to these, there are mediating structures that are integrated into the dialogues and soliloquies. This assumes that the dramatic figure is able to distance itself from the dramatic action and comment on it 'from the outside'. The criterion of epic quality is the degree to which the speaker is abstracted from the situation and its time–space *deixis*. This can lead to a split between the self as a protagonist directly involved in the dramatic situation and the self as a distanced commentator thereof. In extreme cases this leads, on the one hand, to the actor stepping outside his role in order to break the illusion and, on the other, by the 'actor' who steps forward as an epic mediary from behind his role.

With the help of a number of specific examples we should now like to demonstrate the varying degrees of distance possible. That these examples are largely taken from comedies is not coincidental, but rather a further reflection of the special affinity between comic and epic structures. In the works of Plautus, for example, the internal communication system is interrupted on numerous occasions.[51] A particularly common phenomenon is the servant or parasite figure, characterised by his garrulous affabillity towards the audience, which he takes into his confidence and regales with his opinions of the other figures. An example of this is the parasite Artotrogus' behaviour towards his master in *The Braggart Warrior* (*Miles Gloriosus*):

> ARTOTROGUS: Begad, sir! It really was a mere nothing compared with other deeds I could mention – (aside) that you never did. (To audience, disgustedly, as the soldier stalks magnificently about) If anyone ever saw a bigger liar and a more colossal braggart than this fellow, he can have me for his own with full legal rights.[52]

After one sentence of flattery directed at his swaggering dialogue partner, the subsequent aside (see below, 4.5.3.) is addressed directly *ad spectatores*, to whom he communicates his real opinion. In doing so, Artotrogus creates a mediating communication system through which the audience is informed of the ambivalence of his position and is shown what to think of the braggart warrior. Despite such remarks *ad spectatores*, the dramatic illusion is nonetheless not really affected, since Artotrogus, in his commentaries, never steps outside his role as the scheming parasite but merely exposes his true feelings about his false flattery. By allowing Artotrogus to address the audience directly, Plautus' intention is not to make it consciously aware of itself as a theatre audience, or of the action presented as a theatrical performance, but to treat it as if it were a chance group of observers who happen to witness a real situation.

The illusion is broken when the actor steps outside his role and exposes *ex persona* the action on stage as theatre, himself as an actor and the spectators as a theatre audience. This is what happens in a speech by the witnesses in Plautus' *Poenulus*:

> We know that already – if only these spectators knew. It's for their benefit we're doing this play here now; they're the ones for you to instruct, so that they'll know what you're doing when you do it. Don't bother about us: we know the whole business, seeing we all learned our lines along with you, so as to be able to talk back to you.[53]

This speech is motivated on the internal level by the witnesses' refusal to discuss the plan of intrigue with Agorastocles for a second time. At the same time, however, it breaks it by observing the action directly from the external communication level. The audience is not the direct addressee, but is nonetheless the explicit theme of the speech, and the speakers are no longer the fictional witnesses, but actors. To be more precise it should be added that the expressive subjects still remain fictional. They enact fictional actors' roles (S2) in the same way that the audience they invoke (R2), which takes the remarks made *ex persona* at face value, is not the same as either the implied or the empirical audience (R3/4) which sees through – or at least is supposed to see through – the asides or remarks *ad spectatores* as just another kind of fiction.[54] The function of this mediating communication system is to make the audience aware of the theatrical performance as a theatrical performance and thus to 'alienate' it. Of course, in this case, alienation does not create critical distance, as it does in Brecht, but playful exuberance and comic discrepancy.

The examples of epic structures in dialogue cited above are remarkable for their transparency and clarity. However, any thorough analysis must also include the techniques employed to impose mediating elements of information and commentary on to the internal dramatic action and yet which no longer establish an explicit or clearly signalled distinction between the two levels.

Examples of these are the narrative utterances that have become conventionalised in the form of expositional narratives (see below, 3.7.2.) and messengers' reports (see below, 4.2.2.).[55] According to our definition, these types of narrative do not belong *per se* to the epic communication structures in drama since they are situated in the internal communication system. However, an epic mediating communication system can always arise either if the narratives have no plausible addressee on the internal dramatic level or if they appear to be so weakly or superficially motivated that the audience cannot but see itself as the primary addressee.

3.6.2.4. Non-verbal epic tendencies

Finally, we would like to turn our attention to non-verbal epic structures. In comedy it is often possible to observe a style of acting in which the actor prefers to distance himself from his part, subordinating it to his artistic virtuosity rather than submerging himself in it completely. In doing so, the actor fulfils a clear mediating function with regard to the role he is performing. In fact, one might say that he is consciously 'demonstrating' it, rather than 'performing' it. This feature is particularly common in the *commedia dell' arte*, for example, in which the static aspect of the characters and the statically presented half-masks subvert all attempts by the actor to identify himself with his role, and lead to a clear element of tension between the skill with which the actor is able to demonstrate his role to the audience and the role itself. Of course, the intention behind this is very different, but in practice it anticipates the Brechtian theory of an anti-identificatory style of acting and his concept of a 'gestus of showing'.

In terms of stage-design, this manner of acting corresponds to the exposure of theatrical machinery and apparatus in order to create an anti-illusionist awareness of the set as a set, and the props as props. This emphasises the difference between the reality of the objects and the objects they represent, and imbues them with epic mediating qualities (see below, 7.1.).

3.6.2.5. The repertoire of epic techniques

A feature common to the epic communication structures discussed above is that they all undermine concepts of drama that preserve its absolute autonomy with regard to author and audience. Their apparent disparity is a result of the fact that they can occur on all the various levels and layers of the dramatic text. Taken as a whole, they represent the repertoire of formal epic techniques applied to the communication processes. As such they only cover one aspect of 'epic theatre', since in this particular context it has not been possible to analyse the epic tendencies that abolish finality and create a sense of totality. Essentially, this repertoire is open and may be expanded at any time by the addition of newly developed presentation methods. Beyond that, our description of this repertoire cannot even claim to be comprehensive as far as existing texts are concerned. Our intention here, as indeed elsewhere in this introductory study, was not to offer an all-embracing and comprehensive analysis, but to concentrate on the crucial elements of this systematic method. In order to provide a clearer overview, then, the structures discussed in the preceding sections have been collated graphically in the form of a diagram (see p. 85).

3.7. Successiveness and the transmission of information

3.7.1. Simultaneity and successiveness

So far in our discussion of the transmission of information and the communication structures of dramatic texts we have tended to ignore the fact that a dramatic text is a process. For it is a truism that a dramatic text realises its information potential successively in a strictly regulated pattern of successive elements. Time is therefore one of its prerequisite operational dimensions.[56] This invalidates such analytical methods as the 'spatial approach' adopted by the exponents of New Criticism, who regard a

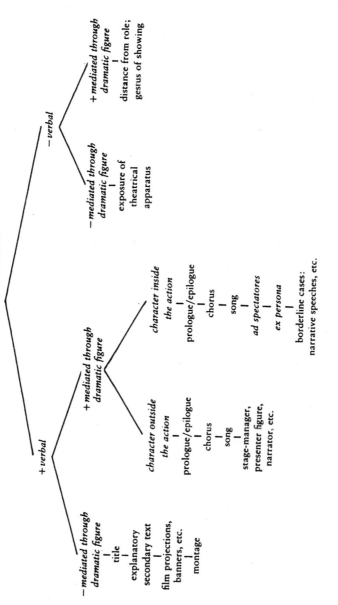

Epic communication structures

+ verbal
  − verbal

+ verbal:

− mediated through dramatic figure
  |
title
  |
explanatory secondary text
  |
film projections, banners, etc.
  |
montage

+ mediated through dramatic figure

  character outside the action
  |
  prologue/epilogue
  |
  chorus
  |
  song
  |
  stage-manager, presenter figure, narrator, etc.

  character inside the action
  |
  prologue/epilogue
  |
  chorus
  |
  song
  |
  ad spectatores
  |
  ex persona
  |
  borderline cases: narrative speeches, etc.

− verbal:

− mediated through dramatic figure
  |
exposure of theatrical apparatus

+ mediated through dramatic figure
  distance from role; gestus of showing

dramatic text retrospectively as a timeless or supertemporal spatial structure of corresponding and contrasting elements.[57] This view systematically fails to register the successive element in the transmission of information – something that we felt obliged to do temporarily to heighten the clarity of our systematic presentation – and inflates this into a permanent and predominant analytical principle thus ignoring one of the key aspects of a dramatic text.

The transmission of information in dramatic texts has two temporal axes: the axis of simultaneity – whereby at any one time pieces of information are transmitted through the various codes and channels simultaneously – and the axis of successiveness – whereby pieces of information are transmitted accumulatively one after another through the various codes and channels. We should now like to concentrate on two elements that are particularly prominent in the chronological dramatic process and in which the successive aspect of information transmission is particularly significant: namely the exposition and the dénouement.

3.7.2. The transmission of information at the beginning of the drama

What we understand as the transmission of information at the beginning of a play largely coincides with the classical theoretical concept of the exposition, one of the most intensively analysed formal aspects of drama.[58] If, however, we define exposition as the transmission of information to do with the events and situations from the past that determine the dramatic present, then it becomes immediately clear that, on the one hand, exposition is not restricted to the introductory phases of the text and, on the other, the transmission of information in the initial phase of the text is not necessarily confined to serving some sort of expository function.

3.7.2.1. Exposition and dramatic introduction

It is therefore advisable to distinguish between the exposition proper and the dramatic introduction – or what E. T. Sehrt describes metaphorically as the 'dramatic upbeat'.[59] In addition to the primarily informative and referential function associated with the exposition, the introduction also serves the phatic functions (for an explanation of the terminology see below, 4.2.5.) that are used to stimulate the audience's attention and to attune it to the atmosphere of the fictional world of the drama. Of course, the dramatic introduction may coincide entirely with the exposition but it can often also occur separately and/or successively as two isolated phases of the text. Every one of Racine's tragedies is an illustration of the way exposition and dramatic introduction may coincide. In Shakespeare's plays, on the other hand, they often occur separately. The opening scene of *The Tempest*, for example, confronts the audience with the spectacular and emotionally charged portrayal of a shipwreck in a storm, thereby stimulating its interest. Nonetheless, because the events leading up to the shipwreck remain unclear at this point, the audience becomes interested in what is to follow, and it is not until Act 1, Scene ii, in a calm expository dialogue, that Prospero informs his daughter Miranda, and thus indirectly the audience, as to the background to this dramatic opening scene.

The equation of exposition and dramatic introduction demanded by normative dramatic theory can only be applied to a historically extremely limited type of drama. The underlying notion behind this kind of equation is a particular interpretation of exposition based not on the criterion of information transmission but on rhetorical traditions that divide the text clearly into strictly separate *partes orationis*. In the same way that – in a speech constructed according to the rhetorical rules – '*exordium, narratio, argumentatio, refutatio* and *peroratio*' are coordinated as a rigidly arranged series of isolated units, a dramatic text should be divided up according to the triadic pattern of '*protasis – epitasis – katastrophe*' or Gustav Freytag's five-part pattern of 'introduction – the rising movement – climax – reversal – catastrophe', in which these elements are separated from one another by the division of the drama into acts.[60] However, any interpretation based on the criterion of information transmission must regard this as a special case that simply cannot be generalised into an absolute rule in a systematic theory of drama.

3.7.2.2. Isolated versus integrated exposition

A more successful way of classifying this special case is to locate it in a typological spectrum of exposition forms that is derived from the position of the expository information in the text as a whole. The sort of exposition we have just been talking about would occupy a position at one end of this typological spectrum – that is, when all of the information on the events leading up to the opening scene is transmitted in a clearly defined block at the beginning of the play. The criteria governing this type therefore require that information is transmitted in the initial position, in isolation and clustered together in a block. One example of this is the expository information in Racine's *Andromaque*, which is presented entirely in the dialogue between Oreste and Pylade in Act I, Scene i. It is not until after a clear change of scene, marked by the exit of Pylade and the entrance of Pyrrhus and Phoinix, that the developmental potential of the situation is translated into action (I,ii).

The opposite extreme occurs when the expository information is no longer bound up with the introductory phase of the text, but is integrated into the plot as it develops and is thus divided up into a number of smaller units.[61] However, even this type is generally characterised by a stronger concentration of expository information in the initial phases of the text and a gradual decline over the rest of it. It is nonetheless possible to suspend even this restricted emphasis on the beginning of the text. This occurs in dramas with a strictly analytical structure, in which the plot is constructed as a constantly evolving process exposing the conditions inherent in the opening dramatic situation. Sophocles' *Oedipus the King* is an example of a text in which the expository information is concentrated towards the end of the text. The *anagnorisis*, or recognition, that Aristotle described in his *Poetics* (chs. 11, 14 and 16) is another way of transmitting expository information in the final phases of the text, in so far as the 'recognition' refers to facts that condition the opening dramatic situation and that are new, at least in part, to both the figures and the audience.

3.7.2.3. The dominant form of temporal reference

Another way of classifying the types of exposition is to establish the context in which the expository information is embedded. In doing so, it is particularly important to establish the dominant form of temporal reference.[62] Whenever reference to the past predominates, the expository information dominates the context and the dramatic present remains subordinate to it. This dominance is most strongly evident whenever the expository information remains completely unmotivated on the internal dramatic level – as, for example, when it is mediated epically in the prologue by a figure situated outside the action. Thus, the speaker of the prologue in Plautus' *Poenulus* – who remains outside the action and maintains close contact with the audience – simply adopts a narrative *gestus* to relate the background events to the play. It is not until the closing lines of the prologue that he provides the transition into the opening dramatic situation. He does this by relating his story to the locale (the houses in Calydon facing each other) and hinting at the possible conflicts inherent in the subsequent opening scene of the drama. In this case, reference to the past is completely dominant, since there is as yet no dramatic present.

The dramatic present carries considerably more weight in Plautus' *Captivi*, though here, too, reference to the past is still the predominant factor. Appearing alongside Philocrates and Tyndarus, the two enchained prisoners of war, the speaker of the prologue takes their current predicament as a point of departure for a narrative explanation of the events that caused this state of affairs in the first place. Both cases are examples of the positional type of block-like isolation; indeed, there is generally a marked affinity between the predominance of the past in expository passages and the block-like isolation of expository information from the rest of the text.

In cases where reference to the present predominates, the expository information is motivated by the current dramatic situation and remains functionally subordinate to it. The background information conditioning it is not evaluated in any systematic way and the only aspects of it that are mentioned at all are those that are immediately relevant to the existing dramatic situation. This situation is determined not only by the act of narrating background information but also by activities and events that are independent of it. Thus, in the opening scene of *Curculio* – to take another example from Plautus – the transmission of expository information is embedded in the action that precedes a nocturnal courtship scene. Phaedromus is cajoled by his servant Palinurus' insistent questioning into enlightening both him and the audience as to the character of his beloved, the obstacles that stand in the way of his courtship and the measures he has already taken to evade them. The expository narration of background information is preceded by the exposition of facts that define the introductory situation: the identities of the two dialogue partners and the relationship between them are established in the way they address each other. and their overall verbal behaviour. Locale and time are established by references to them in the dialogue.

This convention of defining the expository situation is parodied by Ionesco in the first speech of *La Cantatrice chauve*:

> MME SMITH: Tiens, il est neuf heures. Nous avons mangé de la soupe, du poisson, des pommes de terre au lard, de la salade anglaise. Les enfants ont bu de l'eau anglaise. Nous avons bien mangé, ce soir. C'est parce que nous habitons dans les environs de Londres et que notre nom est Smith.[63]

As in the example taken from Plautus, and indeed in countless other dramatic texts of world literature, the time, place and figures involved in the dramatic situation are all mentioned in the opening dialogue. In this particular case, however, the fact that this expository information is completely unmotivated parodies and exposes it as an over-used convention and makes the audience aware of its role as the intended receiver of the information given. In most texts this is more or less skilfully disguised by the use of motivation.

The dramatic present containing expository information can either be static – as it is in the leisurely chat after dinner in *La Cantatrice chauve* quoted above – or it can be part of a more dynamic situation that is already moving towards an as yet unknown future. The integration of expository information into the kind of context that refers to the future represented for Goethe – and Schiller too, who agreed with him on this – the ideal form of dramatic exposition:

... but it seems to me that this is what makes the exposition so problematic for the dramatist since he is usually expected to provide a continuous process of forward movement, and in my opinion the best dramatic material is one in which the exposition already forms a part of the development.[64]

As an illustration of this particular type we have selected Shakespeare's *Macbeth*. The tragedy opens impressively with the three witches meeting in a thunderstorm. The first speech, 'When shall we three meet again?' immediately opens up a future dimension and the expository information on the battle still raging between the Scottish and Norwegian armies is also drawn into this future perspective. They shall indeed meet again,

> When the hurlyburly's done,
> When the battle's lost and won.   (I,i,3f.)

The terms of this appointment also provide for the expository introduction of the central figure – 'There to meet with Macbeth' (I,i,7). Although this forward-moving impetus is slowed down by the two messengers' reports in the following scene, in which the events of the recent past predominate, the very next scene (I,iii), in which Banquo and Macbeth meet the witches, integrates the expository information once again into a strongly forward-looking context: the witches' prophecies combine expository information with a predominant reference to the future, and in the ensuing dialogue between Banquo and Macbeth, and then in Macbeth's soliloquy, the characteristic qualities of the two figures are revealed in their differing reactions to this future perspective.

3.7.2.4. Monological versus dialogical exposition

A third approach towards classifying the types of exposition involved is to establish whether the expository information is mediated monologically or dialogically and also how the speaker positions are occupied. Thus, in the case of monological exposition, the speaker can be a figure from either outside or inside the action. The first of these would imply the epic transmission of expository information (see above 3.6.2.2.) of which the best-known form is the expository prologue spoken by a prologue figure located outside the action. Examples of this, namely Plautus' *Poenulus* and *Captivi*, were mentioned in our discussion of temporal reference. In such cases, the exposition appears as an element preceding the action and isolated from it and the expository information is presented narratively in a single block. In most cases, however, this kind of *prologus argumentativus* is not subsumed into the expository narrative, but rather often combines this with exordial functions such as welcoming the audience and getting it into an appropriate mood, and with the presentation of a poetological programme. It also serves to establish the close contact between the speaker of the prologue and the audience. This type of exposition gradually leads the audience away from reality and into the fictional reality of the play, and yet at the same time exposes its very fictionality. However, its most important function consists in relieving the internal communication system of the need to transmit expository information.

What is true of the words spoken in the expository prologue by a figure situated outside the action also applies to those spoken in the expository prologue by a figure from within the action. Examples of this in Plautus are Mercury's expository prologue in *Amphitryon* and Palaestrio's prologue in *The Braggart Warrior*. In these cases the exposition is no longer completely set apart from the play proper and this makes it possible to structure the transition from the narrative exposition to the dramatic action as a smooth and uninterrupted process. This tendency towards integration is particularly clear in the prologue to *The Braggart Warrior*. In this play, the prologue has been shifted from its customary initial position and occurs in the second scene. As a result, in his expository prologue, Palaestrio is able to refer to a situation that has already been established in the opening scene. The link with the ensuing scene is even stronger, for after welcoming the audience and presenting the background information in narrative form, Palaestrio gradually comes round to introducing the figures and locale associated with the dramatic present. Finally, he abandons his position of epic distance and enters into the dramatic situation in which, from Act II, Scene ii, he takes an active part.

It is important to distinguish between this purely epic form of exposition in the monological prologue and, on the other hand, expository information conveyed in soliloquy delivered within the fictional action. An example of this is the famous opening soliloquy by the central character in Shakespeare's *Richard III*. Even when it is delivered from the front of the stage in close proximity to the audience, with whom the figure establishes an epic relationship through the use of mime and gesture, its verbal structure nonetheless remains within the bounds of the internal communication system. This alone would suffice to explain why the expository information transmitted in this scene is more strongly integrated into the dramatic action than it would have been in an expository prologue. The double repetition of the word 'now' in the first part of the soliloquy (lines 1, 5, 10) indicates that the predominant point of reference is the present, and expository references to the past are included in the structure as points of comparison and contrast between the past and the present. In the second part (lines 14–27), Gloucester contributes towards a closer definition of the dramatic situation by describing his own character, and justifies his villainy by invoking his disability and his resulting experiences as an outsider figure. Finally, after hinting at various intrigues either planned or already in operation, he then moves on to speculate what that future has in store for him (lines 28–40). As soon as Clarence is mentioned in this context, he appears in person and a dialogue between the two men ensues. In this way, the isolation of the monological exposition from the context of the dramatic situation is diminished even further. Of course, the transition from soliloquy to dialogue, and from an audience-orientated to an 'autonomous' scene still marks a decisive break.

This break can only be avoided by embedding the expository information in a dialogue – thus creating a dialogical exposition. The simplest solution – one which achieves no more than a minimum level of integration of exposition and dramatic situation – consists in placing alongside the bearer of expository information a dialogue partner whose sole function is to stimulate the transmission of information by asking questions and making comments, and who disappears from the play once this function has been fulfilled. This rather transparent way of dramatising the expository dialogue was classified by the later Latin theoreticians of classical comedy as a 'protatic figure'. Donatus' definition of a protatic figure in his commentary to Terence's *Andria* coincides with our own. According to him a protatic figure is one,

quae semel inducta in principio fabulae in nullis deinceps fabulae partibus adhibetur.[65]

That Terence's *Andria* employs a dialogical version of an essentially monological exposition is clear from a comparison of Terence's play with its source: Menander's *Andria* presents the same expository material in the old man's soliloquy, whereas Terence introduces the freed slave Sosias as a protatic dialogue partner for him.[66] The monological quality is also apparent from the dialogue structure, for – in purely quantitative terms – the speeches are clearly balanced in favour of the old man Simo. It is Simo who also provides the impulse for all of the dialogical exchanges, with Sosia restricted either to asking questions that provoke Simo into giving more expository information, or to reacting to it with exclamations of astonishment. From a functional point of view, the protatic figure is thus not a genuine dialogue partner, but a thinly veiled stage representative of the audience's hunger for information.[67] In this function then, the protatic figure displays a latent tendency to send information epically in a similar but less blatant manner to the expository prologue.

On the other hand, even this kind of dialogical exposition entails some kind of break between the exposition and the dramatic action proper because the expository dialogue is separated from the rest of the text by the one and only appearance of the protatic figure. In French classical drama, however, this whole problem was solved by the introduction of an expository dialogue between one of the major figures and his or her confidant(e).[68] Unlike the protatic figure, the confidant is not restricted to a single scene, but accompanies the hero throughout the play. Racine, for one, adopted this hero–confidant configuration for the expository dialogue in every one of his tragedies. One of them will therefore suffice as an example. In *Andromaque*, most of the expository information is transmitted in the introductory dialogue between Oreste and Pylade (I,i) and its function in the external communication system is disguised more successfully than was the case in our previous example as a result of its being more subtly motivated. The unexpected meeting of the two friends after six months separation (line 7) makes the information on the background events and the current situation psychologically and pragmatically plausible, and goes some considerable way towards eliminating the imbalance in the relationship between the two dialogue partners. Both Oreste and Pylade mediate expository information and both ask and answer questions. Nonetheless, it would be mistaken to speak of a genuine equality between the dialogue partners, because both Oreste's long narrative description of the background to his courtship of Hermione and his political mission (lines 37–104) and Pylade's shorter report on the background to the situation at the court of Pyrrhus (lines 105–32) are only relevant to the plot inasmuch as it affects Oreste. At no stage in the text is Pylade able to command the interest of the audience for himself alone; he is restricted to functioning as a bearer and receiver of information and as an adviser to Oreste.

Expository information can be integrated into the structure of a genuinely 'dialogical dialogue' (see below, 4.5.1.2.) – that is, not merely in a more or less blatantly 'monological dialogue' – independently of the status of the dialogue partners. It is just as likely to occur in dialogues between two minor figures as it is between two major figures or indeed between major and minor figures. As an illustration of this we have therefore chosen the less obvious case of a dialogue between two minor figures in order to show that even when expository information is transmitted by peripheral figures, it can nonetheless be integrated into the text as a whole and can be motivated dialogically in a number of suggestive ways. Thus, in Hugo von Hofmannsthal's play *The Difficult Man*, the first pieces of information on the background and the current situation are mediated in the introductory dialogue between the two valets Lukas and Vincent. These two are not restricted to this scene alone; they reappear in varying configurations at several points in the text. Nor are their respective functions restricted to the bearing of expository information. The tension between Lukas, a discreet man who knows the wishes of his master intuitively, and the self-confident and impertinent Vincent, on whom all nuances of feeling are utterly wasted and who has applied for a job as valet to Count Bühl, is merely another variation of the central thematic contrast between differentiated sensibility and trite vapidity. In this context, the two valets also 'serve' as implicit pointers to the character of their employer. The fact that Bühl had made Lukas his valet many years before and sacks Vincent towards the end of the drama after a short probationary period pinpoints his own position within this scale of values. Unlike protatic figures or confidants, the two valets are not intended merely to accompany the central figure; they also pursue their own ambitions and desires, thereby initiating sequences of events that are interesting in themselves. This is particularly true of Vincent who, in applying to be taken on as a valet to Count Bühl, strives to inform himself carefully in advance (I,i) and then, on being accepted, immediately attempts to gain favour by ingratiating himself with his employer, only to be fired by him at the end (III,xii).

Whilst Lukas explains the various duties entailed in his new job, Vincent is clearly intent on discovering as much as possible about his new employer. It is this that motivates the transmission of expository information in the introductory dialogue – even on the internal dramatic level. This dialogue is characterised by the tension between the two valets caused by Vincent's blatant interest in obtaining indiscreet insights into the private lives of the members of his employer's family. Lukas, on the other hand, is only prepared to discuss the specific details of the job and thus feels repeatedly obliged to defuse Vincent's pestering curiosity:

> VINCENT (coming further in): What does he study? Estate business? Or what? Political affairs?
> LUKAS: This door by the wall is for the secretary to come in by.

In this manner, Lukas' discretion and tact repeatedly frustrates the audience's – and Vincent's – thirst for information and introduces an element of suspense into the transmission of expository information. By indulging in disrespectful speculation as to the count's personal affairs, Vincent repeatedly provokes Lukas into correcting him:

> VINCENT: . . . When a man won't ever see forty again –
> LUKAS: His lordship will be forty next year.[69]

By selecting minor figures as bearers of the first pieces of expository information, it is possible to show the main figures and their past histories from a comically abbreviated perspective – from the 'servants' perspective'. Bühl's amorous adventures in the past and his possible erotic ambitions for the future are trivialised into arguments for or against the likelihood of Vincent obtaining a secure and comfortable job. This is then compensated for and seen in a more subtle light after the addition of expository contributions from Bühl himself and his former mistress Antoinette Hechingen. The tension that develops between the various contrasting perspectival reflections on past events give rise to a phenomenon that Peter Pütz has aptly described as 'perspectival exposition'.[70]

3.7.3. The transmission of information at the end of the drama

In analogy with the theory of exposition that is applied to the beginnings of dramas, classical theorists also developed a number of concepts to help classify the endings. Aristotle's theories of *lusis* (resolution), *peripeteia* (a dramatic change in the plot), *anagnorisis* (recognition) and *catastrophe*,[71] were succeeded by the *inversio* and *solutio* of the Latin theoreticians and then, much later, by the *dénouements* of the dramaturgists of French classicism. The relations of these concepts to one another can scarcely be said to be unambiguous or unified in any way, despite the fact that, in the eighteenth century, a distinction was made between *dénouement* and *catastrophe* which defined the former as the final *peripeteia* and resolution of the intrigue, and the latter as the situation reached as a result.[72]

3.7.3.1. Closed endings in drama

This particular aspect of information transmission is concerned above all with the concepts of *anagnorisis*, *solutio* and *dénouement*. These three share a common conception of dramatic plot, according to which a figure or group of figures find themselves in a distressing situation as a result of either intrigue, self-deception or lack of information. This situation then culminates in either a happy or a tragic ending, after additional information has been introduced – such as new perspectives on the events leading up to the play or a sudden change in the plot itself. When this happens, the structure of discrepant awareness also generally changes, in so far as the informational discrepancies between the dramatic figures and those between the figures and the audience are reduced to a minimum or are abolished altogether.

We should like to call this type – which is the norm in classical theories of drama – the closed form of dramatic ending. In its purest form, the closed dramatic ending is clearly marked by the resolution of all open questions and conflicts and the abolition of informational discrepancy. In stage terms, this is often emphasised scenically by the implementation of dramatic conventions such as the appearance of the whole cast, speeches that summarise the plot and look forward with anticipation to a secure future, dance and other festivities, or comments addressed directly to the audience. On the thematic level, this is manifested in the resolution of all conflicts and ambivalence in the moral values expressed in the play, thereby clarifying once and for all the intended reception-perspective. Its most consistent form is expressed in the convention of 'poetic justice' that became the norm in the poetics and the dramaturgical theories of the seventeenth and eighteenth centuries. According to this convention all ethical conflicts that are still unresolved at the end of a play must be decided in favour of those who conform to the norm and by punishing those who contravene it. The didactic intention behind this is to encourage the audience to associate with good and avoid evil.

This kind of closed dramatic ending may be subdivided into two categories, depending on whether the informational deficits and value conflicts can be necessarily or plausibly resolved from the information provided in the text itself, or depending on whether they are resolved by the outside intervention of a figure who has played no part in the text hitherto. The classical form of this second type is the spectacular appearance of a *deus-ex-machina* in classical tragedy (especially in Euripides).[73] Thus, in the original, lost version of the ending of Euripides' *Iphigenia at Aulis*, the goddess Artemis appears and announces that she intends to replace Iphigenia on the sacrificial altar with a hind, thereby solving Agamemnon's moral conflict, who had been prepared to sacrifice his daughter to Hellas. Similarly, Plautus has Jupiter descend on a cloud at the end of *Amphitryon* in order to enlighten the confused husband as to the true state of affairs.

Although these kinds of *deus-ex-machina* solutions were generally dismissed in the dramatic theories of the sixteenth and seventeenth centuries, they nevertheless continued to appear in the dramatic texts of the period – though in secularised form. In Molière's *Tartuffe*, for example, in the face of the completely helpless and impotent Orgon and the universally triumphant Tartuffe, the peripeteia required to bring about an ending that accords with the principles of poetic justice is only achieved by the unexpected arrival of a royal commissioner who announces that the impostor has been unmasked by the king and, in addition, informs the assembled figures that the most recent and apparently threatening phases of Tartuffe's intrigues had already been under royal surveillance. On the external level, by reactivating the theoretically spurned *deus-ex-machina* device in this way, Molière is expressing his reverence for Louis XIV.

3.7.3.2. Open endings in drama

As a reaction against the closed form of dramatic ending, playwrights have developed the open form. This is especially common in plays of the modern period.[74] This deviation from the classical norm – marked by a refusal to supply an ending in which all the informational discrepancies are eliminated and all the conflicts resolved – can have a number of different functions. First, it can be the result of a changed view of what a plot should be, namely that it is no longer based on a single constellation of crisis or conflict but is concerned to demonstrate a lasting condition for which – as the plays of Samuel Beckett indicate – a resolution or closed ending would be unthinkable. At best, it is represented as a cyclical, repetitive process

that returns to where it started (see below, 7.4.4.3.). A second possibility –
and one that was used by Brecht, for example – would be an ending that, in
failing to supply a resolution, delegates the responsibility for this to the
audience. A clear example of this is the ending to *The Good Woman of
Setzuan*. At a complete loss as to how they might unite their ethical
demands with the ability to survive in this world, the gods escape upwards
by fleeing back to heaven on a 'pink cloud' (a deliberate reversal of the
deus-ex-machina ending) and thus demonstrate in exemplary and vivid
fashion their inability to resolve the problem. At the end, this is expressed
even more explicitly by the speaker of the epilogue:

> You're thinking, aren't you, that this is no right
> Conclusion to the play you've seen tonight?
> . . .
> We feel deflated too. We too are nettled
> To see the curtain come down and nothing settled.[75]

Of course, these questions are not quite as inconclusive as the text
suggests, for even though the author does not supply any explicit solutions
or instructions, the audience, to whom the problem has been delegated, is
not condemned to helplessness, but is invited, on the basis of implicit
interpretative signals from the author, to criticise the system that has
created this dilemma in the first place.

The open-endedness of this play refers exclusively to the thematic aspect
of the conflict of norms. There are, however, other texts, particularly of
the modern period, in which the author does not resolve even the most
basic factual questions. One example of this is Tom Stoppard's *Jumpers* in
which the unconventional decision consciously to withhold important
information at the end of a play is particularly explicit. The plot of
Jumpers follows that of the conventional detective story – but with one
significant modification. The murder of the philosophy professor McFee
that is enacted on open stage at the beginning of the play is left unsolved at
the end. The resulting informational discrepancy between the unidentified
murderer and the other figures and the informational deficit on the part of
the audience form the structural equivalents of the epistemological message inherent in the play. One of the closing speeches enunciates this
message with programmatic clarity:

The truth to us philosophers, Mr Crouch, is always an interim judgement. We will
never even know for certain who did shoot McFee. Unlike mystery novels, life does
not guarantee a dénouement; and if it came, how would one know whether to
believe it?[76]

The convention of the dénouement is thus cited explicitly by one of the
characters. Its violation in an open ending is justified as both an attempt to

approach the open-endedness of reality and the consequence of epistemological scepticism.

3.7.4. Information and suspense

In this discussion of the various ways that information can be sent successively we should also like to examine the whole question of dramatic suspense. By doing so we would hope to establish a greater degree of precision and practicability in the ways this concept is applied so as to undermine the tendency to equate suspense with some form of conflict or future-orientated finality.[77] It is important to make it clear from the outset that, within the framework of the present study, we do not intend to regard suspense primarily as a category of the reception process within the external communication system, but as a relation within the text and as the 'suspense potential' of the text itself. The notion that suspense corresponds to the realisation of the suspense potential of a text in the reception process depends on a large number of individual and supra-individual parameters (such as the individual's level of attention, the supra-individual reception context and the external conditions of performance etc.) which could only be comprehended completely by means of an as yet non-existent system of pragmatics. Thus, the suspense in the receiver increases with the degree of his or her individual identificatory involvement in a figure and/or situation, and decreases with the degree to which he or she is distracted by disruptive elements on both the internal and external dramatic levels.

3.7.4.1. Suspense and partial awareness

As an element in the linear sequential development of the plot, suspense potential can only be present when the figures on stage and/or the spectators in the auditorium are only partly aware of what might happen next.[78] Suspense potential cannot occur if the figures and/or spectators are completely aware of the ensuing plot sequences – a situation that probably seldom arises – nor if the fictional future is left completely open and unpredictable. Thus, suspense always depends on the existence of an element of tension between complete unawareness on the one hand and a certain level of anticipatory expectation based on certain given information on the other. A completely uncertain future would imply that it is impossible to project an anticipatory horizon of expectation and thus eliminate one component of the area of tension, whilst complete awareness would dispel all ignorance and eliminate the other. In the first case there would be no probing questions as to the future events; in the second they would be unnecessary.

3.7.4.2. The parameters of suspense

In establishing that the suspense potential of a dramatic text results from the partial awareness of the figures and/or receivers as to what will happen next, we have done no more than paraphrase the general conditions applying to the build-up of suspense potential. At the same time, we have not yet explained on which factors the intensity of the suspense potential depends. We must therefore give some indication of the parameters that condition the intensity of the suspense. To do so we decided to select one representative text: H. G. Clouzot's film version of Georges Arnaud's *Le Salaire de la peur* (1952). We chose this particular example because in the genre of the 'thriller' to which this text belongs the creation of suspense, as the name of the genre clearly indicates, is the predominant aim. The fact that it is not a dramatic text in the strict sense of the word (see above, 2.3.) is of little relevance to our analysis.

One factor that directly influences suspense is the extent that the receiver can identify with the fictional protagonist of the ensuing plot sequences. The stronger the identification, the more committed the audience becomes in the way they follow the plans made and the decisions and risks taken by the fictional protagonist, and the more he or she will look forward with anticipation to the ensuing plot sequences. The degree of identification and empathy is not left to the audience entirely, but it is also determined by the text itself. Thus, in Clouzot's film, the relatively lengthy introduction showing the social milieu of the stranded adventurers and tramps in Guatemala is not just designed to provide an element of social criticism, but, above all, to establish a certain level of identification on the part of the receiver with the problems, fears, hopes and the other intimate details of the private lives of the central figures. Of course, encouraging the audience to identify with the dramatic figures in this way is a technique that is by no means restricted to the genre of trivial thrillers. It occurs just as often in classical tragedy, in which great care is taken to make the situation, the protagonists and the motivation of the hero plausible to the audience early on in the text.

As far as the plot sequences themselves are concerned, the suspense potential increases in proportion to the amount of risk involved. In *Le Salaire de la peur*, the four central protagonists risk nothing less than their lives. Should they succeed in transporting the load of highly explosive nitro-glycerine, then they will receive a – for them at least – substantial financial reward. Their failure to do so might result in their deaths. A compromise solution seems out of the question. The reality of this risk for the 'hero' Gérard is demonstrated by the fact that, in the course of their perilous journey, one of the articulated lorries does in fact explode, killing its crew, and that Gérard is severely injured himself negotiating a difficult manoeuvre and dies shortly before they reach the destination. This all-or-nothing, death-or-glory approach can also be a feature of classical drama. The hero of the classical tragedy is also threatened and finally overtaken by death, and even in comedy the hero's attempts to achieve the *summum bonum* of lasting marital bliss are tempered by the awareness that failure would empty his life of all meaning. Even the classicist theory of the 'dramatic fall', according to which the tragic hero must be of an elevated social position in order to make his downfall appear as a particularly radical and devastating change in fortune, can also be seen as a technique that maximalises the risk in order to increase the suspense.

A further influence on the intensity of the suspense potential is the quantity and clarity of the future-orientated information which both figures and audience are able to use to develop their respective anticipatory hypotheses. Such future-orientated information is transmitted explicitly in the open discussions of plans, in prophecies, dreams and oaths, and implicitly in the form of psychic or atmospheric omens.[79] It is the knowledge of plans and potential obstacles to their realisation that produces that form of partial awareness of what will happen next that we identified as a fundamental prerequisite of the development of suspense potential. Thus, in *Le salaire de la peur*, the transport of the explosives and the dangers and obstacles facing it are discussed and planned in great detail, but it is this very detail that makes the intrusion of unforeseen difficulties all the more likely. An additional significant element of future-orientated information is the deadline by which the undertaking must be completed. We know that it must be completed by a certain time because the explosives will otherwise be detonated by the heat of the midday sun. The transport becomes a race against time, and the mere passing of time a consciously perceived and threatening process which constantly stimulates new hypotheses as to the chances of a successful completion of the journey. Conversely, suspense potential cannot develop when there is little or no future-orientated information, even if the author introduces the most drastic shock effects and total risk. Countless picaresque adventure dramas and sensationalist melodramas are examples of this negative element, in which the completely unpredictable may produce isolated moments of suprise or *coups de théâtre*, but not suspense. The link between future-orientated information and the intensity of the suspense potential is confirmed in the most positive sense in the films of Alfred Hitchcock, that master of suspense, or in Harold Pinter's comedies of menace (such as *The Birthday Party*), in which a high degree of suspense potential is built up by the intensive and skilful manipulation of an audience's expectations – without the expected horror ever actually having to occur.

An additional significant parameter on which the intensity of the suspense potential depends is the informational value of the ensuing plot sequence. In theory (see above, 3.1.1.) the informational value of an event decreases if the probability of its occurring increases. Conversely, it is true that the less probability there is of an event taking place, the higher its informational value will be. That is, an event predicted in the anticipatory hypotheses of the figures and/or the receivers on the basis of certain given information has a suspense potential that stands in inverse proportion to the probability of it actually taking place. Again, *Le Salaire de la peur* is an illustration of this. In view of the information on the perilous nature of the transport – the sensitivity of the explosives, the bad roads, the psychological condition of the drivers and the deadline etc. – a successful completion of the journey becomes highly improbable but, as a result, has a high informational value. This high informational value may be presented as the sum of a number of binary decisions that have to be taken at various points along the journey. Will they succeed in clearing away the rock that is blocking the road? Will they succeed in getting the articulated lorry out of the oil sludge? A successful outcome to each of these individual problems has a high informational value because, according to the information available, an outcome of this kind is highly unlikely.

In this discussion we have only been able to give a rough and rather imprecise sketch of the theoretical aspect of suspense, but it is important to add that it cannot be studied in isolation. It must also be studied in connection with the other parameters. Taken in isolation, it would, for instance, be easy to conclude that the greatest possible suspense potential is that created by an utterly improbable and therefore unpredictable event. Unfortunately, this would contradict the statements we made with regard to future-orientated information. There is obviously an upper limit to the maximalisation of the informational value in the intensification of suspense. This limit is probably situated at the point where low probability becomes complete unpredictability. Beyond it, the area of tension between non-awareness and the development of anticipatory hypotheses – upon which suspense is based – collapses.[80]

3.7.4.3. Short- and long-term suspense

Up to now, we have confined our discussion to the parameters that determine the intensity of one particular arc of suspense. However, the suspense potential that exists at a particular point in a dramatic text is generally the result of the interplay of several arcs of suspense. These can vary in length. Long-term suspense, which is often a feature of closed dramas, arches over the structure of the whole text, whereas short-term suspense merely embraces shorter plot sequences on an individual basis. *Le Salaire de la peur* is characterised by an all-embracing form of long-term suspense focussed on the ending and is complemented and sharpened by separate incidences of short-term suspense. In turn, these are intensified by the overall long-term suspense. Thus, suspense potential is not simply the sum of the incidences of long- and short-term suspense, since each complements the other. At the same time, in texts that do not contain this mutual complementation, the suspense potential at any given point will always be less and the overall suspense potential will be calculated simply as the sum of the incidents of short-term suspense. The interplay of several arcs of suspense and the variation in their length and intensity creates considerable variety in the suspense potential in the course of the text. Thus, it is vital to create the basis for the formation of anticipatory hypotheses, and thus for suspense potential, at the beginning of the text − not least by the transmission of expository information. In dramas with closed endings the suspense potential will finally completely disappear at the end following the resolution of all the problems and conflicts.

3.7.4.4. Can suspense be measured?

In view of the large number of parameters involved and the problems involved in trying to quantify them, there would appear to be little point in attempting to 'measure' the intensity of suspense potential. I. and J. Fónagy's attempts to establish a 'measure of dramatic suspense' are no use whatsoever in this respect since all they have managed to record is the number of arcs of suspense interacting at any one point in the text, but not their intensity or the levels of interference. The sole parameter they adhere to is the following: 'The suspense becomes greater in proportion to the number of questions involved and decreases when the question under discussion has been resolved.'[81] As a consequence of their complete reliance on the number of the arcs of suspense involved and their failure to take the type and importance of the questions, the length of the arc of suspense and the intensity of the receiver's identification level into consideration, they have come up with figures that obviously conflict with our own intuitive experience. How can it be seriously maintained that Shakespeare's *King Lear* keeps the audience in twice as much suspense (level 12.2) as *Hamlet* (6.2) and Racine's *Iphigénie* even more than twice as much (14.0)? If one is to assume that the whole point of a scientific analysis of suspense is to explain and reflect accurately the reception experience then this approach is completely invalidated by the results it comes up with.

4. Verbal communication

4.1. Dramatic language and ordinary language

4.1.1. The overlapping of two levels

What dramatic speech[1] shares with ordinary speech in an everyday dialogue is the fact that it is intimately bound up with the immediate context or situation that the participants in the dialogue find themselves in. This sets both of them apart from the varying degrees of situational abstraction that is characteristic of narrative or expository speech. Dramatic speech is nonetheless 'semantically much more complex' than speech in an ordinary conversation because inherent in the former there is

... yet another factor: the audience. This means that to all the direct participants of the dialogue is added another participant, silent but important, for everything which is said in a dramatic dialogue is oriented towards him, toward affecting his consciousness.[2]

However, the semantic complexity of dramatic speech is not the result of its orientation towards the receiver alone, but also of its orientation towards the sender. This again results from the overlapping of the internal and external communication systems: a dramatic speech does not only have two addressees; it also has two expressive subjects. One is the fictional expressive subject manifested in the dramatic figure, and the other is the real expressive subject, namely the author. The all too common habit of naïvely confusing the two expressive subjects in such a simplistic way as to equate an utterance by a dramatic figure with proverbial words of authorial wisdom, together with the corresponding tendency of authors to transform a character into a 'mouthpiece' for their own opinions and views, which is the case in many a *drame à thèse*, only serve to emphasise the need for this fundamental distinction. Of course, the degree to which figure orientation may dominate over authorial orientation, or vice versa, varies considerably. The wit expressed in an Oscar Wilde comedy constantly draws the audience's attention to the wit of the author, whereas the plays of the naturalist school, such as those by Ibsen, are attempts to establish the absolute dominance of figure orientation and eliminate all references to the author (see below, 4.4.1. and 2.).

103

4.1.2. Dimensions of deviation

Dramatic speech also deviates from ordinary speech in its employment of an aesthetically functionalised language. Its deviatory character is revealed in the way it violates the norms of the linguistic primary codes (by the use of innovative word formations or archaisms, for example) and in the introduction of other structural features (such as rhetorical stylisation or metre). Thus, the language of the French classical tragedy is very different to ordinary language – and not only because of the use of metre. Distance from everyday speech is also a prominent feature of the modern verse-dramas of T. S. Eliot and Christopher Fry. At the same time, however, this distance can be reduced to the point of assimilation – which is the case in naturalist theatre, in the contemporary English 'kitchen-sink' dramas and the German neo-naturalism of Rainer Werner Fassbinder and Franz Xaver Kroetz. But even when playwrights come as close as they possibly can to a faithful reproduction of ordinary speech, there is always an element of deviation – if only in the fact that in reproducing it they expose and clarify its characteristic stylistic features. In the plays of Kroetz, this technique of verbal reduction becomes a stylistic principle in itself which is employed to demonstrate the close link between the restricted verbal codes of his figures and their restricted awareness:

> MARY: It's all over if ya gotta drag everythin' through the dirt.
> KARL: Nothin's over.
> MARY: You're taking advantage cause ya have me. Ya take it out on me cause ya don't like me no more, cause ya can't find another.
> KARL: Cause I'm fed up with ya.
> MARY: Don't think I don't know it. Don't think I'm stupid.
> KARL: Ya'd talk different if ya knew the way ya looked.
> MARY: Ain't got no mirror.
> KARL: Go buy yaself one.
> MARY: Ain't got no money.
> KARL: Then I'll buy ya one.[3]

In addition to the historically and typologically extremely diverse ways that dramatic speech might deviate from ordinary speech, there is a second dimension that is concerned with the deviations from the established conventions of dramatic language. If the first dimension of deviation can be defined in terms of the synchronic juxtaposition of dramatic and ordinary speech, the second may be defined within the diachronic coordination of conventions governing stage language. To clarify what we mean we can return to the above-mentioned examples. In resurrecting the poetic ornamentation of the Elizabethan verse-drama and transposing the stylistic practices of modern poetry on to drama, Fry's verse-dramas represent a conscious and radical departure from the pointed arguments and witty prose of the earlier problem plays by G. B. Shaw and John Galsworthy and the West End comedies by the likes of Noël Coward and Terence Rattigan. Following in the anti-idealist tradition of Marieluise Fleisser and Ödön von Horváth, Kroetz's dramatic language is directed against the norms and elaborate codes of a dramatic language which is orientated towards the codes of the ruling classes. Dramatic speech is thus always located in the area of tension that occurs between at least two dimensions of deviation, as a result of which a reduction of the level of deviation from ordinary language is often in inverse proportion to the level of deviation from the established conventions of dramatic language, and vice versa.

4.2. The polyfunctionality of dramatic language

4.2.1. Polyfunctionality

A dramatic utterance always fulfils several functions in the internal communication system simultaneously, though one of these may dominate over the others.[4] We can illustrate this by taking one sentence from the dialogue from Kroetz's play *Michi's Blood* that was quoted in the previous section:

> KARL: Ya'd talk different if ya knew the way ya looked.

The dominant feature here is the appellative function directed at the partner: Karl wishes to influence Mary; he hopes to make her reconsider and revise her relationship with him. At the same time, however, this speech also has an expressive function: Karl's character is reflected in his use of language; his language characterises him. This expressive self-characterisation is in part intentional (he wishes to appear as the superior partner who does not actually need to be with the unattractive Mary), but it is also in part involuntary and unintentional (his verbal usage exposes him as a member of a lower social class and as a man of limited intelligence and brutal tendencies). Finally, this speech also fulfils a referential function: Karl presents his interpretation of the relationship between himself and Mary and portrays her as an unattractive woman.[5]

Unfortunately, the three functions discussed in this first paragraph do not do justice to the complexity of language. In order to achieve a more sophisticated framework for analysis we should therefore like to return to Roman Jakobson's model of verbal communication that we introduced and applied in our analysis of the relations that take place in the external communication system (see above, 2.4.2.). Each of the positions in his communication model – sender, receiver, content, message, channel and code – corresponds to a communicative function. The emotive or expressive function associated with presenting one's own position to the object is linked with the sender and the 'conative' (or appellative) function that is used to exert influence is linked to the receiver. The referential function used to present a speech object is associated with the speech content, whilst the poetic function that refers back reflexively to the specific essence and structure of the sign is linked with the message – as the verbal supersign. The phatic function employed to create and maintain the communicative contact is associated with the channel and, finally, the metalingual function used to focus on the code to make the audience aware of it is linked to the code itself.

These categories will become clearer and more definite when we actually apply them to the analysis of dramatic speech. Of course, at the same time it must be remembered that these functions operate in both the internal and external communication systems. The hierarchical structure of the functions within the internal communication system and the relationships between them that apply to each individual utterance do not normally coincide with those that apply to the same speech within the external communication system. Important functional discrepancies do actually occur. In Macbeth's letter to his wife (I, v), for example, the referential function predominates in the internal communication system as a result of Macbeth's overriding concern to inform his wife of the witches' prophecy and the impending visit of the king. Because they are already well aware of all this, however, the spectators are primarily concerned with the appellative function directed at Lady Macbeth as the receiver, in so far as they are interested above all in seeing how she will receive and react to the news.

4.2.2. Referential function

The referential function dominates strongly in the conventional forms of dramatic report such as the expository narrative (see above, 3.7.2.), the messenger's report (see above, 3.6.2.3.) and teichoscopy (see below, 6.2.2.2.). These particular elements of the plot are presented in the purely verbal form of the narrative which, for economical or technical reasons, cannot be enacted directly on stage.

If this kind of narrative report is only given a referential function in the external communication system because the information it conveys is redundant in the face of the addressee's existing level of awareness in the internal communication system, then the result will be a tendency to produce epic communication structures. Even if the reporting figure does not go so far as to step outside his role or address the audience directly and explicitly, the receiver will still regard himself as the primary addressee in view of the absence of a referential function for the report in the internal communication system.

The dramas of both classicism and naturalism avoided such epic tendencies. In these plays, the referential function of spoken reports is not redundant in either the internal or the external communication systems. We can demonstrate this by quoting the report of Max Piccolomini's heroic death delivered by the Swedish captain in Schiller's *Wallenstein's Death* (IV, x):

> We lay, not thinking we should be attacked,
> In camp at Neustadt, with but slight defences,
> 3020 When towards evening there arose a cloud
> Of dust towards the woods, our vanguard rushed
> Into the camp and cried, The enemy!
> We scarcely had the time to leap into
> The saddle, when the Pappenheimers came
> 3025 Full gallop through the outworks in their charge,
> And soon across the ditch as well, that ran
> Around the camp, they sprang in hostile frenzy.
> But reckless bravery had led them on
> Before their comrades, far behind them marched
> 3030 The infantry, only Pappenheims had dared
> To follow boldly where their bold commander led. –
>   . . .
> Ahead and on the flanks we now attacked
> Them with the force of all our cavalry,
> 3035 And drove them back into the ditch, wherein
> Their swiftly-mustered ranks our infantry
> Presented them a bristling wall of pikes.
> Now neither forwards could they move, nor back,
> Hemmed right between us in a fearful press.
> 3040 The Rhinegrave called out to their leader then
> To yield himself in honourable surrender,
> But Colonel Piccolomini –
>   . . . we knew
> Him by his helmet's crest and flowing hair,
> 3045 All loosened by the swiftness of his charge –
> Points to the ditch, and sets, the first of all,
> His noble steed to leap it, after him
> The regiment – but ah! it was too late!
> His mount, pierced by a halberd, rears itself
> 3050 In pain and fury hurls its rider down,
> And over him goes thundering the charge
> Of horses, heedless now of rein or bridle.
>   . . .
> But then, when they had seen their leader fall,
> 3055 The troops were seized with a despairing rage,
> Now no man thinks of how he may be saved,
> Like savage tigers now they fight, their fierce

Resistance spurs our side to the attack,
And on the struggle goes, and will not end,
3060 Until the last of them has met his death.

Both Thekla, the addressee of the report in the internal communication system, and the audience have known since Act IV, Scene v that Max has been killed in the battle against the Swedes, but neither Thekla nor the audience is aware of the actual circumstances of his death. They are first communicated in this messenger's report. In this case, then, the predominance of the referential function is guaranteed by the fact that the speaker, in accordance with the conventions of the messenger's report, only appears in this particular scene and thus can have no pretensions in the direction of arousing interest in himself as a dramatic figure. He also scarcely even attempts to present himself in any expressive function. Hence the complete absence of personal pronoun in the first person singular. Instead, he submerges his own individuality into the collective 'we' and remains in the background, both as a narrative medium and as a participant in the action he relates. In his report he does not try to emphasise the appellative function and speak to the addressee directly, but restricts himself to presenting the most vivid account possible of what happened. To illustrate the events, the speaker employs a number of deictic references to time and space, ensures that all details serve the context of the events being related, structures the narrative in a particular rhythmic and syntactic way so as to reinforce mimetically the hectic nature of the events, and recalls past events with a vigour that culminates in the change in tense from preterite to historic present (lines 3046ff. and lines 3056ff.).

Although the referential function predominates in the captain's report it is by no means the only one. For the vivid style of the report is not just intended to make it as lively and precise as possible, but also to stimulate and maintain the attention of the listeners in both the internal and external communication systems and to maintain communicative contact between speakers and listeners. Admittedly, this phatic function is more important in the external communication system than it is in the internal, because Thekla, as Max's fiancée, would presumably follow the story of his tragic end with total involvement whatever its outer form might be. The degree of her commitment to her beloved, which the captain had been aware of since her fainting fit on first hearing the news of his death (IV, v and ix), also explains the appellative function of the report: the captain wishes to spare the bereaved more grief than is absolutely necessary and, in the introductory dialogue, declares himself unwilling to talk about the painful events at all. Later on, he expresses the wish to break off his report – in a brief dialogical exchange between lines 3052 and 3053 – and strives to console Thekla by emphasising Max's heroic behaviour. Thekla's mimetic and gestural reactions to the report – signalised in the secondary text after lines 3031 and 3042 – are the correlative of this appellative function. The captain's tactful and protective behaviour demonstrates that he, too, has an expressive function after all. He is not an entirely neutral narrative medium and is characterised implicitly by the style and manner of his report.

Finally, the captain's report also has a poetic function – though only in the external communication system. The aesthetic structure of the speech – the metre and rhythm, the pattern of repeated vowels and consonants, the rhetorical figures (such as the polyptoton in line 3031) and the above-mentioned techniques of illustration and recall etc. – means that the verbal supersign is relieved of its automatic connection to what is being described and draws attention to itself in reflexive self-reference. This poetic function is also associated with Schiller's desire to locate this report in the historical tradition of dramatic messengers' reports and his hope that the audience would recognise it as a particularly complex example.

Thus, we have seen that even a dramatic speech in which the referential function predominates can fulfil other functions. Conversely, it is of course also true that the referential function is a feature not only of reports, but also of every dramatic speech. Thus, in our analysis of the functions of dramatic speech we must always remind ourselves of the already postulated axiom of its polyfunctionality and of the need to describe both the ways the various functions might dominate and the hierarchical correlations linking them.

4.2.3. Expressive function

The expressive function of an utterance relates back to the speaker of a speech and is always of great importance, especially within the external communication system, since the technique of bringing a figure to life by the choice of what he or she talks about, his or her verbal behaviour and style are some of the most important characterisation techniques in drama (see below, 4.4.2. and 5.4.2.3.). An utterance has an expressive function in the external communication system even when the speaker's primary intention is to describe a state of affairs, persuade the dialogue partner to do something or to establish communicative contact. Ben Jonson's emphasis on the close connection between speaker and utterance is thus especially true of dramatic speech:

Language most shows a man: speak that I may see thee. It springs out of the most retired, and inmost parts of us, and is the image of the parent of it, the mind. No glass renders a man's form, or likeness, so true as his speech.[6]

On the other hand, as a conscious feature intended by the speaker, the expressive function does not have any permanent role. It may be found in a particularly pure, and therefore dominant, form in abrupt exclamations – as, for example, in the following exchange between Franz and Weislingen in Act V of Goethe's *Götz von Berlichingen*:

> FRANZ (beside himself): Poison! Poison! From your wife! – I! I! (He rushes off)
> WEISLINGEN: Marie, go after him. He is desperate. (Marie exits) Poison from my own wife! God! God! I feel it. Martyrdom and death![7]

The elliptically abbreviated form of Franz's exclamations still have the important referential function of informing his master that he has been seduced by Adelheid into poisoning him. At the same time, however, their repetition (known in rhetorical terms as *geminatio*) does no more than refer back to the speaker and his condition of extreme excitement. This also applies to Weislingen's exclamations, which merely express his reactions to the events rather than any intention of informing or influencing the other figures.

Another form of dramatic speech in which the expressive function frequently occurs in isolated and dominant form is the soliloquy of reflection and deliberation. Without going into the particular problems of monological speech here (see below, 4.5.), it should be noted that the predominance of the expressive function results from the speaker's desire to articulate his own self-awareness as a way of clarifying his own position to himself, of justifying his actions or reaching a decision. This applies to the following remarks by Macbeth in one of his numerous soliloquies, for example:

> I have almost forgot the taste of fears.
> The time has been my senses would have cool'd
> To hear a night-shriek, and my fell of hair
> Would at a dismal treatise rouse and stir
> As life were in't. I have supp'd full with horrors;
> Direness, familiar to my slaughterous thoughts,
> Cannot once start me.   (V, v, 9–15)

This speech scarcely refers to any specific situation outside the consciousness of the speaker, and the large number of pronouns in the first person singular clearly demonstrates that in these attempts at self-articulation, the speaker is not only the subject but also the object of his speech. The monological speech situation also hinders the growth of a referential or appellative function.[8]

4.2.4. Appellative function

Conversely, it is true that of all these functions it is the appellative function in particular that is dependent on dialogue and the importance of this function increases in proportion to the degree the dialogue partner is involved (see below, 4.5.1. and 4.6.). The more the speaker tries to influence or change the mind of the dialogue partner and the more he or she reacts to the latter's reservations and objections, the stronger the appellative function will be. One special form of exerting influence or persuasion is the imperative, or command, which of course assumes the existence of a certain relationship of authority and dependency in the dialogue partners. In the types of dramatic speech in which the appellative function predominates, the general nature of dramatic speech as verbal action (see above, 1.2.5.) becomes especially evident: acts of persuasion and imperatives represent speech acts which, independently of whether the attempt to persuade is successful or not, or whether the imperative is carried out or not, actually alter the dramatic situation (see below, 4.3.). It is therefore not surprising that a predominant appellative function is particularly common in dramatic speech and that dialogues in which one partner attempts to persuade or win over the other have been virtually obligatory components of plays over long periods in the history of drama.

Dialogues with a predominantly appellative function are often used to mark dramatic climaxes with a high level of suspense. An example of this is the dialogue between Odoardo and Emilia in Lessing's play *Emilia Galotti* (V, vii). Emilia sees suicide as the only solution to her tragic dilemma and attempts to persuade her father to hand over the very same dagger with which he had just intended to kill Gonzaga and Marinelli:

> EMILIA: In heaven's name, no, father! This life is all the wicked have. No, father, give me, give me that dagger.
> ODOARDO: Child, it is not a hairpin.
> EMILIA: Then a hairpin will serve for a dagger! It does not matter.
> ODOARDO: What? Is that what we have come to? No, no! Remember: for you too there is nothing more precious than life.
> EMILIA: Not even innocence?
> ODOARDO: That can resist any tyrant.
> EMILIA: But not every seducer. Tyranny! Tyranny! Who cannot stand up to tyranny? What men call tyranny is nothing; the seducer is the true tyrant. I have blood in my veins too, father, warm young blood like any other girl. My senses are senses too. I cannot promise anything; I cannot vouch for myself . . . Give it to me, father, give me that dagger.
> ODOARDO: And if you knew what it was like, this dagger!
> EMILIA: And even if I do not know! A friend unknown is still a friend. Give it to me, father, give it to me.

ODOARDO: What then if I give it to you – there! (Gives it to her)
EMILIA: And there! (She is about to stab herself but her father snatches it from her hand again)
ODOARDO: See, how quick! No, that is not for your hand.
EMILIA: Then it is true, I must take a hairpin if I – (She puts her hand to her hair to find one, and takes hold of the rose) You, still here? Off with you! You do not belong in the hair of a – what my father wants me to become!
ODOARDO: Oh my daughter!
EMILIA: Oh my father, if I could only read what is in your mind! But no, it cannot be that either, or why did you hesitate? . . . Long ago I believe there was a father who, to save his daughter from shame, took steel, the first that came to hand, and plunged it into her heart – gave her life a second time. But all such deeds are deeds of long ago. There is no such father in the world today!
ODOARDO: There is, my daughter, there is! (Stabbing her)[9]

The predominance of the appellative function in Emilia's speeches is shown by the double repetition of her appeals to her father to give her the dagger, and the intensity of her appeals is increased by the use of rhetorical figures. The constant repetition of direct forms of address – 'my daughter', 'my father' etc. – and the brevity of the individual speeches also serve to intensify the references to the dialogue partner, and thus the appellative function. Emilia repeatedly introduces new arguments in her attempt to change her father's mind and there is, in fact, not a single speech – and not even a single section of her speeches – that is not subordinate to the overall appellative function, either in the form of a demand or arguments in support of that demand. Thus, she claims that denying her the dagger would not prevent her from committing suicide since other weapons would be available to her, that to die counts for little in comparison to the loss of her innocence, that her innocence is powerless when confronted with the force of seduction, that the dagger, whoever gives it to her, is the gift of a friend, that a father who denies her her death in such circumstances disgraces himself morally since he is thus condoning the loss of her innocence. Finally, the argument that ultimately convinces her father is her reference to the story of Virginius and Virginia as an example of a heroic father-ethos. She does not develop this chain of arguments independently, however, but rather by constantly responding to the objections and counter-arguments of her dialogue partner, as her repeated references to individual words, phrases and sentences from her father's speeches clearly indicate.

Although the appellative function has been shown to be probably the most important one in the internal communication system of dramatic texts, this is generally not at all true in the external communication system. In comparison with expository or narrative texts, the appellative function of dramatic texts that is directed at the receiver generally seems to be much less pervasive – didactic dramas and *drames à thèse* apart, of course. It is significant, however, that the direct appeals to the audience inherent in these last two categories frequently presuppose the establishment of a mediating communication system by the introduction of epic commentator figures or figures that are supposed to act as a kind of authorial mouthpiece. This aspect cannot in any way be generalised into a constant feature of the genre and the appellative attitude towards the audience has been manifested historically and typologically in a number of extremely diverse ways. These range from the dramaturgical theory of objectivity (such as naturalism) which merely strives to communicate plain facts to the audience without indulging in direct appeals to a dramaturgy of partisan commitment, whose appeal is ideologically unambiguous, and from texts designed to satisfy the receiver's desire to be amused to those that confront him with ethical questions.

4.2.5. Phatic function

Unlike its appellative counterpart, the phatic function, which is associated with the channel between speaker and listener and is designed to create and maintain the contact between them, is of greater relevance to the external communication system. By 'channel' and 'contact' we do not just mean the purely physical link which enables the dramatist to convey information from sender to receiver; we are also referring to the psychological willingness of both parties to communicate with each other. Thus, the phatic function is served in the external system by such diverse factors as the spatial lay-out of stage and auditorium so as to guarantee the best possible acoustics and visibility (see above, 2.2.1.), the title and the use of advertising to arouse interest, and, finally, the receiver's involvement in the play as a result of either the structures of suspense, the use of epic communication structures and the possibilities for identification with one or more of the figures in the text itself.

On the internal level, the phatic function helps create and intensify the dialogical contact between the various figures. Thus, some of the phenomena that we have already included in the appellative function also function phatically. Examples of this are occasions when the dialogue partner is addressed by the speaker in order to ensure that communicative contact will occur or when he reacts to the former's utterances, thus confirming the communicative contact. However, the phatic function becomes especially important when, in the wake of disrupted communication, contact first has to be established, or when 'maintaining contact' becomes the predominant or even the sole concern of dialogical communication. This last characteristic is particularly common in modern plays, in so far as they frequently portray the increasingly problematic nature of human communication and the attempt – and failure – to break out of a sense of solipsist isolation and alienation by entering into a dialogical relationship. Thus, the dialogues in Beckett's *Waiting for Godot* seldom reveal any intention on the part of the two tramps to discuss their own characters in any depth, to convey information or to influence anyone. Instead, their incessant chatting often merely has the function of enabling them to stay in contact with one another and simulate a kind of communication for which, in reality, the prerequisite conditions have already been withdrawn:

> (Silence)
> VLADIMIR and ESTRAGON (turning simultaneously): Do you –
> VLADIMIR: Oh, pardon!
> ESTRAGON: Carry on.
> VLADIMIR: No no, after you.
> ESTRAGON: No no, you first.
> VLADIMIR: I interrupted you.
> ESTRAGON: On the contrary.
> (They glare at each other angrily)
> VLADIMIR: Ceremonious ape!
> ESTRAGON: Punctilious pig!
> VLADIMIR: Finish your phrase, I tell you!
> ESTRAGON: Finish your own!
> (Silence. They draw closer, halt)
> VLADIMIR: Moron.
> ESTRAGON: That's the idea, let's abuse each other.[10]

The extreme reduction of the expressive function, i.e. the almost complete absence of references in the individual utterances to an individual expressive subject, is shown here in the similarity and interchangeability of the speeches. The referential function is restricted to a discussion of the intention of saying something – though this intention is itself no more than a purported one from which everyone strives to escape; and the appellative function, which usually features strongly when insults are exchanged, has been eliminated since the two figures have no real intention of insulting each other. The insults, like the attestations of politeness, are all part of a word-game construed to pass the time. Speaking has become an end in itself, a purely phatic form of communication whose sole remaining purpose is constantly to reassure the figures that a channel of communication does actually still exist. That they are not even aware that this is itself a failing only emphasises the fact that this dialogue has been reduced to one single function.

4.2.6. Metalingual function

The metalingual function is associated with the code and, like the phatic function, is generally only present in latent form. However, situations do arise – in both ordinary speech and dramatic dialogue – in which it can step into the foreground. This always occurs whenever the verbal code used is explicitly or implicitly developed as a central theme. On the internal dramatic level, the motivation behind such attempts to draw the audience's attention to the verbal code may often stem from a disruption in the communication process – that is when communication no longer functions because of excessive discrepancies between the codes, or, more precisely, the subcodes of the individual dialogue partners, thus causing them to speak about their language in metalingual terms. These discrepancies are often conditioned sociologically, as, for example, in the following dialogue between the homeless alcoholic Loach and Ash, the former teacher, in Peter Nichols's play *The National Health* (1970):

> ASH: . . . My wife couldn't have children. . . .
> LOACH: Was it to do with her underneaths?
> ASH: I'm sorry.
> LOACH: To do with her womb, was it?
> ASH: Yes.
> LOACH: Womb trouble.
> ASH: That sort of thing, yes.[11]

Loach, inhibited by the awareness of the discrepancy between his own and Ash's linguistic registers, between his own 'restricted' and his partner's 'elaborated' code (Basil Bernstein), is obviously searching for a word referring to the lower abdominal region of a woman which would not be an insult to a more delicate taste, and he hits upon the unusual circumlocution of 'underneaths'. Ash, in turn, finds the whole subject matter of female sexuality and female sexual parts highly, if not traumatically, embarrassing. He either does not understand Loach's reference, or, more likely, pretends not to have got the point of his question: 'I'm sorry.' In a second attempt to make himself understood, Loach falls back on the standard expression 'womb' and now Ash cannot but acknowledge having got the message. His curt 'yes' is, however, at the same time a stylistically encoded signal that he does not want to pursue this matter any further and enter a discussion of the painful details of his wife's sexual anatomy. Loach, insensitive to Ash's clear signals that the communication is terminated, goes on and elaborates: 'Womb trouble.' Again, Ash does not take up Loach's expression but, as he is hoping to win over Loach's friendship and therefore does not want to emphasise the difference between their respective codes and registers, concludes the conversation with the non-committal comment, 'That sort of thing, yes.'

Although the technique of drawing attention to the verbal code in this way is particularly common in modern dramas, it is by no means entirely new, as a detailed analysis of Shakespearean dialogues would demonstrate. Furthermore, in order to foreground the metalingual function, it is not necessary to make the verbal code explicit. It suffices to refer to it implicitly, either by juxtaposing a number of contrasting codes or by emphasising one particular code that clearly deviates from the generally accepted norm, thus making the audience aware of the code in the communication process.[12]

However, metalingual references to the code, whether implicit or explicit, do not always have to be associated with disrupted communication – as the above examples might possibly suggest. On the contrary, the predominance of the metalingual function may also be motivated by a high degree of verbal virtuosity or games with the rules of the code. Word- or language-games of this sort are especially common in comedy, something to which the innumerable puns in the dialogues of Shakespeare's comedies testify.

In the external communication system the metalingual function has a bearing not only on the primary verbal code, but also on the conventions of dramatic texts as a system of secondary codes. In such cases, then, it is not the reference to language but that to drama and the theatre that allows the metalingual function to become predominant. Here, too, the references to the code can be either explicit or implicit. The most explicit way of doing this is to establish a mediating communication system, which is what happens in the Brechtian type of epic theatre (see above, 3.6.2.); however, it can also be conveyed to the audience in a more indirect form through the speeches of the figures themselves, as the following extract from Lessing's comedy *Minna von Barnhelm* (V, ix) illustrates:

> FRANZISKA: And now, madam, it's time to stop teasing the Major.
> MINNA: Stop your pleading! Don't you know that the knot will untie itself at any moment?[13]

In her use of the knot metaphor, Minna von Barnhelm is referring to the traditional notion that dramatic intrigue must first be allowed to thicken before being resolved. Her metaphorical and indirect reference to dramatic convention is then taken over by the spectators who apply it directly to the play itself. By Act V, Scene ix, he or she is entitled to expect that the knot will soon be unravelled in the form of the dénouement, in accordance with the conventions of the classical comedy of intrigue.

Finally, the devices that can be used to foreground the metalingual function implicitly in the external communication system are 1) the contrastive juxtaposition of differing conventions in a single text, as may be observed in Shakespeare's *Midsummer Night's Dream* in the contrast between the play-within-the-play with its extremely primitive structure of dialogue, figures and plot, and the formally complex main play; and 2) the high degree of deviation from dramatic conventions familiar to the receiver. Thus, in the early plays of Edward Bond, for example, the receiver is constantly aware that the language used has been reduced drastically in comparison to the language of classical drama. Similarly, to an audience unschooled in literary history experiencing a play by Corneille for the first time, for example, the high level of verbal stylisation will appear as an unfamiliar and rather baffling convention and may direct the audience's attention back on to the code itself.

4.2.7. Poetic function

The poetic function is manifested in the way a message refers to itself, and thus draws the audience's attention to its structure and constituent parts. In ordinary speech, this dimension is dispelled by the fact that the message is made to refer automatically to the object. Normally, the poetic function only applies to the external communication system and not to the communication processes taking place between the various figures. Failure to recognise this situation may lead to serious misinterpretations in attempts at practical criticism. One example will serve as an illustration of such a misunderstanding. Shakespeare's *Richard II*, especially after Act III, Scene ii, contains a number of speeches by the central protagonists that are characterised by their great poetic intensity. This has led a number of notable critics such as Mark Van Doren[14] to regard King Richard himself as a poet who, in his tendency to indulge in poetic speech, neglects political action and thus fails tragically as Regent. The arguments against this interpretation are already inherent in the fact that the causes of his failure are portrayed as a series of misjudged political decisions made in the first two acts, and that his speeches do not attain their high level of poetic intensity until his fall has already been sealed. This interpretation is also undermined in principle by the fact that the poetic function of these speeches operates predominantly in the external, rather than the internal, communication system. To put it simplistically: the poetry here is Shakespeare's, not Richard's, and it is not appreciated as poetry by Richard's dialogue partners on stage but by the audience in the auditorium.[15] The fact that Richard's speeches do not essentially reach this level of intensity until Act III indicates that in view of Richard's passivity and reduced freedom to act, Shakespeare now focusses on the stream of consciousness in the mind of his hero. In addition, by giving him such a poetically charged language, Shakespeare wishes to arouse more sympathy on the part of the audience for the failed hero.[16]

Of course, it is possible to make broader generalisations on the basis of the evidence produced by this example. Thus, the poetic function of metre in a verse-drama, for example, is only relevant to the external communication system and not to the internal system for, if the opposite were true, the figures would presumably express their astonishment at this 'unnatural' manner of speaking.[17] This does not mean, though, that there is no poetic function that can be effective on the internal level, but to achieve it would require explicit or implicit references to it in the utterances of the dramatic figures: explicit in so far as speakers or listeners describe a particular utterance as aesthetically stylised and poetic (which is repeatedly the case in Shakespeare's *Love's Labour's Lost*); implicit in so far as the speeches of one particular figure, in marked contrast to the others', are conspicuous for their high degree of poetic stylisation. The second of these applies, in part, to King Richard's speeches, whose imagery and euphony set them clearly apart from the prosaic sobriety of those of his opposite number, Bolingbroke. Our allocation of the poetic function of Richard's speeches to the external communication system must therefore be qualified – though not to the extent that we would agree with the exaggerated thesis that Richard and the poet are the same person (see below, 4.4.1.).

4.3. Verbal communication and action

4.3.1. The identity of speech and action

If we agree with A. Hübler's definition of action as 'the transition from one situation to another in the sense of a development, a transition which, depending on the kind of situation involved, is selected deliberately from a number of different possibilities rather than simply causally determined'[18] then it is clear that this kind of deliberate change in the dramatic situation often takes place in the utterances of one of the figures. In situations that involve giving an order, betraying a secret, uttering a threat, making a promise, persuading another figure to do something or any other similar speech act, a dramatic figure completes a spoken action which changes the situation and thus the relationships of the figures to one another intentionally.[19] Such spoken action, or actional speech, is common in dramatic texts and it clarifies that identity of speech and action that we discussed in the context of the performative aspect (see above, 1.2.5.) and the predominance of the appellative function (see above, 4.2.4.). Of course, dramatic texts also contain actions that are enacted non-verbally rather than verbally (such as embraces, stabbings or threatening gestures). But even these types of wordless behaviour are generally accompanied by verbal acts that help to plan, justify or declare the intention behind the non-verbal act.

4.3.2. The non-identity of speech and action

4.3.2.1. Speech related to action

From this, it is already clear that the distance between speech and action is likely to be variable. Complete lack of distance – that is, when they are identical – is a special case that, in dramatic texts, deviates both quantitatively and qualitatively in relevance from other kinds of texts. Although dramatic speech is always performative speech – speech as a form of action – as defined by speech-act theory, the identity of speech and of action designed to change a situation does not apply to every dramatic speech. Thus, although commentative attempts to explain or justify an action are also actions that take place in language, they are nevertheless definitely not identical to the action commentated on itself, which is supposed to alter the dramatic situation. This kind of commentative speech is a form of reference, or contrast between speech and action, that frequently occurs in dramatic texts, whether it takes the form of the active figure commenting on either his action or that of another figure or whether there is an epic mediating commentary. In all such cases the speaker distances himself to some degree from the situation in which he finds himself in order to reflect on it. On the occasions when speech and action are identical, however, he remains completely immersed in the situation that he hopes to change by speaking.

4.3.2.2. Speech unrelated to action

When speech is contrasted with action it is not identical to it but nonetheless still refers to it directly. The distance between speech and action can be increased further by abandoning such direct references to action that are features of commentative speech. It is then possible to say that speech and action are unrelated and that they run parallel to each other. Thus, there are certain dialogue passages in dramatic texts – especially in comedies and modern dramas – which are structured like a conversation[20] and which, because they have been distanced from the dramatic situation as a self-contained phatic conversation-for-conversation's-sake, constantly revise their thematic orientation. Examples of this are the witty banter of servants and clowns in Shakespeare's comedies and the dialogues in the plays of Samuel Beckett. The latter are based on the axiom that an action that is intended to alter the dramatic situation is impossible, thereby negating a priori the whole notion that speech can be related to action.

4.4. Verbal communication and dramatic figure

4.4.1. Restrictions in the correspondence between language and dramatic figure

In our discussion of the expressive function of language (see above, 4.2.3.) we drew attention to the significance of language in the constitution of the dramatic figure. That is, it is as a result of what a dramatic figure says and how it says it that it is able to portray itself, whether willingly or unwillingly, consciously or unconsciously, explicitly or implicitly. It is only in this way – assisted by a number of non-verbal devices of self-portrayal – that the receiver is able to regard it as a tangible figure with a distinct personality.

4.4.1.1. The superimposition of a poetic function on the expressive function

Although it has never been entirely negated as a principle, this correspondence between speech and figure – the figure-relatedness of speech – has continued to be defined fairly narrowly in the history of drama and in fact should generally be restricted. Once again, these restrictions result from the overlapping of two communication systems in drama. Thus, in French classical tragedy, for example, the whole idea of the correspondence between speech and figure is undermined by the aesthetic principle of linguistic and stylistic homogeneity that is manifested in the external communication system. The figures essentially all speak in the same kind of rhetorically elevated and metrical style. As such, this verbal and stylistic homogeneity reflects the social homogeneity of the dramatis personae and thus succeeds in relating language to figure. At the same time, however, the psychological individuality of each figure is restricted to certain stylistic nuances. Generally speaking, the tendency towards linguistic homogeneity occurs in the closed dramatic form[21] and in the verse-drama, in which the rhythmic homogeneity in itself reflects the aesthetic principle of uniformity.

By contrast, the correspondence between language and figure is realised much more strictly in naturalist theatre in which, in accordance with the principle of linguistic differentiation, each figure is associated with its own personal verbal style. Between these two extremes – absolute linguistic homogeneity and complete differentiation – there is a broad spectrum of intermediary levels that have been used in drama at one time or another. Two of these intermediary positions are represented by the development of typified class-orientated sociolects (such as the introduction of 'lower' style and prose for servants etc. and an elevated style for their masters) and the indication of individual idiolects.

Clearly, this spectrum of possibilities is determined by the variation in the relationship between the expressive function in the internal communication system and the poetic function in the external system: when linguistic homogeneity occurs, the poetic function predominates; when linguistic differentiation occurs, however, it is the expressive function that predominates. In deducing the character of a particular dramatic figure from its language one need not examine every single stylistic feature of its utterances since these are not entirely self-referential. As a *modus procedendi* it would therefore be more sensible to subtract from the linguistic and stylistic inventory of a figure's utterances all the features they share with the utterances of the other figures – in other words, to take into consideration only the deviations from the language of the other figures as the characteristic verbal features of a particular figure.

4.4.1.2. The superimposition of epic communication structures on figure reference

The level of immediacy in the relationship between figure and language also depends on the particular conception of figure that has been chosen (see below, 5.4.1.5.). As far as a consistently naturalist, psychological conception of figure is concerned, the level of a figure's awareness always remains within the bounds of what is plausible in the psychological and spatial context. Therefore, a figure's speech capability or level of articulation never transgresses these boundaries either. If the dramatist wishes to be consistent in realising this programme he must avoid any additional aesthetical structuring of the language that is not motivated in the internal communication system and be prepared to tolerate a very low level of articulation in figures who are not sophisticated speakers within the fictional framework. The generally accepted and yet unrealistic eloquence of the figures and the aesthetic structure of their utterances is thereby replaced by a reduced level of articulation that may even go as far as complete muteness and by the linguistic characteristics of normal speech (fractured syntax, dysfunctional repetitions, lexical limitations, vagueness, pauses etc.). In his programmatic essay 'Writing for the theatre' (1964), Harold Pinter emphatically confirmed this radically mimetic conception (even though a closer analysis of his own texts would expose aesthetic structures that contradict it):

Given characters who possess a momentum of their own, my job is not to impose upon them, not to subject them to false articulation, by which I mean forcing a character to speak where he could not speak, or making him speak of what he could never speak.[22]

If this kind of conception of dramatic figure and language presupposes a direct link between figure and language and if it is then possible to evaluate every detail of linguistic form and verbal behaviour in terms of a psychological and ideological symptom, then a 'transpsychological' conception of figure eliminates this kind of direct or unrestricted link. Thus, having abandoned the principles of Ibsenesque naturalism, G. B. Shaw wrote in 1923:

> Neither have I ever been what you call a representationist or realist. I was always in the classic tradition, recognising that stage characters must be endowed by the author with a conscious self-knowledge and power of expression ... and a freedom from inhibitions, which in real life would make them monsters of genius. It is the power to do this that differentiates me (or Shakespeare) from a gramophone and a camera.[23]

If a dramatic figure is permitted to express itself in an unnaturally articulate way, then the dramatist is merely employing a historically based dramatic convention. It is this that Shaw stubbornly defends here. It may be described as a process that takes place within an utterance in the course of which a mediating communication system is superimposed on the internal system which the dramatist uses to analyse and interpret the dramatic figures. The high level of awareness and articulacy that these dramas exhibit should therefore not be linked directly and unreservedly to the figure alone, since – by analogy with added aesthetic structures such as verse – they also reflect some degree of authorial intervention.

4.4.1.3. The superimposition of references to the situation on figure reference

A further factor restricting the correspondence between speech and figure, and thus the possibility of inferring the disposition of a dramatic figure from its utterances, is a consequence of the fact that the utterances of a dramatic figure are determined not by its disposition alone, but also by the situation in which it finds itself at any particular time. Thus, the utterances of a particular figure do not need to be stylistically homogeneous and may vary stylistically according to the particular dramatic situation and the intention behind a particular utterance.

The virtuoso skill with which figures such as Tartuffe or Richard III don their various verbal disguises demonstrates the contextual variability of individual verbal style very clearly indeed. However, we have selected an example in which the stylistic differences are less the result of some ulterior strategy on the part of the figure involved than of the direct pressure of the situation in which he appears. The following two quotations express the two different ways that Brabantio, Desdemona's father in *Othello*, reacts to the loss of his daughter – the first takes place immediately after he has discovered that she has eloped (I,i) and the second before the Venetian Senate (I,ii):

> It is too true an evil. Gone she is;
> And what's to come of my despised time
> Is nought but bitterness. Now, Roderigo,
> Where didst thou see her? – O unhappy girl! –
> With the Moor, sayst thou? – Who would be a father? –
> How didst thou know 'twas she? – O, thou deceivest me
> Past thought! – What said she to you? – Get more tapers;
> Raise all my kindred. – Are they married, think you?   (I,i, 161–8)

> O thou foul thief, where hast thou stow'd my daughter?
> Damn'd as thou art, thou hast enchanted her;
> For I'll refer me to all things of sense,
> If she in chains of magic were not bound,
> Whether a maid so tender, fair and happy,
> So opposite to marriage, that she shunn'd
> The wealthy curled darlings of our nation,
> Would ever have, to incur a general mock,
> Run from her guardage to the sooty bosom
> Of such a thing as thou – to fear, not to delight.
> Judge me the world, if 'tis not gross in sense,
> That thou has practis'd on her with foul charms,
> Abus'd her delicate youth with drugs or minerals
> That weakens motion. I'll have't disputed on;
> 'Tis probable, and palpable to thinking.   (I,ii, 62–76)

The first passage is spoken by an extremely agitated man who, surrounded by his servants on the street at night, does not feel obliged to express himself with any degree of formality. Stylistically, this is reflected in the agitated rhythms that repeatedly break up the alternating flow of blank verse and the union of sentences and lines, in the brevity of the sentences and the associative rather than logical way that they are linked together, the numerous parentheses, the verbal gestus of insistent questioning that either anticipates or hastily ignores the answer and, finally, his complete preoccupation with the actual events from which he seems to be incapable of distancing himself in any rational way. The second passage, on the other hand, is characterised by a completely different stylistic texture that has been conditioned, above all, by the completely different circumstances in which it is spoken: we are faced with a speech delivered in court and as such it exhibits a high level of rhetorical formality and logical consistency in the argumentation. It is spoken by a man who is more distanced in time from the theme of his discourse and who is thus able to adopt a more rational stance towards it. The question he asks is not left unanswered, and the answer is justified in two passages (lines 64–72 and 73–7) by an appeal to the norms of reason in the form of evidential proof. This desire to establish some form of rational explanation is reflected in the more restrained rhythms, the extensive hypotaxes, the insistent succession of parallel phrases (lines 67f., 72, 74f. and 77) and the use of a more abstract vocabulary (see the words linked with the vocabulary of thought in lines 65, 73 and 77, for example).

Of course, despite these profound differences in stylistic texture and verbal behaviour, both of these speeches are allocated to the same speaker, namely Brabantio, who speaks differently in different speech contexts. He therefore cannot be characterised on the basis of one or other of the two passages in isolation, but by the way his speeches change stylistically according to the contexts in which they occur. As such, the amplitude of the various stylistic registers reflects the breadth of his emotional responses.

4.4.2. Characterisation through language

In turning our attention to the way a figure's disposition is revealed in his or her verbal utterances it is necessary to distinguish between a number of different layers. Two fundamental distinctions that must be established are whether the verbal forms of self-presentation remain implicit or explicit and whether the implicit form of self-presentation is voluntary or involuntary. Although these forms of self-presentation overlap in almost every utterance, their value as signals endues them with a categorically different kind of status for the receiver.

4.4.2.1. Explicit self-presentation

Explicit self-presentation (see below, 5.4.2.2., on 'self-commentary') occurs when a figure consciously outlines its picture of itself and this may happen in the context of either monologue and dialogue. The information that the receiver obtains from the figure in this way is neither objective nor binding and should be evaluated as elements of a subjectively coloured form of self-presentation – that is, of course, if one ignores the nonperspectival technique of 'objective self-presentation' that was a convention in medieval and occasionally even in Elizabethan drama.[24] However, as a conscious form of self-presentation, it is essentially distorted with regard to the figure concerned and thus does not coincide with the authorially intended reception-perspective for this particular figure. Furthermore, in examples of explicit self-presentation within a dialogue there is an additional distorting factor embodied in the strategic intentions of the speaker who, after all, frequently attempts to influence his or her dialogue partner by means of a particularly stylised form of self-presentation. This kind of distortion may even be a feature of monologues or soliloquies as instances of either tragic or comic self-deception. Thus, to grasp the intended image of the figure, the receiver must adjust the information he or she receives from that figure by activating the mechanisms of perspective guidance that we discussed in 3.5.3.

4.4.2.2. Implicit self-presentation

The situation is different when we turn to the implicit, unconscious or involuntary forms of verbal self-presentation (see below, 5.4.2.3.). As such these are not subjectively distorted and reveal to the receiver the figure's temperamental and ideological disposition directly. Of course, the receiver has to cope here with various forms of implicit verbal behaviour and is therefore confronted with the more complex task of having to interpret symptoms rather than decode signs (see above, 1.3.2.).

One kind of symptom, from which we can infer a figure's disposition, also forms a part of what is known as paralinguistics, by which, to take but one example, a dramatic figure may be characterised on the basis of voice-quality alone. Thus, we generally associate a high piercing voice with resolution or fanaticism and a soft-spoken person with a dreamy or sensitive disposition. Although this paralinguistic aspect is seldom mentioned in the secondary text of the literary work it is nonetheless always relevant in performance.

Stylistic texture as a part of the implicit characterisation process, on the other hand, is established as a feature of the literary text. An example is unnecessary in this case since we attempted to demonstrate this point in our analysis of Brabantio's two speeches (see above, 4.4.1.3.). Nonetheless, we would still like to catalogue the most important questions raised by this kind of textural analysis.

First, we are faced with the general question of whether the language of a particular dramatic figure approximates that of a social or regional subcode – that is, to ask whether its use of either standard English or dialect, an elaborate or restricted code or a particular set of technical terms (whether legal, nautical, medical or whatever) places it in a particular social context. A similarly transphrastic aspect of style (one that transcends individual sentences) is the question of the way individual sentences of a speech relate to one another. Whether they are connected in a strictly logical way, whether they form a more associative series or just a loosely knit jumble, they always shed light on the structure of a figure's level of awareness. Finally, all significant deviations from the normal frequencies in the areas of syntactic and lexical selection and combination can also serve to delineate a figure: the frequency of certain sentence types (such as statements or questions), the predominance of hypotaxis or parataxis, active or passive forms, the use of parallelisms and antitheses, an abstract or concrete vocabulary, figurative or literal speech, the emphasis on certain semantic groups and the frequency of idiomatic or clichéed expressions etc. In this, the characterising function is not restricted to merely identifying the various figures; it also serves to expose their respective temperaments and dispositions.

A last aspect is the one that is concerned above all with the way the speeches of the different figures interact. These relationships enable us to add the verbal behaviour of a particular figure to our list of characteristic features. According to this, a figure is defined by the way he responds to the preceding speech and reacts to the conversation as a whole: a figure that is bound up in his own idiosyncrasies and interests will tend to ignore the preceding speech and continue 'in his own vein' and frequently change to monological speech; conversely, a figure concerned with rationality will explicitly respond to the preceding speech and discuss the arguments contained in it. A more detailed discussion of the various possibilities open to the dramatist is not necessary at this point since we shall be returning to them later on in connection with the structures of dialogue (see below, 4.6.4.). In the mean time it will suffice simply to provide additional concrete examples of the concept of verbal behaviour. Thus, the length of speeches can help define a figure – as someone who is either talkative and gossipy or who weighs up every possibility. A strong tendency towards monological speech can indicate egocentricity. The frequent interruption or cutting short of the speeches of the dialogue partner may reflect impatience or the desire to dominate, and the frequent use of maxims or abstract analyses of the situation often reflects dispassionate rationality. The tendency to deceive or the ability to adapt one's own verbal characteristics to those of the dialogue partner and/or the situation (partner tactics) are also a part of the broad tapestry of characteristic verbal behaviour.

4.5. Monological speech

4.5.1. Monologue and dialogue

4.5.1.1. Situational and structural differentials

On closer examination, the concept of the monologue, which is one of the most frequently defined concepts in dramatic theory, may be shown to be ambiguous.[25] The only thing that the various standard definitions of monologue actually have in common is the fact that they define it as the opposite of dialogue and that they then assign every dramatic utterance to one or other of these two formal categories. The definition of monologue thus depends on how this contrast between monologue and dialogue is understood. The research conducted to date essentially contains two main criteria. First, there is the *situational* criterion, which refers to the speaker's solitude. This means that there is no actual addressee on stage and that the figure is thus left to talk to himself. Secondly, there is the *structural* criterion, which refers to the length and degree of autonomy of a particular speech. According to the first criterion, then, a longish report or a long speech are not monologues since they are addressed directly to other figures on stage. However, according to the second, they definitely are monologues, since they are self-contained, autonomous speeches of a reasonable length. Anglo-American criticism has established a terminological distinction between these two concepts and describes the first type as a *soliloquy* and the second as a *monologue*:

... monologue is distinguished from one side of a dialogue by its length and relative completeness, and from the soliloquy ... by the fact that it is addressed to someone.... A soliloquy is spoken by one person that is alone or acts as though he were alone. It is a kind of talking to oneself, not intended to affect others.[26]

These two criteria represent two different kinds of classification principles. The situational criterion permits an unambiguous form of binary classification, since the question whether a speech is addressed to another figure on stage or not can almost always be answered with either 'yes' or 'no'. It can be answered in the negative either if the figure is alone on stage or imagines he is alone or if he ignores the presence of other figures whilst speaking. According to the situational criterion, all these cases are examples of soliloquy; all others are dialogues. The structural criterion is a different matter altogether: the question whether the criterion of length and inner unity is satisfied or not cannot be answered simply with an unambiguous 'yes' or 'no', but only with a 'more' or 'less'. A binary form of classification is therefore not possible here and has been replaced by a sliding scale of values registering the levels of 'more' or 'less'.

4.5.1.2. Soliloquy versus monologicity; dialogue versus dialogicity

Having established a distinction between soliloquy and dialogue according to the situational criterion we can now begin to chart the scale of possibilities that separate the ideal type of monologue and the ideal type of dialogue by examining the level of monological or dialogical quality in each case. One of the consequences of adopting these two criteria is that when we actually turn our attention to specific dramatic utterances we can expect to discover dialogical soliloquies and monological dialogues.

However, the standard definition of monological speech (extended length and internal coherence) is still too vague to enable us to attempt a more sophisticated analysis. Furthermore, its links with the situational criterion have not yet been explained. Greater clarity can be achieved by referring back to J. Mukařovský's dialectical contrast between dialogue and monologue.[27] According to Mukařovský (pp. 87–8), a dialogue always rests on the polarity or suspense between 'several or at least two contextures' which 'interpenetrate and alternate in dialogic discourse':

Because there is more than one participant in a dialogue, there is also a manifold contexture: although each person's utterances alternate with those of the other person or persons, they comprise a certain unity of meaning. Because the contextures which interpenetrate in this way in a dialogue are different, often even contradictory, sharp semantic reversals occur on the boundaries of the individual replies. The more vivid the dialogue, the shorter the individual replies, and the more distinct the collisions of the contextures. Thus arises a special semantic effect for which stylistics has even created a term: stichomythia.

This shows how the structural criterion develops out of the situational criterion, i.e., the participation of either just one speaker or several speakers: in dialogue we have the semantic changes of direction between each of the utterances and in monologues one unified semantic direction; in dialogues the individual utterances tend to be brief, whereas in monologues they are generally longer. As a result, Mukařovský also recognises the need to replace the binary contrast between dialogue and monologue with a graded scale of values and, analogous to our own concepts of mono- and dialogical speech, to speak of a greater or lesser degree of 'monologicity' or 'dialogicity' (pp. 103f.).[28] The more frequent and radical the semantic changes of direction are in a particular passage, the stronger its dialogicity becomes and vice versa. Furthermore, Mukařovský is correct not to equate the concept of the subject with that of the figure (pp. 96–102) and demonstrates that several contexts can 'interpenetrate and alternate' even within a single utterance of one particular figure. Thus, the speaker of a soliloquy may address himself as 'you', which can then produce a conflict between several viewpoints ('contextures') in one and the same soliloquy – such as the contrasts between body and soul, heart and mind, duty and desire, past and present, etc. This imbues monologues or soliloquies with a dialogical quality which increases in proportion to the frequency and radicality of the semantic changes of direction. And conversely, in a dialogue between figures who are in complete agreement, it is possible to see them as a single dramatic subject. Because it lacks the semantic changes of direction, this kind of dialogue may be said to have a high level of monologicity.

4.5.1.3. Monological tendencies in dialogue

From this it is possible to define an ideal form of 'dialogical dialogue' as an undisrupted form of two-way communication between two or more figures who represent polar opposites and whose interrelations are marked by a high level of tension. As a result these figures constantly refer to one another in their speeches and, because of their overall equal status, they are able to interrupt each other at any time. This means that their speeches are also equal in quantitative terms.

This definition can be used as a starting-point for an analysis of the various factors that encourage the development of monological tendencies in dialogues. The presence of monological tendencies in dialogues can be the result of disrupted communication which, in turn, may be either because the channel between the dialogue partners is severely disrupted or even non-existent (i.e., if they are physically or psychologically unwilling or unable to communicate), because they employ strongly diverging codes, thus causing incomprehension or grave misunderstandings, or, finally, because their referential contexts are so different that the minimum consensus required for communication to take place is missing. Modern plays in particular contain a wealth of examples of such phenomena.

The tendency to produce monological structures also occurs if our second definition of the ideal form of dialogue, namely the tension that exists in the interrelations between the various figures, is suspended. If complete consensus occurs there can be no semantic changes of direction, which means that the monological quality has become so strong that it is almost possible to speak of a monologue divided into a number of parts, as is true of the following dialogue from Maeterlinck's one-act play *Interior* (1895):

> THE STRANGER: See, they are smiling in the silence of the room...
> THE OLD MAN: They are not at all anxious – they did not expect her this evening.
> THE STRANGER: They sit motionless and smiling. But see, the father puts his finger to his lips...
> THE OLD MAN: He points to the child asleep on its mother's breast...
> THE STRANGER: She dares not raise her head for fear of disturbing it...
> THE OLD MAN: They are not sewing anymore. There is a dead silence...[29]

Despite the fact that there are two different speakers, this passage really only represents a single contexture and this becomes evident when we redistribute the speeches or alter the boundaries between them. The meaning of the dialogue will not be affected in any far-reaching way.

The next condition covers the way the speakers refer to each other, and this is related to the appellative function in particular. If the latter is no longer present, the dialogue will collapse into a series of unrelated speeches, whose speakers take little or no notice of each other and talk at cross-purposes. N. F. Simpson's *One Way Pendulum* (1959) pushes this to an extreme. The result is an absurd farce, in which each figure is bound up in its own idiosyncrasies to such an extent that long passages consist merely of a series of disconnected monologues being passed back and forth. Despite everything that is said or happens around her, Aunt Mildred is obsessed with one subject alone – her travel plans and her frustration at being confined to a wheelchair.

Finally, the abolition of equality and the resulting predominance of one figure also encourages the development of a monological tendency because the context of the predominant figure overwhelms the others both qualitatively and quantitatively to such an extent that it is virtually impossible for semantic changes of direction to take place. This kind of predominance has been institutionalised in the public speech, for example, in which from the outset one particular individual figure assumes the function of speaker and the others those of more or less passive listeners, whose interventions are generally restricted to intermittent heckling. As a result, the frequent presentation of public speeches in drama – the two funeral orations in Shakespeare's *Julius Caesar* (III,ii) are examples of this – always introduces a strong monological quality to the dialogue.

4.5.1.4. Dialogical tendencies in soliloquies

The analogous but converse phenomenon – the presence of dialogical forms in soliloquies – is always based on the fact that the identity of speaker and listener which defines the soliloquy is dissolved into a contrast between speaker and addressee, thereby producing a contrast between different semantic contexts. The pure reflexive quality that is characteristic of soliloquies can be suspended if the speaker indulges in apostrophes to a god, an object or an imagined being – a technique that features in all of the soliloquies in Aeschylus and Sophocles, and in most of Euripides'. Although the imagined addressee created by this kind of apostrophising does not answer back directly, semantic changes of direction nonetheless occur within the soliloquy in so far as the speaker imagines the reactions and thus the semantic context of the addressee.

A more pronounced dialogical tendency occurs when the speaker is split into two or more conflicting subjects. This form, which might be described as an interior dialogue, often emphasises the contrasting positions of two subjects by the use of particular pronouns – that is, by apostrophising the self in the second person singular – and it thus expresses the split between the rational philosophical self and the self that is caught up in a real situation. An example of this form of self-apostrophisation occurs in the following passage from Euripides' *Medea*:

> ... but I will
> not suffer my hand to fall idly.
> Ah! Not this, my spirit, do not do this!
> Let them alone, wretched woman, spare your children!
> They will live with you there and be a joy to you.   (lines 1054–8)

The conflict between natural maternal love that regards the murder of one's own children as the most heinous crime and the impulsive desire for revenge that regards the protection of one's children as cowardice provokes a quick succession of radical semantic changes of direction. This internal conflict is clearly marked by the emphatic repetition of 'not', the self-apostrophisation and the switch from one personal pronoun to another.

Finally, on a different level, there is a further dialogical tendency that attempts to establish a dialogue partner by addressing the audience. Since the speaker is not addressing another character on stage and the communication process is one-way, the situational criterion of the soliloquy is fulfilled. However, the speaker departs from the internal communication system and in his comments 'aside' *ad spectatores* switches over to a mediating communicating system (see above, 3.6.2.3.). By addressing the audience and taking its semantic context into consideration, the dramatist has created a dialogical soliloquy. The dialogical tendency is even felt when the audience fails to react to the speaker's remarks *ad spectatores* in an appropriate manner (by applauding or heckling, for example) because the addressee is in fact not the empirical audience but a fictional one that only exists in the remarks *ad spectatores* in the first place.

4.5.2. Soliloquy

After these preliminary discussions, we should now like to develop a typological framework for the various historical forms of the soliloquy that will complement our first attempts to chart the dialogical elements in soliloquy.

4.5.2.1. Convention versus motivation

The soliloquy is based primarily on a convention, an unspoken agreement between author and receiver, which – unlike conditions prevailing in the real world – allows a dramatic figure to think aloud and talk to itself. Of course, thinking aloud and talking to oneself are phenomena that do occur in the real world, though talking in this manner for too long is generally thought to be a pathological deviation from the norm and those who are not pathologically disturbed generally restrict their thinking aloud to brief exclamations. Thus, as a dramatic convention, the soliloquy goes way beyond reality in so far as it stylises a pathological extreme into a normal form of communicative behaviour. This convention cannot be justified by any sort of mimetic relationship to reality (because otherwise the whole illustrious gallery of dramatic heroes would have to be presented as a collection of pathologically disturbed individuals!) but by the functions that it is able to fulfil. These functions are generally the same as those served by the mediating communication system in narrative texts. It is possible, therefore, to regard the soliloquy as a convention that is employed in order to compensate for the absence of this mediating communication system in drama.

Thus, soliloquy is frequently used as a vehicle for transmitting information on previous or future events in concentrated form. This was true of Roman comedy, in which soliloquies were often used to provide the audience with a continuous commentary on the plot and thereby help it to follow the various intrigues which, because of the frequent use of deceptions, disguises and misunderstandings, were often somewhat confusing. In narrative texts, this kind of information is generally mediated by the narrator. The latter is also charged with revealing the figure's consciousness and enabling the audience to participate in its silent thought processes. In drama, which is essentially restricted to the figures in their roles as speaking subjects, these aspects are revealed to the audience through the convention of thinking aloud in a soliloquy. For, although the figures of a drama are able to communicate their thoughts to one another, their dialogical messages lack the intimate immediacy and undisguised openness that is possible in the convention of the soliloquy. Finally, on top of all these mediating functions, the soliloquy also serves several functions of a structural and formal kind: it can form a bridge between two separate scenes, thus preventing the break in the action caused by an empty stage; as an entrance or exit soliloquy it can look forward to or summarise future developments in the plot, and in all positions it can be used to slow down the action and create an element of reflective distance.[30]

It would be difficult to integrate the wide variety of functions served by the soliloquy into dramatic texts in any other way. This explains the longevity of this highly artificial and unrealistic convention. Nonetheless, in the context of the rationalist philosophies and aesthetics of the seventeenth and eighteenth centuries, a number of critics began to object to the artificiality of this convention, even though their criticisms were not formulated in any poetologically explicit way. The result was that French classical tragedy tended to eliminate the narrative soliloquies that contravene the natural norms in such a glaringly obvious manner and to replace them with dialogues with confidants – though, of course, these retained a highly monological quality. And Lessing went even further. Not only did he exclude all purely narrative soliloquies; he went so far as to construct the sort of soliloquies that were designed to reveal something of a figure's interior awareness more 'naturally' either by imitating the style of spontaneous speech (see below 4.5.2.2.) or by establishing an interior dialogue. Both of these devices were strongly influenced by the example set by Shakespeare's celebrated soliloquies. However, the emergence of realist and naturalist aesthetics in the nineteenth century meant that the soliloquy had to be abandoned as a dramatic convention altogether and was in fact rejected in explicit poetological terms. Thus, in a letter to Georg Brandes, Ibsen was able to boast that he had never had to resort to the convention of the soliloquy in his play *Brand* (1866):

I have paid particular attention to form, and among other things I have accomplished the feat of doing without a single monologue, in fact without a single 'aside'.[31]

Of course, the rejection of the soliloquy as a dramatic convention did not mean the rejection of the soliloquy in its entirety for, as we have seen, the soliloquy also plays a certain part in the reality of normal verbal behaviour. The soliloquy can therefore still be used as long as it is realistically motivated. That is, as a brief exclamation, as a soliloquy by a pathological individual or under certain special conditions such as semisleep, extreme tiredness or intoxication. In his preface to *Miss Julie* (1888), August Strindberg elevated this idea into a dramaturgical programme:

Our realists have excommunicated the monologue as improbable, but if I can lay a proper basis for it, I can also make it seem probable, and then I can use it to good advantage. It is probable, for instance, that a speaker may walk back and forth in his room practising his speech aloud; it is probable that an actor may read through his part aloud, that a servant-girl may talk to her cat, that a mother may prattle to her child, that an old spinster may chatter to her parrot, that a person may talk in his sleep.[32]

The preceding paragraphs are not intended to be understood merely as an isolated historical analysis of the soliloquy from the seventeenth to the late nineteenth centuries but rather as part of a systematic typological analysis. For the soliloquy as a convention, as it occurs in classical drama, and the 'realistic' or motivated soliloquy as permitted by naturalists, are not two different historical forms of one and the same structure, but two categorically different semiotic structures. Whereas the conventional soliloquy forms part of the secondary code – that is, the code that regulates the communication process between author and receiver in the external communication system – the motivated or realist soliloquy has a firm basis in the communicative conditions of the internal communication system. In this way, the motivated soliloquy is often interpreted by the audience as a symptom: the very fact that a figure indulges in monological speech exposes him as being unable or unwilling to communicate dialogically. This modification of the soliloquy's position in the semiotic system of drama also explains why monological speech actually seems to have been given greater significance after the 'banishment' of the conventionalised soliloquy by the proponents of a naturalist aesthetics. This tendency has continued into twentieth-century drama. In fact, there are even some modern texts – known as monodramas – whose primary text consists solely of the soliloquy of a single figure. Beckett's *Krapp's Last Tape* (1958) is an example of this. The soliloquy in this case is therefore not just a formal element required by the medium, devoid of meaning in itself, but also expresses themes such as the disruption of communication and the isolation and alienation of the individual.

Of course, the contrast between the conventionalised and motivated types of soliloquy is by no means absolute. Once again, they present two extreme forms spanning a spectrum of possible intermediary forms. Shakespeare's soliloquies, for example, definitely remain within the monological conventions that applied to Elizabethan drama.[33] At the same time, however, they also exhibit the tendency to explain the solitude of the speaker and his or her utterances by invoking the speaker's psychological disposition and social situation: thus, the fact that Hamlet expresses himself in soliloquies is not just a technical device used to give the audience an insight into his mind. It also reflects his sense of isolation, his problematic individuality and his tendency to indulge in introspection.

4.5.2.2. Premeditated form versus spontaneous improvisation

The contrast between conventionalised and motivated soliloquies tends to concide with the stylistic and textural contrast between soliloquies with a clear disposition that often follow rhetorical patterns and those in which the associative and cumulative flow of verbal utterances is intended to simulate the spontaneity of ordinary speech. For whilst the first give the impression of dispassionate rationality and a premeditated closure of content and form, the second are intended to convey the impassioned simultaneity and movement of feelings, thought and speech.

As an example of a soliloquy with a clear and coherent disposition we can examine Don Rodrigue's first soliloquy in Corneille's *Le Cid* (I,vii). As far as the metre is concerned, the soliloquy is divided clearly into six ten-line stanzas, but even its argumentation structure reveals a clear and simple lay-out: in the first three stanzas Rodrigue outlines the dilemma facing him – namely the tragic conflict between his obligation to his father and that towards his beloved. In the second group of three stanzas he decides to act in accordance with his *honneur* rather than his *amour*. To be more precise, stanza 1 presents the situation (*narratio*), in stanzas 2 and 3 he discusses the two alternatives open to him (*argumentatio*), in stanzas 4 and 5 he rejects suicide as a possible way of escaping his dilemma (*refutatio*) and stanza 6 contains his decision to avenge his father and renounce his beloved (*conclusio*). Thus, even this more sophisticated and rhetorically disposed analysis produces an axially symmetrical division of the various parts and displays a strictly logical progression from the presentation of the situation to the final decision. The balance and harmony of the rhetorical framework stands in markedly unrealistic contrast to the psychological disposition of the speaker and thus emphasises the 'trans-psychological' (see below, 5.4.1.6.) conventionality of this soliloquy all too clearly.

As a contrast to the above, we should now like to examine the soliloquy that constitutes the scene 'The woods beyond' in Georg Büchner's play *Woyzeck*:

> WOYZECK: On and on! For ever! On, on, on!
> Stop the music. – Shh. (Throws himself down.)
> What's that? – What's that you say? What you're
> saying? . . . Stab . . . Stab the she-wolf dead.
> Shall I?
> Must I? Is it there, too? In the wind even.
> (Stands up.) It's all round me. Everywhere.
> Round, round, on and on and on . . .
> Stab her. Dead, dead – dead!! (Runs out.)[34]

Like Rodrigue, the speaker here is faced with a decision: Woyzeck, who has just witnessed Marie's dance with the Drum Major, is driven by jealousy into committing a crime of passion. But whereas Rodrigue reaches his decision on the basis of rational reflection, Woyzeck is at the mercy of his own 'nature' and the voices of the elements. He is no longer in control of his own actions and has lost all capability for dispassioned rationality. It is this that provides the motivation for the soliloquy itself: tormented by voices and visions and close to madness, he escapes to an isolated spot where he gives vent to his feelings in a series of stammered exclamations. His soliloquy lacks both the metre and the firm syntactic structure of Rodrigue's expansive, hypotactic sentence constructions. In place of a logically constructed series of arguments there is a stream of fragmented and associated words that are emphatically repeated in a whirlpool of turbulent obsessions and reminiscences that have been sparked off by the 'On and on' that Marie had shouted to the Drum Major during their dance.

The examples we have chosen are a particularly drastic illustration of the contrast between a clear disposition and associative, disordered spontaneity. However, an examination of all existing dramatic soliloquies will reveal, once again, that the majority of soliloquies should be classified as intermediate forms on the spectrum between these two poles. It also shows that although conventionalised soliloquies generally tend towards a clear disposition and motivated monologues towards disorder or the hidden order of spontaneity, this correlation sometimes appears blurred or distorted and occasionally even reversed.[35]

4.5.2.3. Soliloquies of action and reflection

The formal or structural typologies discussed above must be complemented by one of a more functional kind. Various attempts have been made in this direction in the literature on the subject and the result has been a number of new concepts such as the 'lyrical soliloquy', the 'soliloquy of reflection', the 'soliloquy of decision', the 'soliloquy of planning' and the 'soliloquy of conflict'. The disadvantages of such attempts at classification rest in the fact that – because of the disparity of the criteria employed – it is difficult to establish any sort of clear-cut distinction between these concepts, and that the number of categories can be expanded at will. Our own functional typology will therefore be constructed according to one criterion only, namely the relationship between speech and action (see above, 4.3.).

According to this criterion we generally distinguish between soliloquies that are actional and those that are non-actional, or reflective. In the former, the soliloquy constitutes in itself an act that changes the situation. In this type of soliloquy, the speaker generally feels that he or she is faced with a number of different possibilities for action and then selects one of them to follow. In this, even the revocation of a decision constitutes an action. Both of the examples discussed in the previous section – the soliloquies of Rodrigue and Woyzeck – clearly belong to this category.

Non-actional or reflective soliloquies may be divided into two subtypes: the informative and the commentative. They can be distinguished from each other by the different ways they relate to the action. In informative soliloquies, the audience must first be informed of particular events and situations, whilst in commentative soliloquies an event or situation that the audience is already familiar with is interpreted subjectively from that figure's perspective. Both of these types differ from actional soliloquies in that although they refer to the action they do not really constitute an action or change the dramatic situation in themselves. Both forms of reflective soliloquy often contain examples of epic communication structures (see above, 3.6.2.3.). In the informative soliloquy – and this is particularly true of the expository soliloquy – the audience is made familiar with a particular series of events in the most direct way, and the less the transmission of information is motivated on the internal communication level the more obvious this epic function becomes. As far as the commentative soliloquy is concerned, the epic effect increases in proportion to both the distance between the commentary and the dramatic situation and that between the speaker and his active role within the plot. In extreme cases, the result might be a speech *ex persona* in which the commentary goes way beyond the figure's level of awareness and develops into a commentary that can be detached from the speaker and convey the authorially intended reception-perspective in epic form.[36] In such cases, the soliloquy assumes the functions of the mediating commentary in much the same way as the chorus in classical drama.

Of course, once again, actional, informative and commentative soliloquies should be understood as ideal abstractions, extreme types in which one particular function predominates in isolation. In most soliloquies actional, informative and commentative elements combine with each other in varying proportions. Indeed, soliloquies may often be divided into sections in each of which a different element predominates. That the actional soliloquy in *Le Cid* should correspond to one of the ideal types so closely is therefore by no means the rule. In fact, even here, the actional element does not occur in complete isolation because Don Rodrigue's reflections on the various alternatives open to him also represents a kind of commentary on the action.

4.5.3. Asides

Asides or *apartés* are not always soliloquies; nor do they always take the form of monological speech. Nonetheless, we should like to introduce them to our analysis at this particular juncture because they are similar to soliloquies in a number of important ways.[37]

4.5.3.1. The monological aside: convention versus motivation

The type of aside that bears the greatest resemblance to a soliloquy is one like the following example from Calderón's *La dama duende*. Having lost his guard in a duel with Don Manuel, Don Luis reflects upon his position in an aside:

> DON MANUEL: That is no lack of courage,
>   But only the failing of fortune and chance.
>   Go and fetch thyself another sword.
> DON LUIS: Thou art as bold as thou art noble.
>   (Aside) O fate, what should I do now
>   In such a difficult and threatened position?

For should he take my honour
He will, in victory, grant me my life.
I must seek an excuse,
Whether true or false, so that
I may seriously consider which path
I should take to resolve my present doubt.[38]

What this aside has in common with a soliloquy is the fact that it is not addressed to another figure on stage. However, it differs from it in so far as the speaker is neither alone on stage, nor does he imagine he is alone, nor has he forgotten that he is in the presence of others. As a result, this type of aside appears to be a convention that contravenes the circumstances of real life even more than the conventionalised soliloquy. For, not only is this extended period of thinking aloud psychologically unrealistic, but it also breaks all the laws of acoustics, according to which a speech that cannot be heard by a dialogue partner on stage is much less likely to be heard by the audience at the back of the auditorium. On the basis of its structural and communicative affinity with the conventional soliloquy, we should like to describe this type of aside as a conventionalised monological aside. Like the conventionalised soliloquy, the conventionalised monological aside enables the author either to present the figure's thoughts directly (as in the example cited above) to give a frank commentary on a particular situation free of any strategic considerations (often expressed by scheming figures who thus emphasise the comic or tragic irony of that situation) or to convey information on the intentions of a figure or the background to a particular situation in an economical way.

A special form of the conventionalised monological aside is contained in the following passage from Shakespeare's *Julius Caesar*:

CAESAR: Good friends, go in and taste some wine with me;
   And we, like friends, will straightway go together.
BRUTUS: (aside) That every like is not the same, O Caesar,
   The heart of Brutus earns to think upon!   (II,ii,126–9)[39]

This is similar to Don Luis's aside in that one of the dialogue partners breaks out of the dialogue into an aside. The difference in this case is the fact that, as the apostrophe to Caesar indicates, the aside is actually addressed to the dialogue partner, at least outwardly. Of course, it nonetheless remains a monological aside since Caesar is not supposed to hear Brutus' remarks. However, the artificial dialogical quality only serves to emphasise the tragic impossibility of genuine dialogical contact between Brutus and Caesar.

Brutus' aside remains a conventionalised aside, even though its brevity makes it considerably more plausible and less artificial than Don Luis's. Naturally, by analogy with the motivated soliloquy, there is also a moti-

vated monological aside which, as a short, unpremeditated and spontaneous exclamation in reaction to a particular situation remains within
the naturalist bounds of plausibility. In addition to this kind of abbreviated and spontaneous comment on the dramatic situation, a further way of
motivating an aside is to present a reaction to it on the part of the dialogue
partner in the form of an 'intercepted aside', in which the partner notices
the speaker's aside but without understanding what was said.[40]

4.5.3.2. The aside *ad spectatores*

Like the soliloquy, the aside can also be imbued with dialogical elements if
it is addressed *ad spectatores*, and, in the same way that the soliloquy *ad
spectatores* can break through the internal communication system and
establish an explicit mediating communication system by addressing the
audience, the aside *ad spectatores* is also assigned a definite epic and
mediatory function. The fact that this type of aside is generally – but not
exclusively – found in comedy accords with the oft-mentioned affinity
between comedy and epic forms of information transmission (see above,
3.6.). It may be detected in plays as early as the comedies of Menander and
then with high frequency in Shakespeare's comedies and even later. The
speakers who are keenest to make contact with the audience are generally
scheming villains or servant figures, as the following example from
Shakespeare's *The Merchant of Venice* illustrates:

> OLD GOBBO: Master young man, you, I pray you, which is the way to
> master Jew's?
> LAUNCELOT GOBBO (Aside) O heavens! This is my true begotten
> father, who, being more than sand-blind, high-gravel blind, knows
> me not. I will try confusions with him.
> GOBBO: ... Can you tell me whether one Launcelot, that dwells with
> him, dwell with him or no?
> LAUNCELOT: Talk you of young Master Launcelot? (Aside) Mark me
> now; now will I raise the waters.   (II,ii,30–43)

Although Launcelot's first aside cannot yet be described as an aside
directed at the audience, it nonetheless serves the obvious epic function of
(directly) informing the audience, because, although the pointers towards
the identity and blindness of Old Gobbo – appearing here for the first time
– remain unmotivated on the internal level, they nonetheless represent an
important precondition for the understanding of the ensuing scene, and
because, by revealing the plan of intrigue through the word 'confusions',
Shakespeare introduces a technical term from the comedy of intrigue and
thus the secondary code of the external communication system. In the first
aside the audience is addressed only implicitly in the primary text,

although this may easily be made more explicit by the use of mime and gesture. In the second aside Launcelot addresses the audience more explicitly by using a verbal gesture of pointing and an imperative. One of the functions of these asides is to inform the audience about the background to the dramatic situation and the speaker's plans and thus both to create a level of suspense for what is to follow and to ensure that the audience has an informational advantage over the victims of the intrigue – an important factor in the creation of a comic effect. At the same time, however, they also serve to build up comic distance and to strengthen the atmosphere of bonhomie by encouraging the 'complicity' of the audience, or the phatic contact between the audience and the scheming figures.

4.5.3.3. The dialogical aside

The final form of aside, the dialogical aside, does not really belong in a discussion of the soliloquy or monological speech and represents a special form of dialogue (see below, 4.6.3.2.). However, we would like to discuss it at this point because, like the monological aside and the aside *ad spectatores*, it is based on the convention that although a speech is heard by the audience it is not 'heard' by certain characters on stage. The acoustic and physical implausibility of such a convention can be reduced or even eliminated fairly easily – as with the aside *ad spectatores* – by grouping the figures in a particular way on stage. All that needs to be done is to group the figures participating in the dialogical aside together at the front of the stage, well away from the other figures. In fact, this is the most common arrangement used in the performance of dialogical asides, and examples of it are the asides in which Malcolm and Donalbain decide to flee from Macbeth's reign of terror, thereby initiating the counter-plot (*Macbeth*, II,iii,119–24) and that between Sir Toby, Sir Andrew and Fabian in the eavesdropping scene in *Twelfth Night* (II,v,21–158). These two examples, one from tragedy, one from comedy, are characteristic of the way a dialogical aside may be motivated on the internal dramatic level: it is generally conditioned by conspiratorial dialogue or dialogue in an eavesdropping situation.[41]

4.6. Dialogical speech

4.6.1. Prescriptive versus descriptive poetics of dialogue

In normative theories of genre, dialogue is regarded as the basic form in drama. Soliloquies and non-dialogical, epic communication structures are generally regarded as mere 'additives' that may or may not be acceptable. Thus, Hegel wrote: 'The complete dramatic form is the dialogue.'[42] This prescriptive elevation of dialogue to an idealised norm implies a conflict-orientated theory of drama (whereby dramatic conflict is expressed in the contradictions of the dialogues), which, however, only applies to one part of the historical corpus of dramatic texts. This theory simply does not apply to modern drama, for example, and so it generally tends to disregard it. The emphasis on conflict simultaneously elevates the actional dialogue – that is, one in which each speech contains an element of action designed to change the situation – to the ideal norm and condemns the non-actional dialogue – that is, one in which subjects are discussed regardless of whether they have any direct bearing on the action, as is the case in the playful and witty dialogues in comedy, for example – as undramatic deviations. The supra-historical and systematic aspect of our own analytical framework prevents us from making such restrictive value judgements. Moreover, the results of our differentiated analysis of the more relative quality of the contrast between soliloquy and dialogue and the monological and the dialogical that we developed in 4.5.1. forbid such absolute antinominal ideas.

4.6.2. Quantitative relations

First, we shall turn our attention to an analysis of the quantitatively measurable relations between the various utterances in a dialogue. The results of this will show that such quantitative relations are not purely surface phenomena but that they are conditioned by the semantic deep structure of the text and, in turn, themselves condition the deep structure.

4.6.2.1. Duologue and polylogue

This is true of the quantitative division of dialogues into duologues (dialogues conducted by two figures) and polylogues (dialogues conducted by three or more figures). The relevance of this distinction has not been sufficiently acknowledged in previous studies of dramatic dialogue. The difference between a dialogue between two figures and one between more than two is not merely quantitative – it is also qualitative. In a polylogue it is possible to present certain relationships that could not be conveyed in a duologue. One example is a triadic relationship between two figures arguing with each other and a mediator or commentator figure. For this reason, polylogues are potentially of a more complex semantic structure than duologues, something that is also confirmed by the fact that in the development of both Greek and medieval drama the polylogue was preceded by the duologue.

4.6.2.2. Frequency of interruption and speech length

In a quantitative analysis it is also possible to determine the length of each individual speech or utterance and thus the frequency with which interruptions occur in dialogue – that is, the frequency of the semantic changes of direction that result from a change of speaker. In Greek tragedy this frequency could vary considerably, stretching from stichomythia on the one hand, in which the speaker changes after each line of verse, and speeches as long as 110 lines, such as the messengers' reports in Euripides.[43] These variations do not just occur within a single text; the average frequency of interruption may also vary according to the historical period and genre involved (in comedy, for example, the average frequency tends to be higher than in tragedy). It may also vary from author to author (the average length of the longer speeches in Aeschylus comes to 20 lines and in Euripides to 25 lines) and within the works of a particular author (the extremes in Sophocles come to an average of 20 lines in *Oedipus the King* and 29 in *Trachiniae*). The average frequency of interruption represents a parameter whose importance for stylistic studies of individual figures, periods and genres has still not been fully realised. The variation in the frequency of interruption in the course of a single text is also an aspect of form that has generally received little attention from the critics.[44]

Dialogues with a high frequency of interruption exhibit a clear tendency to reflect a close relationship between the dialogue partners. That is, the higher the frequency, the more marked the dialogical and actional quality of the verbal interchange. As an example of this we have chosen the stichomythia in the exchange between the chorus and Orestes that introduces the court-case in Aeschylus' *Eumenides*. The extreme brevity of the speeches in the ensuing exchange is actually mentioned by the chorus itself at the beginning of the dialogue, thereby exposing stichomythia as a literary artifice:

> CHORUS: We are many, but our speech shall be brief.
> (To Orestes) Do thou make answer to our questions one by one.
> (lines 585f.)

What then follows is an interrogation in which each reply that Orestes gives to the questions thrown at him by the chorus is then used by them as a basis for the next question. The distinct dialogical quality that results from the close relationship of the speakers to each other also corresponds to the equal lengths of the speeches accorded to the dialogue partners, the symmetrical arrangement of the speeches and the fact that Orestes is not just confined to answering questions, but can also ask his own – as when he questions the ethical presuppositions of the chorus in lines 605–6. Even when they speak on the same subject, the result is a sharp semantic change of direction after each line because they interpret the situation under discussion – namely Orestes' matricide – from completely contrasting perspectives. The fast interplay of utterances in this scene relates solely to the central conflict and this technique of focussing on a particular conflict is also used in the other functional types of stichomythia in classical tragedy, namely disputation, persuasion and information.

However, we would be guilty of making an inadmissable generalisation if we were either to elevate this particular historical function to a general norm, to regard stichomythia rather one-sidedly as a structure of conflict in dramatic speech or, in turn, to regard conflict-charged speech as the ideal form of dramatic speech. This is undermined by the very fact that stichomythic structures – or, to put it in more general terms, dialogue with a high frequency of interruption – also occur when the dialogue is based on consensus. The following dialogue from Shakespeare's comedy *As You Like It* will serve as an illustration of this:

> PHOEBE: Good shepherd, tell this youth what 'tis to love.
> SILVIUS: It is to be all made of sighs and tears;
>   And so am I for Phoebe.
> PHOEBE: And I for Ganymede.
> ORLANDO: And I for Rosalind.
> ROSALIND: And I for no woman.
> SILVIUS: It is to be all made of faith and service;
>   And so I am for Phoebe.
> PHOEBE: And I for Ganymede.
> ORLANDO: And I for Rosalind.
> ROSALIND: And I for no woman.   (V,ii,76–86)

Although the individual speakers differ in the objects of their love they are united by their enamoured condition. In fact, it is exactly this consensus that is emphasised by the stichomythical succession of the speeches and the anaphorical links between them. Furthermore, as an artificial principle of stylisation, the repetition of the order of speakers – Silvius, Phoebe, Orlando, Rosalind (we omitted the second repetition for reasons of space) – serves to emphasise the parallel development of the two love-plots and, as a result of the anaphoric parallelisms, the comic quality of the way the lovers' desires coincide.

Since dialogues with a high frequency of interruptions tend to be strongly orientated towards the dialogue partner or bound up with the dialogical situation, and since the frequent semantic changes of direction have the effect of increasing the tempo, dialogues made up of longer speeches exhibit the opposite tendency and produce monological elements with a high level of self-reference, a greater degree of abstraction from the dramatic situation and a slower tempo. This difference becomes particularly clear whenever the frequency of interruption shows considerable variation within a closed scenic context, as it does in the opening scene of Molière's *Tartuffe*, for example. The polylogue between Madame Pernelle, Elmire, Mariane, Damis, Dorine, and Cléante begins as a tempestuous series of short utterances in which the enraged Madame Pernelle repeatedly interrupts her dialogue partners' excuses before they have time to express them and regales one figure after another with a stream of insulting accusations. The argument centres around a number of differing interpretations of Tartuffe's role in Orgon's household and the individual utterances are confined to this subject matter alone. As the dialogue progresses, however, the discussion becomes less heated, the speeches become longer and thus also more coherently articulated expressions of the various figure-perspectives. At the same time, although they do not actually lose sight of the given dramatic situation, it is nonetheless placed within the broader context of the background events that led up to it and the social effects that resulted from it. Finally, towards the end of the scene, the situation is assessed in more abstract and general terms.

4.6.3. Temporal relations: succession and simultaneity

The temporal arrangement of the various speeches or utterances and dialogues normally takes the form of a succession, a linear series of individual utterances and dialogues. However, this principle may be varied or broken both within a single dialogue and between a number of dialogues.

4.6.3.1. The relation of one utterance to another

Even when utterances are arranged successively there are often partial overlaps that lead to the partial simultaneity of different utterances when one figure interrupts another. This kind of interruption occurs repeatedly, as we have already indicated, in the opening scene of *Tartuffe*:

> DORINE: Si ...
> MME PERNELLE: Vous êtes, mamie, une fille suivante
>   Un peu trop forte en gueule et fort impertinente;
>   Vous vous mêlez sur tout de dire votre avis.
> DAMIS: Mais...
> MME PERNELLE: Vous êtes un sot en trois lettres, mon fils:
>   C'est moi qui vous le dis, qui suis votre grand-mère.   (I,i,13–16)

This pattern, in which the speaker is interrupted by Mme Pernelle, is repeated in an unbroken series three more times and creates a comic effect solely as a result of the mechanical repetitions directed at a succession of different dialogue partners; at the same time, as a form of verbal behaviour it also says something about the speaker, characterising her as someone with a self-righteous will to dominate.

However, the succession of utterances may also be completely disrupted by the introduction of simultaneous speech, as is the case in the following dialogue from Beckett's *Waiting for Godot*:

> VLADIMIR: You must have had a vision.
> ESTRAGON: (turning his head) What?
> VLADIMIR: (louder) You must have had a vision!
> ESTRAGON: No need to shout!
> (They resume their watch. Silence)
> VLADIMIR and ESTRAGON: (turning simultaneously) Do you –[45]

The effect here is also comic. It is based on the fact that although neither speaker has anything to say to the other they nonetheless suddenly speak simultaneously. This is an utterly conventional dialogue structure often used in slapstick and farce (genres that Beckett frequently invokes) and it can manifest itself in either identical simultaneous speech – as we have here – or non-identical simultaneous speech. The second type was also used by Beckett; in fact it is the predominant dialogue structure at the beginning and end of *Play* (1963), in which the extreme monological quality of the three figures' speeches is emphasised by the fact that they speak simultaneously.

Disrupting the succession principle to produce simultaneity acts as a kind of mirror-image to the reverse process of 'stretching' the pattern of succession by introducing pauses or silence between the individual utterances.[46] Like simultaneous speech, the use of fairly lengthy pauses between individual utterances can hardly be said to be a recent innovation in modern drama. Nonetheless, it was modern drama that first began to employ it with such innovative consistency. Whether the pauses are situated within a speech or between speeches, or whether they are filled with mime and gesture or are left devoid of non-verbal communication – they always reflect some degree of disrupted communication, the monological imprisonment of a dramatic figure in the world of its own imagination, an inability to establish contact with others, or even linguistic impotence. Although classical dramas also contain periods of silence, they do so with the primarily rhetorical function of creating a 'pregnant pause' used in order either to create suspense, to emphasise certain aspects or to allow time for the audience to react. Successful verbal communication is thus regarded as the norm and is not undermined by this kind of silence. The silences that occur in modern plays, by contrast, often serve to focus attention on the impossibility of speech. The innovative quality of this kind of silence has been emphasised by the Bavarian playwright Franz Xaver Kroetz in the preface to his plays *Home-Made, Bloody Minded* and *Men's Business*:

I wanted to break with a theatrical convention that is unrealistic: constant chatter. The most marked behavioural characteristic of my figures is silence – because their language simply does not function. . . . Their problems go back such a long way and are so far advanced that they are no longer capable of expressing them verbally.[47]

4.6.3.2. The relationships between dialogues

As far as the temporal relationship of one dialogue to another is concerned, we can also assume that the unmarked norm is a linear succession of speeches or utterances. Once again, there are deviating structures of simultaneous speech which are not just restricted to modern drama. We have already drawn attention to the way that two dialogues may be presented simultaneously in the context of the aside – i.e. the dialogical aside in an eavesdropping scene that enables the listeners to comment on the primary dialogue or soliloquy spoken by the figure(s) overheard (see above, 4.5.3.3.). Overlapping a primary dialogue or soliloquy with a secondary dialogue or soliloquy in such a way as to provide a commentary on it is by no means restricted to eavesdropping scenes, however. The temporal overlapping of two or more dialogues is a common feature of densely populated scenes, in which the polylogue is often divided into several separate conversations simply by the way the figures are grouped together on stage. Separate conversations amongst groups of scheming figures hatching their plot in the presence of the intended victim, or the satirical commentaries of observer figures are just two examples of the ways structures of this kind can be integrated into a dramatic text. Instances of overlap, or even of simultaneity, occur in large numbers in the dialogues of Ben Jonson's satirical comedies. For our purposes it will suffice to draw attention to one particularly graphic example from *The Alchemist* (IV,v,24–32) when in the course of the soliloquy in which Dol Common feigns madness Face and Epicure Mammon discuss the causes of her madness. This simultaneity of soliloquy and dialogue is signalled by the stage-direction 'They speak together' and the typographical juxtaposition of the various speeches.

The simultaneity of dialogues in Peter Handke's play *Quodlibet* (1969) actually appears as the predominant principle guiding the structure of the whole text. The eleven speaking figures are on stage throughout and, within the framework of a kind of soirée, stroll up and down chatting to each other in constantly fluctuating groups. The dialogues of the various groups, recorded randomly and suggestively by the author, constantly overlap, and this simultaneity produces semantic cross-references of which the figures themselves are unaware but which are revealing to the audience – such as, for example, the series of oblique references to concen-

tration camps: 'gold filling', 'shower', 'loading-ramp' and 'soap', etc.[48]
Once again, a characteristic feature of the innovations in experimental
theatre is the tendency to undermine dramatic convention (in this case, the
successivity of dialogues) and to elevate this negative tendency to one of
the consistently predominant aspects of dramatic structure.

4.6.4. The syntagmatics of dialogue

There are three possible analytical perspectives for the syntagmatic analysis of a dialogical utterance: 1) how the individual parts of the utterance
interrelate, 2) the relationship of the utterance to the previous utterances
by the same figure, 3) the relationship of the utterance to the previous
utterances by the other figures.

4.6.4.1. How the individual parts of the utterance interrelate

The first analytical perspective – the interrelationship of the individual
constituent parts of an utterance – need only be discussed briefly here since
we have already analysed the most important aspects of it in connection
with the soliloquy. Like a soliloquy, an individual dialogical utterance can
be coherent in its semantic orientation and the way it refers to the dramatic
situation. However, it can also contain semantic changes of direction and
changes in the situational references. This kind of utterance is thus in-
herently dialogical in character, in so far as its various segments can be
assigned to different layers of awareness, different types of figure potential
or different roles for the speaker. In this, the semantic changes of direction
may exhibit the transparent tectonics of logical argument or rhetorical
patterns of disposition. At the same time, they may elude rational control
and follow the hidden rules of association (see in this context our illustrations of the analogous distinction in soliloquy, 4.5.2.2.). In the first case,
we expect the sentence structure to contain hypotaxes and conjunctions
that link phrases and sentences logically. In the second we expect to see
parataxes, anacolutha, pauses, asyndetic series of phrases and sentences,
and logically ambiguous combinations using the copula 'and'.[49]

4.6.4.2. How an utterance relates to the previous utterances by the same figure

The question of the way an utterance relates to the previous utterances by
the same figure implies the more far-reaching question of the semantic
coherence and stylistic homogeneity of the sum total of utterances by one
figure in both a single dialogue and the dramatic text as a whole. This
question is particularly important for the verbal constitution of a particu-

lar figure (see above, 4.4.2.), because his perspective is established in the semantic equivalences that exist between all his utterances, and also because the recurrence of certain stylistic features delineates the contours of the figure's identity and distinguishes him from the other figures. How well this generally functions is shown by the fact that the identificatory information on the speaker in the printed text is generally redundant after the figures are introduced for the first time – that is, although it facilitates the reading process it is not indispensable to it. These equivalences or similarities between the utterances of a single figure may be realised and emphasised by the use of verbatim repetitions, either when a figure quotes one of his previous utterances, for example, or – a much more widespread convention in comedy or farce – when he reacts idiosyncratically to the most diverse events or situations by using an ossified or clichéed turn of phrase. The fact that the repetition of identical phrases often appears as a comic deviation indicates that the verbal equivalences are normally manifested more flexibly, in a more balanced mixture of identity and variation.

4.6.4.3. How an utterance relates to the previous utterances by the other figures

The most important of these three perspectives for the analysis of dialogue is the third because it strives to identify the specifically dialogical quality: the question of how an utterance relates to the previous utterances by the other figures, or, to be more precise, and thus facilitate analysis, to the immediately preceding utterance by the dialogue partner. Here, too, it is conceivable to establish a scale of possible relationships, stretching from one extreme – identity – to the other – complete unrelatedness. We have already discussed these two extremes in connection with monological tendencies in dialogue (see above, 4.5.1.3.). In the first case there is absolutely no change in semantic orientation between one utterance and the next because both partners have access to the same relevant information and their attitudes to this information also coincide (this is known as 'consensus dialogue'). In the second there is total semantic incoherence between successive utterances and this is the result either of the two figures talking completely at cross-purposes ('talking past each other') or of the fact that there is no channel linking them, or of the discrepancies between their respective codes ('disrupted communication').

Since we have already given an example of a consensus dialogue elsewhere we shall restrict ourselves to a single concrete example of the opposite, namely an instance where two speeches in a dialogue are completely unrelated. We have chosen the beginning of Act II, Scene ii of Chekhov's *The Cherry Orchard*:

LOPAKHIN: We must decide once and for all: time won't wait. After all, my question's quite a simple one. Do you consent to lease your land for villas, or don't you? You can answer in one word: Yes or no? Just one word!

LIUBOV ANDREYEVNA: Who's been smoking such abominable cigars here? (Sits down)

GAYEV: How very convenient it is having a railway here. (Sits down) Here we are – we've been up to town for lunch and we're back home already. I pot the red into the middle pocket! I'd like to go indoors now and have just one game . . .

This passage is even interesting from the point of view of our first analytical perspective, namely the internal structuring of the individual utterances. In this respect the two speeches of Gayev and Lopakhin clearly contrast with one another. Every single one of Lopakhin's sentences is pragmatically subordinate to a single overriding intention: to force a positive and binding answer to his proposals to revitalise the economy of the estate. They are therefore linked together in a rhetorically transparent relationship to form a single logical argument. This is emphasised by the recurrence of certain lexical and semantic features. In Gayev's speech, by contrast, there is a complete semantic break after the first two sentences, a break that is marked by a pause. After the first two sentences, which refer to his plan to travel into the city in order to negotiate a credit facility at the bank, and which are also stimulated by the immediate situational context of the scene (the railway-line and the distant city can be seen in the background), Gayev, in the next elliptical sentence, turns his attention to his favourite pastime, playing billiards. The relationship between these two sections is purely associative and is not expressed explicitly in the text: the thought of his obligations, which he attempts to make more attractive by remembering the more pleasant aspects that go with it, immediately gives way to thoughts of leisure.

The structural differences between these two speeches do indeed serve the characterisation process: Lopakhin's verbal style and behaviour imply a business-like consistency and utilitarian rationality and thus characterise him as a representative of the new upwardly mobile merchant class that is competent, hard-working and sober. Gayev's verbal style and behaviour, on the other hand, betray him as an inconsequential, emotionally unstable and work-shy representative of a landed gentry in decline.

If we now turn to the relationship between each speech and the one preceding it, it is noticeable that there are no semantic equivalences of any kind: the figures talk past each other, in that neither Andreyevna nor Gayev reacts to what the previous speaker has said but start on a different subject. This is particularly striking in Andreyevna's speech since Lopakhin had asked her a direct and decisive question and forbidden any kind of excuse or vague answer. Instead of responding to that question in some way, as might have been expected, Andreyevna makes a reference to the context of the external situation – namely the smell of the cigar that Yasha had lit in the previous scene. However, at the same time, it is exactly the exaggerated unrelatedness of her speech and Lopakhin's that shows that her behaviour is connected to Lopakhin's speech in some pragmatic way after all. The complete semantic break must be evaluated as a refusal to communicate and as an expression of her unwillingness to answer the question. Thus, the phenomenon of talking at cross-purposes is not necessarily purely monological in character but can also represent an indirect and implicitly formulated gesture indicating the absence of any willingness or ability to communicate. Finally, Gayev's speech does not refer to either Lopakhin's or Andreyevna's but is a reaction to the external situation: the railway-line and the city on the horizon. The two semantically separate parts of his speech do refer to speeches he had made earlier, though, namely his plan to travel into town to arrange the credit facility (II,xv) and his constant reference to billiards (most recently in II,xv). The fact that the number of times he refers back to his own utterances outweighs his references to the utterances made by his dialogue partners must be understood as a manifestation of monological verbal behaviour which, within the framework of a dialogue, is a symptom of disrupted communication.

The kind of dialogue structure we have been describing here was actually elevated to a dramatic programme by August Strindberg in his preface to *Miss Julie*. He claimed that this was the only way to achieve an authentic portrayal of dialogue in ordinary speech, in comparison to the conventionalised dialogues in pre-naturalist drama which falsified the true process of communication between human beings:

In regard to dialogue, I want to point out that I have departed somewhat from prevailing traditions by not turning my figures into catechists who make stupid questions in order to call forth witty answers. I have avoided the symmetrical and mathematical construction of the French dialogue, and have instead permitted the minds to work irregularly as they do in reality . . . Naturally enough, therefore, the dialogue strays a good deal . . .[50]

Normally speaking, the relationship between one speech and the next lies somewhere in between the two extremes of identity and complete unrelatedness. The second speech generally picks up certain elements in the first, but places them in a different context. Frequently used patterns that link one utterance with the next[51] are those linking a question and an answer, or refusal to answer; an imperative and an expression of the willingness or unwillingness to carry it out; a piece of information and the positive or negative reaction to it; a statement and the confirmation, negation or qualification of the statement, etc. Thus, the first speech always gives the second speaker the opportunity to choose between two alternatives. However, both of these, that is, both a positve and a negative reaction signify a response to the first speech and create semantic equivalences.

Negation and qualification, as opposed to assent, are particularly common features of conflict-orientated classical drama. H. G. Coenen has conducted an extremely detailed examination of this in the dialogues of Racine's tragedies and has established a complete repertoire of variants.[52] Coenen's analysis tackles two main aspects: the choice of the point of reference in the preceding speech or utterance, and the way that point of reference is then treated in the second speech or utterance.

The point of reference for the second speech is often the 'sign content' of the first. In its most obvious form, this is the reference to the subject matter, though of course the latter's original status in the first speech may be either modified or ignored. This can often have a comic function, as for example when the first speaker mentions the partner's beloved in passing, and the lover, in his reply, then ignores most of the original context in order to speak about the only thing that interests him: his beloved. A more precise response to the first speech results from a reference to the 'idea', the failure of which to coincide with moral norms, with the laws of logic or with an actual state of affairs may become the subject of the speech. When reference is made to the 'secondary content', the main content of the first speech is ignored and, instead, attention is drawn either to the speaker's attitude towards the primary content or to his or her non-verbal behaviour. One way of referring to it is the *captatio benevolentiae*, for example, which recognises the emotional state of the dialogue partner in a conciliatory way, only to reject his or her actual wishes.

In choosing the 'sign' as a point of reference, the speech is not responding to the content itself but to the fact that this subject has been raised in the first place. It is therefore not in its content but in its actional role that the first speech is taken up by the second. This includes speeches that play off the preceding speech act against its contents – for example by criticising the first speech for the fact that the act of naming someone's merits actually diminishes or obliterates them. This also includes the kind of speeches that are then criticised for being inappropriate to a particular situation (with respect to place, time, speaker or addressee) – that is, for contravening the norms of *decorum* or *aptum* – and the exposure of certain speech intentions such as disguise, deception and lying. Finally, a speech may also refer critically to the inappropriateness of the first speaker's reaction to an earlier speech or utterance.

In the dialogues of classical drama, references to the 'communication process' itself play no more than a subordinate role, because they only occur when dialogical communication is disrupted. Even then, they only occur occasionally, as for example when attention is focussed on a figure's speechlessness in the face of the monstrous nature of the events related. In modern drama, by contrast, references of this kind are very common indeed and are reflected in the predominance of the phatic and metalingual functions (see above, 4.2.5. and 4.2.6.). Finally, there are also imaginary points of reference – that is, points of reference that do not actually exist in the first speech but which are read into it, either intentionally or unintentionally by the second speaker, with the result that its affect or intention may be misinterpreted. These imaginary points of reference are often the cause or consequence of a comic or tragic misunderstanding.

In processing the chosen point of reference the second speaker employs two basic strategies: he can show that the opposite is true or invalidate his dialogue partner's arguments. The latter implies a weakened form of negation, because it does not put forward an opposing view, but confines itself to demonstrating the inadequacies of the arguments used by the opponent to justify his position. Should he or she wish to show that the opposite is true, then there is a whole series of rhetorical and dialectical patterns of argument that the speaker can fall back on. The most important of them are the patterns that appeal to some other authority (for example by invoking the *communis opinio*, or public opinion, which contradicts the views held by the first speaker, or by using an *argumentum ad hominem* that cites an earlier opinion expressed by the first speaker which completely contradicts the one expressed by him later on) and the technique of *demonstratio ad oculos*, by which it is possible to demonstrate the contradiction between the speaker's words and what is actually happening. Other arguments that may be used are those that refer to the preconditions so as to undermine and thus contradict what has been said, and those that refer to future consequences in order to show that if those consequences do not actually occur then the reasoning that predicted them was faulty. Finally, there is the ironic technique of *reductio ad absurdum* which draws a contradictory or absurd conclusion from the first speaker's arguments.

In order to invalidate the first speaker's arguments, the second speaker can either completely reject the *propositio* as a universally valid principle (as, for example, by passionately rejecting the norms of reason or of ethical behaviour) or he can acknowledge its basic validity but go on to question their applicability in the case under consideration.

Coenen's typology assumes throughout that dialogical communication is actually taking place successfully. However, this is often not the case, particularly in modern dramas. These often contain dialogue structures in which the figures do refer back to the preceding speech, but in such a way as to break certain semantic and pragmatic rules. An important class of this kind of law violation is related to the set of presupposition rules. We would like to borrow R. C. Stalnaker's definition of presuppositions as 'propositions implictly supposed before the relevant linguistic business is transacted'.[53] Thus, the fundamental presupposition behind the command, 'Give me the book on the table' is the fact that there is a book on the table and that the speaker is justified in asking the addressee to do something. If one or other of these presuppositions is absent the command is meaningless and the addressee can only react to it verbally in any meaningful way by actually drawing attention to the violation of the presupposition. In the dialogues of Ionesco's 'theatre of the absurd', the sort of nonsensical statements that violate the laws of presupposition are especially common, as the following brief extract from *La cantatrice chauve* illustrates:

> M. SMITH: (toujours dans son journal) Tiens, c'est écrit que Bobby Watson est mort.
>
> MME SMITH: Mon Dieu, le pauvre, quand est-ce qu'il est mort?
>
> M. SMITH: Pourquoi prends-tu cet air étonné? Tu le savais bien. Il est mort il y a deux ans. Tu te rappelles, on a été à son enterrement, il y a un an et demi.
>
> MME SMITH: Bien sûr que je me rappelle. Je me suis rappelé tout de de suite, mais je ne comprends pas pourquoi toi-même tu as été si étonné de voir ça sur le journal.
>
> M. SMITH: Ça n'y était pas sur le journal. Il y a déjà trois ans qu'on a parlé de son décès. Je m'en suis souvenu par association d'idées![54]

On the basis of the given situation – M. Smith reading his newspaper – Mme Smith is bound to presuppose that her husband has read the news of Bobby Watson's death in the newspaper and that his comment 'c'est écrit' is to be understood as 'c'est écrit dans le journal'; however, in M. Smith's next speech but one this presupposition is emphatically denied. The reason for her astonished reaction to it ('air étonné') is probably caused by the additional presupposition that the news of the death is something new to her and that she – in accordance with the speech-act of the question – has not been informed as to exactly when Bobby Watson died. Both of these are also repudiated in her husband's next speech. If she then goes on to agree with his correction and declare that she had not been surprised at the news of Bobby Watson's death, but at the fact it had not appeared in the newspaper until now, then this exposes an insolvable contradiction between this fact and the first question she asked when the death actually occurred. In the rest of the dialogue, omitted here, the semantic presupposition that the name 'Bobby Watson' actually refers to one particular individual is ultimately completely undermined. For, it turns out that every single male and female member of one particular family bears this name. This simultaneously goes against two presuppositions that are based on socio-cultural norm: normally first names are used, on the one hand, to distinguish between the various members of a family, and, on the other, to identify their gender.

The violations of the presupposition rules that we have exemplified here, represent the central verbal means of creating the absurdity that Ionesco refers to in his theoretical writings and to which the theatre of the absurd owes its name. It appears as a historical transformation of the comic: like the comic it is based on a discrepancy, in this case the discrepancy between the contrasting presuppositions held by the figures and/or the discrepancy between the presuppositions held by the receiver and those held by the figures.

4.6.5. The rhetoric of dialogue

4.6.5.1. Drama and rhetoric

In our analysis of the paradigmatic and syntagmatic dimensions of dramatic dialogue we can also invoke the categorisation structures of rhetoric, and it is not even necessary that the text under analysis has already been produced within a rhetorical system of norms and forms, since there is an affinity of intention between rhetorical speech and the classical form of dialogical speech in drama. Both strive 'to use words to effect a change in the situation'.[55] However, the model of rhetorical speech cannot be applied to drama without certain reservations as it is based on a specific speech situation, namely one-way monological communication between a single speaker and a number of listeners. Normally, this situation simply does not arise in dramatic dialogue even though it may occasionally occur (more frequently in classical drama) in the context of a 'set speech'. Thus, whilst it is understandable that rhetorical analyses have hitherto essentially been confined to analysing these set speeches in drama, this also means that the heuristic potential of rhetoric has not yet been completely exhausted.[56]

4.6.5.2. *Logos – ethos – pathos*

As the theory of effect-orientated speech, rhetoric has as its primary purpose the art of persuading or convincing (*persuasio*). The basic strategies developed to achieve this are conceived in such general terms that they preserve their applicability even when we have moved on from the fundamental model of the public speech and they may therefore also be used in the analysis of dialogical speech in drama. The three basic strategies result from the question whether the predominant point of reference is the speech object (*logos* or *pragma*), the speaker (*ethos*) or the listener (*pathos*). This triadic pattern partially overlaps with the referential, expressive and appellative functions of Roman Jakobson's communication model (see above, 4.2.), but in view of its function as a means of persuasion its content is more narrowly defined.

The intention underlying the *logos* strategy is to convince by responding to the existing situation in a partisan way. Depending on the object this response is either narrative and descriptive or argumentative. The most important techniques of partisan argumentation were discussed in the previous section on the relationship between an utterance and the preceding utterance made by the dialogue partner (see above, 4.6.4.3.). The rhetorical guidelines for a partisan narrative or description are conceived with the intention of establishing vividness and clarity since it is these qualities that are the most likely to move the listener into a positive or negative reaction. As far as drama is concerned, the techniques used in the *logos* strategy are applied in particular to argumentative monologues and dialogues, the narrative mediation of background action (exposition) or hidden action.

The *ethos* strategy is based on efforts to establish the reliability and credibility of the speaker, who is then able to develop his own moral integrity or factual authority into the main argument in support of the correctness of his views. If this moral integrity and factual authority do not actually exist they have to be fabricated by the speaker. This kind of self-stylisation as an altruistic, morally flawless, factually expert and yet guileless giver of advice is a common feature of dramatic texts. One famous example of this, renowned for its rhetorical brilliance, is Mark Antony's funeral oration in Shakespeare's *Julius Caesar*:

> I am no orator, as Brutus is,
> But, as you know me all, a plain blunt man,
> That love my friend . . .
> For I have neither wit, nor words, nor worth,
> Action, nor utterance, nor the power of speech
> To stir men's blood; I only speak right on.   (III,ii,217–33)

By stylising himself as a straightforward fellow human being, lacking the subtle skills of oratory, Mark Antony is able to win his listeners' confidence and make them amenable to his arguments. The contrast between this self-image and reality is not perceived by the listeners in the internal communication system; on the external level, however, the receivers are aware of the manipulative strategy with which Mark Antony, in accordance with the principle of *celare artem*, intends to mask his suggestive rhetoric the public negation of which, unbeknown to his Roman listeners, actually demonstrates its existence. What we have attempted to show here by citing a 'set speech' also applies to dialogical exchanges in drama: every one of the great conspiratorial figures in drama – Shakespeare's Richard III and Iago, Ben Jonson's Volpone, Molière's

Tartuffe, to name but a few – create a mask of positive self-stylisation in the course of the dialogues between them and their victims. Of course, whilst these positive self-images are taken at face value by their opposite numbers on stage, the better informed spectator is able to see through their strategic function. The victim of the intrigue ascribes to the scheming villain the positive quality of moral integrity, whilst the spectator perceives his skill in the art of deception and rhetorical bravado.

Finally, the *pathos* strategy is designed specifically to arouse strong emotions in the audience, with the intention of converting it to the speaker's position. This presupposes an advance knowledge of the psychological and ideological disposition of the audience because it is only by taking this into consideration that the speaker's *pathos*, whether genuine or false, can exert an effect on the audience. Amongst the verbal techniques used in the rhetoric of *pathos* are an exaggerated style full of metaphors and other rhetorical devices, appellative structures, such as the rhetorical question (the answer to which, because it is already implied in the question, is almost forced on the audience), the apostrophe to the listener or the impassioned exclamation. Non-verbal techniques used include the showing of emotive objects – such as when Mark Antony holds up Caesar's cloak full of dagger holes (III,ii,170ff.) – or expansive and emotionally laden gestures.

Modern dramas also contain elements of *pathos* that are deliberately designed to appeal to the audience's sentiments or arouse its emotions – that is, if *pathos* is understood not as a historically specific repertoire of verbal techniques but as something that is created with a particular effect in mind. Thus, in modern texts, the classical techniques used in the rhetoric of *pathos*, such as exaggerated style and the use of direct appeals to the audience, are often replaced by a new *pathos* of understatement.

4.6.5.3. Figurative speech

To conclude this chapter we should like to address ourselves to a more thorough examination of one linguistic aspect that has been discussed by others in some detail in the context of rhetorical theory, and has been shown to be of special importance for verse-drama in particular. We are referring to figurative or metaphorical speech. At this stage we do not need to reproduce the sophisticated rhetorical system of tropes and figures since our analysis will be confined from the outset to dealing with a small number of the forms of figurative speech: the tropes of metaphor, simile, synecdoche and metonymy. And in doing so, our intention is not to classify them systematically, but to investigate their functions in the dramatic text.

As far as the functions of metaphorical, or figurative, speech are concerned, the controversy over Shakespeare's imagery that has continued to preoccupy critics since the 1930s is of paradigmatical significance. In this, there are essentially three main conflicting positions: one view is that the repetition of a number of leitmotif-like sets of images are keys to the personality of the author, in so far as frequently repeated figurative expressions (such as those taken from the semantic sets associated with sea travel, jurisprudence and gardening, for example) are believed to be involuntary expressions of the interests and opinions of the author.[57] The type of image analysis conducted by the New Critics, by contrast, refers essentially to the functions enacted *within* a literary work. These critics abstract from the temporal dimension of dramatic texts and project the dynamic development of plots and figures into a static and spatial structure of corresponding and contrasting images. In this kind of 'spatial approach', the dramatic text is no longer seen as the mimetic multimedial representation of action sequences and different configurations, but as an 'expanded metaphor'.[58] This technique of isolating the complex structures of image and metaphor from the dramatic context and from all references to plot and figure contrasts with the third and last view which actually sets out to investigate the integration and functionalisation of metaphorical speech in the dramatic text, reflecting at the same time on the medial conditions peculiar to drama, namely linear development over a certain period of time and multimediality.[59] This third perspective comes close to our own view, which is an attempt to give an analysis of the communicative relevance of individual textual structures in drama, though our study will also be able to integrate a number of conclusions reached by the exponents of the spatial approach.

Within the context of rhetorical theory, figurative speech is assigned three main functions: ornamentation, the illustration or concretisation of a particular situation and emphasis that is used to direct the audience's attention. In turn, all three are functionally subordinate to the overall intention of creating 'persuasive' speech. In drama, these three functions may employ figurative speech in both the internal and external communication systems. However, it can also develop additional functions that are specific to drama.

Thus, figurative speech in drama can have a characterising function. It can become part of the verbal techniques of implicit self-presentation (see above, 4.4.2.2.). However, the fact that a figure often speaks figuratively need not necessarily be a characteristic feature but can be a part of the stylistic code of the whole work. This is the case whenever the whole primary text – as is often the case in verse-dramas – is characterised by a high concentration of metaphorical structures: i.e., when all the figures frequently speak metaphorically. Although the fact that a figure speaks metaphorically can no longer have a characterising function in such cases, certain preferences in the choice of 'tenor' and 'vehicle' definitely can.[60] This can be demonstrated convincingly by citing Shakespeare's Othello and Iago as examples. Both figures constantly have recourse to metaphorical imagery, but whereas Othello generally evokes hyperbolic, expansive images full of intense light and colour, and usually applies them to himself, Iago's imagery is frequently applied to others whom he compares to lower and often repulsive forms of animal life (flies, spiders, goats, wolves, etc.) and the baser bodily functions.[61]

The images in the speeches of a number of figures may often combine to exert a space-creating function which complements the concrete plasticity of the stage-set and conveys a sense of awareness of the overall spatial context within which the action takes place. In this function – the function of 'word scenery' – figurative speech can compensate for the inbuilt constrictions on the presentation of space in drama.[62] It does not just employ metaphor as a form of verbal support to the restricted stage-sets used in the Elizabethan theatre, for example, but also places the particular facet of life portrayed in the drama in its overall geographical, social or even cosmic context. Although this extension of the space portrayed on stage can also be achieved by the use of non-figurative speech, figurative speech allows the dramatist to refer to the near or distant surroundings in a much less 'constrained' manner, because it does not require some form of strict factual motivation. We have selected a further example from the corpus of Shakespeare's plays, because Shakespeare often combines the functions of focussing the scenically presented locale and transcending it in order to place it in a broader context. This is particularly clear in *The Tempest*, in which the flora and fauna of the island, the earth and the atmosphere above it are repeatedly invoked metaphorically and 'painted' with a plethora of detail, at the same time as the nearer and more distant surroundings, the sea with its waves and depths full of corals and pearls, and the far-off coasts of Africa and Italy are deliberately preserved in the consciousness of both the figures and the audience. Not only does this help to create the situation and the concrete tangibility of the locale, it also places the events taking place on the island itself in a more direct relationship to the elementary forces and imbues them with symbolic, representative value (see below, 7.3.1.).

At this point the space-creating function is expanded into the more general thematic function. In this function the use of imagery enriches the thematic implications of the events and provides metaphorical models for the interpretation of the way the plot develops in the course of the whole drama. In *The Tempest*, this applies especially to the metaphorical leitmotifs of the 'storm' and the 'sea', whose central importance is reflected in the title itself. The tempest in I,i sparks off a whole chain of sea- and storm-images involving transformation, menace and rescue that provide a metaphorical commentary on the fates of the various figures and the dialectics of guilt and forgiveness.

Such metaphorical leitmotifs also have an integrating function in that they bind figure to figure and situation to situation and thereby establish a number of contrasts and parallels. It is in the drama of open form that these 'metaphorical bonds' achieve the integration on a textural level that had been abandoned on the structural level of scene succession.[63] In the interrelationship between concretely presented objects and events and their verbal manifestation in metaphorical images, the latter may be elevated to stand as central symbols – like the storm in *The Tempest*, for example.

In *The Tempest* a scenically presented event is followed by a series of images related to it. In other dramatic texts, however, the opposite phenomenon may occur, in which figurative expressions may actually look forward to or predict future events. By indicating what is to come in advance, in such a way as to create anticipatory hypotheses in the mind of the receiver, but without conveying any concrete advance information, this particular type of metaphor fulfils the function of creating suspense (see above, 3.7.4). The technique of anticipating a tragic ending metaphorically by lacing the atmosphere of the opening scene with ominous imagery is a particularly common feature of tragedy. Shakespeare's Juliet, who compares her love with lightning ('Which doth cease to be / Ere one can say "It lightens",' II,ii,118f.), and Oscar Wilde's Page to Herodias, to whom the rising moon appears as a 'dead woman' 'looking for dead things'[64] are just two examples of the way metaphorical speech can arouse suspense and generically orientated expectations. The speakers are often not completely (and sometimes not at all) aware of the ominous implications of their metaphors. This results in discrepancy between the level of awareness in the dramatic figures and that in the audience, and this, in turn, can sometimes create dramatic irony (see above, 3.4.4.).

5. Dramatis personae and dramatic figure

5.1. The interdependence of plot and figure

Traditionally, the relationship between figure and plot in drama has been examined above all with the question in mind as to which has precedence, plot or figure. Without wishing to examine the historical development of this question in any detail, we should nonetheless like to point out that the tradition of theoretical works that insist that plot takes precedence over figure stretches from Aristotle's *Poetics* (ch. 6) via Gottsched's *Versuch einer kritischen Dichtkunst* (II,ix and x) through to Brecht's *Short Organon on the Theatre*, whereas the opposite position, which Lessing, in Part 51 of his *Hamburg Dramaturgy*, claimed could only apply to comedy, was not defended with any conviction until the appearance of the *Sturm und Drang* movement, epitomised by Jackob Michael Reinhold Lenz's *Anmerkungen übers Theater* and Goethe's address in honour of *Shäkespears Tag*,[1] and then later on in the dramaturgical writings of naturalism.

However, in our own analysis we are not so much concerned with the question as to which category takes precedence over the other − whether from the point of view of production or reception − since this question is a historical variable. Our concern are the problems associated with the constant structural interdependence of the two categories. In the same way that the concept of action implies the notion of an active subject and, conversely, the concept of person or character implies the notion of action − whether it is active or passive, external or internal − in drama the presentation of a figure without even the most rudimentary plot and the presentation of a plot that does not contain even the most drastically reduced form of figure is inconceivable. If plot is defined as a series of changes in a situation, and situation as a given relationship that exists between a number of figures both to each other and to a concrete or ideal context, then the dialectical relationship linking plot and figure becomes obvious.

5.2. The status of dramatic figures

5.2.1. Figure versus person

Contrary to the generally accepted conventions, we have been speaking of dramatic 'figure' rather than 'person' or 'character', and we have done this to establish a terminological counterweight to an equally common tendency to discuss dramatic figures as if they were people or characters from real life, and thus to emphasise the ontological difference between fictional figures and real characters. The connotations of the word 'figure', which hints at something deliberately artificial, produced or constructed for a particular purpose, and evokes the impression of functionality rather than individual autonomy (one is reminded of the figures used in a game of chess) actually go some way towards justifying this particular interpretation. For unlike real characters who, of course, are influenced by their social context, but who on reaching maturity are able to transcend it, dramatic figures cannot be separated from their environment because they only exist in relationship to their environment and are only constituted in the sum of their relations to that environment.[2] Social conditions can influence or determine the life of a real person, but, in drama, the fictional context serves the function of actually defining the fictional figure. What this means can be illustrated by the following comparison: whilst it is perfectly reasonable to ask in real life what Mr Smith would do in Mr Jones's position and vice versa, the question as to how Hamlet would behave in Othello's position and Othello in Hamlet's reflects a complete misunderstanding of the special status of fictional figures and can be no more than a form of unverifiable speculation.[3]

The fact that, unlike a real person, a fictional dramatic figure is a deliberate construct is also clearly demonstrated by the fact that the set of information that determines a figure in a dramatic text is finite and closed, and, at best, can be exhausted, but not extended by precise analysis, whereas the amount of information that can be gathered about a real person is theoretically infinite. A consequence of this limit to the amount of information available on a fictional figure is that from the outset each individual piece of information becomes much more important. Even the most incidental piece of information can therefore be of fundamental significance in the analysis of a dramatic figure. In judging real people, on the other hand, one can assume that some data are relevant and others coincidental and irrelevant. Thus, any significance that can be attached to the name of a real person appears to be largely accidental and does not give any indication of the character of that person. In the case of a fictional figure, on the other hand, one assumes, correctly, that a name such as Brand, the central figure in Ibsen's play of the same name, reflects a particular characteristic associated with that fiery figure.

5.2.2. Restrictions in the portrayal of figure in drama

Of course, what we have been saying here on the distinction between figure and character or person does not apply to dramatic figures alone, but is also true of all fictional figures, including those in narrative texts. In drama, however, because of its multimediality and the physical presentation of a figure on stage, the danger that these distinctions might be forgotten or obscured seems to be particularly great – and this is true despite the fact that the conditions imposed by the dramatic medium mean that the possibilities for a detailed, all-embracing portrayal of character are more limited than they are in narrative texts such as the novel. In this context, Käthe Hamburger has spoken of the 'fragmentary quality of dramatic characterisation' and, at the same time, has shown that this fragmentary quality may itself be seen as an approximation to the conditions of reality under which we actually perceive our fellow human beings in the real world,[4] thereby encouraging further the confusion of fictional figure and real person.

The more clearly fragmentary quality of a dramatic figure in comparison to a figure in a novel is a consequence of the more restricted length of a dramatic text and the medially more limited possibilities of opening up a 'view from within' or of exposing the inner mind of a figure to the receiver by going beyond the information articulated either verbally or nonverbally. In narrative texts, by contrast, the social factors determining particular figures, their development, psychological disposition and ideological orientation may be unfolded in as much exhaustive detail as is desired and the inner workings of the consciousness can be exposed by the narrator at will. In his 'Versuch über das Theater' ('Essay on the Theatre') (1908), Thomas Mann used this as his main argument against those who tried to subordinate the novel to drama:

Novelists are often accused of being able to get away with crude simplification and deliberate abbreviation, with superficiality, vagueness and a lack of insight but really these criticisms could be levelled at the theatre with much greater justification than at the novel. It is no coincidence that it is drama and not the novel that has managed to produce those stereotype figures or theatrical scarecrows that can have absolutely no pretensions to individual completeness, such as the 'Father', the 'Lover', the 'Conspirator', the 'Naïve' and the 'Comic Old Man'. . . . The novel is more precise, more complete, more knowing, conscientious and profound than drama in everything that concerns our insight into the body and soul of man, and, far from concurring with the view that it is drama that is the most genuine and three-dimensional of the literary genres, I confess that I regard it as the art of the silhouette, and I therefore feel that narrative is the only true complete, round and three-dimensional channel for presenting mankind in literature.[5]

Thomas Mann's deliberations on the respective advantages and disadvantages of drama and the novel need not concern us here since we are not interested in establishing a normative generic hierarchy. However, leaving the evaluative aspect of his conclusions aside, it is possible for us to agree fully with his arguments. The absence of a narrator or a mediating communication system means that the possibilities of presenting the bio-graphical and genetic dimensions or the inner consciousness of a dramatic figure are greatly reduced.[6] If we initially ignore the various attempts made to increase these possibilities, such as the introduction of epic communica-tion structures and conventions like the unmotivated soliloquy, then the consciousness of a particular figure can only be portrayed to the extent that it can be articulated by the figure himself in a situatively and psycho-logically plausible manner. This emphasis on what is articulated – and in classical drama at least this primarily means what is articulated verbally – reflects a certain one-sidedness. The figures in drama appear predominantly as people who portray themselves rather than exist in their own right – that is, they generally appear in terms of the way they interact with others rather than as solitary individuals and they generally appear as speakers. Friedrich Dürrenmatt, a modern dramatist who is very much aware of the possibilities for the non-verbal characterisation of a figure, has confirmed these limitations:

In contrast to narrative literature, however, which is able to describe man as he is, the art of drama portrays man with a limitation that cannot be circumvented and stylises man on the stage. This limitation is called forth by the art form. The human being of drama is a talking person, that is his limitation, and the purpose of the action is to compel him to a particular speech.[7]

More recent attempts to add a deeper psychological dimension to the dramatic figure by introducing new conventions such as thinking aloud by association – as, for example, Eugene O'Neill attempted to do in *Strange Interlude* (1928) – actually confirm these limitations and must be evalu-ated as an attempt to find functional equivalents to the methods of por-traying the inner consciousness that have been developed in the modern novel: interior monologue or stream of consciousness.

5.2.3. Figure as the focal point of contrasts and correspondences

Our first attempt to provide a more precise definition of what we mean by dramatic figure was made from the negative perspective. We emphasised the differences between a dramatic figure and a real person and demon-strated the former's fragmentary quality and the greater possibilities of characterisation open to narrative texts. At the same time, however, a dramatic figure may also be defined positively as the sum of the structural functions it fulfils in either changing or stabilising the dramatic situation and the character (in the neutral sense of identity) of a figure as the sum of the contrasts and correspondences linking it with the other figures in the text.[8] The first aspect will be discussed later on in connection with the category of plot (see below, 6.1.2.) but we should like to investigate the second aspect straightaway. The following analogy will serve to clarify what we mean: each individual piece in a game of chess is defined within the overall framework of all the different pieces and can only be described as the set of all the relevant relationships by which each piece contrasts or corresponds to the others. The rook and the bishop are similar in that they exist in pairs and that they can move in four directions over several squares, they differ in that the bishop moves diagonally and the rook vertically or horizontally. As one of a pair, the bishop is also similar to the knight but differs from the pawns and the king and queen. Another feature that the bishop shares with the knight is the ability to move in four directions, but they differ in the manner of movement and the bishop's inability to jump over other pieces ... With certain restrictions it is possible to apply this analogy to both the dramatis personae (as the ensemble of figures in a dramatic text) and to an individual dramatic figure, even though in this case it is not always quite as simple to present the various distinguishing features as it is in a game of chess. One fundamental difference between chess and drama, however, is the simple fact that in the latter the system of contrasts and correspondences is not established in advance but is built up as the text develops and that the combination of features used to characterise a particular figure need not remain constant throughout the text. In spite of these differences, however, the analogy with chess makes it clear that it would be advisable to commence our discussion of the dramatic figure by examining the super-ordinate system made up of the ensemble of figures – otherwise known as the dramatis personae.[9]

5.3. Dramatis personae, configuration and figure constellation

5.3.1. Dramatis personae

If the dramatis personae can be defined as the sum of all the figures that appear in a play, then this includes not only the minor figures who speak perhaps no more than once but also the non-speaking figures or 'figure collectives', whose function as set- or prop-like accessories can only be distinguished from that of the actual set or props by the fact they do not convey any purely iterative information.[10] On the other hand, this definition of dramatis personae does exclude those figures who are referred to verbally in the speeches of others, but who never actually appear on stage. Although it is indeed possible for these 'backstage characters', which are only spoken about without them ever actually being seen on stage, to be given individual qualities and even to influence the plot – as the kitchen-girl Nell does in Shakespeare's *Comedy of Errors* (III,ii,71–153) or Dick and Lottie Potter in Alan Ayckbourn's *Absurd Person Singular* – the simple fact that they are presented verbally rather than multimedially means that they have a status that can be clearly distinguished from that of the figures of the dramatis personae.

5.3.1.1. Size

An important, if purely quantitative, parameter for the dramatis personae is the number of different figures it contains. This may vary from the monodrama to the densely populated plays with large crowd scenes. In this respect, the artistic intention of the dramatist cannot always be given free rein since the economic, organisational and architectural conditions imposed by the theatrical set-up generally involve certain restrictions. Thus, the size of a company of actors, for example, can only permit a certain size of dramatis personae, though of course the doubling or trebling of parts that do not overlap scenically enables a playwright to expand the number of possibilities available.[11] Furthermore, the limited length of a dramatic text also discourages playwrights from presenting large numbers of figures – at least in comparison with the social novels of the nineteenth and twentieth centuries. Naturally, an extension of the dramatis personae does not always need to be motivated by the intention of presenting a comprehensive image of reality; it can also serve a rather naïve or self-indulgent tendency towards extravagant spectacle – as in the historical 'epics' from Hollywood, for example, whose unofficial trade mark was the 'cast of thousands'.

5.3.1.2. Quantitative relations of dominance

It is also possible to calculate the relations of dominance within the dramatis personae by establishing the length of time that a dramatic figure spends on stage and the extent of its participation in the primary text. Both of these criteria produce a scale of values for each figure in the dramatis personae, though they do not necessarily have to coincide. Neither do they represent an absolutely dependable criterion for dividing the dramatis personae into major and minor figures, since the length of time spent on stage and the level of participation in the text do not always necessarily coincide with the importance of a particular figure for the development of the plot. Nonetheless, these criteria do represent an important parameter for establishing whether a particular figure is either a central or peripheral element of the dramatis personae since they influence the focus and thus help control the perspective (see above, 3.5.3.2.).[12] At the current level of research it is not possible to grade the figures of the dramatis personae precisely according to their importance for the development of the plot since there are still no sophisticated preliminary studies of the 'grammar' of plot. As long as these do not exist, the more subtle distinctions such as those between 'major figures', 'supporting figures', 'minor figures', 'episodic figures' and 'assistant figures' can only be guessed intuitively and not defined operationally.[13] If we were to quantify the extent to which a particular figure predominates, we would probably have to examine each figure for the number of different ways it relates to the other figures and for the number of triadic plot episodes in which it appears as an active subject (see below, 6.1.2.).

5.3.1.3. Qualitative correspondences and contrasts

Having examined the quantitative relationships within the dramatis personae we shall now turn to the way the dramatis personae is structurally arranged and classified according to the qualitative correspondences and contrasts between them. Since, in this respect, the relevant qualitative features vary from text to text and from one historical period to the next, we felt it was necessary to select one particular type to serve as a model for the rest. Our choice fell on the English Restoration comedy, a genre in which a certain stereotype arrangement of the dramatic figures makes it easier to expose the relevant and salient features. Thus, the pattern of correspondences and contrasts outlined in the following paragraphs do not merely apply to one individual text but are typical of a corpus of texts from a particular historical period – despite the fact that we have restricted our choice of representative examples to William Wycherley's *The Country Wife* (1675), George Etherege's *The Man of Mode* (1676) and William Congreve's *The Way of the World* (1700).

The first and most general features that structure the dramatis personae of the Restoration comedy are also relevant for dramas of most other historical periods. This is particularly true of the contrast between 'male' and 'female', the importance of which is frequently emphasised by the fact that the list of dramatis personae printed before the primary text is structured on the basis of this criterion. Naturally enough, in the love intrigues of Restoration love-chase comedies, this contrast is given central prominence since it is the motivating factor behind all developments in the plot. The division into groups of male and female figures reveals clear differences in the norms of courtship behaviour specific to each sex, though of course the specific qualities associated with each sex are made problematic in Restoration comedy by the use of gender inversion in figures such as the effeminate man and the tomboyish girl epitomised by Sir Fopling Flutter and Harriet in *The Man of Mode*.

A further anthropological constant is that represented by the opposition of 'old' and 'young', though the actual roles played by the different

generations are historically variable. This opposition was not only prevalent in Restoration comedy; it applies to the genre of comedy as a whole,
whose archetypal structure is determined by the victory of life over death
and youth over old age.[14] The young figures presented in Restoration
comedy normally have an unproblematic and uncomplicated attitude
towards sexual libido, whereas the older figures are generally characterised by a number of deviating attitudes towards love: there is the old man
who compensates for his impotence by being ambitious at work (Sir Jasper
Fidget in *The Country Wife*), the ageing rake who makes strict moral
demands on his young wife that are purely preventative and defensive (Mr
Pinchwife in *The Country Wife*), the figure of the old man in love, the
senex amans of Latin comedies, whose comically inappropriate passion
and desire undermine the younger figures' plans and who thus has to be
thwarted (Old Bellair in *The Man of Mode*). Amongst the older female
figures we have the ageing coquette, who attempts to hide her erotic
appetite behind a mask of demurity (Lady Wishfort in *The Way of the
World*), the lady of virtue, whose virtuous behaviour is merely the result of
a lack of opportunity to be otherwise (Lady Woodvill in *The Man of
Mode*) and the ageing beauty who strives to keep her lover by means of
possessive jealousy and the liberal use of cosmetics (Mrs Loveit in *The
Man of Mode*). As far as the development of the plot is concerned, all these
older figures share a common function as 'blocking characters' who, as the
adversaries of the younger figures, must be outwitted, exposed or disem-
powered. Because of the discrepancies either between their age and their
youthful libido, or between their mask of virtue and their promiscuity,
they also create a comic effect. Here too, then, the dramatis personae is
divided into two groups according to one key feature – the generation to
which they belong – and yet within the overall unity or correspondence of
one group it is possible to identify a number of additional distinguishing
features that differentiate more subtly.

A third feature of suprahistorical relevance is that of social class, which,
in Restoration comedy, revolved around the contrast between gentry and
non-gentry. In turn, the second of these groups, which is considerably
smaller than the first, may be divided into two subgroups: the servant
figures, who are functionally subordinate to the aristocratic society of the
gentry, and the representatives of middle-class professions (doctors,
lawyers, clerics and merchants). The contrast between gentry and non-
gentry largely coincides with the contrasts between 'business' and 'pleasure' and between unspecialised, social wit and a one-sided, and thus
comic, specialisation.

These three suprahistorically relevant features – gender, generation and
social class[15] – whose actual content, as we have seen, is historically
variable, are complemented by other distinguishing features whose rele-

vance is historically more restricted. In Restoration comedies one of these features is the contrast between 'town' and 'country'. The significance of this may already be deduced from the titles of plays such as *The Country Wife* or from speaking names such as Mrs Townley (in *The Man of Mode*) alone. The allocation of a particular figure to 'town' or 'country' is thus one of the more important distinguishing features. However, unlike gender, generation or social class in Restoration comedy, it need not be a permanent feature and may change as the plot develops. In fact, it is possible for one strand of the plot to be taken up with one figure moving from 'country' to 'town' and crossing the semantic barrier between them – as the heroine of *The Country Wife* does, for example (see below, 7.3.1.). In such cases, the difference between town and country is presented as a contrast between cultivated sociability, enlightened wit, liberal sexual mores and fashionable elegance on the one hand, and boredom, boorish entertainments, dullness, conservative sexual morals and an old-fashioned lack of sophistication on the other. This is epitomised by the contrast between Mirabell and Sir Wilfull Witwoud in *The Way of the World*.

An additional pair of distinguishing features that was often used to classify the dramatis personae is the contrast between 'nature' and 'affectation', though of course by nature we do not mean some form of uneducated or unsophisticated 'original condition', but rather a highly refined ideal of spontaneous elegance in appearance and behaviour that has become 'second nature', as it were, linked with an anti-idealist affirmation of human sensuality that may be refined aesthetically, but not sublimated ethically in the love-game. As far as actual cognitive abilities are concerned, this opposition is presented in the form of a contrast between 'wit' and 'non-wit'. A figure exhibits 'wit' if he is able to combine 'fancy' and 'judgement' to form a harmonic synthesis, and at the same time respects the flexible and complex rules of urbane decorum. Both of these abilities come as second nature to a wit. Effort is no longer needed as the wit, in his games, has everything under control. Included in the group of figures characterised by their 'wit' in Restoration comedy is the central pair of lovers, who, as 'gay couples' or 'railling lovers', transform the courtship scenes into a witty game, even when they themselves are deeply affected emotionally by love (Dorimant and Harriet in *The Man of Mode*, Harcourt and Alithea in *The Country Wife* and Mirabell and Millamant in *The Way of the World*.

As counterweights to this positive norm there are the non-wit figures whose comic effect derives from their very lack of wit. They may be divided into two subgroups according to whether their lack of 'wit' is the result of complete ignorance or whether they attempt to adopt an affected artificial pose in order to appear witty, despite the fact that they are either partially or completely lacking in the qualities of fancy, judgement and a sense of decorum ('Witwoud'). In *The Way of the World*, one of the representatives of the last group bears the telling name 'Witwoud'. In all three of these comedies, the representatives of the 'witless' subgroup are mostly recruited from the figures associated with the country or the middle-class.

As far as sexual behaviour patterns are concerned, the contrast between nature and affectation is represented in the opposition of libertines on the one hand, and hypocrites and braggarts on the other. Whilst the libertines, under the influence of Thomas Hobbes's sceptical, materialist philosophy, reject all Christian or Platonic ideologies of love and regard their own sexuality simply as an appetite that, like any other, must be satisfied as pleasurably as possible, the representatives of 'affectation' run counter to this 'natural' position either by hiding their appetites behind a mask of virtue or by ostentatiously blowing it up into something vast and insatiable. In this respect, the central pair of lovers is again on the side of 'nature' (though they exhibit characteristically male or female variations of it), whereas their adversaries are characterised by various forms of affectation.

Finally, in the area of fashion and etiquette, the contrast between nature and affectation is reflected in that between natural and playful elegance and the affected artificiality of narcissistic dandies and vain fops such as Sir Fopling Flutter in *The Man of Mode*.

In the above paragraphs we have managed to identify and establish, albeit rather sketchily, the most important features that structure the dramatis personae of a Restoration comedy, though, of course, we have merely hinted at the pragmatic aspect – that is the assessment of these contrasts between various features by the author and the audience – in the evaluative character of our own comments. This pragmatic aspect could be further clarified by showing that there were equivalent patterns of opposition in the philosophical and socio-ethical debates and the social behavioural norms of the period. At the same time, it would also be possible to establish further distinctions in the patterns of opposing features within the texts themselves by investigating and uncovering additional and increasingly sophisticated distinguishing features. However, our primary concern here has been to demonstrate that the structure of the dramatis personae may be represented as a matrix of opposing features, and each individual figure as a set of distinguishing features. We can show this by taking two figures from *The Way of the World* and contrasting their respective characteristics in tabular form:

Mirabell	*Lady Wishfort*
+ male	– male
+ young	– young
+ gentry	+ gentry

+ town	+ town
+ nature	− nature
+ wit	− wit
+ libertine	− libertine (hypocrite)
+ elegance	− elegance

In the same way that their different sets of distinguishing features may be used to draw a distinction between Mirabell and Lady Wishfort, it is also possible to distinguish between Mirabell and the other figures in the play, though of course, the contrasts are repeatedly emphasised by the existence of a few shared or corresponding features (in this case 'gentry' and 'town'). Nevertheless, the same set of features associated with Mirabell also applies to Dorimant in *The Man of Mode*, and in fact, in all the other comedies there are equivalent figures corresponding either entirely or in part to the remaining figures in *The Way of the World*. This is an important indication of the structural homogeneity and stereotype quality of the Restoration comedy as a historical subgenre of drama – a quality that has actually stimulated us into citing this particular group of texts as an exemplary corpus of texts in our analysis.

5.3.2. The constellation of figures as a dynamic structure of interaction

However, the structure of the dramatic personae is not exclusively associated with contrasts and correspondences that interrelate in a purely static manner. It also includes a number of dynamic structures of interaction that we should like to describe as figure constellations. Naturally enough, these are not completely independent of the patterns of opposing features since, after all, these can facilitate the possibility of action taking place. Thus, the contrast between 'male' and 'female' creates the opening for a love intrigue, for example, and the contrast between 'wit' and 'witless' the possibility of a gulling intrigue, in which the simpleton or fop is outwitted or exposed by the wit. Besides, the figures are characterised principally by their positive, neutral, or negative attitudes towards other figures and it is not always possible to trace the causes of these back to the similarities or contrasts between their respective distinguishing characteristics.

One model for the resulting structure of conflicts is the widespread distinction between the hero and his opposite number, or between the protagonist and the antagonist. In his *Morphology of the Folktale* V. Propp expanded this into the three functions of hero, accomplice and adversary.[16] An even more sophisticated model has been suggested by E. Souriau in *Les Deux cent mille situations dramatiques*.[17] He begins by identifying six primary functions in drama, not all of which need to be realised all the time, and whose performers – whether individuals or groups of figures –

may change with the dramatic situation. Dramatic figure and dramatic function are therefore not identical, though of course in each given situation the participating figures and the dramatic functions they perform are closely bound up with one another. At the same time, though, one individual figure may fulfil several functions simultaneously and, conversely, one function may be realised by several figures. The three functions of hero, accomplice and adversary also appear in Souriau's model: as a *force thématique* which strives to establish a certain value for itself or someone else – or at least strives to avoid a negative value, as a *rival* or *opposant* who competes with or resists the *force thématique* and as *complice* who can link up with each of the other dramatic functions. These three aspects are complemented by the functions embodied in the value so desired (*représentant de la valeur*), of the referee or judge able to decide to whom it is allocated (*arbitre*) and by the figure who actually receives this value (*obteneur*).

5.3.3. Configuration

By configuration we mean the section of the dramatis personae that is present on stage at any particular point in the course of the play. A change in the configuration leads to the constitution of a new scene (see below, 6.4.2.2.). This use of the term stems from the works of Solomon Marcus, one of the leading exponents of a mathematical analysis of drama which up to now has been primarily concerned with examining configuration structure as something that can be understood in quantitative terms alone.[18] In the following sections we shall tackle some of the questions raised by this type of research but, at the same time, we shall largely dispense with the laborious mathematical descriptions of complex parameters for the simple reason that the often trivial results scarcely seem to justify the amount of effort involved.

5.3.3.1. Size and duration of the individual configurations

There are two parameters used to characterise each configuration: its size (that is, the number of participating figures) and its duration. The two extremes of the first parameter are represented by the 'empty' or zero-configuration,[19] and the ensemble-configuration. In classical drama, the zero-configuration occasionally occurs when the stage is empty between two scenes. Modern dramas, on the other hand, often contain zero-configurations of greater duration (see above, 2.3.). The ensemble-configuration occurs relatively frequently in texts with a small dramatis personae – in plays with two or three figures, for example – and is then not particularly marked; in texts with an extensive dramatis personae, however, it represents a rare exception which, in French classical drama and also the Elizabethan comedy, became an established convention in the final scene.[20]

The duration of the individual configurations can vary as much as their size. In extreme cases it is possible for one configuration to cover the whole text. An example of this is Samuel Beckett's *Happy Days* (1961): here, the dramatis personae consists of an elderly couple, Winnie and Willie, who are on stage thoughout the two acts. The extreme length of this configuration serves to make the uneventfulness of their existence obvious in scenic terms, and the fact that the ensemble-configuration remains constant throughout reflects their state of complete isolation from the outside world. If configurations of such extreme duration create the impression of time elapsing painfully slowly, time that must be laboriously filled with ritualised, meaningless activities, then, by contrast, configurations of short duration generally have the effect of raising the tempo (see below, 7.4.5.). It is not surprising, therefore, that the average duration of configurations used in boulevard comedies or farces is generally very short and that the exits and entrances often follow one another extremely rapidly.

5.3.3.2. Configuration structure

The identity of a dramatic figure takes shape and evolves in the series of configurations in which it participates, and the contrasts and correspondences that develop between one particular figure and the others become clear when they are meaningfully juxtaposed on stage. In order to clarify the way the configurations evolve within one particular text and to facilitate the identification of the number of configurations in which a particular figure participates – to make them more accessible to analysis – we shall present the configuration structure in the form of a matrix whose lines correspond to individual figures and whose columns correspond to the individual configurations. Thus, if a particular figure is present in a certain scene the appropriate space in the matrix is filled with '1', and if that figure is not present, with '0'. As an example, we have selected an act from a play that has already been discussed above, *The Man of Mode* by George Etherege. The first act may be divided into configurational segments of varying duration in which a total of seven different figures participate: the protagonist Dorimant (D), his *valet de chambre* Handy (H), an Orange-Woman (O), his friend Medley (M), his Shoemaker (S), his friend Young Bellair (Y) and a Footman (F). An analysis of this act, which forms a closed time–space continuum, produced the configuration structure on page 173.

In this matrix, the individual figure is represented as a 'word' in a binary code – that is, as a definitive, finite series of the numbers 1 and 0. Although it does not occur in our example, it is possible for two or more figures to

	1	2	3	4	5	6	7	8	9	10	11	12	13	14	15	16
D	1	1	1	1	1	1	1	1	1	1	1	1	1	1	1	1
H	0	1	0	1	1	0	1	1	1	1	0	1	1	1	1	0
O	0	0	0	1	1	0	0	0	0	0	0	0	0	0	0	0
M	0	0	0	0	1	1	1	1	1	1	1	1	1	1	1	1
S	0	0	0	0	0	0	1	1	0	0	0	0	0	0	0	0
Y	0	0	0	0	0	0	0	0	0	1	1	1	0	1	0	0
F	0	0	0	0	0	0	1	0	0	0	0	0	0	0	1	0

have the same number series. In other words their entrances and exits coincide completely. Two well-known examples of such scenically concomitant figures[21] are Rosencrantz and Guildenstern in *Hamlet*. Conversely, alternating figures are those that never have a single '1' in common. In our example, this applies to the Orange-Woman and the Shoemaker, who, in accordance with the ritual of the *levée*, offer their services to Dorimant one after the other. The scenic alternation of figures often plays a crucial part in comedies using doubles or other forms of mistaken identity. Thus, the confusions in Shakespeare's *Comedy of Errors* are based on the fact that the two twin masters and the two twin servants appear on stage alternately right up to the dénouement.

Finally, a scenically dominant figure is one who does not only participate in all of the configurations with another figure, but in addition participates in a number of other configurations. In this sense, of all the figures in our example above it is Dorimant who dominates over the rest because he is the only figure whose matrix cells only contain the number 1. Thus, as early as the first act, it is possible to identify him as the central protagonist on the basis of this configurational structure alone.

In comparing the number of series of each individual figure there is a simple method of calculating the scenic distance between them if we follow the code-theorist Hamming in assuming that the distance between two words of a binary code corresponds to the proportion of positions in which the 'words' have different numbers.[22] Thus, in our example, the shortest scenic distance (4) is that between Dorimant and Medley, and this reflects the special affinity between these two figures. They only differ in a few minor areas and are closely linked as friends and confidants in a single configuration. The scenic distance between Dorimant and Handy is also relatively small, a fact that is determined by the type of configuration involved – in this case the master–servant relationship.

If we now turn to the structure of the configuration series, then it becomes clear that – if we omit the fourth configuration, since it only takes up two lines of text – it is structured initially according to a law of expansion. The act begins with a soliloquy by Dorimant and this is then expanded progressively by the appearance of Handy, the Orange-Woman, and Medley into a series of configurations with one, two, three and four figures respectively. As the act progresses, Dorimant is confronted with additional figures, in particular the Shoemaker and Young Bellair, though there are never more than four figures on stage at any one time. The process that results in the stage being slowly filled with figures and the protagonist being confronted with a stream of new figures is clearly designed to facilitate the exposition of Dorimant's character. The growing and fluctuating configurations create and realise a number of comparisons and contrasts and thus a whole series of distinguishing features, with the result that by the time the intrigue proper begins in Act II, Dorimant has already been presented to the audience as a rounded and multifaceted figure. This functional link between the configurational structure and figure exposition becomes even clearer if we consider the social status of the new figures that join him on stage: representatives of a lower social class constantly alternate with figures who are equal in rank to Dorimant (H/O – M – S/F – Y). As a result, it is possible both to establish Dorimant's social position within a varied social system and to establish the contours of his personality from the way he behaves towards social equals and inferiors.

The type of configurational structure presented here – that is, one which expands at the beginning and then tails off again towards the end – is one that was particularly common in the plays of a classical tradition that strove to produce structural symmetry and perfection. There are many other ways of structuring the configurational patterns – apart from sequences that are not quite so transparently structured as this one. One particularly interesting example in this context is Arthur Schnitzler's play *La Ronde*, in which the configurational structure actually reflects the metaphor of cyclical movement implied in the title. The text has the following configurational structure:

	1	2	3	4	5	6	7	8	9	10
The Prostitute	1	0	0	0	0	0	0	0	0	1
The Soldier	1	1	0	0	0	0	0	0	0	0
The Parlourmaid	0	1	1	0	0	0	0	0	0	0
The Young Gentleman	0	0	1	1	0	0	0	0	0	0
The Young Wife	0	0	0	1	1	0	0	0	0	0
The Husband	0	0	0	0	1	1	0	0	0	0
The Sweet Girl	0	0	0	0	0	1	1	0	0	0
The Poet	0	0	0	0	0	0	1	1	0	0
The Actress	0	0	0	0	0	0	0	1	1	0
The Count	0	0	0	0	0	0	0	0	1	1

In this erotic counterpart to the *danse macabre*, the constant repetition of two-figure configurations that are linked in the form of a chain returns to the beginning of the cycle when the Prostitute reappears in the final configuration. This and the pervading motif of sexual union serve to demonstrate the way social differences are levelled in the face of the sexual act. Despite the fact that these configurations are so similar, the contrasts between them still make it possible to isolate a number of subtle distinctions in the area of sexual behaviour and ideology, namely double values, false virtue, the desire to possess, hypocritical idealism, etc.

From the evidence of the configuration structure alone it is quite clear that this is not the type of dramatic text that develops a linear plot divided amongst a set of figures in the way that is implied in the conventional interpretation of the word plot. It is a dramatic text with an extremely episodic structure in which each figure is both a primary and/or episodic figure to the same extent. The episodic quality of the drama is reflected in the low level of configuration density,[23] which can be calculated by establishing the relationship between the number of matrix cells with the number 1 and the total number of matrix cells. In Schnitzler's *La Ronde*, this relationship is $20 \div 100 = 0.2$, whereas in the first act of *The Man of Mode* it comes to $49 \div 112 = 0.44$. The maximum configuration density possible is 1.0, which is rarely achieved, and then usually only in dramas with a restricted dramatis personae. One of these is Samuel Beckett's *Happy Days*, mentioned above, which has the simplest of configuration structures:

	I	II
Winnie	1	1
Willie	1	1

A further important parameter is the relationship between the configurations that are possible and those that are actually used. A dramatis personae consisting of 'n' figures can generate '2^n' possible configurations. A dramatis personae of 10 figures would therefore produce 1024 variations, for example. Of course, in the vast majority of cases a dramatic text does not implement any more than a small fraction of all the theoretically possible configurations, though of course it should be remembered that the configurations selected from the paradigm of all possible configurations are not chosen at random, but with a particular purpose in mind. Since, statistically speaking, all of the possible configurations are equally likely to be chosen, the fact that some are chosen and others not takes on a degree of informational significance.[24] Naturally enough, this significance is increased if configurations occur more than once. These repetitive configurations are a common feature of dramatic texts and attract the receiver's attention in a special way since they clearly deviate from any kind of chance selection. Thus, in *Macbeth*, for example, the single configuration consisting of the soliloquising hero (I,vii; II,i,ii; III,i; V,iii,v, vii,viii) and the double configuration consisting of Macbeth and Lady Macbeth (I,v,vii; II,ii; III,ii,iv) are repeated several times, thereby underlining their central importance for the form and content of the drama. By repeating an identical configuration it is possible to demonstrate and clarify the change in the way the figures relate both to each other and to themselves.

5.4. Figure conception and characterisation

In the previous section we showed how a dramatic figure is constituted and defined through the sets of relationships connecting it with the other figures of the play in the varying constellations and configurations. We would now like to concentrate on the dramatic figure in isolation. In doing so we shall divide our analysis into two levels: figure conception and figure characterisation. Figure conception refers to the anthropological model that the dramatic figure is based on and the conventions involved in turning this anthropological model into fiction. Figure characterisation refers to the formal techniques of information transmission that are used to present the dramatic figure. With the help of the communication model for dramatic texts it is possible to set up a suprahistorical repertoire of techniques used in figure characterisation. The historically specific qualities of a particular text can then be understood as a specific selection taken from this repertoire. Figure conception, by contrast, is a purely historical category, a historically and typologically variable set of conventions, since it is not possible to relate the broad spectrum of historically realised images of man and their dramatic manifestations back to a suprahistorical repertoire of possible variations.

5.4.1. Figure conception

5.4.1.1. Three dimensions

In the chapter on dramatic figure in his *Dynamics of Drama* B. Beckermann identifies three dimensions that are relevant to a typological analysis of figure conception: breadth, length and depth.[25] By breadth he means 'the range of possibilities inherent in the dramatic figure at the commencement of the presentation' (p. 214) – that is, the number of possibilities for development open to the figure, its openness or immobility. By length he means the development it will actually go through as a result of a process of change, intensification or a number of revelations, and by depth he means the relationship between its external behaviour and inner life. However, since they are expressed in such general and undifferentiated terms, these three dimensions can only serve as a set of general guidelines for our own analysis, within which we would like to propose a series of opposing models for the analysis of figure conception.

5.4.1.2. Static versus dynamic figure conception

Beckermann's notions of breadth and length provide a framework for distinguishing between statically and dynamically conceived figures. Statically conceived figures remain constant throughout the whole of the text. They never change, though of course the receiver's perception of them may gradually develop, expand or even change under the influence of the inevitable linear process of information transmission and accumulation. Dynamic figures, on the other hand, undergo a process of development in the course of the text; their sets of distinguishing features change, either in a continuous process or a disjointed series of jumps. Thus, with the latter it is not just the receiver's views of these figures that change in every phase of the text − according to the information available − but the figures themselves.[26] This purely descriptive juxtaposition of two contrastive possibilities for figure conception has often been forced into an evaluative hierarchy. In *Mein Wort über das Drama* (1843), the German playwright Friedrich Hebbel defended a normative position that regarded the dynamically conceived figure as the only true dramatic figure:

The matter of the greatest importance . . . is the way the characters are treated. They should never appear as complete products who merely go through the motions of all kinds of relationships and who, although they participate superficially in happiness and misfortune, are nonetheless incapable of either attaining or losing any depth of personality or inner essence. This is the death of drama, a death suffered before birth. For drama can only live by demonstrating to us how the individual assumes form and a centre of gravity in the struggle between his own personal world will and the common world will. The latter modifies and transforms his actions (the expressions of freedom) by introducing a circumstance (the expression of necessity) . . . This is the only way that drama can live.[27]

Not surprisingly, this kind of normative statement is itself conditioned historically and can only be understood in the intellectual and social context of a particular historical image of man. Thus, Hebbel's call for dynamic figures clearly derives from his own idealist vision that each individual has an autonomous will that is in conflict with the necessities imposed by the world around him. If this dynamic conception of figure generally presupposes an image of man that is marked by the notion of an autonomous consciousness, then a static conception of figure is often based on an ideology of social, biological or psychological determinism. Furthermore, the selection of a dynamic or static conception of figure is also conditioned typologically in that the figures in comedies are often conceived of as static, for example. Their comic quality often manifests itself in the rigidly automaticised and inflexible way they react to situations that demand a greater degree of adaptability, whilst the figures in tragedies are often able – if too late – to attain new levels of wisdom and new ideological positions. However, not even this division can be applied universally (after all, there are also tragic figures who fail exactly because of their inflexibility and comic figures who do actually change frequently and develop freely) and can only be invoked for certain historical modes of comedy and tragedy.

5.4.1.3. Mono- versus multidimensional conceptions of figure

Our second pair of contrasting features has been borrowed from E. M. Forster's *Aspects of the Novel* – namely his much-quoted distinction between 'flat' and 'round' characters, or mono- and multidimensional figures. This distinction applies as much to dramatic figures as it does to those in a novel since it is independent of the communication structure of the text.[28] Monodimensional figures are defined by a small set of distinguishing features. In its most extreme form this set is reduced to a single idiosyncratic characteristic which, thus isolated and exaggerated, turns the figure into a caricature. One example of this is Mrs Malaprop in Sheridan's comedy *The Rivals* (1775), who is identified by the characteristically inflated view she has of her own intelligence and attractiveness and the corresponding verbal idiosyncrasies linked with her vain attempts to show off by using words of foreign origin which she has completely misunderstood and thus repeatedly uses incorrectly. This characteristic is reflected in her own name and is referred to immediately when she is mentioned for the first time (I,ii). Her own utterances, and the remarks made about her by others, merely serve to confirm this impression. They are therefore largely redundant as far as the transmission of expository information is concerned, though of course this redundancy creates the comic effect of rigid repetition.

Our example of an extremely monodimensional figure also shows quite clearly that her monodimensional quality, or 'flatness', is based not only on the fact that the set of features defining her is very small, but also that this set is unified and homogeneous – every single piece of information we receive about Mrs Malaprop points towards her vain, exaggerated sense of self-esteem – and that none of the figure-perspectives without her supply any evidence of a distinguishing feature that is any different. By contrast, a multidimensional figure is defined by a complex set of features taken from the most disparate levels and may, for example, concern his or her biographical background, psychological disposition, interpersonal behaviour towards different people, the ways he or she reacts to widely differing situations and his or her ideological orientation. Each figure-perspective and each situation reveals new sides to a figure's character, with the result that his identity is revealed to the receiver as a multidimensional whole with a wealth of different facets and distinguishing characteristics.

5.4.1.4. Personification – type – individual

If we wish to make the step from ideal types to actual dramatic texts, the binary opposition of mono- versus multidimensional conceptions of figure need to be resolved in a continuous spectrum of intermediate forms. In historical analyses of drama there are three main forms that have been considered to be particularly important: personification, type and individual.

The most abstract of these in comparison to a real person is personification, the predominant form of figure conception in the medieval morality dramas and also in the Roman Catholic propaganda plays of the Jesuits. In these cases the set of information that defines the figure is extremely small and designed in its totality to illustrate an abstract concept with all its implications. Thus, the personification of a vice in a morality play, for example – let us say *superbia* – is fully subsumed in the function of illustrating the causes and effects of that vice. Both the appearance of such a figure and his or her utterances and behaviour are totally determined by this function and there is not a single piece of information pertaining to that figure that cannot be allocated to the paradigm *superbia*. Since we are dealing here with an allegorical procedure and since personifications of this kind do not usually appear in isolation but in the context of an allegorical paradigm, such as the paradigm of the Seven Deadly Sins, they are more precisely defined by their exact position within that system.

The type, on the other hand, is not quite so one-dimensional because here the figure embodies a whole set of qualities – which can be larger or smaller – rather than just one single quality or concept. He or she does not represent one single quality but a sociological and/or psychological complex of features. Although overlaps often occur in actual cases, such types can have two different origins: they are either selected synchronically from contemporary characterology and social typology or they stem from the diachronic tradition of preconditioned dramatic figures (stock figures). Thus, as an example of the first, the conception of figure in Elizabethan and Jacobean drama (Shakespeare, Ben Jonson, *et alii*) was often determined by the characterological types of humoral psychology and, thus, the genre of character portraits that were taken up again around 1600 by the imitators of Theophrastus made a whole repertoire of socially defined types – such as the 'country squire', the 'scholar', the 'courtier', etc. – available to the dramatist. On the other hand, one particularly well-known example of a dramatic stock-figure is the *miles gloriosus*, the boastful, swaggering and yet cowardly 'warrior', whose origins can be traced as far back as the comedies of classical antiquity.[29] Even though this type varies from text to text there are nonetheless certain basic characteristics that remain constant.

If the 'type' is divorced from individual qualities so that it can be used to represent some universal or typical supra-individual quality, the intention underlying a figure conceived as an individual is to bring out the features that are unique and contingent. These can only be grasped if the author produces a wealth of detail that characterises the figure, so that its individuality can be presented on as many different levels as possible – appearance, speech, behaviour, biography, etc. – going beyond the social, psychological and ideological clichés inherent in a particular type. It was this kind of figure conception that predominated within the dramaturgy of naturalism. Here the figure is no longer an allegorical personification exemplifying a certain concept and no longer an illustration of a particular social or psychological type, but represents itself in all the complexities and contingencies of reality.

5.4.1.5. Open versus closed figure conception

The contrast between open and closed figure conception touches on, though does not coincide with, the contrast between mono- and multi-dimensional figures. This contrastive model which, once again, merely marks the extreme positions on a spectrum of possible intermediate forms has been borrowed from Eric Bentley, though without taking over the strongly evaluative implications of his interpretation:

The 'great' characters – Hamlet, Phaedra, Faust, Don Juan – have something enigmatic about them. In this they stand in stark and solemn contrast to – for example – the people of the present-day psychological play who are fully *explained* . . .

   If the final effect of greatness in dramatic characterisation is one of mystery, we see, once again, how bad it is for us, the audience, to demand or expect that all characters should be either predefined abstract types or newly defined concrete individuals. A mysterious character is one with an open definition – not completely open, or there will be no character at all, and the mystery will dwindle to a muddle, but open as, say, a circle is open when most of the circumference has been drawn. Hamlet might be called an accepted instance of such a character, for if not, what have all those critics been doing, with their perpetual redefining of him? They have all been closing the circle that Shakespeare left open.[30]

In principle, we can agree with this distinction between 'fully explained' and 'enigmatic' characters, despite the fact that the image of the incomplete circle is a misleading one for describing open figure conception. After all, an incomplete circle is not really open in the sense that a 'mystery' is since there is really only one way that it can be completed. By contrast, one of the crucial components of an open figure – and Bentley's reference to the figure of Hamlet and the numerous interpretations that have been applied to him over the centuries makes this quite clear – is his fundamentally irreducible ambiguity. The figure conception implied in Bentley's image can therefore only be applied to the type associated with the closed figure conception and this, in turn, must be divided into two subtypes: a closed figure conception in which the figure is completely defined by information that is explicit, and one in which it is completely defined by information that is partially explicit and partially implicit. In the first case, the figure is defined explicitly and unambiguously for the receiver, in the second it is also unambiguous, but in a way that is only implied, thus encouraging the receiver to interpret for himself. In both cases, the receiver regards the defining set of information as complete without any insuperable contradictions within it.

Open figure conception is a different matter altogether. From the receiver's perspective the figure becomes enigmatic either because relevant pieces of information – explaining the reasons for a figure's actions, for example – are simply omitted, the information defining the figure is perceived by the receiver as being incomplete, because the information contains a number of unsolvable contradictions or because these two factors (incompletion and contradiction) function together.

It is noticeable that in distinguishing between two subtypes of closed figure conception and the open conception we have established a pattern of distinguishing criteria that is analogous to the tripartite pattern of perspective structures (see above, 3.5.4.). This is not accidental and the reason for it derives from the fact that the figures in dramas with an a-perspectival structure tend to be conceived as closed and explicit, those in dramas with a closed perspective structure as closed and implicit, and those in dramas with an open perspective structure as open. And in the same way that the appearance of a particular type of perspective structure is bound up with certain social and intellectual contexts and implies a particular social function for the text, the appearance of, for example, openly conceived figures cannot simply be determined by what Eric Bentley understood as the 'greatness' of the playwright. It presupposes the existence of a certain anthropological model. In the case of Hamlet, for example, this would be the philosophical context of an introspective scepticism in the Montaigne tradition.

5.4.1.6. Transpsychological versus psychological figure conception

The last distinction we should like to establish at this point refers to the role played by a figure's consciousness in relation to his emotions and passions, his subconsciousness and his physical existence. In this we have been influenced by some remarks made by K. Ziegler on 'personality structure' – i.e. figure conception – in classical drama. In Ziegler's words, it is characterised by the fact that

> in psychological terms, human beings exist virtually exclusively in the sphere of their consciousness – that they are decisively influenced by what they consciously know and express about themselves. Of course, in the context of the classical drama of the early modern period the notion of individual consciousness should not be interpreted 'psychologically' but 'transpsychologically' in the sense of the baroque concept of reason as a function of the objective ordering and content of ideas. That is, not so much as a unique and idiosyncratically individual character or an irrational and complex collection of natural qualities as a positively – or negatively – evaluated position in the hierarchical structure of ethical, metaphysical or religious values and meanings – or indeed lack of values and meanings.[31]

Thus, by a transpsychologically conceived figure we mean one whose level of self-awareness transcends the level of what is psychologically plausible, whose utterly rational and conscious forms of self-commentary can no longer be accounted for in terms of the characteristic expression of an utterly rational and conscious being. Instead, the dramatic figure has become a medium of epic commentary which integrates it into a prescribed system of values (see above, 3.6.2.3.). In this case, then, the figure's subjectively restricted perspective is broken in the context of an a-perspectival dramatic structure in so far as the figure is able to discuss itself and its situation with a degree of explicitness and self-awareness that it could not possibly have acquired from 'own' experiences alone (see above, 3.5.4.1.). This kind of transpsychological conception already existed in the theatrical convention associated with the objective or 'direct form of self-explanation' in medieval morality plays and, occasionally, in the dramas of Shakespeare and his contemporaries. It is also frequently found in satirical figures which then function simultaneously as both the subject and the object of the satire. And it has also been observed in certain figures of Schiller's dramas, who are able to articulate their tragic dilemma with such a level of self-awareness that they then transcend it. Thus, V. Klotz was right to point out that figures in closed dramas often possess such a high level of self-awareness that – as with the wildly passionate love of Racine's Phèdre, Orestes' flight from the Furies and the jealous hatred of Schiller's Don Manuel and Don Cesar – they are able to distance themselves analytically from their passions at the same time as falling victim to them.[32]

The opposite is true of naturalist and realist dramas, in which the figures are actually conceived as multidimensional individuals and not as idealised representatives of mankind. For this reason the figures' respective levels of awareness are restricted and relativised by the emphasis on the irrational qualities of their emotions and moods, on the unconscious influences exerted by milieu and atmosphere, and on the subconscious influence of collective drives and traumatic experiences. In such dramas, the structure of the dramatis personae itself actually encourages a reduced level of awareness for the simple reason that the central figures are often from a lower social class with the result that their capability of rational thought is relatively underdeveloped and their ability to conduct an articulate discourse relatively unsophisticated. Pathological states such as madness or feverish visions and states of a partial loss of self such as semi-sleep, dreams and intoxication serve to expose the workings of a figure's subconsciousness. Intense physical influences such as sickness and extreme climate, and the strong impressions such as those created above all by the immediate senses of smell, taste and touch undermine the significance of the consciousness and reduce idealist claims for the autonomy of consciousness to the level of the absurd.

Once again, then, this supports the view that the appearance of a particular conception of figure is ultimately bound up with certain social and intellectual contexts, though of course in this particular case – to put it in rather simplistic terms – it is possible to maintain that there is a special affinity between idealistic philosophies and a figure conception that emphasises a transpsychological or distanced level of awareness on the one hand, and between a materialist philosophy and a figure conception that emphasises the physical qualities and the un- or subconsciousness on the other.

5.4.2. Characterisation

5.4.2.1. Repertoire of characterisation techniques

The repertoire of possible characterisation techniques may be derived from the repertoire of theatrical codes and channels demonstrated in 1.3.2. However, before commencing our illustrated presentation of the most important characterisation techniques we should first like to present the repertoire of these techniques in the form of a diagram in order to provide the reader with a clear overview of the various aspects that will be discussed below. For although this repertoire has been derived from the general repertoire of codes and channels, we nonetheless feel that it is advantageous in view of the more precise nature of the problems under discussion here – namely the transmission of information with regard to the dramatic figures – to classify this information according to, in part at least, a different set of distinguishing criteria. Of course, some of the points on the diagram could easily be expanded or differentiated further but in the context of this introduction we would like to restrict our discussion to the most relevant of these distinctions.

The overriding classification criterion here stems from the question whether the information used to delineate character is transmitted by one of the figures ('figural') or whether it can only be associated with the position of the implied author as its expressive subject ('authorial'). Whichever is true, we then have to identify whether this information has been sent implicitly or explicitly.[33] In this way we arrive at four classes of characterisation techniques: explicit-figural, implicit-figural, explicit-authorial and implicit-authorial.

5.4.2.2. Explicit-figural characterisation techniques

All explicit-figural characterisation techniques are verbal. They may be divided into two categories: the self-commentary, in which a figure functions simultaneously as both the subject and the object of information transmission, and the outside commentary, in which the subject of the information transmitted is not identical with the object. A self-commentary (see above, 4.4.2.1.) is one in which a figure explicitly articulates the way it sees itself, whereas an outside commentary is one in which one figure is characterised explicitly by another. The various pieces of information on a particular figure sent to the audience either by that figure itself or by another need not coincide. In fact, in most cases they do not coincide, or if they do then only in part, since they are always bound up with a particular figure-perspective.

In turn, self-commentaries must be divided up into those that are mono-logical and those that are dialogical since each of these two types of explicit self-characterisation possesses a different level of credibility. For although both the monological and the dialogical variants are bound up with a particular figure-perspective which may be subjectively distorted, dialogical self-commentaries contain additional distorting factors, such as the various strategic aims and tactical considerations adopted by the figure towards its dialogue partner and which often persuade that figure to provide a deliberately false interpretation of its own actions and motives. Thus, in dialogical self-commentaries, the possibility of deliberate pretence or the deceit of others is added to the possibility of involuntarily deceiving oneself.

Naturally enough, the differing status of monological and dialogical

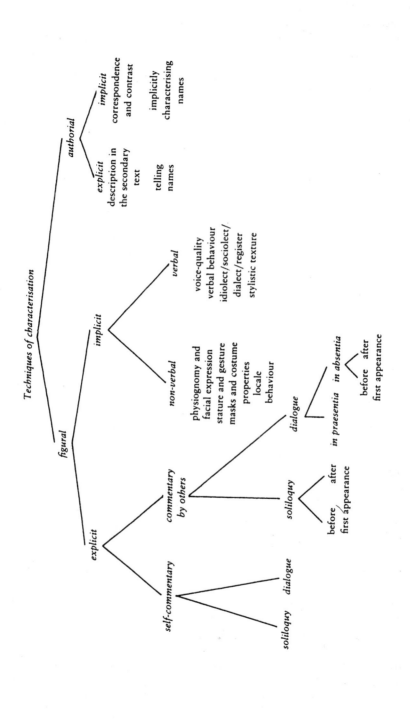

Techniques of characterisation

figural

authorial

explicit
description in
the secondary
text

telling
names

implicit
correspondence
and contrast

implicitly
characterising
names

implicit

non-verbal

physiognomy and
facial expression
stature and gesture
masks and costume
properties
locale
behaviour

verbal

voice-quality
verbal behaviour
idiolect/sociolect/
dialect/register
stylistic texture

explicit

commentary
by others

self-commentary

dialogue

soliloquy

dialogue

soliloquy

before
first appearance

after

in praesentia   in absentia

before   after
first appearance

commentaries applies in equal measure to the outside commentary. In this case, however, it is important to establish whether the dialogical outside commentary is conducted in the presence or absence of the figure being discussed because in the first case strategic and tactical distortions will occur more frequently. Finally, the status of the outside commentary also differs according to whether it is presented before or after the first appearance of the figure under discussion. The first of these represents a common convention used by the playwright to prepare the audience for the figure's appearance. In his *Essay of Dramatic Poesie* (1668), John Dryden referred to this fact in the context of an analysis of a comedy by Ben Jonson:

when he has any character of humour wherein he would show a *coup de maistre*, or his highest skill, he recommends it to our observation by a pleasant description of it before the person first appears.[34]

The special status of this kind of outside commentary consists in the fact that since the audience has not yet been able to make its own assessment of the figure, it does not have access to the information that would enable it to place that figure in any sort of perspective. As a result, the audience is obliged to await the entrance of that figure in a state of expectant suspense, a state that can be intensified if the audience is confronted with a number of different and contradictory outside commentaries. Brilliant examples of this are the build-up to Olivia's entrance in Shakespeare's *Twelfth Night* (I,i–v) and the preparations for the appearance of Tartuffe which are in fact drawn out over two whole acts (I,i–III,i).

Explicit self- and outside commentaries cannot be considered in isolation, however, since they always involve a greater or lesser degree of implicit self-characterisation. The manner in which a figure comments on itself can serve as an implicit characterisation technique, though of course the information conveyed explicitly can be decisively undermined or even contradicted by that conveyed implicitly. And, by analogy, the way one particular figure comments explicitly on another also contains elements of implicit self-characterisation.[35] From this it should be clear that the aim of such a systematic analysis of characterisation techniques is not to demonstrate how particular isolated units occur in individual sections of a text, but to expose certain processes in the way they constantly overlap or are superimposed on one another.

At this point we should like to provide a concrete example to support the arguments developed in the preceding paragraphs. We decided to select a contemporary drama, Peter Nichols' *The National Health* (1969). Our choice was guided by the fact that, although this is a drama in the conventional realist tradition, it nonetheless experiments with epic forms (such as the play-within-the-play, epic commentator figures, etc.) and therefore employs a wide range of different characterisation techniques.

As the title suggests, the action takes place in a national health hospital. The dramatis personae is divided into two main groups: the patients on the one hand, and the doctors, nurses and hospital staff on the other. The events portrayed represent everyday life in a hospital ward. Embedded in this primary dramatic level is a trivial television soap opera about the romantic world of doctors and nurses that bears the title 'Nurse Norton's Affair'. As far as the primary dramatic level is concerned the author has chosen to concentrate on the presentation of the dramatic figures and their differing attitudes towards their hospital environment rather than on plot. The focus of interest is distributed relatively equally amongst the various figures, thus eliminating the distinction between primary and secondary figures. We can therefore select any one of the figures at random to serve as an example — in our case, Ash, a patient suffering from stomach ulcers who, as a former teacher who had been forced to resign because of his homosexual tendencies, is now plagued by his present job as an office worker, the separation from his wife and the strained relationship with his adopted son.

Like all of the figures on the primary dramatic level, Ash is conceived statically. His character and his opinions have been shaped irrevocably by his milieu, his physical condition and his life story. The figures in the play-within-the-play, by contrast, are conceived dynamically. Their ability to change their behaviour and opinions overnight guarantees an edifying solution to the superficially tackled problem of race. By contrasting these two different figure conceptions, the author is voicing an implicit criticism of the ideological presuppositions behind trivial drama and is also implying an anti-idealist world-view. Ash appears as a multidimensional individual (again in contrast to the monodimensional figures of the play-within-the-play) whose character is obvious to all, right down to his subconsciousness. Despite this multilayered quality he is nonetheless perceived by the receiver as a closed figure that can be defined clearly and completely on the basis of the sum of all the information provided.

Compared to other figures, Ash is particularly prone to producing explicit self-commentaries in his dialogues. Thus, quite apart from the specific contents of these commentaries, their very frequency is enough to portray him implicitly as a character who tends to reflect upon his own fate and yet who is also looking for dialogical intimacy and the sympathy of others. This sets him apart from the other patients, who are lacking in any degree of reflective distance towards themselves and who are completely absorbed with themselves in a monological way. The recurring themes of Ash's explicit self-commentaries are his illness — he introduces himself to Loach, the new arrival, with grim self-irony as 'Mervyn Ash, tummy ulcer' (p. 17) — and, almost obsessively, his life history:

Handling the young is my vocation. My first year at teachers' college was a
benediction. I felt: I have come home, this is where I belong. Amongst people of my
own kidney . . .

I've always been able to handle boys. Why did I leave it? You may well ask. A
matter of preferment. Nepotism. Muggins here didn't give the secret handshake,
never got tiddly in the right golf-club. I didn't have the bishop's ear. You scratch my
back, I'll scratch yours. I wasn't smarmey enough by half.   (pp. 30f.)

The fragmentary quality and implausibility of this first commentary on his
past is such that the audience is able to see through it, even though there
has not yet been any definite information that might contradict Ash's
self-interpretation at this point. In fact, it is exactly this lack of information
that stimulates the audience into making up its own hypotheses and
sensitises it to any implicit pointers towards character in Ash's utterances.
His self-commentary becomes clearer in a subsequent dialogue, once again
with Loach, whom he has constantly been trying to take into his confidence:

When I was forced to give up teaching, I had a mental break-down. They made that
an excuse for getting rid of me, but it was they who'd caused it. In fact, I could lay
my perforated ulcer directly at their doorstep.   (p. 68)

This clearly demonstrates that Ash did not simply resign from his job but
was sacked against his will. But, as is true of all his utterances, he never
refers explicitly to the actual reason for his dismissal, namely homosexual
behaviour. Thus, one of the most important pieces of information that is
required for the definition of this figure has been excluded from the
explicit information given and is encoded in a more implicit mode of
characterisation. In the same vein is the implicit information that the
receiver must decipher from what Ash explicitly articulates with regard to
his philosophy of life – his 'belief in reincarnation', his 'belief that we can
store up character in life after life until we attain perfection' (p. 69), and his
elitist views on education and the value of self-improvement (p. 107). Such
statements are understood by the audience as a desperate attempt on the
part of Ash to give his life meaning and to justify his existence to himself.

The audience's ability to recognise that Ash's explicit dialogical self-
commentaries are strategically and perspectively distorted does not only
derive from the implicit information provided by Ash. It also derives from
Ash's monological self-commentaries. For although these are very short,
as befits the realist context, they nonetheless provide a clear insight into his
un- and subconscious, and are justified psychologically as speech during
sleep – again in accordance with realist convention. His two monological
exclamations:

No . . . no . . . please don't do that . . .   (p. 9) and

That boy – I warn you . . .   (p. 35)

are gestures of resistance and warning which bring to the surface the
suppressed homosexuality he successfully manages to avoid when talking
about himself in his conscious, waking hours.

Explicit outside commentaries hardly occur at all as characterisation
techniques in *The National Health*. Most of the dramatic figures are so
preoccupied with themselves and their respective ailings that they generally take little notice of each other, existing alongside rather than together
with the others and speaking in monologues. This explains why Ash is the
object of an explicit outside commentary on two occasions only, and the
subject of those commentaries, Barnet, a hospital porter, operates outside
the world of the patients and functions as an epic commentator figure on
the periphery of the dramatic fiction. In both cases the outside commentary is dialogical and is conducted in the presence of Ash. In both cases the
subject of the commentary is Ash's homosexuality:

> BARNET: I think they [i.e. homosexuals] can be useful members of
> society, long as they sublimate their libidos. Look at male nurses.
> FLAGG: You're a male nurse.
> BARNET: I'm an orderly, thank you. No connection with the firm next
> door, Fairies Anonymous. Ballet dancers. Scout masters. Teachers.
> There you are. Teachers? We had a master when I was a kid, name of
> Nash, we called him Nance. Everyone knew but him.
> ASH: I bet he did know.
> BARNET: What?
> ASH: His nickname. You always do. The boys think you don't but you
> do.
> BARNET: Did you know yours?
> ASH: Cinders.
> BARNET: Short for Cinderella, was it? . . .
> ASH: No. (Laughs) A play on words. My name Ash, you see. Cinders –
> Ash.   (pp. 99f.)
>
> BARNET: I suppose young Ken arouses your old interest in boys?
> ASH: Once a teacher, always a teacher, eh, Kenny?   (p. 104)

In these dialogues, Barnet blatantly expresses the things that Ash is trying
to conceal. In doing so he does not merely explicitly characterise Ash as a
homosexual, however; he is also implicitly characterising himself as someone who revels in obscenity, who does not miss any opportunity to indulge
in sexual innuendoes and who completely disregards all rules of tact.

5.4.2.3. Implicit-figural characterisation techniques

Implicit-figural characterisation techniques are only partially verbal because a dramatic figure is presented implicitly not only through what it says and how it says it, but also through its appearance, its behaviour and the context within which it operates (clothing, properties, interiors, etc.). Playwrights have repeatedly emphasised the importance of these implicit characterisation techniques. Lessing did so in Part 9 of his *Hamburg Dramaturgy*, for example:

In everyday life it is undoubtedly extremely insulting to view the characters of others with complete distrust and one should strive to lend credence to the testimonies professed by honest people amongst themselves. But should the dramatic poet be given the benefit of the doubt in quite the same way? Certainly not, though his job would be much easier if we were to do so. What we want to see on stage is who people are and we can only see this from their actions. . . . True, a private individual cannot perform many great acts within the space of twenty-four hours. But who is demanding great acts anyway? The character of a man may be manifested in the most insignificant action – and from a poetic point of view the greatest acts are those that shed most light on that character.[36]

Whilst Lessing preferred to emphasise the way a figure is characterised by its actions, Hebbel concentrated on the way implicit characterisation occurs through use of language. He completely rejected explicit self-commentaries and demanded instead that the dramatic figure should be presented implicitly and indirectly through the various ways it uses language to refer to its environment:

When the poet attempts to delineate character by allowing his figures to speak for themselves then he must be on his guard not to let them speak about their own inner selves. All utterances must refer to something external. It is only then that they can really express the inner workings of the character's mind most colourfully and powerfully, because that inner self can only be formed as a reflection of the world and life.[37]

As we see here, the relationship between explicit and implicit characterisation techniques has already been discussed in some detail in normative dramatic theories. As such it may therefore be seen in the broader context of a more generally conceived pair of contrasting features which in Renaissance England were paraphrased as the rhetorical categories of 'telling' and 'showing'. The decision to favour the predominance of implicit techniques is thus tantamount to emphasising the 'showing' of specific things and encouraging the audience to think for itself, rather than the more abstract 'telling' that does not require much audience involvement. In rhetorical terms, the justification for such a decision is the greater degree of 'evidence' and sensuous immediacy, and thus the greater persuasive powers wielded by techniques that are concrete and implicit.

In recent years critics have become more aware of the significance of implicit self-presentation thanks in particular to the advances made in sociology and the theory of interpersonal communication. Niklas Luhmann has provided a concise summary of the results of these developments in the following argument:

All action ('action' here in the broadest sense of the word) in the presence of others is also communication; it does not merely make the action and its immediate consequences visible but also gives an indication of who the person conducting the action actually is.[38]

Of course, the categories established in studies of this kind and the conclusions they come to – further examples are Goffman's *The Presentation of Self in Everyday Life* (1959) and Watzlawick, Beavin and Jackson's *Pragmatics of Human Communication* (1966) – cannot be applied to the analysis of fictional figures without a number of significant reservations. This is because the fictional model will inevitably abbreviate and stylise empirical reality – though the degree to which this occurs varies historically. The situation in dramatic texts is complicated further by the fact that there are two different levels of communication – one between the fictional figures and one between the figures and the audience – with one superimposed on the other. Nonetheless, if these categorical differences are taken into account, then a deeper understanding of sociological concepts and communication theory can be extremely useful in any attempts at a sophisticated analysis of the communication processes in drama. Examples of this might be the interplay of voluntary and involuntary self-presentation (Goffman) or of the superimposed aspects of content and relationship (Watzlawick).

We no longer need to provide a theoretical analysis of the various layers of implicit verbal self-characterisation since these were discussed in connection with the verbal constitution of figure (see above, 4.4.2.2.). We can therefore turn to an illustration of the three aspects of voice-quality, verbal behaviour and stylistic texture, using Peter Nichols' *The National Health*, once again, as our model.

Of these three aspects, voice-quality is the one that is least accessible to analysis because, in this particular play at least, it has not been prescribed in either the secondary text (in the form of a stage-direction, for example) or in the primary text (in the form of a reference to Ash's voice quality by another figure, for example). However, there is no doubt that in performance this aspect is important in the area of characterisation. Thus, Robert Lang, who played Ash in the first performance at the National Theatre in London (16.10.1969) used a voice that was soft and cultured and yet which occasionally became shrill and hectic. The intention was to express both Ash's cultural pretensions and sensitivity on the one hand and his psychological instability on the other.

The verbal behaviour of a figure is generally prescribed in the literary text but the producer and the actors can introduce pauses and variations of tempo to create a variety of subtle nuances. The frequency of Ash's self-commentaries in dialogues has already been identified as a characteristic feature of his verbal behaviour, exposing him as a reflective, problematic character – not least to himself – for whom it is important to be appreciated and liked by his dialogue partners. In fact, it is always Ash who is on the look-out for, and then initiates, dialogical contact with his fellow patients. The fact that he attempts to make this verbal contact as personal as possible by repeatedly addressing his dialogue partners by their first names or nicknames only serves to underline his need for contact with others. In doing so, he never violates the rules of tact and responds politely to his conversation partner, refusing to allow himself to be provoked by the crude vulgarities of others, and is constantly concerned to achieve balance and understanding.

Since he masters an elaborate verbal code, the stylistic texture of his utterances separates him from his conversation partners who speak the restricted code of the lower classes. By constantly clinging to the social stylistic norms associated with speaking 'nicely' (p. 107) and using a 'decent voice' (p. 21) free of dialect, which he refers to metalinguistically, Ash makes it clear that he regards this form of cultivated language as a status symbol, the symbol for a social status that, in real terms, he has already lost. Thus, through language he is still able to identify with the 'upper class' although he has already been banished from it. He frequently employs abstract nouns and introduces complex syntax, and his utterances are often articulated with a high level of logical coherence. However, the frequent use of foreign words, fairly obscure biblical references – to the Gadarene swine, for example (pp. 11 and 103) – and Latin quotations in his dialogues with partners who cannot possibly understand them reflect a certain level of affectation and need to impress that is often comic. The comic aspect is occasionally emphasised by the introduction of abrupt contrasts in style and register:

> ASH: . . . People with dependent natures, we have to draw our strength
>   where we can.
> LOACH: Man needs a mucker.   (p. 69)

This aspect culminates in the penultimate scene, in which Ash waxes lyrical about the 'tongue Shakespeare spake' to the dyslexic Ken, the victim of a motor cycle accident (p. 107).

The implicit non-verbal form of self-characterisation can only be determined in part from the literary text (see above, 2.1.). Physiognomy and mime, stature and gestures are largely dependent on the physical qualities and theatrical capabilities of the actor who has been selected by the director as most suitable for the particular role under consideration. The choice of Robert Lang to play Ash was a successful one in that this actor's long, oval, soft and slightly bloated face convincingly conveyed the feminine sensitivity of the character, and Lang's cultured use of his hands complemented Ash's efforts to maintain a level of verbal culture and preserve a set of social signals which he could use to preserve his identity. Such gestures are not specifically prescribed in the text itself, but there are a number of other characteristic aspects which are, such as the occasions when Ash places his hand on Loach's knee (pp. 69 and 86) – a physical manifestation of his need for intimacy and contact which betrays his homoerotic tendencies.

Ash's costume is predetermined by the dramatic context as either pyjamas or a bathrobe, and yet even here it is possible to bring out certain characteristic differences with regard to the elegance of the cut or quality of the material used. Even the properties (see below, 7.3.3.2.) assist the characterisation process and in this text they are especially relevant for the hospital personnel. In *The National Health* they merely serve to indicate the job a particular figure does, in contrast to the conventionalised, symbolic properties in non-realist drama which are used to define a figure more comprehensively – a king by a crown and sceptre, an old man by a stick and a scholar by a book, for example.[39]

In the same way, the locale (see below, 7.3.) can also function as a form of implicit self-characterisation if, for example, the setting reflects the state of consciousness of a particular figure (such as Lear and the blasted heath) or if a figure is characterised metonymically by a particular interior that has been furnished as a voluntary or involuntary expression of that figure's personality. Thus, in Ibsen's *The Wild Duck*, the figure of Consul Werle is characterised by the interior presented on stage, a manifestation of his status and taste as a wealthy, upper-middle class citizen, even before his first appearance:

Werle's house. An expensively and comfortably furnished study; bookcases and well-upholstered furniture; in the middle of the room a desk, on it, papers and ledgers; lighted lamps with green shades provide a subdued light. At the back, open folding doors with curtains drawn back. Beyond, a large, elegant drawing-room, brightly lit by lamps and candelabras . . .[40]

Finally, the character of a dramatic figure is also revealed implicitly through its behaviour and actions. However, this is such an enormous subject that we can only deal with it successfully in this context by selecting a few concrete examples from the text under discussion. Thus, the way Ash behaves towards his fellow patients and the hospital personnel is characterised by a level of helpful generosity and polite formality which reflects his conscious wish to adhere to the behavioural norms of the upper class. The attitude he adopts towards himself is one of self-pity interlaced with irony and, at the same time, he strives to compensate for his instability and vulnerability by yearning for order, correct behaviour and discipline. His actions are all determined by the single overriding aim of establishing strong and close friendships. In doing so he attempts to deny, both towards himself and others, the homosexual motivation upon which his efforts to win over Loach, and then Ken, are founded, sublimating it in an idealised vision of friendship and pedagogical eros and thus to make it socially acceptable.

5.4.2.4. Explicit-authorial characterisation techniques

Explicit-authorial characterisation techniques are not used in *The National Health*. All this means is that Peter Nichols has chosen to forego the opportunity to provide an explicit description of his figures in the secondary text, a technique which became a common feature, especially in modern drama after George Bernard Shaw (see above, 2.1.2.). Historically, this technique was derived from the list of dramatis personae which was then expanded epically by the addition of commentaries on the figures. Underlying the implementation of such techniques is the assumption that the printed literary text can, in its own right, influence the reception of a drama in a way that goes beyond its usual function of merely providing a set of instructions for the director.

A second technique of explicit-authorial characterisation is the use of telling names. Names such as Mr Pinchwife, Lady Wishfort, Mrs Loveit and Sir Wilfull Witwoud – i.e. those encountered in our analysis of the Restoration comedy – serve to define a figure even before his or her first appearance on stage and apply a label that is as permanent as it is critically intended.

5.4.2.5. Implicit-authorial characterisation techniques

In between this kind of explicit speaking name and names that have absolutely no characterising function there is a whole spectrum of possible intermediary variations. Van Laan has described these intermediate ones as 'interpretative names'[41] to distinguish them from explicit speaking names, and this also identifies them as manifestations of an implicit-authorial characterisation technique. The difference lies in the fact that an interpretive name is plausible in realist terms – that is, it accords with the conventions of real names – and also in the fact that the characterising reference to the figure remains implicit. In an earlier section (5.2.1.) we cited an example of this kind of name that will also apply here: the name of Ibsen's pastor Brand. In Norwegian, 'Brand' is an utterly conventional name, meaning both 'fire' and 'sword'. Both of these meanings are thus intended as implicit references to Brand's character with his energetic attitude of 'all or nothing' in his struggle against the compromises of orthodox theology and the established church. The distinction between his name and an explicit speaking name is reflected in the simple fact that its function as a characterisation technique can be completely overlooked by the receiver, something which in the case of an explicit speaking name such as Sir Wilfull Witwoud would presumably be out of the question.

However, the most important form of implicit-authorial characterisation is the emphasis on the contrasts and correspondences that exist between one figure and the others. We drew attention to this in our analysis of the structure of the dramatis personae (see above, 5.3.1.3.), though of course at that point we were concerned to demonstrate the fact that these relationships actually existed, whereas now we should like to establish what form they take in actual texts. Thus, these correspondences and contrasts can be perceived and articulated by the figures themselves, so as to stimulate the receiver into making contrastive comparisons for him- or herself. To give one example: Ash assures Loach that they are similar in their social dysfunctionality and isolation ('We're in a very similar boat', p. 85), though of course it is actually the differences in their respective social backgrounds, their education and intellectual awareness that are implicitly brought out instead. Another possibility is to confront several different figures with a similar situation, either simultaneously or consecutively and thus to establish their individuality by comparing the differing ways they react to it. In Act I, Scene i of *The National Health*, for example, an elderly lady wanders from bed to bed holding short evangelical sermons and handing out religious leaflets in the hope of converting the patients. The various ways the patients react to this promise of salvation – laconic dismissal by the dying Mackie, complete incomprehension on the part of the senile Rees, Foster's scepticism and Ash's well-meaning open-mindedness – represent an economical dramatic technique employed by Peter Nichols that enables him to demonstrate the ideological positions and interpersonal behavioural patterns of a whole series of figures early on in the play.

Finally, it is also possible to characterise the figures contrastively by showing the different ways they address a particular figure or theme – in *The National Health* this might be the state-run health service, for example.

In all of the cases cited here – and they do not by any means represent a comprehensive repertoire – the figures are contrasted with each other and are thus characterised implicitly, in such a way as to establish a clear pattern of situational or thematic correspondences.

6.   Story and plot

6.1. Story, plot and situation

6.1.1. Story

6.1.1.1. Story as the basis of dramatic and narrative texts

Ever since Aristotle's *Poetics* (chs. 6 and 14) – that is, from the very beginnings of dramatic theory – critics have agreed unanimously that the macrostructure of every dramatic text is founded on a story, though of course the concept of what actually constitutes a story has given rise to a whole range of different interpretations varying considerably in precision and breadth. At this point we should like to define 'story' formally as something that requires the three following ingredients: one or more human or anthropomorphic subjects, a temporal dimension indicating the passing of time and a spatial dimension giving a sense of space. Interpreted this way, story provides the foundation underlying not only every dramatic text, but also every narrative. On the basis of this criterion alone, then, it is not possible to distinguish between these two types of text, though it does set them apart from both argumentative texts, whose macrostructure is based on a logically or psychologically coherent flow of argument (essay, treatise, sermon, 'reflective poetry' etc.) and from descriptive texts that describe concrete and static objects or states of affair (topography, blazon, character description etc.). It is possible to distinguish between the three categories on which the macrostructure of a text may be based – story, argument and description – by establishing whether the temporal and spatial dimensions are present. The following matrix should clarify what we mean:

	story	argument	description
temporal dimension	+	−	−
spatial dimension	+	−	+

Our interpretation of story refers to the subject of the presentation rather than the presentation itself. As the subject of the presentation it provides the basis for the presentation and it can be reconstructed from the presentation by the receiver. From this, we can conclude that a number of different dramatic texts can be based on one and the same story and also that the same story may even be presented as texts in different media. The story underlying Christopher Isherwood's novel *Goodbye to Berlin* (1939), for example, has been translated into the medium of drama as *I am a Camera* (1954) by J. Van Druten, the medium of the stage-musical as *Cabaret* (1966) by J. Masteroff, J. Kander and F. Ebb, and, under the same name, into the medium of film-musical by Jay Allen and Bob Fosse (1972). The story is thus much less specific and less concrete than any of the versions that are presented in a dramatic or narrative text. It represents the structure of invariable relations shared by every one of its existing or hypothetical versions. In this sense, the sort of abbreviated summary of the 'contents' sketching out the important features and relationships that appears in reference works or literary dictionaries is closer to the story than to the dramatic text itself. But not even this kind of 'abstract' is identical to the story, which can only be grasped by means of an even more abstract and schematic model. However, the methodologies that have been developed in the fields of structural anthropology, folklore studies and *récit* theory to create such a model are still in an early stage of development.[1]

6.1.1.2. Story versus *mythos* or plot

Plot is for the presentation what story is for the subject of the presentation. Whilst story consists in the purely chronologically arranged succession of events and occurrences, the plot already contains important structural elements, such as causal and other kinds of meaningful relationships, segmentation in phases, temporal and spatial regroupings etc. This distinction was established by the Russian formalists, who isolated the two concepts of 'fable' and *sujet*, and was taken up again by J. M. Lotman:

Fable refers to the total number of interlinked events that are reported in a work . . . Contrasting with the fable is the *sujet*: the same events, but in their *representation*, in the order they are communicated in the work, and in that combination in which the information on it is conveyed in the work.[2]

Apart from the rather confusing terminological inversion – Tomashevski describes as 'fable' what we call 'story', and *sujet* what we call 'plot' – this coincides with our own distinction. In Anglo-American literary theory it corresponds to the distinction between 'story' and 'plot' that has been developed with regard to the theory of the novel in particular. This distinction stipulates that a 'story' is a chain of events that follows a 'time sequence', whereas a 'plot' is also determined by an additional element of causality.[3]

What we call plot corresponds to Aristotle's concept of *mythos* and is frequently used as a translation of it. Aristotle's *mythos* is the synthesis of events, though of course this synthesis is determined by a whole series of principles of which causality is only one.[4] In the form of the *mythos*, the story becomes a manageable entity, with a beginning, middle and end. Aristotle's definitions of beginning, middle and end make it clear that the mythos represents a unified, self-contained causal context:

A beginning is that which is not necessarily consequent of anything else but after which something else exists or happens as a natural result. An end, on the contrary, is that which is inevitable or, as a rule, the natural result of something else but from which nothing else follows; a middle follows something else and something follows from it.   (*Poetics* ch. 7)

The principle of totality overlaps with the principle of unity of the *mythos*, which Aristotle felt had been guaranteed not because the *mythos* refers to the actions of a single hero, but because the different parts had been welded together in such a way 'that if one of them be transposed or removed, the unity of the whole is dislocated and destroyed' (*Poetics* ch. 8). The principle forced him to reject episodic forms of *mythos* because the various episodes in them are arranged without any consideration of probability or necessity.

Of course, we cannot regard these calls for totality, unity and closed structures of causality as ahistorically normative absolutes since, after all, they reflect particular historically based points of view. In fact, they have been emphatically flaunted in many contemporary plays and openly rejected in anti-Aristotelian dramaturgical theories. Brecht's concept of an 'open' ending to a drama (see above, 3.7.3.2.), for example, contradicts the Aristotelian definition of an ending, and Max Frisch, in this a pupil of Brecht's, criticises the fundamental issues underlying the call for a closed structure of causality in the plot by adopting the perspective of an altered world-view:

Although the sort of plot that tries to create the impression that it could not have taken any other course has something satisfying about it, it nonetheless remains a falsehood: it can only satisfy one particular dramaturgical theory which continues to burden us with its classical legacy: a dramaturgy of submission, a dramaturgy of peripeteia. Whatever the damage caused by this great legacy – not only to our literary judgement but also to our essential vitality – one basically always expects that at some point a classical situation will arise in which one's conscious decisions will simply merge into fate – and yet it never does arise. Of course, there may be a number of great scenes but there is no peripeteia. In actual fact, wherever real life continues we see things that are far more exciting: we can always conclude from chance actions that they could always have developed differently, and that there is no action and no omission that might not be open to future variation. . . . All that remains, then, for a story to be convincing in spite of its chance quality is a dramaturgical theory that accentuates that chance quality.[5]

6.1.2. Action

With the concept of 'story' we introduced a concept of literary theory that has hardly been discussed at all in any great length.[6] The concept of action, and particularly its German equivalent, *Handlung*, on the other hand, is considerably less straightforward since it is encumbered by a long and not completely uncontroversial tradition in dramatic theory.

6.1.2.1. Action – action sequence – action phase

First of all, the word 'action' is ambiguous when used with reference to dramatic or narrative texts for the simple reason that, in its normal usage, it can be used to describe both a single action by a particular figure in a particular situation and the overall action of the whole text. In order to resolve this ambiguity we shall restrict the term 'action' to the first interpretation and describe the second, in which a number of actions are linked together, as an 'action sequence'. When we actually get as far as analysing a text it will be necessary to insert a further level of segmentation, which we would like to call 'action phases', in between the two categories of 'action' and 'action sequence'. The criteria defining these forms of internal segmentation will be discussed in greater detail below, in 6.4.1.

6.1.2.2. Action and story

However, we would first like to define the concept of 'action' more precisely and clarify its relationship with 'story'. We would agree with A. Hübler, who defined action as the 'intentionally chosen and not causally defined transition from one situation to the next'.[7] An action therefore always demonstrates a triadic structure, whose different components consist of the existing situation, the attempt to change it and the new situation. This tripartite pattern is a recurrent feature of most structuralist definitions of action. Thus, Bremond defines the elementary sequence within the course of an action as a series of three steps that go from the situation that allows an action to take place, via the realisation of this possibility to a successful change in that situation.[8] In the same vein Todorov describes the elementary structure of narrative as a transition from one balanced situation to another.[9] Lotman characterises the 'event', a unit in the construction of the *sujet* that corresponds to our notion of 'action', as the 'transfer of a figure across the borders of a semantic field', and again it is possible to distinguish between three separate segments (the figure on the one side of the semantic field, the transfer across the border and the figure on the other side of the semantic field).[10]

Implicit in our concept of action are the three elements that we felt were integral parts of a story (a human subject and the dimensions of time and space), because the 'intentional choice' implies a human subject, the situation a spatial dimension and the transition from one situation to another a temporal dimension. From this we may conclude that every action and every action sequence is a story or part of a story; this does not mean, however, that every story, whether entirely or partially, consists of actions or action sequences. For the otherwise undefined human or anthropomorphic subject of our definition of story is specified in the definition of action as a subject that makes a deliberate choice. 'Story' thus proves to be the broader concept of the two and action is separated from the other components of the story by the specific fact that it includes an intention to change the situation.

6.1.2.3. Action versus event

Once again, we should like to follow A. Hübler's lead and describe these other forms or components of the story as 'events'.[11] These always occur whenever the preconditions for a story have been fulfilled, but not those for an action. This applies to those stories, or parts of stories, in which either the human subjects are incapable of making a deliberate choice or the situation does not allow any change. Naturally, these two possibilities are not mutually exclusive; in fact, it is often the case that one is superimposed upon the other.

The arguments outlined above have two consequences for drama: 1) The story on which a drama is based does not need to exhaust itself in a sequence of actions alone but can – and this is often the case – consist of a series of actions and events. 2) There is another type of dramatic text that is theoretically conceivable and has even become a reality – one whose macrostructure is determined by events rather than actions. This kind of 'actionless' drama has become especially common in recent times. In fact, this lack of action, the reduction of action to events, is one of the most important structural transformations in twentieth-century drama. Naturalist plays were amongst the first to project a concept of figure that saw the individual as a non-autonomous being determined by various genetic and social conditions and thus only capable of making deliberate choices in an extremely limited way. This severely restricted the possibilities for action open to them and led to the event – which affects and takes place with human beings – becoming established as the predominant paradigm of story. This also applies to many modern one-act plays, whose structure is generally determined by a single situation. In these plays, event dominates over action as, by definition, action presupposes a succession of different situations. Of course, the clearest and best known examples illustrating the reduction of the story to a series of events are the plays of Samuel

Beckett. In *Waiting for Godot, Endgame* or *Happy Days* the immutability of the situation in which the dramatic figures find themselves – something that they accept as a foregone conclusion – and their constant verbal and mimetic activity are no longer designed to bring about a change in the situation through action but have decayed into a form of game that merely serves to pass the time. In these plays, then, the events take on the form of a cyclical, repetitive game that has become no more than an aimless end in itself.

6.2. Presenting the story

6.2.1. Restrictions on presenting the story

As we have seen, every dramatic text presents a story which is either a sequence of actions, a series of events or a combination of the two. As was also true of the presentation of figures (see above, 5.2.2.), there are certain restrictions affecting the presentation of stories that derive from the communicative and medial conditions peculiar to drama – the absence of a mediating communication system, multimediality and the collective nature of production and reception.[12] These restrictions become particularly clear when they are compared to those that apply to narrative texts. They, too, present a story, but unlike drama they also are endowed with a mediating communication system, rely exclusively on the transmission of verbal information, are generally produced and received on an individual basis and vary considerably in length.

6.2.1.1. The principle of succession

The absence of a mediating communication system in drama means that the story is presented according to the principle of succession. Although it is possible to present action phases narratively after the event in utterances of the figures, the principle of succession certainly applies to all action phases that are presented scenically (with no more than a handful of deliberately experimental exceptions; see below, 7.4.2.). Within the continuous time–space framework of a scene the presentation strictly follows the order of actions and events as they occur in the story. This principle also controls the sequence of scenes. Generally speaking, two successive scenes present two successive phases of the story and overlaps do not even occur when these phases involve different sets of figures. The principle of succession therefore precludes the use of flashbacks, which are such a common feature of narrative texts and films, and restricts the possibility of scenically presenting simultaneous actions and events to those that are bound to one and the same locale. Thus, a dramatic presentation of a story is associated much more closely with the unambiguous element of succession than a narrative presentation would be, because the latter can switch around whole sections and divide the story into a number of parallel phases of action. If the succession principle is actually violated in dramatic texts then this betrays a tendency to create epic structures or establish a mediating communication system to which these violations – since they have been inserted into the text with the deliberate intention of interpreting the story – undoubtedly belong (see above, 3.6.2.1.).

6.2.1.2. The principle of concentration

One of the consequences of the multimediality and the collective nature of production and reception in drama is the principle of concentration. The predominantly scenic aspect of the way a story is presented in a play makes it very difficult to present that story in abbreviated form (see below, 7.4.3.2.). This, together with the fact that the length of the presentation is restricted by the audience's levels of receptivity and stamina, means the story that is to be presented must be limited in length.[13] The length of a story should not simply be equated with its duration, since the latter may be abbreviated or abridged. More importantly, it refers to the number of different actions and chains of events that combine to make up the story. An additional contributory factor in the concentration principle is the fact that, in dramatic texts, the sociological and psychological influences on the circumstances surrounding the story cannot be treated with quite the same breadth as is possible in narrative texts. For whilst the author of a psychological novel is able to analyse the most complex structures of motivating forces and developments in the characters of its figures in the most minute detail and the author of a sociological novel can present all classes of society and the way the figures are conditioned socially by their milieux as meticulously as he or she pleases, the dramatist must be much more selective. This difference becomes clear when long narrative texts are adapted for the stage. Whilst this process may achieve gains in concrete realism, the original is usually simplified in terms of its psychological and sociological complexity.

6.2.1.3. Theatrical and social restrictions

Finally, there are additional restrictions that result from the multimediality of the dramatic text. These are conditioned not least by the level of sophistication in the theatrical machinery. There are certain actions or chains of events that simply cannot be presented scenically at a given stage of technical development and can only be communicated through the verbal narration of a particular figure.[14] The limit to what could actually be performed on stage was surely reached – or even exceeded – by Ibsen in *Peer Gynt* when, in his stage-directions, he demanded the following scenic presentation of a shipwreck:

Close to land, among surf and skerries. The ship is sinking. Through the fog, glimpses of a boat with two men. A heavy sea breaks over it; it overturns; a shriek is heard, then silence. After a moment, the boat reappears, bottom up. Peer Gynt comes to the surface nearby . . . Clutches the keel. The cook comes up from the other side . . . Clings to the keel . . . They fight; one of the cook's hands is injured; he hangs on tight with the other . . . He screams and slips under . . . Peer Gynt, seizing him . . . His hold loosens.[15]

The realisation of these stage-directions seems to presuppose the technical possibilities of film which, of course, simply did not exist at the time this text was written. It was therefore impossible to translate them into realistic action on stage, leaving the director to interpret them in a more symbolic and stylised manner. The difficulties that this entails are presumably one of the most salient reasons why *Peer Gynt* was and still is performed so rarely, and why it is primarily read as a closet-drama.

In addition to these technical difficulties there are also those imposed by the social norms of propriety, decency and decorum. This often affects the presentation of physical violence or of sexuality – two areas of expression that have repeatedly been suppressed as taboos in the history of drama. Horace was one of those who rejected the idea of presenting brutal acts of violence on stage and recommended that they should be conveyed in narrative form in reports delivered by the figures:

So that Medea is not to butcher her boys before the people, nor impious Atticus cook human flesh upon the stage, nor Procne be turned into a bird, Cadmus into a snake. Whatever you thus show me I discredit and abhor.[16]

Acts that are regarded as acceptable when mediated verbally are simply not tolerated when they are presented in the direct, concrete form that is created by the multimediality of the dramatic text. A further illustration of this is provided by a comparison between the different ways that the erotic and the sexual are presented in narrative and dramatic texts respectively: narrative texts have always been – and still are – given much freer rein than dramatic texts. The corporeal vitality of drama constantly threatens to sweep away the psychological distance required for the aesthetic appreciation of a dramatic presentation[17] and the public character of a dramatic performance lowers the threshold of embarrassment. Neither of these factors applies to the private reception of a purely verbal narrative text.

6.2.2. Techniques of presentation

6.2.2.1. Scenic presentation versus narrative mediation

We have already seen that the story can be presented either directly in scenic form, or it can be mediated narratively in the figures' speeches. We have also pointed out that the second technique of presentation can function as a way of circumventing technical restrictions or social taboos. The differences between scenic presentation and narrative mediation – or between 'open' and 'hidden action'[18] – are twofold: the form of presentation in open action is multimedial and a-perspectival, whereas the narrative presentation of hidden action is purely verbal and linked to a particular perspective. In the first, the audience itself becomes a witness to the events as they are presented in concrete, visual form which it can then interpret according to its own views; in the second it has to rely on 'second-hand information' – that is, on a report whose purely verbal quality makes it much less vivid and objective. This applies to both the 'spatially hidden action' that takes place off-stage at the same time as the action on-stage and to the 'temporally hidden action' that takes place in the periods omitted between the various scenes and acts.

Horace has succinctly contrasted these two techniques in a line of his *Ars Poetica*:

Either an event is acted on the stage, or the action is narrated.

and then goes on to evaluate the different ways they affect the audience:

Less vividly is the mind stirred by what finds entrance through the ears than by what is brought before the trusty eyes, and what the spectator can see for himself.[19]

This evaluation, which claims that direct scenic presentation always has a stronger effect on the audience whilst narrative mediation, at best, is allocated a surrogate function and is implemented only when the events cannot be presented scenically in a convincing way or if they are deemed improper, need not be given our unreserved support. Verbal presentation of hidden action is not always intended to function as a mere substitute for scenic presentation. It is often an important and dramatically economical way of establishing focus and emphasis and creating suspense. Thus, the narrative mediation in a report allows the playwright to reproduce in a condensed form particular phases of the story and thus to present stories of a greater length than would otherwise be possible in a purely scenic presentation. This element of conciseness becomes especially clear in a narratively mediated exposition which enables the author to present the background events in abbreviated form – however involved and lengthy they may be – and thus to concentrate the scenic presentation on the decisive period of crisis within that story (see above, 3.7.2.).

The possibility of being able to choose between direct scenic presentation and narrative mediation also enables the dramatist to emphasise certain phases of the story and keep others in the background. In other words, the choice between these two modes of presentation is one of the important elements in structuring and giving meaning to the plot, and it is these elements in particular that give a story its individual accent and profile (see above, 6.1.1.2.).

Of course, we should not forget that the relationship between open and hidden action is not peculiar to one single work or one single author; it is also typical of a particular period. In some historical periods a greater part of the story will be presented as hidden action than in others.[20] Thus, the plays of Seneca and his Renaissance imitators show a strong tendency towards narrative mediation, as do the dramas of French classicism which suppress 'all kinds of sensually dynamic action as hidden action and only allow them on stage when they have been processed rhetorically and dematerialised through a distancing filter'.[21] The fact that the actions and events in these plays are filtered through the human consciousness may give them greater emotional force and serves to replace external action and events with the inner workings of the consciousness.

Finally, hidden action, especially the kind of spatially hidden action that takes place at the same time as the action presented scenically, can have an extraordinarily powerful effect on the audience and can create a situation of extreme suspense if the events are hinted at acoustically rather than presented directly. It is precisely the fact that these events are not presented scenically that allows the audience to anticipate or fear the worst. P. Pütz has illustrated this point by citing an example from classical Greek tragedy:

When Orestes murders his mother the action is removed from the audience's field of vision and the wails are the only indications of hidden action. The invisibility does not detract from the dramatic effect; in fact it heightens the suspense by filling the spectator's imagination with ideas in which horror is united with the fearful forebodings of ultimate certainty.[22]

Many of the functions discussed here coincide in one of the most famous examples of spatially hidden action in classical German drama – the execution scene in Schiller's *Mary Stuart* (V,x). Of course, there is an obvious pragmatic reason for choosing narrative mediation in this case: it is extremely difficult to present an execution convincingly on open stage. Furthermore, the ghastliness of it would violate the norms of classical aesthetic taste. However, Schiller is able to camouflage this negative substitute function and transform it to his advantage by introducing a

number of positive functions. The execution scene is constructed as a
soliloquy by Leicester, who experiences the execution acoustically in a
room nearby:

> And I still live! I can endure to live!
> Will not this roof collapse upon my head?
> Will the abyss not open to engulf
> The wretchedest of creatures? O, what have
> I lost! O what a pearl I cast away!
> What heavenly joy I spurned and threw aside!
> She's gone; her soul already is transfigured,
> And I am left the torments of the damned.
> Where is the firm resolve with which I came,
> To stifle all the promptings of my heart,
> To watch her die, and coldly stand apart?
> The sight of her awakes forgotten shame,
> Can she in death still pierce me with love's dart?
> Accursed wretch, it is no longer yours
> To yield in meekness to this piteous shock:
> Your path is turned for ever from love's shores,
> Within your breast forever close the doors
> Of mercy, let your brow be like a rock!
> If you would still enjoy your treason's fruit,
> You must not shrink back now; be resolute!
> Pity, be silent; turn to stone, my eye;
> I will be witness, I will see her die
> (He goes determinedly towards the door by which Mary left, but stops
>   halfway)
> In vain, in vain! With horror I am racked,
> I cannot, cannot see this fearful act,
> I cannot see her fall – Hark! What was that?
> They are already there below, preparing
> To do their dreadful work beneath my feet.
> Voices I hear – No, no! Away, away
> Out of this house of terror and of death!
> (He attempts to leave by another door, but finds it locked, and starts
>   back)
> What? Am I bound here by a God's command
> To hear that thing I cannot bear to see?
> The Dean of Peterborough – he exhorts her –
> She interrupts him – Hark! She prays aloud,
> Her voice is firm – Now silence – utter silence!
> I only hear the women weep and sob,
> They are unrobing her – Hark! Now they move
> The stool for her – she kneels – she lays her head –
> (The last words have been spoken in a tone of increasing terror. There is
>   a pause; then suddenly, with a convulsive movement, he collapses
>   in a faint. At the same time, a muffled, long drawn out murmur of
>   voices is heard from below)[23]

This scene is an illustration of the economical quality discussed above, but not because the narrative report has compressed the time-scale of this section of the story – after all, the technique used here[24] actually depends on the simultaneity of the report and the action reported and, thus, the durational equality of the two. It is economical in the sense that it presents two strands of action at the same time: the execution, mediated narratively and acoustically by noises off on the one hand, and Leicester's scenically presented reactions to it on the other, his wavering between a cynical double game and deeply felt, strong emotions. These reactions have an actional quality, though of course we are faced here with an inner action, rather than an external action like the execution itself. The actional quality rests in the fact that his collapse, this tragic moment when he finally becomes aware of the irrevocable consequences of his previous behaviour, brings about a change in the situation – especially in the relationships between Leicester, Mary Stuart and Elizabeth. In this scene, then, we are faced with an actional soliloquy (see above, 4.5.2.3.) and this actional quality is reinforced on the verbal level by the emotionally charged rhetoric and on the mimetic level by the exaggerated movements and gestures.

The parallel presentation of two different chains of events or actions – the narrative report itself and the reported events – is a feature of all narrative presentations of action, even when the actional character of the narrative report is not always quite so strongly accentuated as it is in the example just quoted. In accordance with the principle of performative language that applies to a figure's speech in drama (see above, 1.2.5.), a report in drama always has at least a latent actional character because it reduces the informational discrepancies between the figures and thus causes a change in the situation even when it is an emotionally neutral report delivered by an unpartisan informer figure.

Finally, the decision to present the execution as a spatially hidden action has the function of shifting the focus of the presentation on to the inner action. The emphasis is not on the physical fact of Mary's execution but rather on the inner development that she has undergone and which had been concluded by her transfiguration as a 'schöne Seele' (noble soul) in the preceding scenes (V,vi–ix). By presenting her execution from the perspective of Leicester's reactions to it, Schiller is providing an introduction to the subsequent scenes in which the focus is directed away from the title figure on to Elizabeth, her opposite number, and in which the consequences of this execution occupy the centre of attention.

6.2.2.2. Types of narrative mediation

The narrative mediation of action and event may be classified according to the criterion of the temporal relationship between the narratively mediated story and the narrative report itself. In the first case, it is important to establish whether the narratively mediated phase of the story occurs before or after the 'point of attack', i.e. the beginning of the action presented scenically. If it occurs before, then it is an exposition narrative; if it occurs later, then it is a report of temporally hidden action that is often presented in the form of a messenger's report (see above, 4.2.2.).[25]

In addition to the various types identified by the criterion of temporal relationship, another typology can be established according to the degree of explicitness of the narrative report. We have already discussed this criterion in our typological analysis of the different forms of exposition (see above, 3.7.2.2.–4.) but it is just as relevant for the presentation of hidden action from the entr'acte[26] and the mediation of spatially hidden action. The example we chose – the messenger's report from Schiller's *Wallenstein* (see above, 4.2.2.) – illustrates the type of explicit narrative mediation in the form of a block-like, coherent report. However, hidden action can also be presented verbally in such an implicit way that the terms 'narrative mediation' and 'report' scarcely apply any longer. In other words, there is a number of borderline cases of narrative mediation. In these, the coherent report is replaced by a number of revealing allusions and gestures that the audience is obliged to complete and interpret. An appropriate example of this occurs in Gerhart Hauptmann's play *Rats*, which P. Pütz has analysed as follows:

Act Four culminates in a final conversation between Frau John and her criminal brother whom she has 'put on' to Pauline in order to bring an end to the latter's blackmail attempt. At this moment she does not yet know that Bruno has already done a thorough job . . . The clues that lead to the discovery of what had happened are not obtained from questions but from a number of almost magic effects stimulated by objects and reminiscences. Frau John asks her brother, 'Who was it that gave you such a big scratch on your wrist, Bruno?' Bruno is listening to the sound of the bells coming in from outside as if he had not heard her words at all, and then says, as if absent-mindedly: 'This mornin' at half-past three she still could've heard the bells ringing.' This reveals what had happened off-stage, the very thing that Frau John had suspected and feared.[27]

Although the hidden action is still conveyed verbally, it is no longer referred to explicitly – let alone reported in any detail or with any coherence. This kind of implicitness can be increased even further if the action hidden in the past is no longer mentioned at all and, thus, must be inferred entirely from the change in the dramatic situation.

Similar gradations occur in the teichoscopy, even though the special time structure involved means that the extremes are situated not quite so far apart. Thus, the narrative mediation of Mary Stuart's execution, for example – because of the fact that Leicester is forced to rely on acoustic impressions alone and finds himself in a condition of extreme excitement –

is less explicit, coherent and detailed as, for example, Klara's teichoscopic perspective in Hebbel's *Maria Magdalena* (I,iii). From her window she observes her mother going to church. She is composed and filled with new confidence as a result of her mother's recovery:

How sure and confidently she strides out. She has already almost reached the churchyard – who will be the first person she meets, I wonder? Of course, that doesn't mean anything, I was just thinking. (Starting with shock) It's the grave-digger! He has just been digging a grave and is climbing out, she greets him and is looking down into the murky hole with a smile. Now she has thrown her bunch of flowers into it and is entering the church. (A choral can be heard) They are singing 'Now thank we all our God'.[28]

6.2.2.3. Multiple presentation

The fact that there are two possible ways of presenting a story – scenic presentation and narrative mediation – does not mean that the dramatist is obliged to choose one mode of presentation to the exclusion of the other. He or she can in fact choose to present certain sections of the play *both* scenically *and* narratively.

In all, there are three steps involved in the presentation of an action or a chain of events: first, the verbally mediated anticipatory phase in which the action is planned or announced; secondly, the scenic realisation of the action; thirdly, the verbally mediated retrospective narrative which re-capitulates it or informs the audience of it. It is by no means necessary to make use of all three steps every single time; it is also possible to implement the anticipatory narrative and the scenic realisation, the anticipatory and retrospective narratives, the scenic retrospective and the retrospective narrative or even just the scenic realisation or the retrospective narrative in isolation. The anticipatory and retrospective narratives need not be re-stricted to the speeches of a single figure. It is possible to anticipate a phase of action in the speeches of several different figures, just as it is possible to put a number of different retrospective narratives into the mouths of several different figures.

One of the important functions of multiple presentation is to provide emphasis, because by violating the principle of economy in this way the dramatist draws attention to it as something that deviates from the norm. In addition to this rather general function of providing emphasis, multiple presentation can also serve to create suspense and contrast a number of different perspectives. The function of creating suspense is generally associated with the sequence containing the anticipatory narrative(s) and the scenic realisation since the transmission of future-orientated informa-tion arouses a sense of expectancy – whether of pain or of pleasure – in the audience (see above, 3.7.4.). Contrasts between receiver- and figure-perspectives on the other hand are generally created by the sequences containing the scenic realisation and the retrospective recapitulation since the receiver, as an eye-witness of the scenically presented phase, is able to perceive and compensate for any perspectival distortions in the different retrospective narratives.

In the realm of comedy, in which the emphasis on play for play's sake often ultimately undermines the economy principle, there are numerous examples of this kind of tripartite multiple presentation in the form of anticipation (A), realisation (R) and retrospective (RS). An example of this is the intrigue conducted against Malvolio in Shakespeare's *Twelfth Night*, which takes the form of a chain of interconnected tripartite structures that runs through the text from Act II to Act V in the pattern A-R-RS, A-R-RS, A etc. In II,iii, Maria reveals her plan to Sir Toby Belch and Sir Andrew Aguecheek in which she intends to instigate a letter intrigue in order to expose Malvolio's smug self-satisfaction, and the conspirators – not to mention the audience! – look forward to enjoying a 'sport royal' (II,iii,161). The sense of expectancy that this provokes is not immediately relieved, however, and the audience must sit through a delay until II,v, which only serves to heighten the suspense. The audience then receives advance information on the way the ensuing intrigue will develop: Malvolio is to receive a letter which, it seems, has been sent by Olivia. The letter speaks of her love for him and contains instructions which urge him to behave in a particularly absurd manner. Malvolio's antics would be secretly observed by Toby, Andrew and Feste. However, what then actually happens is not simply a repetition of those verbally transmitted plans in scenic form. Nor is the audience's attention exhausted by the purely comic aspect of Malvolio's amorous fantasies, his pedantic, circumstantial, and yet utterly naïve interpretation of the letter, and the boisterous commentaries and interjections of the eavesdroppers. The physical vitality of the scenic presentation goes way beyond that. The retrospective recapitulation of this scene in the dialogue between the eavesdroppers and Maria, the initiator of the plan, overlaps with preparations Malvolio is making for his next encounter with Olivia. In accordance with the instructions in the letter he intends to confront her – she being ignorant of the true situation – dressed in what from everyone's perspective but his own appears as an absurd costume and behaving in a grotesquely suggestive way. The scenic realisation of this phase of the action is delayed even longer (until III,iv) though in fact this broad arc of suspense is strengthened by a further preparatory announcement by Maria (III,ii,64ff.). In the initial planning phase of the letter intrigue it was not known how Malvolio would react which helped to increase the suspense. Now it is Olivia's behaviour that has become an unknown quantity: how will she react to the sudden and, for her, inexplicable change in her hitherto so strictly puritanical chamberlain? Here too, the scenic presentation actually exceeds the audience's expectations and, again, the contrasting retrospectives from the instigators and the victim of the intrigue respectively overlap with the plans for the next phase of the action, the incarceration of the apparently mad Malvolio. This plan is then realised in IV,ii and presented scenically in the form of an exhaustive comedy of deception involving a visit by Feste – disguised as a priest – to Malvolio's dungeon. The intrigue is exposed as a part of the general dénouement in V,i,270ff. and leads to the final retrospective summary contrasting the perspectives of Olivia who had intervened sympathetically, the participants, who feel the sport had been worth while, and the almost irreconcilably offended Malvolio.

This example shows that multiple presentation does not necessarily lead to uneconomical redundancy in the transmission of information. On the contrary, it represents an important factor in the coherence of a text. It also shows that it is able to create suspense by stimulating and guiding the audience's anticipation and, by contrasting the various retrospective recapitulations, to display comic and/or tragic discrepancies between the various perspectives. Finally, these links between planning and realisation – or between planning and retrospective recapitulation – may have a further function: they can expose as a comic or tragic motif the way a figure is changed by the consequences of his or her actions or the discrepancy between the action as it is planned and the action as it is carried out.

6.3. The combination of sequences

We would disagree with the Aristotelian notion of the 'unity of the plot' (*Poetics* ch. 8) and say that the total number of interrelated actions and events cannot always be traced back to a single sequence of actions or events; it is usually based on a combination of several different sequences. A sequence of this sort is a relatively closed system of chronological and causal relationships. If it is completely closed, the various sequences can only be loosely linked as an unconnected series of juxtaposed elements and thus it corresponds to what Aristotle dismissed critically as an 'episodic plot'. However, if the sequences are not completely closed then it becomes possible to link them in a coherent and meaningful way.[29]

This being the case, one can ask a completely different question, namely whether these interconnected sequences are coordinated on one and the same fictional, dramatic level or whether they are superimposed upon one another on a number of different levels. In theory these seem to be two equally viable alternatives, but in practice the former clearly predominates over the latter. The fiction-enhancing play-within-the-play structures created by superimposing several different sequences on different levels has been employed by dramatists far less frequently than the more normal structure that has just one level of fiction. In certain historical periods, though, such as the Elizabethan theatre, the German baroque drama and the plays of German romanticism, the balance has been redressed in the other direction – at least to some extent.

6.3.1. The coordination of sequences

6.3.1.1. Succession versus juxtaposition

Depending on the chronological relationships linking them, the sequences can be coordinated either according to the principle of juxtaposition or according to the principle of succession. In their extreme forms, juxtaposition occurs when the sequences completely coincide chronologically and succession when they are chronologically completely separate. In the vast majority of cases, however, it is the intermediary forms that predominate, and these occur when there is a partial overlap. In those plays whose structure is determined by the succession principle, this structure has generally been derived from the picaresque or Romance traditions which tended to link a loosely connected series of adventures involving a single central figure. One notable example of this is Ibsen's *Peer Gynt*, in which the hero's experiences in his native Norwegian village (Act I), in the mountains (Acts II and III), in Morocco and Egypt (Act IV), at sea off the Norwegian coast and finally back in his native village and mountains (Act V) are linked as a chain of relatively independent sequences. The one major feature they share is the identity of the central figure, but they are also linked by a number of recurrent thematic motifs, such as the quest for the self, or – in the last act – by the recapitulation of the events of the preceding scenes. An example of the opposite principle, in which the various juxtaposed sequences may interrupt or replace each other as the plot progresses, is Shakespeare's *King Lear*. The subplot involving Gloucester takes place within the same fictional time-scale – and with very little phase displacement – as the Lear plot, and runs closely parallel to it in terms of action, structure and thematic content (for a discussion of the functions of this relationship, see below, 6.3.1.4.).

6.3.1.2. Plot and subplot

Coordinated sequences may be divided into those that are quantitatively or functionally equal and those that form a hierarchical pattern. In the first category, two or more 'plots' are either juxtaposed or strung together successively; in the second, one of these plots is allocated one or more 'subplots'.[30] At the same time, however, it is not always as easy to distinguish between 'plot' and 'subplot' as the widespread application of these terms would appear to suggest. The difference between them is, after all, one of degree rather than type and in some cases this can make it difficult for the receiver to establish whether he or she is faced with a series of coordinated plots or a mixture of plots and subplots. The difference between them is similar to that between primary and secondary figures (see above, 5.3.1.2.). In other words, it is more a question of focus in which the quantitative aspect – the length of the presentation – is extremely important but by no means the only one that is decisive. In fact it is a common feature of comedy in particular that it often contains episodes that are developed and expanded out of all proportion to their functional importance for the development of the theme and the story. This is just another example of the comic impulse to indulge in play for its own sake. Any attempt to establish a hierarchical pattern of plots and subplots should therefore always take the functional aspect into consideration. This kind of functional gradation occurs if one plot sequence is subordinated functionally to another in such a way that, for example, it provides new impulses for the other, the main plot and relativises it by introducing parallels and contrasts. The introduction of new impulses or of parallels and contrasts in this way may also serve to define the relationship between two or more main plots, but unlike the rather one-sided relationship between plot and subplot this would then function as a balanced two-way reciprocal relationship.

We would like to illustrate this by discussing Ben Jonson's *Volpone*, a play that contains coordinated sequences of both plots and subplots. It is no accident that this example should have been taken from the sphere of Elizabethan and Jacobean drama. This particular historical period is an obvious choice because it was one in which playwrights were not over-burdened with normative theories demanding unity of plot. As a result, the techniques used to coordinate a number of plot sequences were able to reach a high level of richness and sophistication.

The macrostructure of Ben Jonson's satire on legacy hunters consists of the juxtaposition of three functionally equally important strands of plot: the three intrigues instigated by Volpone and Mosca against, in turn, Voltore, the lawyer, the ageing Corbaccio and Corvino, the merchant. These three plot sequences are introduced in quick succession in the first act and for several scenes they are allowed to run parallel to each other without coinciding in any significant way. Then, as a result of a number of planning errors on the part of the conspirators and a few unfortunate coincidences, they begin to overlap and coincide more dramatically. Their relationship is not one of plot to subplot. They are three equally matched main plots and this is clear from both the similarities in the way they are introduced in Act I and also their quantitative equivalence. Furthermore, they are also equally matched in terms of theme and plot structure. All three sequences follow a similar pattern (with Mosca's help, Volpone, apparently terminally ill, rich and without heirs, manages to squeeze a whole series of gifts out of an avaricious legacy hunter) and they all vary the same theme: the destructive influence avarice has on all natural relationships. Jonson underlines this equivalence by introducing an allegorical and emblematic framework of animal fable reflected in the names given to the conspirators ('fox' and 'fly') and their three victims ('vulture', 'raven' and 'crow').

In one sense, the interferences that result from the juxtaposition of these three plot sequences have the function of creating suspense and dramatic irony; at the same time, though, they are also combined with satirical emphasis and exaggeration to create a picture of a society dominated by unscrupulous greed. Voltore, the sly lawyer who is unashamedly prepared to bend the law, the senile Corbaccio, who is ready to disinherit his own son, and the jealous Corvino who is willing to gamble with his wife's chastity and honour are not only variations on the theme of a kind of avarice that perverts all moral norms and human relationships; they also represent a universally applicable pattern of behaviour and a satirical picture of the way of the world.

These three parallel plots, which reach a premature conclusion in the court scene in Act IV, vi, are followed by a fourth plot sequence in the last act, which as a kind of comic inversion of the preceding acts, follows the pattern of the duper duped and shows how Volpone himself becomes the victim of an intrigue. Although this plot sequence takes up less space than the ones before, it is nonetheless conducted on the same level for the very reason that the emphatic reversal of roles of swindler and victim constitutes a clear reference to the preceding plot sequences and also because the new conflict between the two conspirators Volpone and Mosca is particularly interesting in itself.

At the same time, the plot sequence involving Sir Politic Wouldbe, Madam Wouldbe and Peregrine clearly has the status of a hierarchically subordinate subplot.[31] One might argue that it is connected with the main plots through the figure of Madam Wouldbe, who is similarly trying to ingratiate herself with Volpone, and through the allegorical framework of the animal fable (Peregrine = falcon and Pol = parrot). It certainly reworks some of the same motifs. Nonetheless, the scenes involving Sir Politic and Peregrine (II,i and ii; IV,i; V,iv) appear as a relatively autonomous kind of digression. They contain their own exposition and the dénouement is separable from the court scenes (V,x and xii) in which the four main plots are resolved. This subplot also proceeds on a different thematic level to the legacy intrigues in the main plots inasmuch as Peregrine's gulling of Sir Politic's interminable references to political conspiracies and technical projects is to be regarded as the punishment of a relatively harmless folly rather than the serious vices of the main plots. This subplot is also isolated from the others configurationally, in that the dialogical contact between Sir Politic and Peregrine and the figures of the main plots is extremely sporadic and because, as Englishmen, they remain outsiders in Venetian society. It is therefore relatively closed, which is supported by the fact that it has often been omitted from stage productions of the text. It has virtually no innate significance and is completely consumed by the function of alleviating the darker satire of the main plots, of providing a burlesque counterpoint to the central thematic structures (identity and transformation) and of complementing the picture of Venetian vices with their English follies.

6.3.1.3. Linking devices

This play can also be used to demonstrate the most important devices used to link coordinated sequences. The most direct and most obvious of these is the overlapping of actions or events, in which one action or event figures in two different sequences at the same time. In *Volpone*, this kind of overlapping or interlocking is particularly important in linking the various main plots and it becomes more frequent as the play develops. Thus, the premature appearance of Corvino and Celia (III,vii) thwarts Mosca's shrewdly laid plans and leads directly to a situation in which Bonario, Corbaccio's son, witnesses Volpone's attempt to seduce and rape Celia, and then saves her, thereby almost exposing the intrigues against both Corvino and Corbaccio.

In addition to – and usually intimately bound up with – the interlocking of a number of different strands of action or chains of events there is a further binding technique that consists of overlapping figure constellations. Thus, the first three main plots in *Volpone* are linked by the very fact that the parts of the conspirators are always played by Mosca and Volpone whereas their victims vary from Voltore to Corbaccio and Bonario, and Corvino and Celia. In the fourth main plot Mosca is the only one to retain the part of a conspirator for, although Volpone still confidently imagines he is one, too, in reality he has already become a victim. The other figures, however, remain the victims they were. By overlapping figure constellations the dramatist is also able to link the subplot involving Sir Politic Wouldbe, his wife and Peregrine with the other subplots by including Madam Wouldbe in the series of visitors to Volpone's sick-bed (III,iv), even if not as a legacy hunter.

In contrast to the linking techniques outlined above, which, taken on their own, are only capable of establishing a rather superficial and obvious form of coherence, situative and thematic equivalences create a deeper, inner connection between the various strands of plot. Thus, in *Volpone*, the links on the levels of action and figure constellation point up significant similarity in situation and theme. The four main plots all centre around the legacy-hunter motif and – as we showed in the previous section – they are all concerned with the subject of avarice perverting the natural and moral order. It should be added that such equivalences are also reflected in the microstructure of the text. Examples of this are the iterative metaphors borrowed from the animal kingdom that do not merely reflect the allegorical and didactic intentions of the fable, but also serve to demonstrate the degradation of man to a predatory and necrophagous animal, thereby inverting the hierarchy of the 'great chain of being'. This thematic equivalence also represents the most important link between Peregrine's intrigue against Sir Politic and the main plot: when Sir Politic hides inside a tortoiseshell in Act V, iv to save himself from supposed police persecution because of his political projects, he unwittingly provides a dramatically vivid example of the same transformation from man to animal that the other figures had undergone on a purely verbal and metaphorical level – though of course there is a subtle distinction between them as the relatively harmless follies of Sir Politic are associated with the relatively harmless image of the tortoise with its emblematic references to the virtues of wise circumspection and silence, whereas those driven by the more serious vice of avarice are identified with more threatening species from the natural world.

6.3.1.4. Functions

In accordance with the methodological assumption that structure and function are interdependent and yet not identical we should now – having dealt with the structures and techniques – like to examine in detail the functions associated with the coordination of sequences. In doing so we shall attempt to grade the possible functions according to how universally or specifically they can be applied.

According to this criterion, the most universally applicable level is presumably the one associated with the aesthetic values of *varietas* and *copia* – or variety and abundance. In Elizabethan theatre, for example, and in the pre-Shakespearean plays in particular, sequences are frequently coordinated in a way that encourages the enjoyment of variety and abundance as ends in themselves.[32] In dramas of this kind tragic sequences alternate with comic sequences and in some cases the playwright completely omits – or at best merely hints at – any kind of connection on the levels of action and the figure constellations. The sudden switch from tragic pathos to burlesque comedy and vice versa and the broad sociological spectrum of the numerous protagonists stretching from the aristocratic figures of the main plot to the servant figures of the subplot in a play such as Richard Bower's *A New Tragicall Comedie of Apius and Virginia* (*c.* 1564)[33] constitute an ideal example of this compound form. The juxtaposition of the tragic and the burlesque is not a device used to play off the various sequences against each other, nor are they linked thematically. It is simply a way of providing comic relief, of liberating and relaxing the audience emotionally and of satisfying its need for variety and abundance.[34]

However, the notion of variety for variety's sake has been wildly exaggerated, especially by the older generations of critics of Shakespeare and his contemporaries. They often simply failed to perceive more far-reaching dramatic and thematic functions. A classic example of this is the debate that revolved around the function of the gate-keeper scene in *Macbeth* (II,iii) with the dialogue between the drunken gate-keeper and Macduff and Lennox, who request admission to Macbeth's castle immediately after the murder of King Duncan (II,ii). Samuel Taylor Coleridge was one who was unable to see this grotesque episode as anything more than a 'disgusting passage' inserted by the actors to please the mob's desire for variety and laughter.[35] It was left for Thomas De Quincey, in his influential essay 'On the knocking at the gate in *Macbeth*' (1823), to put forward the notion that this scene fulfilled the important function of providing a link between the murder scene and a new dramatic counter-movement:

Hence it is, that when the deed is done, when the work of darkness is perfect, then the world of darkness passes away like a pageantry in the clouds: the knocking at the gate is heard; and it makes known audibly that the reaction has commenced; the human has made its reflux on the fiendish; the pulses of life are beginning to beat again; and the re-establishment of the goings-on of the world in which we live, first makes us profoundly sensible of the awful parenthesis that had suspended them.[36]

In this case, then, the immediate juxtaposition of horror and the grotesque has the twofold function of contrasting two extreme aspects of existence so as to magnify the sense of horror felt at the preceding murder scene, and of marking, dramatically, the beginning of a counter-movement involving the powers of life. This interpretation also throws into relief the dramatic ironies of this scene in the way that the gate-keeper's ignorant and drunken talk of his job as the 'devil-porter' of hell and of 'the primrose way to th' everlasting bonfire' reminds the audience of the murder and indeed the murderer himself.

One of the functions fulfilled by the coordination of sequences that affects the overall structure of a work rather than just specific themes is the intensification of suspense (see above, 3.7.4.4.). This occurs whenever an action sequence is inserted into another just as the latter is about to reach what the audience anticipates as the climax. By embedding one sequence into another the playwright is able to broaden the arc of suspense and thus increase its duration and intensity. Once again, Ben Jonson's *Volpone* will serve as an example. In the final scenes of Act III, for example, the positions of Volpone and Mosca reach crisis point as a result of the unforeseen interferences between the various strands of the intrigue that we described above: it seems that public exposure of their villainy is both inevitable and imminent. And yet, the next scene (IV,i) does not bring the expected crisis and the release of suspense that would accompany it. Instead, the author inserts an episode from the subplot involving Sir Politic and Peregrine consisting of a leisurely dialogue that has absolutely nothing to do with the legacy-hunter intrigues and has little dramatic value in itself. The audience is left in a state of suspense until the main plot is resumed in the court scenes in IV,iv–vi.

If there are situative or thematic equivalences linking the various sequences, then they also have what might be described as an integrative function. This was an aspect that was given particular prominence in the context of German romantic aesthetic theory, in which the concept of the organic unity of the work of art, the organic cohesion of all its constituent elements was a central theme. Friedrich Schlegel, for one, admired the consistency with which Shakespeare was able to weld his dramas into organically structured, complex wholes by employing 'those antitheses with which he contrasts individuals, crowds and even worlds in picturesque groups' together with a 'musical symmetry on the same grandiose scale' and 'gigantic repetitions and refrains'.[37] However, the two types of relationships that Schlegel mentions – antithesis and repetition – should not be understood as two autonomous dimensions. They are related dialectically to the extent that contrasts can only be perceived when placed against a background of similarities and, conversely, similarities are not simply based on the repetition of identical elements but always include deviating, and therefore contrasting elements.

However, the various similarities and contrasts have functions other than simply contributing towards the aesthetically pleasing, self-contained beauty of the dramatic structure. They also serve a number of additional, quite specific thematic functions. One of these is mirroring, or the way equivalent sequences clarify and modify each other.[38] In many of Shakespeare's comedies, for example, each of the two or more parallel love-plots is a reflection of the other, and by contrasting two different concepts of love – such as coarse and sensual eroticism, platonic or petrarchian love, ironically muted depth of feeling etc. – the dramatist is able to define them with greater precision and subtlety and to use the one to undermine ironically the credibility of the other.[39]

Since it contravenes the economy principle, the repetition of similar elements also has a decidedly emphatic function which gives the repeated element greater prominence. This applies to the coordination of the action sequences involving Lear and Gloucester in *King Lear*, for example, as August Wilhelm Schlegel realised:

The two cases resemble each other in the main: an infatuated father is blind towards his well-disposed child, and the unnatural children, whom he prefers, requite him by the ruin of all his happiness ... Were Lear alone to suffer from his daughters, the impression would be limited to the powerful compassion felt by us for his private misfortune. But two such unheard of examples taking place at the same time have the appearance of a great commotion in the moral world: the picture becomes gigantic, and fills us with such alarm as we should entertain at the idea that the heavenly bodies might one day fall from their appointed orbits.[40]

The emphasis on, and intensification of, the tragic effect that this produces corresponds to an analogous intensification of the comic effect in comedy. According to Bergson the repetition of situations and events is in itself potentially comic. Moreover, the extreme accumulation and exaggerated pattern of correspondences – a common feature of comic texts in particular – represents a stylisation principle that may be used to expose the play as an artifact by emphasising the obvious artificiality of the symmetries.

The final function in our necessarily incomplete catalogue can again be illustrated by taking the Gloucester subplot in *King Lear* as an example: it is the function of generalisation. Lear's fate, taken in isolation, may appear to be a special case but when a similar fate befalls Gloucester it assumes more universal significance and is generalised suggestively to represent the way of the world. This has already been emphasised by A. C. Bradley:

This repetition does not simply double the pain with which the tragedy is witnessed: it startles and terrifies by suggesting that the folly of Lear and the ingratitude of his daughters are no accidents or merely individual aberrations, but that in that dark cold world some fateful malignant influence is abroad, turning the hearts of the fathers against their children and of the children against their fathers...[41]

6.3.2. The superimposition of sequences

Coordinated sequences are situated on one and the same fictional level. Super- or subordinate sequences, on the other hand, are situated on different fictional levels. What this means is that a primary dramatic level, whose ontological status is characterised by the fictionality of dramatic presentation, contains within it a secondary dramatic level that introduces an additional fictional element. The two most important forms that exploit this hierarchical arrangement of fictional levels are the dream inset, in which the additional fictional element consists of the unreality of the dream and its concrete manifestations on stage, and the play-within-the-play, in which the fictionality of dramatic presentation is strengthened by the introduction of a secondary fictional level in the form of a theatrical performance embedded in the structural framework of the primary dramatic level.

6.3.2.1. Dream inset

Dreams in drama represent sequences of actions or events that are imagined by one of the figures of the play. Like every other kind of sequence
they can be either presented scenically or mediated narratively. The most
common form is the narratively mediated dream,[42] probably because it is
the easiest to realise on stage and does not require any additional conventions of presentation. One borderline case is the dream soliloquy, in which
the speaker does not relate an earlier dream, but actually speaks whilst
dreaming. In this case the dreamer and the act of dreaming are presented
multimedially on stage but the dreamed sequences themselves are narrated
in purely verbal form.[43] In the dream inset, by contrast, the dreamed
sequences are also staged multimedially and the stage is transformed into
the inner chambers of the dreamer's mind. Of course, when this happens it
is crucial that the transition from the superordinate primary dramatic level
to the inserted level of the dream is signalled to the audience and a separate
code of conventions has been developed to do that. However, the signs
used in such cases are iconic, which means that they can even be understood by an audience that is unfamiliar with this dramatic convention.

Two examples will suffice to illustrate this, namely Franz Grillparzer's
The Dream: A Life (*Der Traum ein Leben*) and Arthur Schnitzler's one-act
play *The Woman with the Dagger* (*Die Frau mit dem Dolche*) from the
cycle *Lively Hours* (*Lebendige Stunden*). In both texts, the subordinate
dream sequences are directly connected with the events taking place on the
primary level inasmuch as the experiences encountered in the dream help
the figure to reach a decision in a critical situation. Grillparzer's Rustan
dreams about the corrupting effects and deceptiveness of the search for
fame and fortune and so, upon wakening, he submits himself, liberated
and content, to the unheroic Chippendale-idyll with Massud and Mirza. In
her own particular dream, which is stimulated by a Renaissance portrait of
a woman with a dagger, Schnitzler's Pauline imagines herself in an earlier
incarnation as Paola, the wife of the painter Remigio, and stabs Lionardo,
her lover for one night, to death. Convinced that 'a fate hangs over her
from which she cannot escape'[44] she then grants her present lover
Leonhard the night of love that he so much desires. Whilst Rustan's dream
pre-empts the life of adventure and adulation that he strives after and
anticipates a future that he then decides to abandon when he wakes up,
Pauline's dream, based as it is on the myth of reincarnation, is linked
retrospectively to a previous incarnation which is an almost faithful reproduction of her present situation, thus exposing the present as no more than
a totally predetermined reworking of a familiar kind of tragic triangle of
love. Whilst Rustan's dream enables him to change his course of action for
the better, Pauline's merely reinforces the futility of all autonomous action

in the face of the predetermined inevitability of everything that happens to her.

These differences in the thematic conceptions underlying the two dream insets demonstrate the philosophical distance between Grillparzer and Schnitzler. Nonetheless, we do not need to dwell on them any further because our main concern here is with the formal structural aspects of the way the subordinate sequences are embedded in the text. In this respect there are a number of noticeable similarities. In both Grillparzer and Schnitzler, the embedding and embedded sequences are closely linked by sets of clear thematic and situative equivalents and, in particular, by the fact that the dreamer appears as the active subject of the dream. A further feature shared by these two texts is the fact that the subordinate dream sequence outweighs the superordinate sequence of the primary level, at least in quantitative terms, leaving the latter to serve as a dramatic framework introducing and concluding the dream sequence. From this, it is clear that the hierarchical arrangement of super- or subordination merely describes the ontological relationship between the sequences and not the dramatic focalisation, i.e. the theatrical or thematic predominance of one element over another. The quantitative predominance of the dream inset over the primary dramatic level is considerably more pronounced in Grillparzer's play than it is in Schnitzler's but not even that is an extreme case. On a typological scale which arranges the texts in ascending order according to the length of the inset, and the decrease in the size of the primary dramatic framework, this extreme position would be filled by a text in which the superordinate framework no longer exists and which is completely taken up with the dream. An example of this kind of text is Strindberg's *Dream Play* (without a prologue in the original version).[45] Going beyond Strindberg's preface, in which he said that in his *Dream Play* he had attempted to imitate 'the disconnected but apparently logical form of a dream',[46] we can interpret the drama *in toto* as the scenic presentation of a dream, with the implied author (S3) or receiver (R3) as the dreamer (see above, 1.2.2.), since there is no primary dramatic framework introducing a fictional dreamer figure.

A similar situation occurs in Shakespeare's *A Midsummer Night's Dream* when Puck in his epilogue refers back epically to the title of the play and invites the audience to interpret the play as something it has dreamt:

> If we shadows have offended,
> Think but this, and all is mended,
> That you have but slumbered here
> While the visions did appear.   (V,i,412–15)

However, the difference between this and Strindberg is, of course, the fact that the notion of the play as one single scenically presented dream is not really conclusive in this particular case. It is more like a playful after-thought which does not have any profound effect on the way the text as a whole is received — unless, of course, a director bases his whole *mise-en-scène* consistently, and thus one-sidedly, on the title of the play and the epilogue.

Unlike Strindberg's frameless *Dream Play*, the plays by Schnitzler and Grillparzer, which are examples of a communicatively unambiguous and unproblematic norm, contain a clearly marked dividing-line separating the primary fictional level and the subordinate level of the dream inset with its twofold characteristics of fictionality and fantasy. Both texts prepare the receiver for the concrete physical presentation of an imaginary, psychological reality through the actual utterances of the figure con-cerned. With the words 'I am tired, my brow grows heavy, Weariness o'ertakes my limbs'[47] Rustan sinks down on to a bed to rest and, in the dialogue passages that precede the dream inset in Schnitzler's play, Pauline appears to be 'lost in thought' (p. 706) before she finally sits down on a couch, completely preoccupied with the portrait of the woman with a dagger. The actual transition is then marked by a number of obvious scenic signals both acoustic (a harp is heard which is joined by other instruments playing soft music; the midday bells toll and suddenly fall silent) and visual (the backdrop opens to reveal a wooded landscape through a veil; the stage grows dark, and after a quick change of scene, is illuminated again). Grillparzer goes even further, introducing an emblematic presentation involving a serpent in a palm tree and an allegorical pantomime involving two boys bearing torches, in which the boy dressed in brown (the waking world) gives light to the boy dressed in a multicoloured costume (the dream world) and then extinguishes his torch. Schnitzler, on the other hand, differentiates metrically between the blank verse of the dream set in Renaissance Italy and the prose of the primary action that takes place in contemporary Vienna.

Subordinate dream sequences of this kind can fulfil a variety of different functions, from characterisation, plot motivation and thematic mirroring to implicit references to the theatrical medium itself. The first and last of these are functions specifically associated with this form of plot combina-tion. Thus, like the soliloquy (see above, 4.5.2.1.), the dream inset is an anti-realist convention that eliminates — or at least weakens — the restric-tions imposed by the dramatic medium on the presentation of inner, psychological processes (see above, 5.2.2.). It enables the dramatist to present an extreme form of subjectivisation which binds not only the verbal utterances but also complete multimedially presented sequences to a particular figure-perspective. The relationship between the dreamer and the dream inset is analogous to that between the implied author and the text as a whole. This analogy also underlies the potential of the dream inset to expose the medium of drama by referring to it implicitly. The imaginative quality of the subjective 'psychodrama' of the dream inset – 'psychodrama' here not meant in the psychotherapeutical sense used by Moreno – acts as a metaphorical model for the fictionality of dramatic presentation because what fantasy and fiction share is an element of non-reality or illusion. With that, however, an implicit poetological programme may suggest that the fictionality of drama is not only illusionary like a dream; it may also claim that its view of reality reaches towards the profound truths of a dream.

6.3.2.2. The play-within-the-play

In a play-within-the-play one group of dramatic figures from the superordinate sequences performs a play (the subordinate sequences) to another group of figures.[48] By inserting a second fictional level into the text the dramatist duplicates the performance situation of the external communication system on the internal level. The fictional audience on stage corresponds to the real audience in the auditorium and the fictional authors, actors and directors correspond to their real-life counterparts in the production of the text. In theory, the process of inserting a secondary level of fiction into the primary level can be repeated *ad infinitum* (a third level may be inserted into the second etc.). However, in practical terms the process of raising fictionality to the third, fourth or fifth power is hampered by the audience's limited capability of digesting such a complex hierarchy of sequences and fictional levels. Ludwig Tieck's romantic comedy *When the World is Upside Down* deliberately sets out to explore these limits, to the extent that it even contains fictional spectator figures who discuss this very problem:

Look – here we sit watching a play; in this play more people sit watching another play, and in this third play, the third actors are watching yet another play![49]

What this *tour de force* of romantic irony demonstrates all too clearly is also true of the ordinary play-within-the-play: theatre and drama become their own themes and foreground the nature of the relationship between the real audience and the real performance. Moreover, by foregrounding the dramatic illusion, illusionism may be exposed as problematic. In extreme cases, such as the plays by Tieck or Pirandello, this may be part of a calculated attempt to disorientate the audience by blurring the lines dividing appearance and reality or reality and fiction and may tempt it into thinking of reality itself as an illusory drama in the sense of the topos of the world as a stage (see above, 2.4.1.). One of the fictional spectators in *When the World is Upside Down* is provoked into speculating as follows:

Now just imagine, my friends, how it might be possible that we were actors in some play and one of us began to get everything mixed up. In these circumstances we would be Play No 1. Perhaps that is how the angels see us; if one of those spectating angels could see us now wouldn't he be running the risk of going mad?

This is indeed true, as the real audience is well aware, except that it is wont to seeing itself in the role of the 'angels' and is therefore encouraged to regard itself *sub specie angelorum* as an only seemingly real audience in its own right. Similarly, the plays-within-the-play that Pirandello introduced to complicate the dramatic illusion in his own plays are designed, though for different philosophical reasons, to expose reality itself as a necessarily feigned fiction. In *La lettre* (1924) he wrote:

I believe that life is an extremely tragic farce, for the reason that, without being able either to know or recognise either why or from whom, we carry within ourselves the need constantly to delude ourselves by creating a reality of our own volition (a different one for each person, and never the same for everyone) which is then exposed from time to time as vain and false.[50]

A typological analysis of the play-within-the-play must pay particular attention to two criteria: the quantitative relationship between the primary action and the play-within-the-play and the links between the various figures on these two levels. As far as the second criterion is concerned, J. Voigt[51] has developed a systematic typology that really needs to be no more than sketched out here. The relationship between the hierarchically arranged plot sequences is at its most tenuous when the play-within-the-play is performed by a separate set of figures – that is, when the fictional actors representing the figures in the play-within-the-play either never appear in the superordinate plot sequences at all or, if they do, then only on the periphery. Thus, in the prologue (induction) to Shakespeare's *The Taming of the Shrew*, for example, the drunken tinker Sly is treated like the lord of the manor by a high-spirited court when he wakes up from one of his drinking bouts and they arrange a performance of the comedy proper – the play-within-the-play – for him. However, the arrival of the troupe of actors is merely announced by a messenger (Induction, ii,126–33) whilst the actors themselves only appear briefly in the first scene of the prologue and then later, from I,i solely in the roles prescribed by the play-within-the-play. In *Hamlet*, on the other hand, the arrival of the actors is first announced by Rosencrantz and Polonius (II,ii,312–71 and 385–97), and they then also appear in dialogues with Hamlet discussing their repertoire and the play that they are to perform (II,ii,416–539) before actually getting round to performing their play-within-the-play about 'The Murder of Gonzago' (III,iii,131–254). Nonetheless, as actors they remain clearly separate from the remaining figures on the primary dramatic level since their connection with them is restricted to their function as a troupe of actors that has been invited to give a performance at court.

The connection between the two levels is more direct when the sets of figures are identical – that is, when the fictional actors in the play-within-the-play also appear as figures in their own right in the primary sequences. An example of this is the workmen's play in A Midsummer Night's Dream. The workmen appear periodically throughout the play and are seen preparing and rehearsing their 'tedious brief scene of young Pyramus /And his love Thisbe' (V,i,56f.). Quite apart from his function as the actor in the role of Pyramus, their leader, Bottom, plays a particularly important part in the superordinate sequences because his metamorphosis into a donkey and Titania's love for him (III,i, IV,i) are a part of the conflict between Oberon and Titania and thus the primary dramatic action.

Finally, there is one special structure of identity in which the figures of the play-within-the-play are transformed into figures on the primary level. The play-within-the-play begins with an apparently autonomous set of figures but these then begin to participate or interfere in the superordinate sequences of the primary action. Arthur Schnitzler's grotesque one-act drama The Green Cockatoo (Der grüne Kakadu) is one example of a play that is based on this structure. In this play, set at the time of the French Revolution, a troupe of actors acts out a fictional and quasi-theatrical drama about the world of criminals and revolutionaries in a run-down bar in Paris and with an aristocratic audience that is decadent enough to find pleasure in such horrors. The actor Henri interrupts this play-within-the-play with the news that his wife's lover, the Duke of Cadignan, has been murdered, thereby disconcerting both the fictional and the real audience since it is not known whether this news is supposed to be fact or fiction. The decision on the part of Prospère, landlord and director of the troupe, to take the report seriously leads to Henri discovering his wife's actual infidelity and then going on to murder the Duke.

This series of structural types derived from the relationship between the sets of actors on the two dramatic levels must be complemented by an analysis of the role played by the fictional spectators. These may also participate in the play-within-the-play and in a broad variety of ways. In its most reduced form the fictional audience is simply present on stage and remains silent. Thus, after the play-within-the-play has got under way in The Taming of the Shrew Sly and his fellow spectators speak just once more, and then only briefly (immediately after I,i), before falling completely silent, and it is only their physical presence on stage that signals the doubled fictionality of the presentation. In most other cases, however, the spectators act as commentator figures, by discussing either the poetological implications of the play – as they do in Ben Jonson's Every Man Out of His Humour – or – as they do in Hamlet – the implications of the play-within-the-play for the primary sequences in which they themselves also participate. The relationship between the fictional spectators and the play-within-the-play becomes even closer if the former do not just discuss it amongst themselves but actually enter into a dialogue with the fictional actors, author, stage-designer or director. This occurs repeatedly in Shakespeare's *A Midsummer Night's Dream* and Ludwig Tieck's *Puss in Boots* (*Der gestiefelte Kater*), for instance. This device is only possible if the play-within-the-play contains epic communication structures that constantly undermine the absolute autonomy of its dramatic fiction. Tieck intensifies the anti-illusionist aspect when he allows the 'Jackpudding' or 'Hanswurst' figure to address the real audience as a dialogue partner and has the fictional audience – Fischer and Müller, who imagine they are the ones being addressed – react to his comments with a complete lack of comprehension:

> JACKPUDDING (towards the parterre): Both of us now stand on intimate terms and sympathise in matters of good taste and he [i.e. Leander, the court scholar] attempts to assert, against my opinion that the public in *Puss in Boots*, at least, is well drawn.
> FISCHER: The public? Why, no public appears in the play.
> JACKPUDDING: Better yet! So no public appears in it at all?
> MÜLLER: Certainly not, unless he means the several kinds of fools who appear.   (p. 109)

The sudden breaks in the illusion, the contrast between the totally anti-illusionist stance of the Jackpudding figure that enables him to see through the fictionality of both the primary action and the play-within-the-play and the partially anti-illusionist audience which is aware of the fictionality of the play-within-the-play but not of its own, creates a special kind of comic discrepancy of awareness (see above, 3.4.) in which romantic irony is used to subvert the play as a whole.

The highest level of audience activity is achieved when the audience actually intervenes in the action itself rather than just participating in a verbal dialogue with the actors in the play-within-the-play. One of the earliest examples of this occurs in Beaumont and Fletcher's *The Knight of the Burning Pestle* (1607) when George, the shopkeeper, and his wife – as spectators – send their apprentice Ralph on to the stage of the play-within-the-play to ensure that the shopkeeper-class is at last worthily represented in a heroic drama. Tieck's spectator figure Grünhelm, who hopes to become the comic figure, and the spectators who storm the stage in *The World Upside Down* (pp. 93ff.) were clearly influenced by this model. Pirandello, who was familiar with the writings of Tieck and Friedrich Schlegel, is clearly a playwright in this particular tradition, too.

The quantitative relations between the super- and subordinate plot sequences are as variable in the context of the play-within-the-play as they are for the dream inset. The play-within-the-play either takes the form of a short episode inserted into a more extensive sequence of primary action, which thus carries the predominant focus of the text, or it is both quantitatively and qualitatively superior to the primary sequences, which are then reduced to acting as a kind of frame – sometimes in the form of a prologue or induction. Of Shakespeare's plays, *A Midsummer Night's Dream* and *Hamlet* are examples of the first and *The Taming of the Shrew* is an example of the second. In *Bartholomew Fair*, Ben Jonson employed the first technique, and in *Every Man Out of His Humour*, *The Devil is an Ass*, *The Staple of News* and *The Magnetic Lady* the second.

These two structural types, which are separated by a whole spectrum of intermediary forms, differ in functional as well as qualitative terms. For if the play-within-the-play forms just a brief episode in the play as a whole it is generally closely linked up with the action on the primary level: Hamlet arranges for a performance of 'The Murder of Gonzago' in order to pass judgement on the murderer of his father, and the play enacted by the workmen in *A Midsummer Night's Dream* represents the culmination of the wedding celebrations of Theseus and Hippolyta and the quartet of lovers. If, however, the primary sequences are reduced to little more than a mere frame for the action in the play-within-the-play then this frame serves to intensify the fictional quality of the dramatic form and functions as an alienating device. By enabling, furthermore, the fictional actors and spectators to comment on the central play-within-the-play the frame assumes the function of an epic mediating communication system inserted between the play-within-the-play and the real audience (see above, 3.6.2.2.). In this way Ben Jonson frequently made use of commentaries from the fictional audience to underline the theoretical assumptions underlying his plays, and Brecht, in his *Caucasian Chalk Circle* introduced an outer frame in the form of a discussion on the future of the valley in order to place the chalk circle story into a particular perspective and thus to bring out the exemplary character of this legend-like story with regard to the establishment of law in a socialist community.

To conclude we should like to examine one specific example – the play-within-the-play in *A Midsummer Night's Dream* – to demonstrate the multifunctionality of this segment of the text and, in doing so, to analyse more closely those functions that have not been discussed before. The macrostructure of this text consists of a hierarchically graded pattern of four interlocked sequences – the primary amorous confusions surrounding Hermia, Lysander, Helena and Demetrius, the quarrel between Titania and Oberon, the preparations for Theseus' and Hippolyta's wedding and the theatrical activities of the group of workmen. All four sequences follow a similarly structured pattern involving a transition from a dynamic situation filled with potential conflict and suspense to one that is static and, once reached, marks the end of the text. The conflicts within the quartet of lovers and that between Oberon and Titania are resolved and the preparations for both the marriage of Theseus and Hippolyta and the theatrical performance are successfully concluded. Thus, the play-within-the-play is integrated into a system of equivalent structures and this is emphasised by the fact that it is motivated from within the context of the wedding preparations.

Moreover, it is also linked with the sequences involving the two pairs of lovers in a number of thematic and situative ways. For like the conflict-ridden plot sequences involving the lovers, the tragedy of Pyramus and Thisbe relates the story of a love that is thwarted by parental opposition. Shakespeare invokes the mirroring principle (see above, 6.3.1.4.) to contrast the two different solutions to this kind of conflict – one is tragic, the other comic. Thus, within *A Midsummer Night's Dream* itself Shakespeare created the same highly suggestive contrast between a love-comedy and a love-tragedy that was also suggested by the chronological proximity of *A Midsummer Night's Dream* and *Romeo and Juliet* – both were written around 1595 – in the external communication system.

Of course, the tragedy of Pyramus and Thisbe is only related to *Romeo and Juliet* to the extent that they share a common central motif. In all other respects the workmen succeed in transforming it into an involuntarily comic persiflage of a tragedy. The play-within-the-play is thus assigned two additional functions. These serve the ideals of *varietas* and *copia* in ensuring the presence of carefree, burlesque comedy in a play otherwise dominated by plot sequences whose romance-like sensibilities and poetic quality create few opportunities for laughter. And, as a literary satire, this play-within-the-play also has a parodistical function: the announcement describing the play as a 'very tragical mirth' (V,i,57) is aimed at the kind of unthinking and purely additive mixture of genres in pre-Shakespearean drama that Sidney attacked in his contemporaneous *Apologie for Poetrie* (1595). By repeatedly disrupting the illusion Shakespeare is also parodying a dramaturgical concept in which epic communication structures are the rule rather than exceptions that are associated with a specific function. Moreover, the completely exaggerated and thus meaningless pathos of Pyramus' speech:

> O grim-look'd night! O night with hue so black!
> O night, which ever art when day is not!   (V,i,168f.)

lampoons the conventionalised rhetoric of the Elizabethan Seneca epigones.

It is important to remember, however, that the clumsy ineptitude of the workmen's performance is not simply intended as a parody of the 'primitive' dramaturgical skills of traditional popular drama. It is also designed to demonstrate the inadequacies of *all* theatrical presentations – including *A Midsummer Night's Dream* itself – and to emphasise the role played by the audience's imagination in making the dramatic illusion actually work. When the workmen ask the fictional audience to imagine that a particular actor represents a wall, the moon or a lion, then the difference between this and the level of fantasy that Shakespeare expects of his real audience when, for example, he repeatedly refers to the minute size of the fairies, despite the fact that their appearance suggests otherwise, is one of degree rather than principle. So, here, too, the play-within-the-play refers implicitly to the theatrical medium itself, thereby exposing it and distancing it from the real audience. This is further emphasised on the primary level in comments made by the fictional spectators:

> HIPPOLYTA: This is the silliest stuff that ever I heard.
> THESEUS: The best in this kind are but shadows; and the worst are no
> worse, if imagination amend them.
>
> (V,i,209–11)

Theseus' 'shadows' refer to the fictionality of dramatic presentation which is, after all, one of the key conventions of theatre. In fact, Puck uses this very word in his epically mediated epilogue (V,i,412) and applies it to the text as a whole which he regards retrospectively as a shadow-like dream-play (see above, 6.3.2.1.). And in the context of these implicit references to the fictional and illusory qualities of drama we should not omit the unwittingly comic dimension of the way Bottom and his comrades grotesquely exaggerate their ability to create a theatrical illusion in their play-within-the play and then believe that they must mitigate the effects of the gruesome events on their aristocratic audience by adding their own comments on the illusionary nature of their performance.

Related to the play-within-the-play, but nonetheless categorically separate from it, are the various forms of deception and disguise in both tragedies and comedies that constitute play-acting within the play.[52] This also means that there are figures in the drama playing other roles in the presence of other figures but in this case the roles are feigned rather than fictional. As feigned role-play, play-acting within the play is deliberately intended as a way of deceiving other figures in the play, whereas fictionality is founded on an agreement between actors and audience as to the special ontological status – the illusory quality – of a performance. Deception or disguise is therefore not a subordinate sequence embedded in the primary action in the way that applies to dream insets and plays-within-the-play but is itself a part of that primary action. If we nonetheless discuss it briefly in this context then this is because it produces certain structures that are similar in both form and function to those of the play-within-the-play. This applies especially to the appearance of spectators on stage functioning as commentator figures. Eavesdropping scenes are especially clear examples of this[53] since they show the actions of an innocent victim being observed and commented on by a group of initiated spectator figures (as in *Twelfth Night*, II,v). The same applies to feigned eavesdropping scenes, in which the conspirators act out a scene that they ensure is being witnessed by their innocent victim (as in *Much Ado About Nothing*, II,iii and III,i). In such cases, the spatial arrangement of the groups of figures reminds us of the performance situation in the play-within-the-play and, in addition, the preparation, performance and retrospective discussion of the deception often makes use of theatrical terminology. The fictionality of drama thus becomes a metaphorical model for the falseness of the game of deception and theatre metaphors refer implicitly to the inherent fictionality of drama as a whole which is thus exposed.[54]

6.4. Segmentation and composition

6.4.1. The segmentation of the story and the story-presentation

The macrostructure of a dramatic text – indeed of every kind of text – takes the form of a syntagmatic pattern of its constituent elements. It consists of several larger sections which, in turn, may be divided into subsections almost *ad infinitum*. The number of relevant layers of subdivision varies from text to text. Open dramas, for example, will be constructed much less hierarchically than closed dramas (see below, 6.4.3.). However, the number of levels on which macrostructural segmentation takes place is the same for all narrative and dramatic texts: the story and the presentation of that story (see above, 6.1.1.2.). The deep-structural level – the story on which the presentation is based – is divided up according to certain semantic and logical criteria and the most important layers in ascending order are individual actions or events, phases of actions or events and sequences of actions and events. Structural segmentation on the surface, on the other hand – the dramatic presentation of the story – is marked by changes in configuration, interruptions in the chronological and spatial continuity and additional signals such as lowering or raising the curtain, intervals and, most important historically, the division into scenes and acts.

Having divided this segmentation process into two or more levels, we must now establish how these different types of segmentation correlate. In theory, there are two possible answers. That is, the deep- and surface-structural segments can either correspond to each other or they can contradict each other. Neither of these two extremes – that is, complete corres-

pondence or identity, and complete discord – has ever been a feature of a
dramatic text. Nonetheless, every single text occupies an intermediary
position on a sliding-scale depending on which of the two extremes it
resembles more.

We have decided to focus our critical energies on Racine's *Phèdre* in
order to clarify this whole question. Lack of space, however, will prevent
us from discussing anything more than the most salient structural units.
The surface structure of the text – that is, the literary text used in performance – is divided into five sections, each of which is clearly marked by a
complete change of configuration, the interruption of spatial and chronological continuity, by intervals and the raising or lowering of the curtain.
Apart from the third, which is rather shorter, these five 'acts' are roughly
equal in length and hardly even differ in the number of 'scenes' (the three
inner acts, II to IV, each consists of six, the first and last acts of five and
seven scenes respectively). The structural units 'y' that deviate (slightly)
from 'x' are distributed according to the principle of axial symmetry, with
regard to both length of the acts and the number of individual scenes:
xxyxx or yxxxy.[55]

The question is, of course, whether this clear and symmetrical structure
correlates with the segmentation pattern in the story, whether the division
into acts coincides with the phases of the story on the deeper level. In this it
is important to remember that the story behind *Phèdre* is presented, in line
with the Aristotelian or classicist demand for 'unity of plot', as one closed
plot sequence held together essentially by an uninterrupted causal nexus.[56]
Thus, the surface-structural division into acts cannot, to start with, correspond to any completely or relatively independent units on the deeper level.
Instead, they can only correspond, at best, to less clearly marked divisions
between individual successive and causally linked phases of action.

If we omit the extensive phases of the background events which affect
Thésée, Phèdre, Hippolyte and Aricie and which are related in narrative
form, then it is possible to divide the scenically enacted part of the story
into three phases.[57] The first phase develops the initial situation as a kind
of 'impasse': Hippolyte is in love with Aricie but various dynastic considerations prevent him from courting her or revealing his true feelings to her;
Phèdre, in turn, is in love with her stepson Hippolyte, but she too is unable
to reveal her true feelings because she is bound to her husband Thésée. For
both, the obstacles separating them – embodied in the figure of Thésée –
and the objects of their love seem unsurmountable. As a way out of this
dilemma, Hippolyte plans to run away but Phèdre sees no escape and
languishes with grief. The second phase begins with the news that Thésée is
apparently dead. This news opens up new possibilities for both figures:
Hippolyte finally confesses his love to Aricie and discovers that she har-
bours similar feelings for him. Phèdre confesses her own love for Hippo-

lyte and is rejected. Finally, the third phase begins with the news that Thésée has survived after all, and he arrives soon afterwards. At the instigation of her confidante Oenone, Phèdre reacts by initiating a campaign of defamation against Hippolyte, claiming that he had tried to seduce her, but then, in the conflict between self-preservation and jealousy on the one hand, and ethical principles on the other, she chooses to abide by the latter, rejects Oenone, who immediately commits suicide, and then poisons herself. Thésée reacts to her calumny by sending Hippolyte into exile and placing a curse on him, though in doing so he has to struggle between the loyalty he feels towards his wife and that towards his son. Hippolyte, in turn, reacts to the calumny and the threat of exile by planning to elope with Aricie but, as they flee, Thésée's curse catches up with them and Hippolyte is killed by a sea-monster.

The three phases outlined here may be summarised as the 'impasse' (1), 'the apparent resolution' (2) and 'the resolution' (3). The criterion which appears to be the decisive factor in the way they are divided into segments is the fact that the situation changes completely – that is, a change takes place that is much more far-reaching than those resulting from the actions of Phèdre and Hippolyte. The news first of Thésée's death and then his survival and arrival on the scene therefore correspond to peripeteia in the Aristotelian sense (*Poetics*, ch. 11).

The three action phases that result from this kind of division do not, however, correspond to the surface division of the text into five acts. Phase 1 covers I,i to I,iii, Phase 2 I,iv to III,ii and Phase 3 III,iii to V,iii. A further illustration of the way these two levels of segmentation do not coincide is the fact that the narrative mediation of the action phases associated with the background events is not completed at the end of Act I but continues well into Act II. Not only do the different levels of segmentation not coincide, they are actually structured contrastively. For while the story is divided according to the principle that each phase is longer than the one before, the length of the five sections of the play itself (i.e. the acts) remains relatively constant; and whereas the action phases of the story proceed in a linear succession, the series of acts is, as we have seen, cyclical and symmetrical.

What is the function of this absence of coordination between the two different segmentation processes? Is it really no more than the expression of a conscious desire for form, of a desire to create aesthetic stylisation as an end in itself, as Jacques Scherer claims:

. . . la structure externe a ses lois propres, qui ne sont nullement l'expression des tendances profondes de l'architecture interne de la pièce, mais manifestent au contraire l'imposition à la matière dramatique de formes extérieures, voulues par la conscience esthétique collective des auteurs classiques.[58]

In addition to this, however, it also functions as a way of creating emphasis, of controlling the focus of the presentation and thus of establishing interpretative links that were not yet present in the merely chronological and causal relations of the story. The way the dramatic presentation is divided into segments is therefore an important element in the structural transformation of the story into a plot.

Thus, by transferring the early phases of the story into concise expository narratives, the author shifts the emphasis on to the later phases. In *Phèdre*, the third and last of the scenically presented phases fills two and a half acts, that is half of the complete text. The focus of the play is thus directed at this final phase in which the situation is resolved so tragically. Had the segmentation methods been exactly the same on both levels it would also not have been possible to present the end of each act as climactic moments of dramatic suspense in the way that Racine managed to do.[59] It is the very fact that they do not coincide that prevents the end of each act from becoming a point of rest and that fills it with the precipitatory dynamism necessary to bridge the gaps between the acts. Thus, at the ends of those acts that occur in the middle of a phase of action, the author often questions the future course of events or the figures make some momentous decision that will influence those events; at the end of Act I Phèdre decides to tell Hippolyte of her love for him; at the end of Act II the rumour is circulated that Thésée is still alive after all and has already landed; Act III ends with Hippolyte's plan to tell his father of his love for Aricie and Act IV with Phèdre vacillating between the desire for jealous revenge and established moral norms and with her rejection of Oenone.[60]

These kinds of meaningful similarities in the structure of the individual acts do not merely occur at the ends of acts; they can also appear in other positions in the dramatic structure. Thus, the changes in the situation are measured against the background of various recurring configurations, such as the dialogues between Hippolyte, Phèdre and Aricie with their respective confidant(e)s, the soliloquies of Phèdre (III,ii and IV,v) and of Thésée (IV,iii and V,iv) and the encounters between Hippolyte and Phèdre and between Hippolyte and Aricie. Moreover, each act culminates in one or two 'great scenes' around which the other scenes are arranged: in Act I it is when Phèdre tells her confidante about her love for Hippolyte (I,iii), in Act II her declaration of love to Hippolyte himself (II,v) and in Act III the first meeting between Hippolyte and Thésée. Climaxes are reached in Act IV in the scenes when Thésée places a curse on Hippolyte (IV,ii) and Phèdre wrestles with her jealousy (IV, vi) and in Act V with Théramène's report of the death of Hippolyte (V,vi) and Phèdre's suicide (V,vii).[61] This arrangement enables the author to emphasise certain aspects that were only present in latent rather than concrete form in the story itself, as any comparison with the Phaedra plays by Euripides and Seneca would demonstrate. Overall, the tripartite linear and unequal phase structure is transformed into a five-part, axially symmetrical and balanced act structure, and the beginning of the third phase – the arrival of Thésée – becomes the central peripeteia of Act III; Acts I and II develop the conflict potential which then reaches crisis point and runs down in Acts IV and V.

This paradigmatic analysis of Racine's *Phèdre*, describing the relationship between the tripartite structure of the story and the five-act structure of the play, cannot be applied universally; in fact, it can only be applied to this text. What is universally valid, however, is the way two levels of segmentation are superimposed on each other and this we wanted to demonstrate. At the same time, it will presumably have become clear that, on the level of presentation, the segmentation process is based on a clear set of criteria that are easy to put into practice, whereas the division into phases on the level of the story can often be more problematic. The lack of preliminary studies of the theory of plot explaining the links between individual actions and phases of actions, and between phases of actions and sequences of actions, has forced us to rely on our own intuition in dividing up a story into a number of segments. In this particular rather straightforward case, however, we were guided by the hypothesis that in the formation of phases – just as in determining individual actions – the predominant prerequisite was that a change in the situation should occur, though with the difference that this change had to affect all the figures in the action phases rather than just a few of them.

6.4.2. The segmentation of the dramatic presentation

There are two aspects that a discussion of the surface–structural segmentation of the dramatic presentation must both take into consideration and yet, as far as possible, keep strictly apart: the systematic and ahistorical aspect of segmentation criteria and the historical aspect of segmentation conventions.[62] Since the existence of historical conventions presupposes the existence of certain systematic criteria, we shall first concentrate on the latter.

6.4.2.1. The criteria and signals of segmentation

The smallest units of segmentation are marked by partial changes in the configuration. Thus, the section of a text that exists between two partial changes in the configuration represents the smallest macrostructural unit of segmentation.[63] Every entrance or exit of one or more figures is therefore a significant development on this level of segmentation, and the unit it creates can only be subdivided further by introducing thematic, rhetorical or situative criteria. Thus, the scene involving Hippolyte and Théramène in I,i of Racine's *Phèdre* which ends with the entrance of Oenone is one such unit of segmentation on this level. In scenic terms it cannot be subdivided any further. Thematically, though, it can be split up into smaller units since the theme of the dialogue changes at various points – Thésée (speeches 1–3), Phèdre (4–7), Aricie (7–13) as the reason for Hippolyte's desire to leave and his plan to say farewell to Phèdre (14–15).

On the next level upon the scale, the units of segmentation are marked by a total change of configuration. The first act of *Phèdre*, for example, ends with a configuration consisting of Phèdre and Oenone, and Act II opens with Aricie and Ismène. This total change in the configuration between acts is a characteristic feature not only of *Phèdre* but also of most of the dramas of French classicism.[64] This change usually coincides with an interruption in the chronological continuity as it does here, or, even more clearly, a change in locale. A complete change in configuration may also take place without these accompanying criteria, though not in French classical drama, if the two configurations are separated by a period of time when the stage is empty – the so-called 'zero-configuration' (see above, 5.3.3.1.). This enables the dramatist to change the configuration entirely without interrupting the time–space continuity.

This brings us to the two remaining superimposed segmentation criteria: the omission of time and the change of locale. In a play such as *Phèdre*, which complies strictly with the classicising unity of place, there is not even the slightest change of locale, but in the plays by dramatists such as Shakespeare these two criteria generally appear in tandem.

The criteria we have discussed in the above paragraphs have all been universally applicable. However, there is an additional category of segmentation markers that is associated with specific periods in the history of drama. However, as is always the case when we are faced with purely historical phenomena, lack of space prevents us from providing anything more than a cursory selection of the most important of these. In classical Greek drama, for example, the chorus was used as a marker to divide the text into a series of *epeisodia*. It became even more important in this context with Euripides, when the chorus began to lose its active role and the songs became more isolated from the plot structure. This resulted in the songs assuming the features of a sort of filling inserted into the dramatic structure in order to establish clear divisions between the various episodes of the plot.[65] In the drama of later historical periods a similar function was performed by various types of interludes or entr'actes such as the allegorical dumb shows in Elizabethan drama or the 'Reyen' in the baroque tragedy.[66] Finally, in the plays of Shakespeare and some of his contemporaries, the convention used to signal the end of a scene was often a rhyming couplet, which contrasted with the blank verse of the rest of the text. What all of these different forms share is the tendency of these separating or framing elements to create a more audience-orientated or epic vehicle for conveying information and a greater level of abstraction and generalisation.[67]

The formal conventions we have been discussing here are all well integrated into the text. However, there are at least three other ways of marking the division of the text into sections that are definitely not part of the text: the interval, the curtain and the black-out. The interval is an extended interruption in the flow of the text and, as such, represents the most obvious segmentation signal. It transports the audience from the fictional context of time and space represented on stage back to the context of their own world as an audience and it is this which distinguishes the interval from the – superficially seen – similar type of interruption represented by the 'empty stage' or zero-configuration. After all, the latter is an integral part of the text and is therefore not intended as a way of interrupting the text and its fictional deixis. Because it is a dimension of reality, the length of the interval bears no relation to the amount of fictional time that has been omitted. Instead, it can be a means of grading the segmentation level – that is as long as it is not determined entirely by the need for set-changes and the like. Finally, the curtain, which did not become established as an accepted convention for dividing the text until the eighteenth century, functions like the black-out, as an additional optical signal marking the interval and makes it possible to change the set without completely disrupting the dramatic illusion.

6.4.2.2. Units of segmentation

The smallest unit of segmentation – in German usually called *Auftritt*, and in French *scène* – has no name in English theatrical terminology. It is that unit whose beginning and end are marked by partial changes in the configuration (see above, 5.3.3.).[68] Since this unit is defined in terms of constancy of configuration, we should like to call it, too, a 'configuration', using the concept here in a slightly changed sense: we are projecting its original spatial reference – i.e. the set of characters on stage at a certain point of time – on to the temporal axis of the time-span during which the set of characters remains the same. The importance of the caesura between two such configurations increases in proportion to the importance of the figure making its entrance or exit – in other words, with the significance of the change of situation this brings with it.

The entrances and exits of the figures, which delineate the dramatic segments, can either be motivated in some way or they can be coincidental.[69] In a dramaturgical concept that emphasises the causal nexus between the various strands of plot and chains of events it is the motivated entrances and exits that predominate. The appearance of a new figure is often anticipated by the figures already on stage, or, on entering, a figure may profer a plausible reason for his or her appearance. Similarly, an exit may be explained by references to plans or jobs to do in such a way that the receiver is sufficiently informed as to the future whereabouts and the activities of the departing figure. The reasons behind the entrances and exits thus represent an important source of information on the hidden action that is supposedly taking place off-stage (see below, 7.3.1.2.).[70] Nonetheless, even plays constructed around a dramaturgical concept that requires causal links and necessity often contain a number of coincidental entrances which are often referred to as having happened 'just in time'. The choice of a public locale as opposed to a private interior makes particular configurations easier to explain and chance meetings much less improbable. Thus, the public places that have been used repeatedly in drama since classical times are not merely intended to signal the public character of the story or subject matter; they also serve a function that is more formal and technical.

These thoughts are confirmed if we return to Racine's *Phèdre*. The stringency of the norms imposed by the need for unity of place influenced the choice of a public place as the locale (the square in front of the royal palace in Trézène) since the series of thirty different encounters can only be convincing if the locale is freely accessible to all of the figures. The configuration with which the drama begins (I,i) shows Hippolyte in conversation with his confidant Théramène. The fact that they are together is explained by the very nature of their relationship. And yet it is clear from the tone of their dialogue – they are in the middle of it as they walk on to the stage (or as the curtain rises) – that there is a special reason for this particular conversation, namely Hippolyte's decision to run away. The entrance of Oenone in the following scene is similarly motivated by the fact that she has been sent in advance by her ailing mistress who, although she wishes to go for a walk in the sun, does not want to meet anyone. But her appearance at this particular moment is entirely coincidental and unprepared. The reason behind her appearance also explains both the departure of Hippolyte and Théramène and the arrival on the scene of Phèdre herself. It should also be added that although this explains the departure of Hippolyte and Théramène it does not give any indication of their destination or of what they will be doing there. The great scene between Phèdre and Oenone (I,iii), in which Phèdre confesses her love for Hippolyte, is suddenly interrupted by Panope who brings her mistress the news of Thésée's death and the imminent royal elections in Athens. But she is then immediately dismissed so that Phèdre and Oenone can discuss the implications of these new events (I,v). Finally, the plan to visit Hippolyte is what motivates their exit and thus leads to the empty stage at the end of the act.

Further commentary on the movements of the figures of the play in the remaining four acts is unnecessary since it would not result in any new perspectives. It will have become sufficiently clear by now to what extent motivation and coincidence interact in the succession of different configurations and also to what extent these configurations are linked together in an unbroken chain, the so-called *liaison des scènes*.[71] It is also noticeable that the individual constellations, unlike the individual acts, differ widely in both function and length. The short constellations I,ii, I,iv and I,v, containing brief announcements, messages and agreements, both conjoin and frame the longer entrances (I,i and I,iii) in which long speeches are used to intensify the conflict potential of the situation. This also varies the dramatic tempo (see below, 7.4.5.), which the shorter configurations tend to accelerate and the longer ones to slow down.

The next unit of segmentation can be identified as a series of configurations that ends when all of the figures leave the stage (i.e., when a total change of configuration occurs) and/or when the time—space continuum is interrupted. Critics schooled in the Shakespearean tradition would describe this unit as a scene. Those influenced by a different tradition, embodied in the plays of French classicism, would call it an act. This unit therefore contrasts not only two contradictory terminologies but also two different methods of dramatic composition, for whilst the Shakespearean tradition distinguishes between three different units of segmentation – configuration, scene and act – the French tradition is restricted to the two units, *scène* and *acte*. The relationship between these two traditions may be summarised as follows:

Shakespearean tradition: configuration   scene   act
French tradition: *scène*   *acte*

The French *acte* corresponds to the Shakespearean scene in so far as it is determined by the same criterion, namely the interruption of chronological continuity, though of course the Shakespearean tradition can expand this criterion by adding a change of locale, and the French tradition prescribes a complete change of configuration at the end of each *acte*, which is not obligatory between Shakespearean scenes. On the other hand, the *acte* may also correspond to the Shakespearean act inasmuch as they both represent the highest unit of segmentation and generally divide the complete text into five parts.[72]

This problem is complicated further by the fact that the contemporary quarto editions of Shakespeare's plays only contain embryonic attempts to divide the plays into scenes and no indication whatever as to the beginnings and ends of acts or configurations. Not even the posthumous folio edition of 1623 divides more than just a few of the plays into acts with any degree of consistency. This was not done in any comprehensive way until the eighteenth century. These facts suggest that the significance of the configurations and acts as relevant units of segmentation is problematic as far as Shakespeare is concerned and in fact this has kindled an endless controversy that has been raging and continues to rage amongst Shakespeare scholars.[73] Without going into the results of this debate in any detail it can nonetheless be said that the predominant level of segmentation and thus the unit of dramatic composition, is the scene in the plays of Shakespeare, and the act in the plays of the French tradition. Generally speaking, then, the plays of Shakespeare are constructed as a variable series of shorter elements and are thus more flexible than the plays of the French tradition in which the five acts are cemented together like a row of virtually identical building blocks. And, unlike the French tradition, which divides a play into acts according to a number of clear external criteria, such as the interruption of chronological continuity or a complete change of configuration, the Shakespearean tradition divides a play into acts according to certain internal criteria, such as changes of mood or thematic emphasis or important new developments in the plot.

6.4.3. Composition

This contrast between a flexible arrangement of scenes on the one hand and a more rigid act structure on the other touches on one of the central elements in the theory of dramatic composition. Until the nineteenth century, such theories had an underlying intention which was strongly normative but since the turn of the twentieth century they have experienced something of a transformation in both overall intention and method from normative prescription to typological description. A comparison of Gustav Freytag's influential *Technique of Drama* (first published in 1863)[74] and Volker Klotz's *Geschlossene und offene Formen im Drama* (*Open and Closed Forms in Drama*, 1960)[75] will suffice to illustrate the extent of this transformation. Freytag, whom modern literary critics have ridiculed – often unfairly – as a sort of dramaturgical Beckmesser, was fully immersed in a normative tradition that strove to articulate a set of structural rules which could be applied to every dramatic text by analogy with the rhetorical pattern of the *partes orationis*. His structural model was, like the rhetorical model for public speeches, one of three or rather five parts.[76] His method was deductive: based on a conflict-orientated theory of drama his view was that a plot develops in the dialectical conflict between action and counter-action and thus moves from the exposition of the conflict through the antagonistic climax to the catastrophe. This model, a refined version of the late classical model of *protasis*, *epitasis* and *katastrophe* (see above, 3.7.2.1.), was then applied to a corpus of texts that was so selective that it managed to hide the contradictions between the theoretical model and the various empirical texts. In this way, Freytag managed to exclude comedy and whole historical subgenres, such as medieval drama, the drama of *Sturm und Drang* and the plays of Büchner and Grabbe from his analysis, concentrating instead on the tragedies of classical antiquity (Sophocles etc.) and French and German classicism, and squeezing the tragedies of Shakespeare rather violently into the Procrustean bed of his dramatic categories.

Freytag was attempting to turn what had already become a historically rather restricted method of composition into a normative absolute. He failed to perceive the historical bias of his own perspective and the historical relativity of the norms he was postulating. Volker Klotz, on the other hand, attempts to isolate two contrasting composition techniques from a historically and typologically extremely varied corpus of texts by defining two ideal types – open and closed forms in drama – and then constructing an analytical method based on the categories Wölfflin developed for the history of art and which were then applied to drama by Walzel, Petsch and others. The initial phase of this procedure is empirical and historical in so far as it records a number of structural devices in plays taken from a wide range of historical periods. The second phase is made up of an attempt to define a number of ahistorical constructs by arranging these examples according to various perspectives. These constructs are then integrated into a systematic context from which it is possible to construct a set of ideal types of such purity and consistency that seldom occur, if ever, in historical reality. The idea behind the construction of such ideal types is heuristic in the sense that they provide historical research and interpretation with analytical frameworks and descriptive models. His method is superior to Gustav Freytag's normative perspective in two ways: first, because it does not attempt to elevate one particular composition technique to a normative absolute and secondly, because it describes a number of different ones and is therefore able to refer to a historically broader spectrum of text types, fully conscious of the interdependence between systematic generalisation and historical specificity.

In the following sections, in which we shall be borrowing Volker Klotz's analytical method and presenting the contrast between closed and open structures in drama, we shall restrict our discussion to the analysis of the perspectives of 'plot' and 'composition'.[77] This is because we have already discussed both language structure and figure conception in some detail and shall be investigating the time–space structures in the next chapter.

6.4.3.1. Closed form

The ideal type of closed form is based on a completely self-contained story in which there are no background events to influence the beginning, in which the ending is absolutely final and the presentation of which – the fable or plot – conforms to the Aristotelian demands of unity and totality. Unity of plot, according to Aristotle, means that the drama consists of a single plot sequence or, if there are more than one, that one (the 'primary plot') should predominate clearly over the others, which in turn have no claims to autonomy and which are designed to be completely subordinate to it. In positive terms, the totality of the plot means 'that everything is there that somehow belongs to it (completeness)' and, in negative terms 'that all elements that are not indispensable are omitted (indispensability of the parts)'.[78] A conflict between clearly defined antagonistic forces develops out of a transparent initial situation based on a finite and comprehensible set of facts. This conflict is then led towards an unambiguous solution at the end.

From this it is clear that the ideal type of closed form corresponds most closely to the historical dramatic form that Gustav Freytag strove to prescribe as a normative ideal in the nineteenth century. His theory was that the plot is based on a pyramid-like structure which he represented graphically as follows:[79]

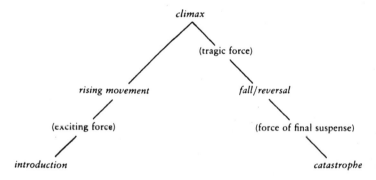

The introduction or 'exposition' presents the initial conflict, which is then intensified by the exciting force – a decisive action by the protagonist or antagonist – and rises towards the climax. A tragic force then initiates the protagonist's downfall or a decisive change in the direction of the plot which, after a delay induced by the force of the final suspense, culminates in the final catastrophe. This sort of model implies a linear, goal-orientated, single-stranded plot, in which each phase and each detail is important only to the extent that it helps the progress of the plot. Detail is subordinated to the whole and this is also manifested in the axial symmetry and balance of the whole composition. The introduction, exciting force and the rising movement are mirrored almost exactly in the catastrophe, the force of the final suspense and the fall respectively on the other side of the central climax. Each constituent part is made to fit into this pattern and this even applies to the dominant segmentation level – the division of the play into five acts, each of which is supposed to correspond to one of the five stages of the plot. It is also supposed to apply to the internal structure of each act, in which the succession of scenes is supposed to provide a replica in miniature of the tectonics of rise and fall.

The plot itself is as lacking in autonomy as its components, and it is designed to provide a clear, concrete illustration of an ideal problem. It is for this reason that the presentation of individualistic or characteristic qualities, however sensual or direct, can never be an aim in itself and must always be subordinate to the overall structure. The concrete external circumstances of conflict must remain in the background behind the overall idea and, as a result, the portrayal of mental processes predominates over physical action. The latter is largely dematerialised and transformed into narratively mediated 'hidden action'.

The ideal type of closed form is therefore a hierarchically arranged structure, in which the plot is determined by the idea and the constituent parts of the plot by the whole. The hierarchical arrangement and symmetry of this structure do not just affect the composition of the plot. They also influence the forms and style of the language used – the predominantly hypotactic syntax, the conceptual transparency of the vocabulary, the clearly constructed utterances and dialogues and the frequent use of parallelisms – and also the restricted dramatis personae, divided into a number of distinctly contrasting and corresponding groups, the figure conception that emphasises fully conscious reflection and tends towards types and, finally, the concentrated economy and abstraction of the time–space structure.

6.4.3.2. Open forms

As an ideal type, open form is devised as a counter-model to that of closed form and is thus determined from a negative perspective. One of the problems that this creates is the question to what extent this idealised type can be applied to specific dramatic texts. This was something that Klotz either ignored or failed to see clearly enough, for although a positively determined idealised form can cover a relatively homogeneous corpus of texts, one determined from a negative perspective must be able to subsume a wide variety of techniques that negate the closed form. For apart from the fact that they all represent departures from closed form, the theatre of *Sturm und Drang*, the plays of Büchner, naturalist theatre, satirical drama, epic theatre and, to extend Klotz's list, the theatre of the absurd and documentary theatre really have very little in common and deviate from it in widely different ways. From this objection it follows that, unlike Volker Klotz, we shall not be so much concerned to devise a comprehensive theoretical model for open form as with identifying the most important variants of deviation and negation with regard to the story and its dramatic presentation.

Since the story presented in plays with a closed dramatic structure is predominantly a causally-linked series of conflicting actions and counteractions, one of the ways of negating it is to replace the deliberate action by an event that befalls the figures or by a numbing immutability that renders them incapable of action (see above, 6.1.2.3.). It was in this spirit that Peter Weiss answered a question put to him by the Brecht scholar Ernst Schumacher on the form and function of plot in documentary theatre:

I don't know what you mean by 'plot'. As far as I'm concerned there is an event taking place on stage; it doesn't need to be part of a plot, it can also be a situation. It doesn't need to start out from one particular point and then develop towards a definite goal or ending.[80]

This undermines not only the primacy of deliberate action in closed dramas, but also, at the same time, the self-contained quality of the story with regard to an absolute beginning and a conclusive ending. Moreover, the 'totality' of the plot, in the sense of its completeness, can never really be a feature of documentary theatre because even when the documentation is as exhaustive and comprehensive as it can be, given its direct reference to historical reality, it will nonetheless and necessarily be no more than a model-like abbreviation of that reality.

The unity of plot that occurs in the idealised type of closed structure can be disrupted if a number of different plot sequences are given equal importance and are thus no longer minor sequences subordinate to a 'main plot'. In such cases the structural openness consists in the fact that the story is no longer presented as a closed, hierarchically arranged whole, but as an ensemble of individual sequences that are relatively autonomous and isolated from one another. The individual sequences are no longer woven together, nor do the various actions and events interfere or overlap – or if they do then only very selectively (see above, 6.3.1.3.) – and as a result the sequences appear to be relatively independent. However, it is possible to compensate for this reduction or even total elimination of pragmatic links between different strands of plot in various ways. In this context, Volker Klotz lists three techniques that are commonly used in drama: the coordination of complementary strands (sequences), conjunction by metaphor and the central self.[81]

To demonstrate how complementary sequences may be related Klotz shows how collective and private strands are juxtaposed in J. M. R. Lenz's *Soldaten* (*Soldiers*) and Frank Wedekind's *Frühlingserwachen* (*Spring Awakening*): the collective strand is used to define the socio-anthropological framework (in this case the situation of the unmarried soldateska and the generation conflict respectively) in a series of separate incidents, whilst the private sequences are used to transform the conditionality of the collective framework into a dynamic series of actions or events (such as the fate that befalls Marie Wesener and the three individual cases Moritz Stiefel, Melchior Gabor and Wendla Bergmann). Klotz uses the expression 'conjunction by metaphor' to refer to the repeated use of leitmotif-like imagery to conjoin a number of otherwise autonomous dramatic situations and sequences (see above, 4.6.5.3.). However, as his examples from *Woyzeck* clearly demonstrate – the image of downward movement and word motifs such as 'On and on', 'Stab her dead' and 'Dance!' – Klotz is not just interested in the iterative use of metaphor since he also includes recurrences of non-metaphorical words and non-verbal signs in his analysis. In the broadest sense, then, this integrational technique, which is designed to act as a counterbalance to the pragmatic openness in the plot, is supposed to forge links by creating thematic equivalents (see above, 6.3.1.3.) that are strengthened by the varied repetition of verbal and non-verbal motifs. – Finally, these otherwise diverging sequences may be unified around a particular figure if every situation is designed to shed light on this central self with all its biological, social, psychological and ideological idiosyncrasies. Unlike the hero in a closed drama, the central self is the centre of attention not because, as the protagonist or central active *subject* it is he or she who initiates the most important actions, but rather because he or she is the *object* of the conditioning elements presented in the various scenes and dramatic situations:

In plays that contain a central self as a structural principle, the protagonist, acting simultaneously as a 'mon-agonist', remains isolated at the centre of a counterworld that closes in on him from all sides. In such cases, the plot does not move forward in the same way that it does in closed drama – namely as a linear progression moving from one specific point to a specific destination in such a way that each step conditions the next and each step moves closer to the destination – but as a series of cycles.[82]

At the same time this refers to a further device that is used to undermine closed structures – the breakdown of linear finality in the plot and its replacement by cyclical, repetitive or contrastive structural patterns. The progression from one scene to the next is not so much a consequence of the pragmatic nexus – which is interrupted by the insertion of scenes that portray the milieu or provide a commentary on the action, in other words, scenes that are completely redundant as far as the plot is concerned but which are atmospherically or thematically relevant – as a deliberate attempt to establish a set of meaningful similarities and contrasts. Short scenes alternate with long and complex scenes, scenes in the open air with intimate interiors, soliloquies with crowd scenes, dynamic stage-action with static stillness, emotional pathos with ironic deflation. For whilst the closed forms of drama develop the story as a linear and continuous progression in a strictly arranged series of scenes and acts, the loose pattern of scenes in open dramas tend to break it up into a series of repetitions and variations.

This is also conditioned by the fact that the acts and scenes have a different function in open dramas than they do in closed dramas. In the latter, the act represents the decisive unit of segmentation and the text as a whole is constructed as a tectonically clearly structured pattern consisting of a small number of units of similar length. In open dramas, on the other hand, it is the scene that is the decisive structural unit, relegating the acts – in so far as they are not omitted altogether – to a secondary role as a loose grouping of scenes. In this way, plays with an open construction form a series of numerous shorter units that vary in length. The analytical method of structuring plays 'from top to bottom' – i.e. from the text as a whole through the acts down to the configurations – is inverted as a synthetic lay-out constructed 'from bottom to top' – from the constituent parts to the complete text. In ideological terms, this structural contrast corresponds to the contrast between the deductive movement in closed dramas – i.e. the development from an idea to its realisation – and the inductive movement in open dramas. In the latter, specific individual qualities determined by the anthropological, social and psychological environment of the dramatic figures are more important than abstract ideas, and these specific individual qualities can no longer be directly subsumed – and even less by the figures themselves – into a more general and ideal structure.

The remaining levels of analysis produce analogous results but we can here do no more than outline them: figure conception is predominantly individualistic and conscious awareness is overshadowed by subconscious and physical behaviour patterns. The language structures are characterised syntactically by the predominance of parataxis and lexically by the large number of non-abstract words; the figures' verbal behaviour reflects the difficulties they experience in articulating their feelings and presentiments verbally, both for themselves and for others. For this reason, communication between the figures is often disrupted: their utterances often simply no longer have any bearing on the utterances of others or they are hesitant, syntactically and logically incoherent and culminate in a non-verbal but pantomimetically eloquent silence. The dramatis personae is large, with a broad social mix and although many of the figures only appear episodically, there is no clear division between primary and secondary figures. Finally, the time–space structures tend to produce expansive panoramas filled with a wealth of precise and concrete details.

7. Structures of time and space

7.1. The reality and fictionality of time and space in drama

Together with the figure and its verbal and/or non-verbal behaviour the concepts of time and space represent the basic concrete categories within the dramatic text. It is this that distinguishes the latter from narrative texts, in which the only concrete aspects are narrative discourse and figural speech, whereas space, and the non-verbal behaviour of a figure are presented in a verbally encoded and abstract form only. As far as the category of time is concerned, however, this contrast has to be qualified in some way: in both narrative and dramatic texts the presentation of time is specific and concrete – in the former as narrated time and in the latter as the actual playing time. However, only in drama can presented time always be clearly defined; in narrative texts it can only appear as a clearly defined category in the context of 'scenic narration'. These differences are a direct consequence of the multimediality of dramatic texts, in contrast to the purely verbal form of presentation employed in narrative texts (see above, 1.3.).[1]

The superimposition of an external communication system over an internal system also occurs within the structures of time and space. The actual space taken up by stage and auditorium on the external level corresponds on the internal level to the fictional space in which the story unfolds, whilst the fictional temporal deixis of the story corresponds to the real temporal deixis of the performers and the receivers, though of course the fact that the present tenses on both levels are identical should not tempt us into confusing the real *hic et nunc* of the audience and actors and the fictional *hic et nunc* of the figures. This overlapping of reality and fiction also applies to every single structural element of the theatrical text: the real actor on the external level corresponds to the figure he or she represents on the internal level, the actual stage set to the fictional locale, the real-life costumes to the fictional clothing worn by the figures and the real property to the fictional objects used by the figures etc.[2] If the form of dramatic communication is 'absolute' (see above, 1.2.3.) then, viewed from the receiver's perspective, the actor is transformed completely into the fictional figure, the stage into the fictional locale and the props and costumes into the corresponding objects in the fictional world.

On the other hand, this 'absolute autonomy' is broken and a mediating communication system established if the specific elements of the theatrical presentation, and thus the presentation process itself, are left visible behind the fiction or maybe even undermine it (see above, 3.6.2.4.). The style of acting demanded by Brecht with his theory of a 'gestus of showing', for example, in which the actor is not completely absorbed by the figure he represents but prefers to 'demonstrate' the behaviour of the figure to the audience, is as much an epic technique of information transmission as scene-changes on open stage, the use of scenery that clearly emphasises its fictional quality, and costumes that do not even attempt to deceive the audience into thinking they are anything else. In such cases, the audience is presented not only with a fictional world with its fictional parameters of time and space but also with the techniques and processes underlying the presentation. The dramatic performance is thus 'alienated' and the illusion broken.

In drama that is 'epic' in this way the audience is constantly being reminded of the tension in the relationship between the real time–space deixis and the fictional one. However, there have also been a number of avant-garde experiments conceived with the conscious intention of exploring the extremes of dramatic form. In these, the attempt is made to overcome this discrepancy by eliminating the fictional deixis completely. In happenings (generally performed outside), for example, the context of an established theatre is given up and in performance art the fictional time–space deixis is eliminated because the performers essentially abandon fiction in favour of a manipulation of real objects by real people in a way that is partially planned and partially spontaneous. All that happenings or performance art have in common with drama as we understand it is multimediality and the collective nature of production and reception. What they lack is the superimposition of one communication system on another and thus the two deictic systems of reference. It is this element of superimposition that has already been identified as the quality that distinguishes dramatic texts from other types.

The converse attempts to eliminate the double deixis by presenting theatre itself in the theatre lead us to Pirandello, but even in his plays a categorical distinction can and indeed must still be drawn between the internal fictional level and the external, real level – despite the apparent identity of fictional locale and actual venue (i.e. the stage itself). The stage used by the fictional actors in *Sei personaggi in cerca d'autore* (1921) for rehearsals is not the same as the real stage situated in front of the audience because on the real stage a play is being performed, whereas on the fictional stage a performance of a play is being rehearsed. This categorical distinction between fictional space and real space, which is merely emphasised by their apparent identity, is repeated with regard to time, though in this case there is not even an attempt to make them seem identical: the fictional rehearsal takes place during the day, whereas the actual performance generally takes place in the evening.

Unlike Pirandello, however, Peter Handke, in his play *Publikumsbeschimpfung* (*Insulting the Audience*) (1966) actually set out to achieve a genuine kind of identity between real and fictional structures of time and space. This is expressly explained to the audience by the figures themselves:

The stage represents nothing. It does not represent any other kind of empty space. The stage *is* empty. . . . You are not looking at a space that is pretending to be another space. You are not experiencing a kind of time that means another time. The time here on stage is exactly the same as yours. . . . The front of the stage is not a barrier.[3]

In the ensuing passage, the omission of a time–space deixis that deviates from reality is then passed off as a way of fulfilling the unities of time, action and space, though in fact unity is interpreted as the deictic unity of stage and auditorium – a marked redefinition of the neoclassical concept of unity as an uninterrupted continuity (see below, 7.2.1.1.):

Since we are talking uninterruptedly and directly to *you*, we and you form a single unit. Under certain circumstances we could therefore say we instead of you. This is what we mean by 'unity of plot'. The stage up here and the auditorium form a single unit since they no longer form two levels. There is no radiation belt. There are not two different places here. Here there is just one place. This is what we mean by the unity of place. Your time, the time of the spectators and listeners form one unit because there is no other time here than your own. There is no bifocal division into fictional performance time and time for the performance. Time is not performed here. There is only real time. There is only the kind of time that we, we and you, have experienced ourselves. Here there is just *one* time. This is what we mean by the unity of time. All three of the circumstances we have mentioned signify the unity of time, place and plot. So this play is classical.

We have quoted from this text so extensively because it explicitly negates the principles underlying the dramatic structures of time and space and the norms of an autonomous form of drama. The figures are no more than 'the mouthpiece of the author' (p. 23) throughout and, with the exception of a short prologue scene, address the audience rather than each other. There is, therefore, no fictional internal communication system in this case – something we normally consider to be an essential component of a dramatic text. Instead, every piece of information is transmitted through a mediating communication system, which is here being used as a vehicle for a discussion of the conventional relationship between the audience and the figures in a metalingual or, more precisely, metacommunicative way rather than merely to convey a fictional story. Typologically speaking, this play can only really be related to the dramatic genre if it is called a 'metadrama' or 'metatheatre' – or, to use Handke's own description of it: a 'speech play'.[4]

7.2. Open and closed structures of time and space

7.2.1. Normative theories

If we define the closed concept of space (or the unity of place) from a negative perspective as the omission of all changes of locale and the closed concept of time (or the unity of time) as the exclusion of all chronological discontinuity then the unities of time and space are principles that apply within each scene in a dramatic text. As a unit of segmentation in drama each scene is nothing but a closed time–space continuum in the play with each scene being marked by a change of locale or a rupture in time (see above, 6.4.2.2.).

7.2.1.1. The unities of time and space as norms

However, this general principle of scenic presentation derived from the absolute autonomy of drama is not what is meant by the well-known historical 'unities' of time and space, which have been such a crucial aspect of dramatic theory since the Renaissance.[5] These call for the most comprehensive form of chronological and spatial continuity over the whole text and preclude all changes of locale or more extended ruptures in time. In defence of their normative application of the 'three unities' of time, space and plot the critics generally cited Aristotle's *Poetics*, but this really only calls for the unity of plot (see chs 7 and 8) whereas the unity of time is only mentioned briefly as a formal tendency in contemporary dramas – 'And then, as regards length, tragedy tends to fall within a single revolution of the sun'[6] – and the unity of space is not mentioned at all. Consequently, a number of more or less stringent interpretations of the principles concerning the unities of time and space were put forward. Some theorists allowed switches of locale between the rooms in one house or even between different localities in one city and a time-span of a whole day or even a day and a night. In 1570, Lodovico Castelvetro, on the other hand, demanded rigorous adherence to the unity of space and went even further than Aristotle in his demand for a unity of time in which the actual length of the presentation is identical to the fictional time-scale of the drama.[7] In the Renaissance, it was only Castelvetro who subscribed to such a strict interpretation, which was in fact an extension of the time–space continuity from the individual scene to take in the whole text.

Theorists justified their normative implementation of the unities of time and space by appealing to the more general principles of plausibility and reason.[8] They felt that changes of locale and sudden jumps in time would overtax the imaginative capabilities of the audience, which, after all, remains in one place continually throughout the performance, and these ruptures would therefore also endanger or even destroy the dramatic illusion. This is not the moment to discuss to what extent these historical rules were applied to individual plays written between 1500 and 1800. It ought to be said, however, that these rules did not always have the positive aesthetic effect of encouraging dramatists to use the stringency of the closed form to create a corresponding internal coherence in their plays. Their influence was also occasionally negative and restrictive, and even threatened the very principles of plausibility and reason that they were designed to preserve. Such restrictions on time and space can lead to situations in which a number of different figures meet at one particular place so frequently that the whole thing becomes increasingly implausible, even if the locale is a public place and generous allowance is made for the power of chance, and to situations in which events take place in such swift succession that they contravene all laws of general common sense.

7.2.1.2. The abolition of the unities of time and space

It was at this point that eighteenth-century criticism took over and finally brought about the complete collapse of this kind of rule-orientated dramatic theories. In 1767 Lessing, in Parts 44 to 46 of his *Hamburg Dramaturgy*, subjected Voltaire's *Mérope* (and the original on which it was based, Scipione Maffei's *Merope*) to a detailed analysis, concentrating on the extent to which Voltaire had preserved the three unities. His concluding judgement was devastatingly critical:

One should just try and imagine that all the events that he allows to take place in his 'Merope' occurred on *one* day and then calculate how many inconsistencies this is bound to contain.

He has written this play in accordance with the letter but not the spirit of these laws. For although the events he has occur in the space of a single day could conceivably happen in that period, no reasonable person would actually do so much in one day. To create physical unity is not sufficient; there must also be a moral unity . . .[9]

In this passage Lessing is still arguing from within the old rule-dominated dramaturgy in that he criticises the stereotypical and meaningless application of those rules, rather than the rules themselves, and compares these manifestations with the more meaningful and organic interpretations of the classical dramatists who wrote their plays quite naturally in accordance with the unity of the plot and the particular theatrical conditions of the time (the constant presence of the chorus on stage, for example):

It is one thing to reconcile oneself with the rules; it is another genuinely to abide by them. The French have managed to do the former; the latter was only truly understood by the ancients. (p. 254)

A decisive factor in the move away from the classicist rule-orientated theories, which was manifested in the dismissive treatment of purely ornamental solutions to the unities of time and space, was the way the dramas of Shakespeare were received in the eighteenth century.[10] With their apparent lack of concern for the normative application of time–space unity and their often panoramic and expansive structures of time and space they were felt to represent a counter-model to French dramatic theory and practice. Their canonisation therefore reflected a substantial shift in the course of dramatic theory. Thus, as early as 1759 Lessing, in the influential seventeenth of his *Letters Concerning the Most Recent Literature*, declared that Shakespeare's plays, in which the external unities of time and space were only realised on a few rare occasions (e.g. *The Comedy of Errors* or *The Tempest*), were actually closer to their ancient predecessors in Greece and Rome than were the dramas of writers such as Corneille and Racine:

Even if this whole question were to be decided according to the laws prescribed by the ancients Shakespeare is a far greater tragedian than Corneille, for, despite the latter's intimate familiarity with and the former's virtual ignorance of the ancients, Corneille only managed to come anywhere near them in his mechanical dramatic technique, whereas Shakespeare succeeded in approaching their fundamental spirit.[11]

At around the same time as Lessing, Samuel Johnson launched an even more fundamental attack on the classicist norms, condemning them as empty and superficial, emphasising their inconsistencies and, most importantly, casting doubt on the very reasons for their existence. Once again, it was the works of Shakespeare that gave him the inspiration to do this. In the 'Preface' to his 1765 edition of Shakespeare, he wrote:

The necessity of observing the unities of time and place arises from the supposed necessity of making the drama credible.
. . .
The objection arising from the impossibility of passing the first hour at Alexandria and the next at Rome, supposes that when the play opens the spectator really imagines himself at Alexandria and believes that his walk to the theatre has been a voyage to Egypt, and that he lives in the days of Cleopatra . . . The truth is that the spectators are always in their senses and know, from the first act to the last, that the stage is only a stage, and that the players are only players.[12]

In other words, the dramatic fiction does not set out to deceive the audience by pretending that the illusion it presents is actual reality. Its fictionality is established in advance as part of the dramatic code of communication between the author and the audience: they come to a conventional agreement as to the play's illusory quality and its special ontological status. Johnson argued, correctly, that within the frame of reference established by this kind of agreement it is irrelevant in principle whether the stage is intended to represent either a single fictional locale throughout or a series of different ones, or whether the fictional time-scale represents either an unbroken continuum or a succession of episodes. By rejecting the inappropriate application of the criteria of plausibility and reason to fictional texts – inappropriate because they fail to take their fictionality sufficiently into consideration – Johnson and other contemporary theorists of drama justified retrospectively the practices not only of Elizabethan and Jacobean drama but also of the theatre of the Middle Ages, and thus enabled drama as a whole to develop historically with a greater degree of formal flexibility.

7.2.2. Dramatic practice

7.2.2.1. Closed structures of time and space

This brief discussion of the history of dramatic theory from the sixteenth to the eighteenth centuries addressed a problem, the normative discussion of which can now only be of interest from a historical point of view. However, it must also be examined within the framework of a systematic and descriptive theory of dramatic form. The relevance of this problem is demonstrated by the fact that, even though the normative view that the unities of time and space were necessary prerequisites that were based on reason has been comprehensively discredited, there are still plays being written that are based on self-contained and concentrated structures of time and space. These plays are particularly common in naturalist theatre and, more surprisingly, perhaps, in the theatre of the absurd as developed by Beckett, Ionesco and Pinter.[13]

We should like to illustrate this briefly by citing *The Selicke Family* (1890), a play by the two German naturalist playwrights Arno Holz and Johannes Schlaf. The three acts of this play span the brief period from Christmas Eve to early on Christmas Day, and they are all set in the rather sparse lower middle-class living-room of the Selicke family. This superficial similarity with the time–space structures of, for example, a tragedy in the French classical style actually serves to emphasise the differences in their respective communicative functions. In Racine's tragedies the unities of time and space are 'unmarked' – that is they do not represent a specific intention for each individual text because as components of the secondary code of this particular historical type of drama they are prescribed for each individual text. The functions associated with it are therefore of a general kind, namely the creation of illusionistic coherence, the concentration of suspense towards the ending and a closed aesthetic structure. In *The Selicke Family*, on the other hand, the closed structures are not prescribed as an obligatory norm; they are not the form normally expected and thus are not 'unmarked'. Nor do they represent a retrogressive attempt to reactivate the classicising form of rule-based dramaturgy because that is undermined in this particular play in other ways: the conception of the figures, the construction of dialogues and the action. Instead, the closed structures serve specifically *thematic* functions: the permanence of the locale – an interior littered with furniture and other objects, isolated from the outside world, from which only a few noises actually permeate – creates the impression of a suffocating narrowness and hopelessness that is in line with the authors' determinist conception of figure. At the same time, the figures are all locked into a milieu that does not permit any kind of change and holds them prisoner in a state of numbing *stasis*. Replacing the type of public locale that unity of place in classical and classicising drama was based on by a private interior is therefore primarily of thematic importance.[14] Similarly, the unity of time in this play has the function of highlighting the inevitability of the events, which are presented as a series of crisis-ridden attempts to release the suspense and tensions that had been allowed to develop well before the play starts.

The tendency in naturalist drama to create closed structures of time and space – i.e. to preserve a single locale and to equate the performance time with the fictional time-span of the play – should also be seen in the context of the poetological programmes of naturalism which, after all, did attempt to bring the fictional presentation as close as possible to empirical reality in order to achieve the greatest possible sense of immediacy in the dramatic presentation:

Art has the tendency to return to nature; this occurs according to the particular prevailing conditions of reproduction and the way they are operated.[15]

As far as the time–space structures of drama are concerned, this particular line of argument – from Arno Holz's *Art. Its Essence and its Laws* (1891) – implies that, whenever possible, the dramatist must avoid sudden changes of locale and interruptions in the chronological continuity, since this technique simply does not correspond to the way we perceive reality and is little more than a crude form of authorial intervention.

7.2.2.2. Open structures of time and space

Each shift of locale and each jump in time actually undermines the absolute autonomy and immediate quality of the fiction presented because they cannot be related to an expressive subject in the internal communication system of the fiction. Instead, they are related to a mediating communication system through which a series of contrasting or corresponding scenes with differing time–space *deixis* is introduced to provide a sort of explanation of and commentaries on those scenes. Thus, a drama with open time–space structures exhibits a clear tendency to create epic structures, not only because the historical convention that demands dramatic concentration is flouted in favour of a type of openness reminiscent of the classical epic (see above, 3.6.1.2.), but also because the discontinuity of time and space in drama implies a 'narrative function' to which this discontinuous arrangement of scenes must be related (see above, 3.6.2.1.). This epic tendency, or narrative function, becomes more strongly marked as the structures of time and space become more open. Here, too, it is possible to establish a sliding-scale moving from the hermetic, strictly interpreted unities of time and space on the one hand to the openness of the more panoramic structures of time and space that Shakespeare used in his Histories, on the other. Of course, the narrative function in such cases differs decisively from the narrator in narrative texts because it remains implicit rather than being linked explicitly to a tangible figure.

Despite this implicit quality, the narrative structure conveys a number of extremely clear evaluative signals that influence the way a text is received. This might be demonstrated in a precise analysis of the time–space structures and their thematic functions in, say, Shakespeare's trilogy *Henry VI*. However, we shall have to restrict ourselves to a few general points. This trilogy presents a broad historical panorama spanning a period of almost forty years and taking in a wealth of different locales on both sides of the Channel. The extreme openness of both time and space, which is reflected in the extensive, multilayered dramatis personae and a large number of simultaneous and successive plot sequences, enables the dramatist to introduce ever-changing patterns of contrasting or comparative elements in order to present expansive lines of development, and the effects of political conflict on all layers of society, from the ordinary people to the princes and bishops in particular. Behind this plethora of individual and apparently disparate episodes and incidents he is able to allow more general historical and philosophical laws to shine through.

Thus, by constantly switching back and forth between England and France in *Henry VI Part 1*, the danger at home (in the shape of the princes' disunity) is related to the threat looming from abroad (in the form of the French army), and the defeat in battle is interpreted as a direct consequence of the strife at home. The political chaos that England as a nation has to endure is interpreted as atonement for the usurpation of Henry IV, and this continues until, purged and brought to reason by the terrors of the Wars of the Roses, England returns to a state of peace and happiness under the Tudors. This is a theme that recurs again and again in a series of different episodes, and the technique of serial repetition – as in the series of episodes that portray the downfalls of several important figures (Eleanor, Gloucester, Winchester, Suffolk) in *Henry VI Part 2* or the sudden changes in fortune in battle in *Henry VI Part 3* – demonstrates the universality of the laws of destiny and political rise and fall. It also creates the impression that long periods of time were passing very quickly. These extensive time-spans enable the dramatist to present lines of individual development – such as the growth of the central figure from a dependent child to a disillusioned and impotent monarch – or the overlapping historical context of the Tudor myth.

The succession of different locales is used to present a vast tapestry of images in which public and private locales, interiors and scenes in towns or open countryside, aristocratic and plebeian environments, England and France are constantly being contrasted. After sequences of scenes from the battlefields, which seem to cover the whole of England and France like a topographical net and emphasise the horrors of war, the scene always returns to London, where the changed constellations of power are ratified, either in the royal palace, Westminster Abbey or the Tower. In view of the way the story develops it is perfectly reasonable for these locales to recur again and again. The garden scenes, on the other hand, or the scenes situated in a garden-like area do not occur quite so naturally and are a deliberate artifice on the part of the playwright. With its biblical connotations of the Garden of Paradise or Eden and its emblematic reference to an ordered and hierarchically arranged social structure, the garden becomes a counter-model to political chaos. In Act II, Scene iv of *Henry VI Part 1*, which takes place in the Temple Garden, the feud between the houses of York and Lancaster is stylised into a symbolic struggle between the white rose and the red rose, and the locale both provides the props for it, and establishes an ironic link between its significance as an emblematic manifestation of order and the Wars of the Roses it heralds. In Act II, Scene ii of *Henry VI Part 2*, the Duke of York chooses his garden as the place to present the dynastic background to the current events as a conflict between various legitimate and usurpatory interests, and in Act IV, Scene x, Jack Cade's anarchistic rebellion ends in Iden's (*sic!*) garden, the name of the garden's owner serving to draw attention to the biblical reference. Finally, in Act II, Scene v of *Henry VI Part 3*, Henry VI, away from the battlefield, dreams of an arcadian existence as a shepherd until the mirror-like dual appearance of a 'Son that hath killed his Father' and a 'Father that hath killed his Son' returns him to a world in which the most fundamental human bonds have been severed and in which his own wishful daydreaming is evidence of his culpable failure as sovereign.

7.2.2.3. Discordance in structures of time and space

Up to now we have tended to regard the closed or open structures of time
and space as interlinked phenomena, as if, for example, closed structures
of space always imply closed structures of time. And in practice this is
indeed what usually happens. However, there is a category of texts in
which the structures of time and space are discordant – that is, where one is
open and the other closed. One extreme example of a text in which unity of
space is combined with a time structure that exhibits a radical discrepancy
between the actual performance time and the fictional time is Thornton
Wilder's one-act play *The Long Christmas Dinner* (1931). In this play the
locale, the dining-room in the house of the Bayard family, remains constant throughout and presents the decline and fall of the family over a
period of ninety years. This long period of time is presented scenically in
condensed form as a montage of an accelerating series of Christmas
dinners.[16] The opposite situation that occurs when the time structures are
closed and spatial structures are left open, is more difficult to realise
scenically, however, since it depends on the presentation of chronologically simultaneous and yet spatially separate events. This can only be done by
omitting all forms of closed causal connection and, in addition, by clearly
signalling the abolition of the established convention that demands that
events take place in the same chronological order in the play as they did in
the story (see below, 7.4.2.). An example of this kind of structure was cited
above in connection with our discussion of the epic montage technique,
namely the presentation of the preparations for war made by Germany,
France, Russia and England in Joan Littlewood's *Oh! What a Lovely War*
(see above, 3.6.2.1.). In this case, however, the discrepancy between the
closed time structure and the open space structure is restricted to a relatively short section of the text. In fact, to our knowledge there is not a single
text that was written according to this principle throughout.

7.3. The structure and presentation of space

The function of space in dramatic and also in narrative texts is not simply
confined to the fact that every story needs a setting, or to the secondary,
subordinate function of providing an environment in which the participating figures can act out the story.[17] This is particularly true of drama,
which, after all, presents space not only verbally but also in some concrete
visual form. In the twentieth century this has been brought emphatically
into the public consciousness by the emphasis on the structuring of space
in naturalist, expressionist and futurist drama and by the stage-designs
and writings of Adolphe Appia, E. Gordon Craig, Oskar Schlemmer or
Ferdinand Léger, who came to the theatre from the world of architecture

or the visual arts. For although Oskar Schlemmer's abstractionist dictum 'the art of the theatre is the art of space' can only be applied unreservedly to the historically specific programmes of the Bauhaus movement,[18] it is nonetheless generally the case that drama is *also* an art of space.

7.3.1. The semantic interpretation of space

The additional functions of space are not merely restricted to the fact that it creates a certain environment conditioning the figures' actions and that it can actually characterise those figures (see above, 5.4.2.3.), but they also include its 'model-forming role' (J. M. Lotman):

Behind the presentation of things and objects that form the environment in which the figures of the text perform there is a system of spatial relations, namely the structure of the topos. This structure is, on the one hand, the principle governing the way the figures are organised and distributed within the artistic continuum and, on the other, it functions as a language employed to express a number of other non-spatial relations in the text. In this fact resides the special model-forming role of aesthetic space in the text.[19]

Because spatial opposites are construed as models for semantic opposites, space is charged with semantic interpretations that basically distinguish fictional space from real space. This distinction exists independently of whether the fictional space closely follows the naturalist principle of mimesis and reproduces real space as faithfully as possible or, conversely, whether it is alienated from it in the form of extreme stylisation. There are three types of spatial relationship that are relevant here: first, there are the binary opposites of left and right, back and front, top and bottom within a single scenically presented locale, then, there is the spatial relationship between the scenically presented locale and the space 'off-stage' and, finally, there is the relationship between the different scenically presented locales. The semantic interpretation of space is therefore possible in a drama with a single locale – i.e. a play with a closed structure of space – as well as in a play which moves from locale to locale in an open structure of space.

7.3.1.1. The relationships within a single locale

As far as the spatial relationships within a single locale are concerned, the juxtapositions of different figures or groups of figures are already inherent in the dialogical form of the drama. The presence of several figures on stage at the same time who communicate dialogically with one another implies some form of spatial relationship of distance or proximity, and the opposition of left and right can be interpreted semantically in terms of conflict or consensus.[20] At this point, however, we would like to concentrate on the connotations implied in the relationship between top and bottom since the vertical spatial axis is not consistently realised in dramatic texts. When it is realised, it is therefore more strongly marked than is the case with the horizontal axis.

Shakespeare's *Richard II* is a particularly impressive example of this and the contrasting developments associated with Richard's fall and Bolingbroke's rise to power are reflected not only in purely verbal imagery, such as the analogy of the pair of scales or the well with two buckets with their opposition of upward and downward movement, but also in gestural and scenic leitmotifs such as kneeling or bowing which are similarly determined by this form of vertical opposition. Thus, the contrast between top and bottom is transformed into a spatial model of the feudal hierarchy that is destroyed by both Bolingbroke's usurpation and Richard's failings as a ruler. This spatial opposition is expressed most clearly in the climax in Act III, Scene iii, in which Richard is invited by Bolingbroke to step down from the battlements of Flint Castle and into the 'base court':

> NORTHUMBERLAND: My lord, in the base court he doth attend
> To speak with you; may it please you to come down?
> KING RICHARD: Down, down I come, like glist'ring Phaethon,
> Wanting the manage of unruly jades.
> In the base court? Base court, where kings grow base,
> To come at traitors' calls, and do them grace.
> In the base court? Come down? Down, court! down, king!
> For night-owls shriek where mounting larks should sing.
>
> (III,iii, 176–83)

The spatial contrast between the upper stage and the stage platform, which was an important feature of the Elizabethan stage, is interpreted semantically as a feudal and moral contrast, with the result that Richard's fall crosses not only a spatial dividing-line but also a semantic frontier and thus marks the central peripeteia of the whole text.[21]

7.3.1.2. The relationships between stage and off-stage

It is often, though not exclusively, the case in dramas consisting of a single locale that the spatial contrast between the stage and the off-stage area is modelled to represent a central semantic opposition. This sort of semantic interpretation of the contrast between interior and exterior space is particularly common in modern dramas written under the intellectual auspices of existentialism, and they often make considerable play of archetypical notions of space such as the uterus, caves and labyrinths.[22] The very titles of plays such as Sartre's *Huis clos* and *Les séquestrés d'Altona* or Pinter's *The Room* and *No Man's Land* reflect the central importance of the spatial opposition of interior and exterior space. In Beckett's plays, for example, the space off-stage is often left so vague and undetermined that the locale presented on stage seems to have been sealed off and isolated from every kind of narrower or broader spatial context and the events therefore take on the features of an existential model. In Sartre's *Huis clos* the exterior space becomes a place to escape to, but one which is inaccessible to the figures locked inside, condemned to be with each other for ever. In Pinter's plays, on the other hand, it is generally the interior or stage space that is interpreted in positive terms as a place of escape, with the off-stage area harbouring all sorts of vague and anonymous threats heralded by every knock at the door, telephone call and the appearance of each new figure.[23]

7.3.1.3. The relationships between a number of different locales

The relationships linking different locales produce the clearest and most tangible contrasts because several different and often contrasting locales are presented visually in the course of the play. Shakespeare's plays, which are dramas of movement virtually throughout, contain innumerable examples of this, and of all his plays it is especially the comedies that exhibit a particularly transparent spatio-semantic arrangement.[24]

The majority of his comedies are based on a simple spatial antithesis by which the various locales are divided into two groups, and this antithesis is manifested in the story constantly moving back and forth between the two areas. The cities of Verona and Milan and the forest near Mantua in *The Two Gentlemen of Verona*; the palace and the city of Athens and the 'wood near it' in *A Midsummer Night's Dream*, the ducal court and the Forest of Arden in *As You Like It* – all of these plays are variations of the essential contrast between an urban, courtly civilisation on the one hand, and the 'green world' of nature on the other. By contrasting civilisation and nature in this way the author has reduced the semantic interpretation of the spatial contrast down to its most abstract level. Seen in more concrete terms, the court and the city represent an area of potential conflicts that are then resolved 'playfully' in the forest, which serves as a place of escape. Urban, courtly society is dominated by the laws governing everyday reality, but these can be suspended in the world of the forest; in the former, death threatens, but the 'green world' is an area of regeneration and rebirth.

Thus, in *A Midsummer Night's Dream*, the lovers, facing the threat of death, flee Athens for the nocturnal forest where, in dreamlike unreality, the world is set aright, the lovers find each other and then, as changed people, return to a changed Athens. The play has a clearly cyclical structure in terms of locale, a feature that is also at the heart of the other comedies, though most of them are not constructed with quite the same degree of symmetry as *A Midsummer Night's Dream*. The order of the locales may be shown graphically as follows:

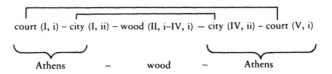

court (I, i) – city (I, ii) – wood (II, i–IV, i) – city (IV, ii) – court (V, i)

Athens   –   wood   –   Athens

The central wood scenes are placed between two perfectly symmetrical scenes set in Athens, though of course the clarity of this structure divided up according to the changes of locale is somewhat obscured by the dysfunctional division of the play into five acts that was undertaken by later editors.

7.3.1.4. Fictional locale versus real spatial context

There is one type of relationship that exists on a different level to the ones dealt with above, namely the relationship between the fictional space and the real spatial context of the intended audience. The decisive parameter clarifying the underlying intention behind the text and the status of the text is distance or proximity. Thus, the spatial distancing of events in Shakespeare's romantic comedies, for example, has the effect of abandoning all claims to realism. None of them – with the unique exception of *The Merry Wives of Windsor* – is set in England and the audience is transported to a series of topographically more or less vaguely defined Mediterranean regions of France, Italy, Sicily, Illyria or Greece. In this, Shakespeare was simply conforming to a convention of Elizabethan romantic comedy and romance which, in turn, had been influenced by a number of different sources and models borrowed from late Greek romance, Latin comedy, the Italian *commedia erudita* and the novella. In *A Midsummer Night's Dream*, this spatial distancing is reinforced by Shakespeare's decision to add chronological distance between the audience and the action by placing the latter in the sphere of the myth. However, the events are brought closer to the audience's world with the presentation of the plebeian world of the workmen, a group of figures that can hardly be said to be Greek in any way whatsoever, and whose presence creates an effect of cosy English parochialism.

Unlike the romantic comedies, satirical comedies tend to be set in contemporary England and London in particular, and so they establish a more direct link with the actual world of the audience. In such cases the spatial approximation of the fictional locale to the real world of the audience is, of course, intimately connected with the author's satirical intention of exposing the evils of a threatening and irksome environment.

Thus, in his own arrangement of his early comedy *Every Man in His Humour* for the folio edition of 1616, Jonson transferred the setting from the Florence of the original version (1598) to England in order to emphasise his satirical aspirations. In doing so, he was merely acting in accordance with a new programme which he had announced cogently in the prologue to *The Alchemist* (1610) with the words, 'Our scene is London' (line 5).

7.3.1.5. The locale and the events

One final aspect of the semantic structuring of space that we should like to discuss in this context is the relationship between the locale and the events that take place within it. This may remain unmarked or implicit, but it may also be determined by a number of clear semantic contrasts or correspondences. King Lear on the storm-blasted heath (III,ii and iv) and the lovers in the moonlit garden at Belmont (*The Merchant of Venice*, V,i) are memorable examples of semantic correspondence, that is, of the harmony between the inner moods and actions of the figures, and the external spatial setting. In both of these examples, the figures are themselves aware of this correspondence and specifically refer to it in their speeches. Of course, the contents of these two examples could scarcely be more different – *King Lear*, with its internal and external turmoil and *The Merchant of Venice* with its emphasis on inner and outer harmony. However, both are based on what John Ruskin described as a 'pathetic fallacy'. This was the notion that nature was in some way in sympathy with man, a notion that represented a widespread topos in European literature and was a particularly common feature of Shakespeare's plays. However, even Shakespeare's plays on occasion contain examples in which the locale and the action contrast dramatically and these were often used to create dramatic irony. The arrival of King Duncan and his entourage at Macbeth's castle, for example, occurs in an atmospheric and spatial context that seems to promise a period of peace, harmony and fertility:

> DUNCAN: This castle hath a pleasant seat; the air
>   Nimbly and sweetly recommends itself
>   Unto our gentle senses.
> BANQUO: This guest of summer,
>   The temple-haunting martlet, does approve
>   By his lov'd mansionry that the heaven's breath
>   Smells wooingly here; no jutty, frieze,
>   Buttress, nor coign of vantage, but this bird
>   Hath made her pendent bed and procreant cradle.
>   Where they most breed and haunt, I have observ'd
>   The air is delicate.   (I,vi, 1–10)

However, the audience has already been informed that this will be the setting for Duncan's murder. There is a similar ironic contrast between the events and the locale in the above-mentioned scene in *Henry VI Part 2* Act IV, Scene x (see above, 7.2.2.2.) which draws together Jack Cade's anarchistic rebellion and a paradise garden, the emblem of both cosmic and political order.

Act III of the contemporary German dramatist Rolf Hochhuth's drama *Soldiers* (1967), with its heading 'The park' was conceived in this very same tradition. It is set in the orchard at Chequers, the country residence of the British Prime Minister, on the day of the fatal 'accident' that befell Sikorski, the head of the Polish government (4 July 1943). In the detailed commentaries in the secondary text, Hochhuth refers explicitly to both the iconographic and emblematic significance and ironic function of the setting:

'God Almighty first planted a garden. And indeed it is the purest of human pleasures. It is the greatest refreshment to the spirits of man; without which, buildings and palaces are but gross handyworks.' Thus begins Francis Bacon's eulogy to the park and at this point the greatest effort should be made to present this landscaped counterpart to the seascape of the first act in accordance with the high standards demanded by this sixteenth-century courtier. For our scenery is intended as an ironic accusation.[25]

This ironic contrast becomes clear as soon as the curtain rises to reveal a stage empty of people: the visual impression of an arcadian idyll is completely undermined by the acoustic impression of a radio announcement about a German offensive on the Russian front. The irony is heightened in the ensuing scenes as the park is transformed into a command centre for marine warfare and the setting for a number of heated debates on the saturation bombing of German cities. The semantic connotations evoked by the locale – the privacy and peace of a *vita contemplativa*, paradisiac or pastoral innocence, order and harmony – are permanently contradicted by the actions and intentions of the figures, especially the central figure, Churchill, who shares the responsibility for Sikorski's death and is responsible for the bombing raids on civilian targets.

7.3.2. The conceptions of space

7.3.2.1. Neutrality – stylisation – realisation

A comparative study of the ways that the dramatic setting or locale has been visually realised over the centuries will reveal a broad spectrum of variations, stretching from abstract neutrality to a sharply focussed realistic type of scenic enactment. Visual realisation in classical Greek tragedy, for example, scarcely went beyond the given stage set, which remained the same whatever the play, and which only occasionally was complemented with additions such as an altar or a tombstone.[26] In Elizabethan theatre the locale was still represented by little more than the permanent stage itself: the stage platform, supporting pillars, trapdoors, doors, upper stage and the 'discovery space' of the inner stage etc. – though various other emblematic items such as mountains, city-gates, caves, tents or supporting platforms became increasingly popular as additional stage properties. Classical French drama and Weimar classicism, on the other hand, already began to implement painted two-dimensional backdrops which helped the audience to identify a specific locale but did not go so far as attempting to present a realistic illusion. They remained little more than a marginal framework which uses abstract stylisation to point at what the locale might be and with which the figures had virtually no physical or haptic contact.[27]

The contrast between this and the concept of space in late nineteenth-century drama could scarcely be more evident. An example is the set prescribed by Strindberg for his play *Miss Julie* (1888), a play that bears the programmatic subtitle 'A naturalistic tragedy'. Before the text of the play proper, Strindberg inserted detailed stage-directions in which he described the scenery in a way that left little to the set-designer's own imagination:

A large kitchen: the ceiling and the side walls are hidden by draperies and hangings. The rear wall runs diagonally across the stage, from the left side and away from the spectators. On this wall, to the left, there are two shelves full of utensils made of copper, iron and tin. The shelves are trimmed with scalloped paper.
A little to the right may be seen three-fourths of the big arched doorway leading to the outside. It has double glass doors, through which are seen a fountain and a cupid, lilac shrubs in bloom, and the tops of some Lombardy poplars.
On the left side of the stage is seen the corner of a big cook-stove built of glazed bricks; also a part of the smoke-hood above it.
From the right protrudes one end of the servants' dining-table of white pine, with a few chairs about it.
The stove is dressed with bundled branches of birch. Twigs of juniper are scattered on the floor.
. On the table end stands a big Japanese spice pot full of lilac blossoms. An ice-box, a kitchen table and a wash-stand.
Above the door hangs a big old-fashioned bell on a steel spring, and the mouthpiece of a speaking-tube appears at the left of the door.[28]

What is noticeable about this secondary text is the 'epic' thoroughness with which the stage set is prescribed right down to the most minute detail – such as the patterned paper lining the shelves. From this it is clear that the set here is no longer just an ephemeral backdrop, but has been injected with a completely new level of significance and meaning for the play as a whole (which we shall discuss in greater detail below). It was felt that the materials used in the setting should be as genuine or authentic as possible so as to create a complete illusion of a real room within the framework of the stage. By breaking up the frontal perspective with diagonal, oblique walls or other elements, the intention was to heighten the three-dimensional sense of space, and by presenting the stage-space simply as one part of a broader locale it was made to suggest a spatial continuum extending beyond the frame of the stage. All this was designed to serve the naturalists' desire to reproduce a true likeness of reality, as Strindberg confessed himself in his extended preface to the play:

As far as the scenery is concerned, I have borrowed from impressionistic painting its asymmetry, its quality of abruptness, and have thereby, in my opinion, streng-thened the illusion. Because the whole room and all its contents are not shown, there is a chance to guess at things – that is, our imagination is stirred into complementing our vision. I have made a further gain in getting rid of those tiresome exits by means of doors, especially as stage doors are made of canvas and swing back and forth at the slightest touch. . . . I have also contented myself with a single setting, and for the double purpose of making the figures become parts of their surroundings, and of breaking with the tendency towards luxurious scenery. But having only a single setting, one may demand to have it real. Yet nothing is more difficult than to get a room that looks something like a room . . . Let it go at canvas for the walls, but we might be done with the painting of shelves and kitchen utensils on the canvas. We have so much else on the stage that is conventional, and in which we are asked to believe, that we might at least be spared the too great effort of believing in painted pans and kettles.[29]

The gap between a neutral space or one that is merely hinted at in stylised form and a realistically reconstructed space is thus very large indeed. Nevertheless, we would rather interpret this distance from a systematic rather than the purely historical point of view because the way the conception of space in Western drama and theatre has developed over the centuries cannot really be described as a linear process that slowly moved towards a realistic presentation of locale. The use of space in medieval drama, for example, was generally more neutral and less prede-termined than the notion that prevailed in plays of classical antiquity, and modern drama in general can scarcely be described as a striving to preserve the naturalist tendency to fill the stage with a plethora of realistic details or to create the illusion of reality. In fact, it covers a variety of different movements that consciously reject that tradition. Examples of this are the abstract and stylised use of space in expressionist drama that were in-tended to reflect inner states or conditions rather than material objects, the deliberate exposure of the artificiality of stage sets and restriction to the most basic necessities in epic theatre and, finally, the sense of unreality in the use of space in 'absurd' plays such as Beckett's *Waiting for Godot*.

7.3.2.2. Functions

Corresponding to these different levels of realism with which a locale can be presented on stage are the different functions of space. We shall begin by examining the kinds of space that are presented most specifically and realistically. At one extreme, this particular conception of space may be invoked in order to create the spectacular visual effects with which, for example, the 'stage extravaganzas' of the nineteenth and twentieth centuries attempted to thrill their audiences. At the other extreme, it may serve to recreate the contingencies of reality. It is this second function that predominates in the theatre of naturalism, where the wealth of material detail which surrounds the figures also has the additional function of emphasising the extent to which the figures are conditioned by external circumstances.[30] By using objects to reflect the circumstances affecting a dramatic figure it is possible to demonstrate its dependence on the conditions of its immediate environment, social atmosphere and its physical and psychological disposition – i.e. that a figure is no longer acting autonomously as a transcendental self but under the pressure of external conditions. If Strindberg, as we have just seen, hoped that his figures would appear as if they had become 'parts of their surroundings' he is using a biological metaphor to express exactly this kind of social determinism that results from material conditioning. Thus, in the contrast between the servants' quarters with the aristocratic, or even feudal, ornamental garden in the background, the locale of *Miss Julie* is already being used to define the sociological tensions against which the tragedy of the central figure unfolds. The sprigs of lilac blossom on the servants' table are not just a gratuitous decorative detail: it is the 'strong aphrodisiac effect of the flowers' that contributes to the stimulating atmosphere of the midsummer night that Julia finds so difficult to resist.[31] In the semantic context of the rather obvious contrast between the interior and the background, the lilac blossom also has a symbolic function: the fact that they have been brought in from the ornamental garden into the servants' kitchen must be interpreted as a symbol for Julie's attempt to 'cross frontiers' (Lotman), for her violation of social barriers. Whilst in this case the conditions imposed by the physical character of the room dominate over the figure, thus transforming the room itself into a sort of active protagonist, there are a number of twentieth-century dramatic texts in which the figures are utterly static and the room and the objects that fill it become the only truly active forces, as Hans Hoppe has demonstrated convincingly with regard to the dramas of Ionesco and others (see below, 7.3.3.2.).[32]

Conversely, if the locale remains neutral or largely unspecified the focus of the presentation shifts towards the figures' inner consciousness, which is then classed as autonomous or 'un-conditioned' as far as the material or objective circumstances are concerned. The idealist conception of the primacy of an autonomous consciousness over the external conditions of social environment and atmosphere goes hand in hand with an emphasis on more general human qualities in favour of the more specific and individual. It is not the uniqueness of an individual that is established by this type of spatial context but the qualities that are representative of a particular class – such as the imposing dignity of a magnificent palatial setting to represent a powerful ruler. In naturalist drama the spatial context shapes and determines the individual figure, but in the plays of Corneille, for example, its function is reflective, which means that it merely reflects the particular figure's status. This shift away from the specific and the individual towards the general and typical also corresponds to the fact that when space is conceived in strongly concrete terms the locales are generally private interiors, whereas here they are generally public spaces that are not associated with one specific individual.

Of course, this does not merely apply to classical French or German drama; it is also true of modern plays whose conception of space is neutral and indefinite. This applies to Beckett's *Waiting for Godot* for example, in which the locale is identified laconically in the secondary text as 'A country road. A tree' and, even in the productions supervised by Beckett himself, the set consisted of hardly more than one, more or less stylised tree. Even the peculiar characteristics of this tree are left so vague that Vladimir and Estragon are able to argue whether it is a tree, a shrub or a bush (pp. 14 and *passim*). Similarly, the country road leads from one unspecified place to another.[33] On the most superficial level, this tree serves the initial function of indicating that the locale is in the open air and that it is therefore a plausible place for two homeless tramps to meet. On a deeper level, though, the emptiness of the stage, which the tree, as a focal point, actually emphasises, reflects the existential condition of the two tramps – their isolation, aimlessness and disoriented solitude. These are, at least from Beckett's point of view, general definitions of the human condition which need not be explained genetically in terms of the specific physiological, sociological, atmospheric or psychological aspects of the figures' lives through a specific environment. Instead, the space Beckett presents is intended as the symbolic reflection of this state and level of awareness. It is exactly because the events are situated in a kind of abstract 'nowhereness' – as Leo Spitzer has described the settings in Racine – that they are elevated to the status of a universally valid model of human existence. As the text progresses, the tree becomes increasingly laden with a series of new symbolic associations. This process, following the pattern of projection from inner to outer experience, takes place in the dialogues between the two figures: the conversation between Vladimir and Estragon on the two thieves on the cross links the tree with the cross of Jesus as a symbol not only of death but also of the hope of salvation and life (pp. 11–13) and in their reflections on suicide they see it as a potential gibbet, though of course in the image of the hanged man's erection life and death once again overlap (pp. 17f.). This symbolism is continued when the apparently dead tree produces a few leaves and Vladimir is prompted into comparing their rustling with the sound of sand and ash (pp. 62f.). It also becomes the tree of paradise since it is impossible to hide behind it (pp. 74f.). However, it is not this symbolic quality in itself that is characteristic of a stylised conception of space because, as we saw in the case of the sprigs of lilac blossom in *Miss Julie*, even in plays whose conception of space is more precise and individualistic, the space presented, or a detail within it, may still serve a symbolic function. The characteristic feature is the fact that the locale has a reflective rather than a determining function. In this particular example, then, space is used predominantly as a way of projecting certain levels of inner awareness and only provides a rather rudimentary image of real space. Some forms of modern drama, such as expressionist theatre, went even further in excluding any reference to real space and in using stage settings to serve as a channel for projecting the inner workings and condition of the soul.[34]

7.3.3. Localisation techniques

Our discussion of the various conceptions of dramatic space has tended to hedge around the actual techniques that are used to present it in the dramatic text. These localisation techniques, by analogy with the characterisation techniques (see above, 5.4.2.) form a closed repertoire that may be derived from the repertoire of codes and channels at the disposal of theatrical texts (see above, 1.3.2.). What has varied over the centuries are the qualitative and quantitative criteria governing the selection of a particular set of techniques from this repertoire. This becomes evident in a comparative study of the conventions used in, for example, Elizabethan and naturalist drama: In Elizabethan plays it was the verbal localisation techniques that predominated, whereas naturalist drama generally resorted to visual or other non-verbal techniques.

7.3.3.1. Verbal localisation techniques

The importance of verbal localisation techniques was mentioned briefly above in connection with implicit stage-directions (see above, 2.1.4.). The expression 'verbal localisation technique' refers to a phenomenon that is generally known as 'word-scenery'[35] or 'spoken space'[36] – that is, the way the spatial context is portrayed or referred to in the figures' utterances. The immediate function of word-scenery in Elizabethan drama, for example, was to compensate for the restricted means in the scenic presentation. It was much more than a simple substitute, however, and this was reflected in the fact that attempts to present visually every single detail of the word-scenery in, for example, Banquo's and Duncan's description of Macbeth's castle in *Macbeth* I,vi (see above, 7.3.1.5.) did not actually heighten the effect. On the contrary they simply distracted the audience from the poetic qualities of the language and reflected a desire to create a uniform effect that undermined the dramatic irony engendered by the contrast between the locale and the events taking place within it. This naïve desire for realism ran counter to Elizabethan dramatic practice and yet became a feature of those heavy-handed Shakespearean productions in the nineteenth century.

This example also reveals one of the fundamental differences between word-scenery and the visually presented stage set. The latter is 'objectively' the same for all figures, whereas the former is generally linked 'subjectively' to one or other figure-perspective. The idyllic, cheerful picture of Macbeth's castle painted by Banquo and Duncan is obviously not an objective view and is no more than an externalisation of their inner moods at the time. Linking word-scenery to a figure-perspective in this way can create a complex web of ambiguity that a specific stage set can scarcely match.[37] One and the same locale may be presented in a number of completely different ways, depending on the different perspectives of the various figures acting within it. This presented writers like Shakespeare with dramatic opportunities that he was able to exploit to the full, especially in his middle and late comedies. In *As You Like It*, for example, the different ways the figures see the Forest of Arden accurately reflect their own perspectives whilst at the same time, as the play develops, the locale itself takes on a multidimensional and complex web of meaning. The preliminary conversations that take place in the first act lead the audience to expect an idyllic pastoral, which combines features taken from the classical myth of the Golden Age and elements of the home-grown Robin Hood tradition. The first scenes, however, that take place in the Forest of Arden abound with references to aspects which, rather surprisingly, seem to undermine ironically the pastoral conventions of the *locus amoenus*. For although the Duke adopts a pastoral tone to praise the advantages of country life over life at court, he also emphasises the genuine hardships imposed by inclement weather which the shepherds and inhabitants of the forest are obliged to endure without sufficient protection (II,i). To the exhausted fugitives the forest seems at first sight to be an inhospitable place and the perspective of Corin, the shepherd, seems to reflect the misery of the English farm labourer of the time more accurately than the carefree happiness of an arcadian world of shepherds and shepherdesses (II,iv and vi). In fact, these negative aspects actually predominate in the figures of Touchstone, the clown, and the cynical Jacques. – In *The Tempest*, with its open perspective structure, the locale has become completely ambiguous, in that a number of extremely divergent views of the island overlap. Instead of adding up to a subtle and sophisticated overall picture, as they do in *As You Like It*, they are now completely at odds with one another:

> This Shakespearean drama does not present the audience with the one single definitive view of an isolated island. Instead each individual figure is given the opportunity to interpret it as he or she wishes – or rather to bring his or her own interpretation to the island because it transpires that the island is a reflection of man's inner barrenness or fertility.[38]

The function of word-scenery is thus not completely taken up with compensating for the lack of an explicit stage set. It may transcend this function and contribute towards figure characterisation, the development of central themes – often in the shape of leitmotif-like images – and, in more general terms, the semantic structuring of stage-space.

The second important type of verbal localisation is represented by the descriptions of the locale outlined in the secondary text.[39] Since these usually take the form of explicit stage-directions or instructions to the set-designer they can normally be translated directly into the multimedial presentation. The range of possible variations stretches from a cursory reference to a locale through to the sort of detailed description that Strindberg provided in *Miss Julie* (see above, 7.3.2.1.).

Quite apart from this sort of quantitative expansion, the secondary text may also assume a relatively high level of autonomy *vis-à-vis* the scenery if it is not restricted to merely providing stage-directions but includes commentaries and interpretations. In such cases the localisation process in the secondary text becomes a part of an independent epic mediation system. We have already shown this in connection with the epic communication structures in drama as they appear in Chekhov's *The Cherry Orchard* (see above, 3.6.2.1.). The almost essay-like proportions of Rolf Hochhuth's discussion of the form and function of the garden that served as the locale for Act III of *Soldiers* is even more extreme in this respect (see above, 7.3.1.5.). Naturally, the insertion of this kind of epically conveyed description of and commentary on the locale is based on the presupposition that the literary text, and thus the purely 'closet reception' of dramas, has gained a certain degree of autonomy with regard to the performed text and its multimedial reception.

7.3.3.2. Non-verbal localisation techniques

The title of this particular section will presumably initially conjure up the notion of a more or less precise and specific presentation of space by means of a stage set (consisting of scenery, accessories and props, lighting etc.). However, we would first like to concentrate our attention on one aspect that is not quite so obvious as the stage set but which is nonetheless of great and universal importance – namely the creation of a sense of space and locale through the actions and activities of the various figures on stage.

On one level of this actional conception of space, the exits and entrances of the figures can be used to indicate certain spatial relationships and to establish a contrast between the fictional space off-stage and the fictional space on-stage. The figures appear to be coming from and going to a number of different places and the different directions they take add spatial sophistication to the off-stage area. These as yet rather vague distinctions can then usually be made more precise and concrete in the verbal utterances of the figures themselves, in the course of which it becomes clear that – to take a spatial arrangement commonly used in Latin comedies, for example – one direction leads to the market place and the other to the harbour. Announcements or retrospective utterances, dialogues between figures entering or leaving the stage giving the impression that they are abruptly started or broken off as the figures cross the 'line' separating the stage and the area outside it, teichoscopic utterances which refer to action taking place simultaneously off-stage, and, finally and quite independently of any narrative mediation on-stage, noises or voices off which can be heard in the auditorium – all of these are techniques used by playwrights to specify and define both the immediate and more distant environment and are extremely important for the way the plot develops.[40]

Thus, in Ben Jonson's *The Alchemist*, which is set almost entirely in Lovewit's house, a succession of customers enter from the street to see the three villains and are sent out again or pushed into adjoining rooms whilst in a further room behind the stage Subtle has set up his alchemist's laboratory in the hope of creating the stone of the wise (a plan that comes to nothing when in Act IV, Scene v there is a large explosion off-stage). This constant flow of people from the surrounding areas of London into the house in Blackfriars seems to identify the latter as a focal point of all kinds of vice and the rest of a plague-ridden London further afield off-stage as a place that has fallen prey to folly, greed and corruption. Nor is Jonson's description of the locale left vague and abstract; on the contrary, he has added a great deal of local colour and a wealth of topographical details. However, quite apart from these additional elements specifying the locale (most of them are mediated verbally by the figures themselves) the very structure of the plot as an intrigue in itself creates and sustains the contrast between the stage and the off-stage area. By definition, this implies that the victims of the intrigue are constantly arriving and departing, in the same way that the three rooms immediately adjoining the stage are also a spatial consequence of the demands imposed on the dramatist by the various intertwining strands of the intrigue. Thus, certain types of plot require certain spatial arrangements.

However, it is not just the figures' entrances and exits that constitute such spatial relationships. These can also be established whilst the figures are present on stage. Their physical presence is in itself enough to give the dramatic text a certain spatial dimension, and their positioning and movements are what brings this space to life – a space that is both created, sustained and restricted by the stage-area. Even the presence of a single, motionless figure on an otherwise completely empty stage creates a set of spatial relationships: a position centre-stage, for example, creates a meaningful opposition to one that is off-centre and, similarly a position up-stage is related to one down-stage. The system of spatial relationships becomes more complex as new figures enter and create an increasing number of possible spatial groupings. The 'distance' between two figures is a consequence of the particular chain of events that led up to this configuration and this makes it possible to interpret the spatial relationship in a number of different and meaningful ways. Thus, if two figures, or groups of figures, are situated far apart, for example, then this may be a physical manifestation of conflict or animosity. It may also express a wish on the part of one of the figures or groups to be an impartial observer, an interested spectator or even an eavesdropper. It is, after all, movement that brings a particular stage-space to life and, as such, both the contrast between stillness and movement and the choreographical arrangement of the various moves – direction, speed and coordination – are 'significant' in that they assume the character of a sign. The two elements involved – the static and the dynamic – combine to realise the potential of the space defined by the borders of the stage and it is this that actually creates dramatic space.

Along with the figures and the set, the properties, or 'props', also form a part of the specific inventory of a dramatic text that enables the author to achieve a convincing three-dimensional quality.[41] In the system of visual signs in drama the prop occupies a central position between the figure and his or her costume on the one hand and the stage set on the other. For whilst costumes are usually inextricably associated with the figures, a prop can be associated either with a figure or the set, depending on whether or not it is drawn into the figure's sphere of action. Thus, elements of the set can temporarily turn into props if they are used by one of the figures and then go back to being a part of the set as soon as the figure relinquishes all haptic contact with them. On the other hand, a prop may also become part of a costume if it is firmly attached to one of the figures, just as, conversely, a costume may become a prop if it is separated from the figure or is brought into the action in a particular way.

In many plays an object may shift from one position to another within the structural spectrum of 'figure – costume – property – set'. Thus, the crowns worn by the kings of England and France in the final scene (V,ii) of Shakespeare's *Henry V*, for which there are no specific instructions in either the primary or secondary texts, are part of the costume that identify those figures as monarchs. The crown of Richard II in Shakespeare's play of the same name, on the other hand, is frequently referred to in the primary text and integrated meaningfully into the gestural action – especially in the crucial abdication scene (IV,i):

> KING RICHARD: Give me the crown. Here, cousin, seize the crown.
>   Here, cousin,
>   On this side my hand, and on that side thine.
>   Now is this golden crown like a deep well
>   That owes two buckets, filling one another;
>   The emptier ever dancing in the air,
>   The other down, unseen, and full of water.
>   That bucket down and full of tears am I,
>   Drinking my grieves, whilst you mount up on high.
> BOLINGBROKE: I thought you had been willing to resign.
> KING RICHARD: My crown I am; but still my grieves are mine.
>   (IV,i, 181–91)

In the context of this gestural game, the crown has become a prop. It is no longer a permanent sign of Richard's regal status, and this game with it, which Richard demonstratively interprets as a visual conceit and which reflects once again the above-mentioned vertical symbolism in the use of space, integrates it into an emblematic process that is designed to underline the central peripeteia – namely Richard's abdication and Bolingbroke's usurpation. Finally, a crown that is neither worn by one of the figures nor integrated into its gestural repertoire but remains linked with the throne as a part of the insignia of royal power contributes towards defining the dramatic setting.

The shifts of position within the spectrum of figure – costume – prop – set can sometimes be even more radical, however. In fact, it is true that a dramatic figure may become object-like and even a part of the set if it only appears as a physical presence and is not permitted any degree of verbal or mimetic expression. This would apply to stage-extras, for example, who often fill the back of the stage, remaining motionless with the sole function of defining the contours of the dramatic space – such as by emphasising the feudal character of the setting. Conversely, it is also possible for an object, or element of the set, to assume the characteristics of a dramatic figure if, as Hans Hoppe (1971) has shown in the case of the modern 'theatre of objects', it is able to develop some form of independent activity. The grandfather clock in Ionesco's *La Cantatrice chauve*, for example, with its irregular and arbitrary chiming succeeds in becoming a law unto itself. It interferes repeatedly in the figures' plans and actions and attains a level of articulation that is in no way less sophisticated than that of the figures themselves, who are only able to utter meaningless successions of sounds.

The number and types of props deployed in a dramatic text are prescribed by the particular conception of space involved. Plays that tend towards neutrality or a high level of stylisation use a very small number of props, but the ones they do use are all the more important because of that. This was already the case in classical Greek tragedy, in which props such as the urn of Sophocles' Electra and Philoctetes' bow are never banished to the periphery but are always endowed with a number of important symbolic functions – such as plot motivation, characterisation, the clarification of a particular situation (as reminders of the past, instruments of dramatic irony etc.). The plays of German and French classicism also tended to be very economical in their use of props and generally only used them to represent things of great significance. A small number of 'heraldic' props to indicate the high social standing of a figure and certain objects introduced to move the plot forward such as a letter, ring or casket are used to represent the large number and wide variety of objects that usually constitute a real-life environment but which are excluded in order to establish the degree of exemplary universality and internalisation intended. Of the three levels of concreteness with which objects can be represented in dramatic texts – 1) as a visible and tangible object, 2) as an object that is referred to verbally either directly, or 3) indirectly (i.e. metaphorically) – it is levels 2) and 3) that predominate in plays of that type and thus tend to dematerialise the dramatic presentation. Beyond that, the only things that are presented physically are concrete objects that are specifically mentioned in the primary text; such plays make no provision for the gratuitous or incidental inclusion of other objects.

In complete contrast to this, the detailed environments prescribed for naturalist dramas, for example, generally call for a wide range of precisely identified objects. And these objects are not simply 'present' on stage but are constantly being integrated into the action in some way. This constant and often incidental haptic contact between the figures and the world of objects (that is, when it occurs instinctively or when such contact is not mentioned in the figures' utterances) is in marked contrast to the distance that is created and preserved between the figures and their physical environment in plays with a neutral or stylised conception of space. However, even if the quantity of material objects used in a play is extremely large, their function need not be reduced to reflecting the contingencies of reality. Even the most apparently trivial and incidental prop can be significant in some way, as the plays of Chekhov, the master of the apparently insignificant and meaningless detail, show.[42]

The long list of props used in The Cherry Orchard includes Gayev's caramels, Ranyevskaya's telegrams, Varya's key-ring, Firs's walking stick and Dooniasha's powder-box. The cigar that Yasha lights in Act II, Scene i reflects the deep impression that the elegant world of Paris has made on him, the servant, in the same way that Dooniasha, with her powder-box, strives to imitate her mistress. At the same time, though, by smoking in Dooniasha's presence, Yasha proves that although he is trying to impress her with his refined urban habits, his command of them is inadequate because he would otherwise never smoke a cigar in the presence of a woman. In other words, there is a great deal of the characterisation that is not conveyed through dialogue but rather through mimetic and gestural activity using certain props. The information conveyed in this way is much more individualised and sophisticated than the more universal qualities associated with a crown or other heraldic kinds of props.

This brief study of the role of a prop in a play has enabled us to illuminate a broad selection of their most important functions. Nonetheless, we should now like to close with a short systematic summary.[43] First and foremost, props are used to reflect the degree of imitative realism or stylisation and, closely linked to that, to characterise dramatic space and the dramatic figures. Beyond that they may be instrumental in moving the plot forward if, for example, they represent something that is coveted by one or more of the figures, if they become an instrument of intrigue or the *corpus delicti* that exposes a crime or misdemeanour. In this function an object may actually become the focal point of the plot, and this is often referred to in the title of a play. Comedies such as Plautus' *Aulularia* (*The Pot of Gold*), Heinrich von Kleist's *The Broken Jug* and Carl Sternheim's *Knickers*, or tragedies such as Franz Grillparzer's *The Golden Fleece* are amongst the first to spring to mind (the fact that we are able to think of more comedies than tragedies in this context is no coincidence and is presumably a consequence of the special affinity between comedy and the world of tangible objects). In fact, when these objects are of such key importance it is often possible to establish a number of semantic links with the central themes of the play: the broken jug in Kleist's play reflects the disintegration of social harmony and man's fall from grace, whilst Sternheim's rather *risqué* article of clothing illustrates the ambivalence and hypocrisy inherent in the manifestations of both prudery and lust. One last function of objects and props is bound up with the way they can contribute to chronological coherence. They can remind either the figures or the audience (or both) of past events and may anticipate the future. An object may signify one aspect of the biographical background of one of the dramatic figures (cf. Yasha's cigar, for example) or may refer to an important moment in the background events preceding the play (the wig belonging to the village judge Adam in *The Broken Jug*, for example) or it may provide a figure with an occasion for reminiscence (Electra's urn in

The Golden Fleece, for example).[44] Reference to the future is often simply implied by the use to which an object may be put (a dagger or a bottle of poison usually lead one to expect an act of violence) or by the fact that its presence is puzzling to the extent that the audience expects a solution. A letter or a locked casket, for example, encourages the audience to speculate as to what it might contain. This is clearly demonstrated in Shakespeare's *Merchant of Venice*, in which Portia's suitors have to select the casket containing her portrait from a selection of three made of gold, silver and lead respectively. In each case the reference to the future implied by each object creates suspense (see above, 3.7.4.), since they pose questions that can only be resolved at some time in the future.

7.4. The structure and presentation of time

7.4.1. Tense: immediacy versus distance

Absolute autonomy, or the absence of a mediating narrator in dramatic texts (see above, 1.2.2.–4.), means that the predominant tense used in drama is the present, whereas in narrative texts it is the past. Thornton Wilder formulated this distinction in the following succinct manner:

A play is what takes place. A novel is what one person tells took place.
The novel is a past reported in the present. On the stage it is always now. This confers upon the action an increased vitality which the novelist longs in vain to incorporate into his work.[45]

Of course, this does not mean that the present tense is the only one used in dramatic texts because, despite the immediacy of the dramatic situation presented on stage, the figures – and the audience – are aware of both a past and a future dimension. Nor does it mean that the fictional present of the dramatic situation coincides with the real present of the audience, in other words that the present tense used in the fictional text reflects the real present of the audience (see above, 7.1.). After all, the absolute autonomy of drama applies as much to the audience as it does to the author.[46]

Nevertheless, like the relationship between the fictional locale and the real spatial context (see above, 7.3.1.4.), the relationship between the fictional time-scale within the play and the real time-scale of the presentation is relevant for the intentions underlying the text. It is important to establish whether the fictional action is set in the unspecified world of myth, a clearly identifiable historical period, in the immediate present of the world of the audience or in an ahistorical, atemporal and unidentifiable period, because the relationship between the text and contemporary reality varies according to the amount of chronological distance between them. Thus, the chronological distance separating the subject matter of

Elizabethan history plays from the contemporary political context, for example, enabled the playwrights to discuss, albeit indirectly, the dynastic and constitutional problems of the time in a way that would not have been possible without this distance, and, conversely, the *hic et nunc* setting of Ben Jonson's *The Alchemist* is used to emphasise the satirical references to the audience's real environment outside the theatre.

However, at the same time it is by no means always the case that the greater the amount of time separating the content of a play and the context of its performance, the greater the level of mediation or indirectness of the relationship between the text and reality, or that a greater proximity or even simultaneity is bound to imply greater immediacy. It is important in each individual case to analyse all the various functions involved in such a way as to take into consideration how precisely the text is located within a specific historical period or how vague the time-span involved is. Thus, neither Elizabethan nor classical French drama were particularly concerned with historical authenticity as far as the costumes, props or set were concerned and this tended to reduce considerably the sense of chronological distance between, for example, the Roman republic portrayed on stage and the England of Elizabeth I or the France of Louis XIV. The historical dramas of the nineteenth century, on the other hand, were generally concerned to present the figures and action with a high level of historical authenticity. These two contrary trends were also reflected in the use of language. Plays written from a historicising perspective tended to contain a large number of lexical, syntactic or stylistic archaisms, whilst those wishing to establish greater chronological proximity often employ anachronisms.

7.4.2. Succession and simultaneity

We shall now turn to the chronological relationships that exist in the internal communication system. These are determined on the basis of two axes: the 'horizontal' axis of the succession of events and the 'vertical' axis of simultaneous events (see above, 3.7.1.). In his fine essay on Shakespeare (1773), Herder pointed out this very fact in the context of an analysis of the time structures in Shakespeare's plays:

It is in the course of his events, in the *ordine successivorum* and *simultaneorum* of his world, that his time and space are contained.[47]

On the axis of succession one incident follows another, whilst on the axis of simultaneity a number of different situations, actions or events coincide to make up the dramatic situation. This simultaneity applies both to actions and events that are presented scenically and those that occur off-stage and which are related verbally, either as they occur or retrospectively. From this it is clear that the vertical axis of simultaneity is the one that implies the category of space.

Succession in drama takes place on two levels: that of the story that forms the basis of the text, and that of the presentation of that story. These two levels need not, and in fact generally do not, coincide because when information is transmitted retrospectively these two series are displaced against each other. And yet such reports of past events are processes scenically presented in themselves and thus ensure a degree of forward movement on both levels of the succession axis.

The three dimensions of time are, in principle, equally balanced. Some theorists of drama tend to think that the future dimension is the one that predominates, but this view only applies to a historically specific type of text which follows a particular norm of future-orientated finality. Thus, the following definition of the dramatic by S. K. Langer certainly can be applied to classical drama, Shakespeare and the plays of French and German classicism, but not to plays that have no plot – that is, those in which information is conveyed successively but only to present a static condition. Drama's 'basic abstraction', Langer claims, 'is the act, which springs from the past, but is directed towards the future, and is always great with things to come'.[48] Peter Pütz, on the other hand, describes the succession process in drama without accentuating the futural dimension as a norm; it can therefore be applied ahistorically:

In each moment of a drama something has *already* happened and there is something that is *still* to happen, that may be concluded and anticipated from what went before. Each new moment takes up some aspect of the past and anticipates future events. Dramatic action is made up of the *successive* realisation of anticipated *future* events and those recalled from the *past*.[49]

As far as the presentation itself is concerned the fictional time-scale of the play passes within the flow of the actual time of the performance, though of course if time is stretched or concentrated this may lead to discrepancies in the respective tempi. This correlation of the linear direction in the chronological succession processes on both levels is true not only within passages characterised by closed time–space structures, but, as a rule, it also transcends the division of a play into acts or scenes. One of the conventions of dramatic texts that is rarely subverted – even in innovative or experimental theatre – is the expectation that the situations presented in successive scenes follow the same successive pattern as the fictional chronology, either in such a way that each follows on directly from the preceding one, or, more usually that they are separated by gaps of varying length. Thus, if two successive scenes or acts in the fictional chronology partially or totally overlap then this is a dramatic deviation from the norm and must be clearly signalled. Friedrich Dürrenmatt has drawn his readers' attention to Johann Nestroy's magical farce *Death on the Wedding Day* (*Der Tod am Hochzeitstag*) as an example of the successive presentation of simultaneous fictional events. In this play the simultaneity of the successive acts is signalled by the fact that the 'action of the second act forms the acoustic backdrop to the first and the action of the first the acoustic backdrop to the second'.[50] Alan Ayckbourn's trilogy *The Norman Conquests* exhibits a similar structure of simultaneity on a larger scale.

The basic principle of correlation between the two levels of succession (presentation and story) is disrupted even further if a play contains situations which on the fictional time axis actually precede those presented in a previous scene or act. A well-known example of this phenomenon is J. B. Priestley's *Time and the Conways* (1937). The title is itself an indication that time is a central theme, and this is then amplified by the radical departure from the conventional principle of succession, which draws the audience's attention to the whole question of time. All three acts take place in the same room in the Conways' house but whilst Acts I and III take place on an autumn evening in 1919, Act II takes place on an autumn evening in 1937. A simple inversion of Acts II and III would restore the more conventional succession principle: Act I closes with Mrs Conway singing a Schumann song and Act III opens with the end of that song, whereas Act II is separated from the others by a long intervening period of eighteen years. By choosing this unusual arrangement the author is able to articulate the contrast between the hopes and expectations of the young generation after the end of the First World War and the frustration of these hopes in the face of reality and he is able thus to emphasise the dramatic ironies inherent in the last act. In doing so, Priestley succeeds in presenting a conception of time which (influenced by the theory of time proposed by the mathematician and philosopher J. W. Dunne) Alan Conway specifically refers to in the play itself – namely the shift of emphasis from successive juxtaposition to static simultaneity by means of a *regressus ad infinitum*.

The principle that the order in which scenes are presented in a play corresponds to the order of the events in the story underlying the play is also disrupted when the author introduces epic communication structures. An epic commentary from a figure from either outside or inside the action (see above, 3.6.2.2. and 3.) 'consumes' real performance time, but at the same time 'suspends' the succession process of the action. This suspension of time can be represented scenically by fixing one particular moment, by 'freezing' the movements of all the figures apart from the commentator. Productions of Thornton Wilder's *Our Town* and Dylan Thomas' *Under Milk Wood* have contained a number of examples of this technique. Soliloquies may also suspend time in a similar way: the thought processes they reflect cannot be measured on any normal time-scale, and yet, they need a certain amount of time to be verbally articulated.[51] Such elements therefore do not actually stimulate the linear development of the plot but serve to deepen and intensify a particular moment.

The axis of simultaneity is constituted in the first instance by information transmitted simultaneously using a number of different codes and channels – that is, by events and situations presented on stage at one and the same time. Furthermore, simultaneity may also be something that applies to events taking place off-stage. In most cases, the information on spatially hidden action is transmitted verbally after the event, but it can also be conveyed simultaneously, either by sending clear acoustic signals from the off-stage area that are audible to the audience, or by getting one of the figures to give a teichoscopic report. In Eugene O'Neill's *The Emperor Jones* (1920), for example, the introduction of noises or voices off is of central importance. The drumbeat of the negro tom-toms, which begins in the middle of the first scene and then grows continuously in intensity, speed and volume right through to the end of the play,[52] becomes an all-pervasive symbol for those archaic and magical powers that first threaten and then overtake the hero.

One way of presenting several simultaneous events or situations on stage at the same time is to divide the stage-area into several parts. The dramaturgically innovative and ingenious playwright Johann Nestroy experimented with such techniques in his local farce *Upstairs, Downstairs, or the Whims of Fortune* (*Zu ebener Erde und erster Stock, oder die Launen des Glücks*) (1835). The two locales mentioned in the title, the ground floor and the first floor of a Viennese apartment building, are presented simultaneously by dividing the stage-area horizontally into two levels, so that the partially simultaneous and partially successive action that takes place on the two levels emphasises the social differences and tensions between rich and poor, the 'upper' and 'lower' classes.

7.4.3. The presentation of time

After this rather general discussion of time and the functions of succession and simultaneity in dramatic texts we should now like to see in greater detail exactly how a playwright creates the fictional chronology and establishes chronological coherence and, finally, also how this fictional chronology relates to the duration of the actual performance.

7.4.3.1. Establishing the chronology

An important aid to establishing the fictional chronology is closely associated with the above-mentioned principle whereby the order of scenes in the play corresponds to the order in which the events in the story behind it take place, unless there are clear signals indicating that there is some degree of deviation from the norm, such as those used to identify flashbacks or previews of future events. However, this only serves to fix the chronology in relative terms because both the actual time (date and time of day) at which a particular scene takes place and the length of time separating two random points in the series of events are left completely unspecified. If the chronology involved is to be established in absolute as well as relative terms then it will be necessary to employ particular techniques of transmitting chronological information.

Once again, these methods of transmitting chronological information may be derived from the communication model and the repertoire of codes and channels that dramatists may draw on. On the most obvious level, this information can be conveyed epically, using the secondary text to specify the time such as the title of Zacharias Werner's fate tragedy *The Twenty-Fourth of February – Der vierundzwanzigste Februar*) or scene headings such as those used by Brecht, or by indicating the time through an epic commentator figure, film-projections or notice-boards etc. However, even plays that do not contain epic communication structures manage to specify the time. A figure may refer explicitly to the time at which an event has taken place or will take place. In Holz and Schlaf's *The Selicke Family*, for example, Frau Selicke remarks at one point 'It's almost quarter-to'.[53] It may also be mentioned implicitly, as in Ben Jonson's *Volpone*: 'Good morning to the day; and next my gold!' (I,i,7). The transmission of information by non-verbal means can also be of great importance in this context. The costumes and set are often used to identify the historical period in which the action takes place and the costumes, set, lighting and even the activities of the figures themselves frequently point towards a particular time of day or year. In naturalist dramas such as *The Selicke Family* there is even a clock on stage which keeps precise and continuous time. These visual signals are complemented by a number of acoustic signals: the final soliloquy of Marlowe's *Dr Faustus* is punctuated by the chimes of a bell indicating eleven o'clock, eleven thirty and midnight, and in the third act of Gerhart Hauptmann's *Rose Bernd*, the humming of a distant threshing machine indicates that the action takes place at harvest time.

In addition to identifying the immediate moment in this way it is also possible to establish the exact chronological arrangement of the various acts and scenes, and thus chronological coherence, by referring to the dates of past and future events. By reverting to expository information it becomes possible to relate the 'point of attack', the beginning of the scenically presented action, chronologically to the background events; similarly, at the end of the play there might be corresponding references to future events taking place 'after' the dramatic presentation has finished. Within the drama itself it is possible to make references to both past and future scenes, as well as the chronologically hidden action that takes place between scenes, and this is what establishes the chronological order fashioned according to the particular needs.

The degree of chronological precision may vary considerably and stretches from a series of scenes whose chronological relationship both to each other and to the rest of the drama is left rather vague to a concise and coherent chronological relationship between the scenes which identifies precisely both the date and the time of day in each case. In closed dramas, for example, the acts are arranged according to a precise chronological pattern, whereas open dramas often contain whole series of scenes separated by varying or unspecified periods of time. The degree of chronological precision may vary even within the space of one text, as a cursory analysis of Shakespeare's *A Midsummer Night's Dream* would show.[54] In this play, the scenes set in Athens at the beginning and end of the play are placed in a fairly precise chronological context: the impending marriage between Theseus and Hippolyta is mentioned in the first two utterances of the play and this is linked chronologically with Act V and the wedding celebrations that are due to begin in two days' time. The second scene of Act I, in which the workmen rehearse their feast performance is also connected chronologically with this point in time. The times when the two pairs of lovers and the workmen arrive in the woods from Athens – and also when they return – are pinpointed with similar precision. Both groups arrange to meet 'tomorrow night' in the woods (I,i,164, 178, 209, 223, 247; I,ii,86ff.) and this informs the audience that the scenes from Act II,i to Act IV,i all take place on the eve of the wedding. The appearance of the ducal hunting party in Act IV,i,101ff. indicates that the morning of the wedding day has already dawned. The ensuing scene with the workmen (Act IV,ii), in Athens once again, is pinpointed chronologically on the basis of the reports that the triple wedding has already taken place. The final scene (Act V,i) covers the three hours between dinner and midnight (Act V,i,33 and 35) and is concluded by the arrival of Oberon, Titania and their entourage, and this had been planned as early as Act IV,i,85 for 'tomorrow night'. In contrast to the high level of chronological precision in the day-time scenes set in Athens, all we know about the chronology of the nocturnal scenes in the woods is that they take place between midnight and early morning without any details as to the precise time at which each scene is supposed to take place. This discrepancy between various levels of chronological precision is a consequence of two different conceptions of time (see below, 7.4.4.). The scenes set in Athens generally follow the chronological rhythms of the real world, but in the woodland scenes conventional chronology is suspended in favour of the timelessness of dreams and the more idiosyncratic sense of time as perceived by the supernatural figures in the play.

From this it is clear that, analogous to the semantic interpretation of space discussed above (see 7.3.1.), we should also attempt a semantic interpretation of time. For if a dramatic text is set at a specific time this is not simply designed as a way of strengthening that text's realistic plausibility and its mimetic link with reality; it also touches on much more fundamental questions. The choice of a particular historical period as the setting for the fictional events already carries with it a number of semantic, connotative implications that are far more important than just measuring the chronological distance between the setting and the contemporary world of the author. They also refer to the socio-cultural stereotypes associated with that epoch – such as the model classicism of ancient Greece, the stoic virtues of the Roman republic and the decadence of imperial Rome, the aesthetic refinement and Machiavellian corruption of Renaissance Italy etc. The reference to certain seasons of the year also has important semantic connotations, and it is possible to identify a number of archetypal affinities between, for example, tragedy and autumn or winter, and comedy and spring or summer,[55] though, of course, these conventions may be deliberately violated for ironic effect.

Thus, in *A Midsummer Night's Dream*, as in all of Shakespeare's comedies, references to spring and summer, the rebirth and renewal of nature after the winter, the natural processes of growth and ripening and seasonal customs such as May or Midsummer celebrations predominate. The consequence of this is that the lovers' plans and actions seem to have become integrated into an elemental natural rhythm centred around fertility, ripening and overcoming death. Seasonal archetypes of this kind may also be found in more recent plays. The five acts of Gerhart Hauptmann's play *Rose Bernd*, for example, follow the seasonal changes from spring to autumn, thereby linking Rose Bernd's tragic fall to the autumnal 'fall' and imbuing it with fateful, natural inevitability. And, finally, as we noticed in the case of *A Midsummer Night's Dream*, the time of day at which the action takes place can also be interpreted in a particular way. Generally speaking, night is associated in a complex manner with the world of the imagination, dreams and the supernatural, and daytime with rationality and the real world. The various parts of the daily cycle are often associated archetypically with particular dramatic genres: in tragedies, night, and especially midnight, is often interpreted as a time of threatening darkness and the morning as a time of sober disillusionment, whereas in comedy the passing of time from morning to noon and night is often interpreted as one that leads from rebirth to maturity and fulfilment.

Pinpointing the chronology in this way can also affect the suspense potential and the tempo (see below, 7.4.5.) of a dramatic text. The introductory phase of a text frequently contains forward-looking references to a particular time in the future and these serve to stimulate a sense of forward movement in the play, place the figures under the pressure of time and thus create suspense (see above, 3.7.4.3.). If that specific point in time is mentioned more than once, especially together with the reminder that it is approaching fast, the effect is repeatedly to reinforce this suspense potential and, in addition, to create the impression that time is passing very quickly. This technique is particularly common in plays with closed time structures, in which the suspense and the tempo are increased by the short span of fictional time. In plays with extremely open structures, on the other hand, the way chronological information is conveyed often creates the impression of a slow and rather aimless process of development, a process that is bound up with the expansive seasonal cycles or the way one generation gives way to the next.

7.4.3.2. Fictional time and actual performance time

With this reference to the contrast between open and closed time structures we should now like to return to our reflections on the relationship between fictional time and the actual time taken by the performance, because the distinction between open and closed time structures is actually governed by this relationship. By actual performance time we mean the duration of the performance, the period of time it takes to perform the play, minus the intervals. In order to eliminate all possible misunderstandings we should like to emphasise that the actual performance time is not the length of time that a scenically presented process would cover in real life (this would be virtually impossible to calculate) but the length of time needed for the performance. Implicit in this definition is the fact that the actual performance time is left relatively imprecise in the literary subtext. It can only be established in the actual performance itself because the style and tempo prescribed in each production may cause a considerable amount of variation in the length of time it takes to perform a particular play.[56] Conversely, the fictional time is usually fixed more or less precisely in the literary text and only needs to be recreated and made clear in the performance itself.

A sophisticated analysis of this question will also distinguish between primary, secondary and tertiary fictional time. Primary fictional time is the total length of time covered by the action presented directly on stage; secondary fictional time is the fictional period that begins with the 'point of attack',[57] the beginning of the action presented on stage, and finishes with the end of the drama but includes any time that has been omitted in periods of chronologically hidden action; finally, tertiary fictional time refers to the fictional duration of the story from the beginning of the purely verbally related background events to either the end of the text or to the point in time mentioned in the play that is furthest in the future. Secondary fictional time is therefore contained within the tertiary dimension and itself contains primary fictional time. However, because the relative sizes can always be defined as 'greater/smaller or the same' these categories may also coincide exactly. This would be true of a text which is characterised by a complete lack of the type of retrospective or anticipatory narrative and by structures of time–space continuity without any cuts in the time-span covered.[58] From this, it may be deduced that the time structure is always closed if the primary and secondary types of performance time coincide entirely, whereas it is always open to a greater or lesser degree if certain phases are omitted in between scenes and acts, thereby creating a discrepancy between the primary and secondary time-spans. The earlier the 'point of attack', the smaller the discrepancy between the secondary and tertiary levels of fictional time, and the two coincide if – an extreme case – the story is presented scenically right from the start. Conversely, the later the 'point of attack' – which is often the case in analytical dramas, for example – the greater the gap between the secondary and tertiary levels becomes.

If we start off by taking a hypothetical drama whose time structure is characterised by the fact that the tertiary time covered by the story coincides completely not only with the primary and secondary time-spans but also with the actual performance time, then it will soon become clear that the discrepancy that normally exists between the actual performance time and the fictional duration of the story presented can be bridged in two ways: first, by means of verbal summary of the events that take place off-stage during, before, or after the play itself; secondly, by compressing the events taking place within a scene and thus abbreviating the primary fictional time in comparison to the actual performance time within the uninterrupted time–space continuum of an individual scene.

The compression of events taking place off-stage refers to the omission from the direct scenic presentation of complete phases of the story – the chronologically hidden action and the events that take place both before and after the play itself. These omissions are redressed with a greater or lesser degree of explicitness, thoroughness and detail by inserting verbal or scenic references to these missing phases. Both the duration and the content of these phases can therefore either be circumstantiated or left more or less vague. Thus, in the third of his *Trois discours sur le poème dramatique* (1660), Corneille expressly allowed the poet the freedom of not always having to explain or justify everything that each individual figure has been doing during the periods that are omitted, and also the freedom to leave the duration of these excluded periods vague if they are not of fundamental importance to the subject of the play.[59]

The compression of events taking place within a scene resembles the speeding-up effect used in film but differs from it in one crucial respect. The speeding-up effect in film is based on the principle that *all* events and movements occur more quickly than they do in reality whereas the compression of time within a scene in drama does not involve speeding up every movement at the same rate – in fact, this would be virtually impossible (with living actors) without recourse to technical means[60] – but it rather excludes or abbreviates certain sequences. This abbreviation is reflected in the fact that although the text announces that particular events will take a certain amount of time, the time they do take up in performance is noticeably shorter.

In fact, dramatic literature contains a large number of spectacular examples of this. The fictional time-span covered by the final soliloquy of Dr Faustus in Christopher Marlowe's play (V,ii) is identified precisely: at the beginning of the soliloquy the clock strikes eleven and Faustus reacts to it with the desperate exclamation 'Now hast thou but one bare hour to live' (line 132); after thirty lines it then strikes eleven-thirty, provoking Faustus' comment 'Ah, half the hour is past; 'twill all be past anon' (line 162) and after no more than a further nineteen lines, at last, the clock strikes midnight, causing Faustus to shout 'It strikes, it strikes!' (line 181). That this discrepancy between the fictional time of one hour and an actual performance time of approximately three minutes is actually noticed by the audience is therefore guaranteed by the clarity and explicitness of the verbal and non-verbal references to the time and by the acceleration of the speeding-up effect in the second half of the soliloquy. This discrepancy, and indeed the intensification of it, is designed to emphasise the subjective quality of Faustus' perception of time. The predominant conception of time is therefore no longer that of an objective empirical chronometer, but has become highly subjective and may differ considerably from the regular passing of time. The dramatic compression of time in this particular scene reflects Faustus' feeling that he does not have much time left and that the moment of his eternal damnation is approaching at a frightening speed. In fact it is this, together with his reflections on the possibility of mercy, that forms the central theme of the soliloquy. The very fact that the soliloquy is purely reflective and presents certain inner processes that do not correspond to any kind of physical action is what makes such a radical compression of the time-scale involved possible in the first place, because inner, psychological events are by definition not subject to measurable units of empirical time. In this particular case, then, the introduction of a discrepancy between fictional and actual performance time is not designed simply as a way of economising in dramatic terms, but actually reflects the discrepancy within the fiction itself between the empirical chronometry (the chiming of the bells) and Faustus' subjective perception of time.

A second example from the realm of Elizabethan drama that can be mentioned briefly in this context[61] is the last act of *A Midsummer Night's Dream*. This is made up of a single scene with closed structures of both time and space, but although it covers a fictional period of approximately three hours between dinner and midnight, the actual performance time takes little longer than half an hour. The discrepancy between the two time-scales is not as extreme as it was in the previous example. In fact it also fulfils a different function and is put together differently. The focal point of this act is the play-within-the-play that relates the story of Pyramus and Thisbe. In real life this would presumably take approximately two to three hours. It is therefore the abbreviation of this play-within-the-play that is Shakespeare's most important device for reducing or minimising the discrepancy between the fictional and real time-scales involved. Here too, the manipulation of time, the impression that three hours have passed in the space of a few minutes, is explained by the events presented on stage themselves: they are static, and instead of introducing new elements of plot their sole purpose is to celebrate the resolution of the conflicts that had already occurred in Act IV. The fact that the basic situation does not undergo any more changes and that the sole situation that does take place is presented as a series of variations and high-spirited play goes some way towards abbreviating the presentation though, of course, the subjective perception of time on the part of the figures – the lovers complain impatiently about 'this long age of three hours' (lines 33f.) before they can consummate their love in the marital bed – is undermined ironically by the compression of that time.

By comparison the converse process – the stretching or slowing down of time – is of relatively minor importance in the context of drama. The slow-motion techniques used in film to slow down or draw out every single movement or action in relation to empirical reality does not really have an equivalent in drama in the same way that speeding-up a film does. Long pauses in a dialogue, or scenes in which the action is reduced to a series of insignificant or irrelevant activities, may create the impression that time is being drawn out, but this does not spring either from a comparison between the fictional time and the actual performance time, or between the fictional time and the time a particular action would take in real life. Instead, this impression is derived from the comparison with the conventionalised compression techniques in plays which tend to abbreviate the action on stage in relation to empirical reality by concentrating on the logically most important causal elements. However, it is only possible to refer to this as a slow-motion technique if the length of the fictional time is clearly signalled and is noticeably exceeded by the actual performance time. For this reason, therefore, it is not technically correct to regard a soliloquy as an example of stretched time, despite the fact that it may articulate a sudden insight or moment of awareness in such a way that the articulation takes up several minutes of performance time. Because these psychological processes cannot be manifested chronometrically, it would be more accurate to say that time is being suspended rather than extended or stretched. Generally speaking, the same can be said of dreams. However, there are examples in which the beginnings and endings of the period of suspended time are clearly marked. In J. B. Priestley's *Time and the Conways* (see above, 7.4.2.), for example, the whole of the second act is presented as Kay's daydream, in which she has visionary premonitions of her own and her family's future. The scenic presentation of this dream takes up a third of the actual performance time, though the dream itself only lasts for a few moments, as the signals at the end of Act I and the beginning of Act III marking the fictional chronology clearly indicate. By inserting Act II between Acts I and III the author therefore manages to stretch the fictional time being presented. Of course, the presentation of the dream itself does not deviate from the norm according to which fictional and real time within a scenic continuum coincide.

The extension or compression of time within the action presented is therefore always dependent on there being a number of references to time in the internal communication system, either in the verbal utterances of the figures or through certain non-verbal signals (such as bells, changes in the lighting etc.), which indicate a marked deviation from the actual performance time. Live theatre cannot create discrepancies between real and fictional time simply by slowing down or speeding up the figures' movements as a film can, because that would just proportionally abbreviate or lengthen the actual performance time. Instead, the manipulation of chronological relationships is always rooted in the chronological information conveyed in the internal communication system. And this opens the door to certain kinds of manipulation that go beyond the types of extension and compression of time we have been discussing here. Thus, a single text may combine contradictory or irreconcilable sets of chronological information – though it should be said that these contradictions generally come to the surface in a philological analysis rather than during a performance of the play in the theatre. The 'double time' technique that appears in some of Shakespeare's plays is an example of this.[62] In *Othello*, for example, it is possible to isolate two different sets of information and indications as to the chronology of the events portrayed. One of these suggests that Othello murders Desdemona within a few days of their wedding and the other that these two events were separated by several weeks. Contradictions of this sort cannot simply be dismissed as errors or carelessness on the part of the author and must be understood in the light of their function within the work as a whole. Because even if the audience in the theatre does not perceive them clearly as contradictions, it is nonetheless influenced in its feeling for the length, rhythm and tempo of the play by double time. Certain phases of the play create the impression that the events follow each other in rapid, tragic and inexorable succession, whilst others give a sense of more expansive and drawn-out psychological developments. The remarks made by Goethe to Eckermann with regard to the contradictions inherent in Shakespeare's plays also apply here:

... he [Shakespeare] regarded his plays as a lively and moving scene that would pass rapidly before the eyes and ears upon the stage, not as one that was to be held firmly and carped at in detail. Hence, his only point was to be effective and significant for the moment.[63]

7.4.4. The conception of time

Although the techniques used to establish dramatic chronology are derived from the communication model for dramatic texts, and may be presented as a closed repertoire, it is not possible to do this for the various conceptions of time. This is because the conception of time underlying a particular text, like the various conceptions of space, figure and plot, is a historical category and, as such, is conditioned not by the systematic pattern of communication structures but by particular intellectual or socio-historical ideas. The simultaneous staging used for medieval religious plays, for instance, on which a number of different locales might be presented at the same time and the tendency to merge biblical events and contemporary reality were founded on the theological conception of a divine scheme or plan of salvation which seems to have suspended the sense of a chronological progression from the past through the present to the future *sub specie aeternitatis*. However, our concern at this point is not simply to accumulate a number of interesting examples; nor is it possible to compile a comprehensive historical survey of all the philosophical changes in the way time is conceived or, closely related to this, of the formal changes in the time structures of drama. Instead, as we did in our discussions of the concepts of figure and space, we shall have to restrict ourselves to a short summary of some of the historically significant polar opposites in the development of the conception of time.

7.4.4.1. Objective chronometry versus the subjective perception of time

In this section we can refer back to certain aspects that we discussed above in connection with the presentation of time. One example of this might be the contrast between a conception of time in which the objectivity of empirical chronometry predominates and one that is based on a more subjective perception of time. An objective conception of time is usually

manifested formally in a set of strict, clearly marked signs that demonstrate the continuous and regular passing of time: the clocks in the Selickes'
living-room and in the classroom of Trevor Griffiths's *Comedians* are
particularly transparent examples of this, whereas the clock in the living-
room of the Smith family in Ionesco's *La cantatrice chauve*, with its
idiosyncratic changes in speed, lampoons this notion to the point of
absurdity. In Shakespeare's *As You Like It* on the other hand, Orlando
states quite emphatically that 'There's no clock in the forest' (III,ii,284)
thereby introducing an ever-changing series of new and varied reflections
on the subjective perception of time in the pastoral world of the Forest of
Arden. This is reflected in the time structure of this play in the fact that the
chronological relationships between the series of scenes are rather loose
and imprecise.[64] As we observed above, contradictions in the chronology
and the extension or compression of the fictional time are generally
associated with a subjective conception of time, and this subjectivity is
something that the figures themselves can be aware of or something that
the spectators can discover and reflect on. Subjectivity is an important
feature of modern drama in particular, something which has presumably
been affected by the nineteenth- and twentieth-century discussions of the
concept of time in the fields of both philosophy and science (Henri Bergson, Ernst Mach and Albert Einstein, for example) and by the competition
for the dramatic genre emanating from the chronologically much more
flexible artistic media of film and the novel.[65]

7.4.4.2. Progression versus stasis

A second contrast that we can establish here is one between a conception
of time in which chronological progression is concomitant with constant
change and one in which time is seen simply as duration – that is, as the
chronological prolongation of a static condition. In plays written before
the modern period it was the progressive conception of time that predominated, because the passing of time was always reflected in the progression in the various strands of plot. Periods of time in which there was
little or no action or movement were usually banished to the intervals –
assuming they were included in the story at all. In such cases, time is
generally conceived as a chronological progression and succession of
events rather than a static condition. However, the conception of time that
predominates in many modern one-act plays, for example, is often 'achro-
nological' – that is, a single static situation predominates over the conventional progressive series of changes in the situation.[66] Thus, the situation
presented at the end of the text does not differ in any drastic way from the
situation presented at the beginning. What does change, however, is the
figures' insight into that situation brought about by the information

conveyed in the course of the text. Durative and iterative events are associated with such a static conception of time, in the same way that action which brings about changes in the situation is associated with a progressive conception of time. The durative or static aspect is signalled quite specifically even in the title of Samuel Beckett's *Waiting for Godot*, for example. Waiting, especially if it is for an event which might happen at any time, or not at all, is a purely static activity and does not involve any changes in the dramatic situation. It is characterised not by an idea of progress but by stasis. Within this static, durative context, actions degenerate to no more than iterative activities designed to pass the time. Vladimir and Estragon therefore play their already all too familiar games over and over again as a way of countering their boredom. There are a few remains of a progressive conception of time – in the second act the tree, which had been bare in the first, now has a few leaves and Pozzo and Lucky have reached an advanced state of physical and psychological decay – but these are to be seen as a kind of contrast only and as such implicitly reinforce the predominantly static conception of time used in this play.

7.4.4.3. Linear versus cyclical movement

Closely related to the idea of stasis or duration is the conception that interprets time as a form of cyclical repetition of identical or similar phenomena. Although there is a certain idea of progression in this concept, it is not the sort of linear progression moving from point A to point B, but a cyclical movement which starts from point A and moves through a number of other positions before returning either to A or to a corresponding position point A^1. This is a conception of time that is based on the natural life-cycles – the cycles of the day, month, seasons and generations. Linear and cyclical developments always occur simultaneously, however, and so it all depends on the author's intention and the audience's perspective as to which of them is seen to predominate.

In the tragedies of French classicism, for example, it is the linear form of progression that predominates. As time passes, the situation is constantly changing. In the plays of Shakespeare, on the other hand, the sense of linear progression is often combined with more cyclical rhythms. This includes Shakespeare's above mentioned predilection for setting the plot in the cycle of seasons; and although the individual plays do not usually manage to take in a complete cycle or a number of cycles, the concept of cyclical repetition is certainly often discussed by the figures themselves. The set of history plays which are linked together by the notion of progress inherent in the teleological framework of the Tudor myth, with the Tudor dynasty interpreted as the culmination of the historical process, is also a prime example of a series of cyclical plot structures describing the repeated usurpation and the ensuing loss of power. In Shakespeare's later romantic comedies the cyclical aspect of a succession of generations became particularly important.

It was not until the drama of the twentieth century that the cyclical conception of time began to predominate, however. Thus, Thornton Wilder's *The Long Christmas Dinner* (1931), for example, condenses the time-scale so drastically that it is possible to present ninety Christmas dinners in the Bayard household. The cyclical repetition of Christmas festivities and the growth and decline of three generations is emphasised by the repetition of the same almost hackneyed expressions and the same procedures and actions. This is designed, on the one hand, to make the audience aware of the passing of time in a way that is more noticeable than if it were presented as a form of linear development. On the other hand, it also suspends time in the eternal repetitions of similar episodes. A second example of this is, yet again, Beckett's *Waiting for Godot*, a play in which the cyclical quality of certain repeated words, actions and gestures underlines the impression of stasis. The cyclical notion that the end always returns to the beginning is illustrated most graphically by Vladimir's nursery rhyme at the beginning of Act II about the dog that went into the kitchen and stole an egg from the cook. The rhyme is not only constructed cyclically, it can also be repeated *ad infinitum*, thereby transforming the passing of time into timelessness. In the context of the macrostructure of the whole text this cyclical quality is manifested in the parallel construction of the two acts. Both begin with Vladimir and Estragon meeting each other and in both they are joined for a while by Pozzo and Lucky, and by the boy announcing that Godot will not be coming on that day. Both acts close with a decision to leave, which is then not realised.

7.4.5. Tempo

7.4.5.1. The literary text and the text in performance

Dramatic tempo is an aspect of drama that is discussed far more often by those involved with theatrical practice than by dramatic theorists.[67] This fact is itself an indication that tempo in drama must be analysed principally on two different levels – the level of the literary text and the level of the multimedial performance of that text. The literary text usually contains an implicit and more or less precisely identifiable tempo that may also be defined explicitly in the secondary text; the multimedially performed text can then latch on to these tempo markers and put them into practice. Equally it may also deliberately violate them. Modern producers are particularly fond of undermining the tempi demanded by the literary text in this way. Scenes that are supposed to be performed at speed are slowed down by the introduction of pauses or other distractions designed to preoccupy the figures, and – conversely – scenes that are supposed to be slow are often rattled through at breakneck speed.

7.4.5.2. Deep structure and surface structure

The natural scientist defines tempo as the ratio of units of length, area or space per unit of time, or the ratio of events per unit of time. The first of these can be applied in the context of dramatic analysis to determine the speeds of various types of movement (mime, gesture and choreography, for example) and the second to measure the tempo at which one event is succeeded by another (frequency of the change of speaker or situation). However, this hypothesis cannot be regarded as complete if it is not possible to distinguish between the two levels of the tempo of a dramatic text – a deep structure level and a surface structure level. These two levels refer back to the distinction we made between the subject of the dramatic presentation – manifested on the deeper level as the story – and the dramatic presentation itself – manifested on the surface level as the plot (see above, 6.1.1.). As far as the surface structure is concerned, the tempo of a particular section of the text is determined by the speed of the movements and the frequency of the changes of speaker, configuration and locale. On the deep structure level, the tempo is determined by the frequency with which the situation changes in the story itself.

The overall impression created by one section of the text – such as a single scene – is determined by the way these two aspects of tempo interrelate. In fact, they may deviate considerably from each other. Beckett's plays, for instance, are full of scenes in which the verbal utterances are delivered at high speed with the figures constantly engaged in some sort of activity whilst at the same time the situation remains completely unchanged. In such cases there would be a marked contrast between the frenetic activity on the surface level and the almost complete stasis on the deeper level – the lowest possible position on the tempo scale. Conversely, a report that is presented rigidly without any sort of flexibility or movement may relate a section of the story that is full of action or peripeteia. In such cases the low surface tempo would contrast markedly with the intense activity on the deeper level. In both cases the overall impression is one of a discrepancy between the two diverging tempi rather than simply one of high tempo. Of course, this discrepancy may itself have a certain function, as it does in Beckett, whose figures attempt to enliven the all too slow passage of time by busying themselves with numerous meaningless and gratuitous activities and delude themselves about the permanence of their situation. However, it can also be dysfunctional and reflect a degree of aesthetic incompetence on the part of the author if the tempo is too forced. It is only when the tempi on both levels are perfectly synchronised that the author is able to create the impression of a consistent tempo, whether high or low. If the tempo is high then this means that every one of the swift series of utterances represents a speech act that affects the situation and that each nuance or change of position, grouping and configuration drives the story onwards towards its final crisis and conclusion.

7.4.5.3. The tempo of the text as a whole

The tempo category that applies to the text as a whole is the ratio of situation changes to the secondary performance time – that is, the period of time that begins with the 'point of attack' and ends with the last scenically presented dramatic situation (see above, 7.4.3.2.). The overall tempo of a dramatic text is therefore dependent on the number of peripeties it contains and on the level of chronological concentration. The classical drama, with its highly concentrated and closed structures of time and space, presents conflicts with a high concentration of peripeteia and achieves a high overall tempo because of its particular structures of time and plot. Other types of drama, characterised by more open and panoramic time structures and plots with fewer peripeties generally proceed at a more leisurely pace. A comparison of two of Shakespeare's comedies, *A Comedy of Errors*, with its concentrated chronology and numerous peripeties and *As You Like It*, with its open time structure and fewer changes in the dramatic situation, shows that this hypothesis is confirmed by the audience's immediate impression in the theatre. The classicising norm embodied in the unity of time is therefore not merely designed to create a closed continuum of illusion; it is also supposed to increase the dramatic tempo and thus precipitate the final dénouement and conclusion.

7.4.5.4. Tempo variations, rhythm and suspense

In most cases, the dramatic tempo does not remain constant throughout, however. In some phases the tempo may slow, in others it may accelerate. It may even be varied within a single dialogue if, for example, a relaxed conversation characterised by long speeches is allowed to develop into an argument made up of a fast exchange of short stichomythic utterances. Conversely, a hectic succession of rapidly changing configurations may give way within a single scene to a more permanent static configuration. Turbulent scenes full of movement are often contrasted with peaceful interludes, and phases in the text in which the plot is moved forward by a rapid succession of changing dramatic situations are sometimes followed by less eventful phases in which reflection and commentary are implemented to consolidate the situation. In other cases, the author may wish to hold up or retard the forward movement of the plot by inserting something like a song, a play-within-the-play or an extended narrative.[68] Each play has an overall average tempo and it is presumably the variation of that tempo above and below average that is implied by the frequently used but seldom precisely defined concept of 'dramatic rhythm'.[69] Variations in tempo may also influence the intensity of dramatic suspense (see above, 3.7.4.), and of course within certain bounds the suspense may be heightened by either accelerating or reducing the tempo – accelerating in so far as the swift changes in the situation may lead to the constant creation of new arcs of suspense, and a slowing down in so far as the arcs of suspense are broadened or expanded. Texts from different historical periods will generally follow different patterns in the way the tempo is varied. In classical tragedy, for example, the plot proceeds at a brisk pace as far as the central peripeteia. This is then followed by a less eventful phase associated with reflection but the tempo picks up again as the catastrophe approaches before, finally, it comes to rest, like a photographic still, in the form of a static closing tableau.

Concluding note

We have reached the end of our survey, having covered in a systematically coherent fashion the main structural aspects of dramatic texts and theatrical communication. The scope of our study has been vast indeed, as we have tried to do justice to both the dramatic and the theatrical dimensions of plays and to illustrate the range of structural possibilities through examples taken from the main periods of Western drama. Thus, if not a history of drama and the theatre in itself, the study provides the structural tools for the writing of such a history, or rather, such histories. Within the grid of its systematic categorisations history has inscribed itself, and even if the often drastic juxtapositions of Latin comedy and the Theatre of the Absurd, of Shakespeare and French classical tragedy, may occasionally have created the impression of a violently a-historical, if not anti-historical, slant to this book, its dedication to the study of individual texts in their historical specificity and of drama and theatre history in general should by now have become clear. System and history, systematic categorisation and historical interpretation, are not mutually exclusive, but presuppose and depend upon each other.

This is the ethos underlying my study and this study will be useful to its reader exactly to the extent that he or she does not just mechanically apply its various categorisations, but adapts and refines them historically. Such a reader will also appreciate that this book is not interested in isolating structures or levels of theatrical communication as an end in itself, but as a prerequisite for showing how they interrelate. We do not dissect to murder, but to stimulate and revitalise our perception of complex interrelationships. In spite of the often elaborate categorisations of isolated structural features, the emphasis has been on how the various levels of verbal and non-verbal communication, of plot and 'character', of time and space, interrelate and on how these internal structures of dramatic texts function within the wider contexts of the theatre as a historically changing institution, of authorial intentions and audience expectations, and of social conditions and ideological frames.

Notes

Preface

1. H. v. Hofmannsthal (1957), II, 433.
2. In this context see the works of the Cambridge anthropologists J. E. Harrison (1913), G. Murray (1912), F. M. Cornfeld (1961) and Th. Gaster (1966), 'archetypical' critics such as F. Fergusson (1949) and N. Frye (1957) and Marxists such as R. Weimann (1978).

1. Drama and the dramatic

1. The bibliography compiled by R. B. Vowles (1956) and W. Wittkowski's research report (1963) faithfully reflect the trends in traditional research. The various dramatic theories propounded by the Russian formalists, the Czech, Polish, French and Russian structuralists, the Copenhagen glossematicians, the linguists and communication theorists, the semioticists and semiologists, the information theorists, cyberneticists and statisticians have all been covered in the bibliographical sections of A. van Kesteren and H. Schmid (eds.) (1975), P. Pavis (1980), K. Elam (1980), E. Fischer-Lichte (1983).
2. For its reception in the Renaissance see B. Weinberg (1953), and in the eighteenth century M. Kommerell (1957). The critical works of the Chicago school of neo-Aristotelians are examples of a modern theory of literature that attempts to preserve and develop the Aristotelian tradition. Their programmatic works have been collected in R. S. Crane (ed.) (1952).
3. One is reminded of the importance of the Japanese *Nôh Plays* for W. B. Yeats and Brecht, and the Balinese theatre for A. Artaud.
4. For the relative neglect of drama at the hands of the Russian formalists see J. Striedter (ed.) (1969) xxiv–xxvi. A more positive picture has been drawn by H. Schmid (1975) in her research report. The representatives of new criticism – that is, those that actually refer to drama – generally concentrate on analysing the structures of verbal imagery and symbolism. A characteristic example of this is the interpretation of *Macbeth* in C. Brooks (1947).
5. The first critics to attempt this published their results in the Prague structuralist journal *Slovo a Slovonost* in the late 1930s and early 1940s. There are German translations of J. Veltruský (1964), P. Bogatyrev (1971), J. Mukařovský (1975), J. Veltruský (1975) and J. Honzl (1975). A comprehensive anthology would undoubtedly be extremely useful, though a short summary has been attempted by K. Elam (1980) 5–20. More recent semiotic studies of importance are those by S. Jansen (1968), T. Kowzan (1968), M. Pagnini (1970), D. and D. Kaisersgruber and J. Lempert (1972), B. Wuttke (1973), E. Kaemmerling (1979), B. L. Ogibenin (1975), P. Pavis (1976 and 1980), F. Ruffini (1978), A. Ubersfeld (1977, 1980 and 1981), K. Elam (1980), E. W. B.

Hess-Lüttich (1982), E. Fischer-Lichte (1983), H. Schmid and A. van Kesteren (eds.) (1985) and P. Pavis (1985). See also the two anthologies edited by A. Helbo and others (1975) and A. van Kesteren and H. Schmid (1975) respectively. The latter also contains a research summary (pp. 41–58) and a bibliography (pp. 318–38) compiled by van Kesteren. See also the bibliography in H. Schmid and A. van Kesteren (eds.) (1984) 511–48.

6. For a discussion of this term see K. W. Hempfer (1973) 26f. and 160–4.

7. *Republic* 394c. Aristotle expressed it in similar terms: '. . . in representing the same objects by the same means it is possible to proceed either partly by narrative . . . or else to represent the characters as carrying out the whole action themselves' (*Poetics* ch. 3).

8. In this we have used the model described by R. Fieguth (1973).

9. In this context see F. Stanzel (1964) 39f.

10. The model used for drama only takes account of dramatic speech. The various forms of non-verbal communication will be examined more thoroughly in 1.3.

11. P. Szondi (1956) 15. See also Henrik Ibsen's programmatic remarks on his play *Ghosts* relating to the absolute autonomy of the drama with regard to the author: 'They endeavour to make me responsible for the opinions which certain of the personages of any drama express. And yet there is not in the whole book a single opinion which can be laid to the account of the author'. (Letter to S. Schandorph of 6.1.1882 in Ibsen (1905) 352.

12. See the discussion of the problem in 'Drama und Dialog' by K. L. Berghahn (1970) 1–13.

13. English translation in E. Bentley (ed.) (1968) 153–7. See also E. Bentley (1965) 96–8 and J. Levy (1969) 141–8.

14. J. L. Austin (1962) 60.

15. F. Dürrenmatt (1976) 75.

16. See A. Sinfield (1977).

17. J. L. Styan (1975) 4.

18. S. Jansen (1968), M. Pagnini (1970).

19. An early example of a play that specifically prescribes the use of olfactory information is García Lorca's 'folk romance' *Mariana Pineda* (1925), in which the secondary text for one particular scene states: 'The atmosphere is determined by the fine, autumnal scent of quinces.'

20. For an analysis of the semantics of gesture in drama, see S. Skwarczyńska (1974) and A. Helbo (1983). A number of important preliminary studies have been published in this very area by the Prague structuralists: on the actors, J. Honzl (1938); on the direction of movement, J. Honzl (1940); on the props and set, J. Veltruský (1964). The non-verbal aspect has also been analysed extensively, if not systematically, by a number of British critics. The most important of these are J. L. Styan (1960 and 1975) and J. R. Brown (1966 and 1972).

21. The classification method and terminology has been borrowed from C. S. Pierce. For a discussion of the 'theatrical code' see also A. Helbo (1975) and K. Elam (1980) 32–97.

22. From this use of weakly normative codes G. Mounin (1970) 87–94 has concluded that linguistic categories cannot be applied to dramatic texts. Although he is correct to criticise the purely metaphorical application of linguistic categories, his rejection of the terms *langage*, *communication* and

code when applied to dramatic texts and his desire to replace them with various behaviourist categories such as *stimulation* and *réponse*, is based on too narrow an understanding of language, communication and code.

23. See J. Veltruský's discussion of these position shifts (1964). For a more sophisticated analysis see below, 7.3.3.2.
24. In this context see A. Villiers (1953).
25. R. Schechner (1966) 27.

2. Drama and the theatre

1. M. Frisch (1977) 184.
2. E. Ionesco (1962) 185. The neo-Aristotelian theorist E. Olson has reduced the importance of the literary text even more drastically. In his view, drama is 'not essentially a form of literature, but rather a distinct art which may or may not employ language as an artistic medium' (1961) 88. In this respect Olson modelled himself on Aristotle (see *Poetics*, ch. 6), for whom speech, or diction, was just one of the six elements that constitute drama. See also W. Flemming (1962).
3. *Dr Johnson on Shakespeare* (1969) 72.
4. For a discussion of reading methods and the relationship between reading and seeing plays, see J. L. Styan (1960 and 1975), J. R. Brown (1966, 1968 and 1972) and S. Wells (1970). The production aspect of this problem has been addressed by R. Peacock (1946) and the contributors to E. Fischer-Lichte (1985).
5. R. Ingarden (1973) 208–10. For the relationship between reading and performance see pp. 317–23.
6. G. B. Shaw (1970) I, 28.
7. A. Chekhov (1954) 334. For the relationship between these two types of stage-directions see J. Hasler (1974).
8. H. v. Hofmannsthal (1955), Prosa IV, 197.
9. In this context see R. Williams (1968) 173–7, and R. Schechner (1971).
10. H. G. Coenen (1961) 42–4.
11. In this context see the relevant contributions in E. Bentley (ed.) (1968) and A. Kennedy (1975) 8–13.
12. The terminology has been borrowed from J. Kaiser (1961) 32–72. See also M. Schäfer (1960), A. S. Cook (1966), W. Steidle (1968), T. Kowzan (1969), K. Scherer (1970) and D. Bevington (1984).
13. See in this context D. Mehl (1975).
14. The terminology has been borrowed, once again, from J. Kaiser (1961) 133–6.
15. R. Southern (1962) has written a concise introduction to this which also considers a number of non-European traditions. In this context, see also J. Orrell (1983) and R. and H. Leacroft (1984).
16. In this context see D. Frey (1946) and H. Kindermann (1963).
17. B. Brecht (1964) 194. The influential propagator of the style of acting which called for 'complete transformation' was Konstantin Stanislavsky. For an introduction to his work see *Stanislavsky on the Art of the Stage* (1950).
18. This aspect is not new by any means, but it always used to be considered in the context of the theory of genre. Thus, in Section 42 of his *Hamburg Dramatur-*

gy, Lessing felt that tragedy called for complete illusion, whereas comedy was permitted to break that illusion and create a degree of distance. Similarly, A. R. Thompson (1946) 88–100 classifies tragedy as 'drama of identification' and comedy as 'drama of detachment'.

19. The narrative function of the camera has been described by K. Hamburger (1968) 176–85 and J. Dubois *et alii* (1974) 288. For a more general discussion of the relationship between drama and film see W. A. Koch (1969).

20. G. Gurvitch (1956). See also U. Rapp (1973) 11f.

21. E. R. Curtius (1961) 148–54; F. Yates (1969).

22. In this context see, for example, E. Goffman (1959) and the anthology edited by B. J. Biddle and E. J. Thomas (1966).

23. See the almost exactly contemporaneous but completely independent works by E. Burns (1972) and U. Rapp (1973); also K. Elam (1980) 87–92.

24. Amongst the more recent studies are those by J. Bab (1931), A. Beiss (1954), G. Gurvitch (1956), J. Duvignaud (1963 and 1970), A. Silbermann (1966), Z. Barbu (1967), A. Häuseroth (1969), D. Steinbeck (1970) ch. 18 (with bibliography) and R. Démarcy (1973). Historical studies that are interesting from a methodological perspective are those by W. H. Bruford (1950) and V. Ehrenberg (1951).

25. R. Jakobson (1960).

26. L. Goldmann (1955).

27. L. Goldmann (1975) 158.

28. See J. S. R. Goodlad (1971) 3–10. U. Rapp (1973) 21–8 classifies the research into a number of theories – the theories of reflection and superstructure, the theory of symbolism, the theory of effect and the theory of integration. For the psychological and social functions of drama see also H. Granville-Barker (1945), P. A. Coggin (1956) and the anthology edited by J. Hodgson (1972).

29. See under 'Director' in J. R. Taylor (1970) 84f. and A. Veinstein (1955).

30. Its development in Britain has been outlined by R. Findlater (1967).

31. For a discussion of the economic problems faced by the theatre and other performing arts see the empirical study of the situation in the USA by W. J. Baumol and W. G. Bowen (1966) and *tdr* 29 (1965) on 'Dollars and drama'. The current situation in the UK has been described by R. Hayman (1973).

32. M. Descotes (1964) has produced a diachronic analysis of this particular aspect.

33. See A. Harbage (1941) and R. Weimann (1967 and 1970); but A. J. Cook (1981).

34. For a more general discussion of this see P. Bourdieu (1970) 159–201. For an analysis of the audiences of television plays see J. S. R. Goodlad (1971).

35. E. Auerbach (1968) 359–94.

36. See D. V. McGranahan and I. Wayne (1947), B. Jones (1950) and S. W. Head (1954), for example.

37. The results of this analysis have been summarised in J. S. R. Goodlad (1971) 140–77.

38. F. Dürrenmatt (1976) 83f.

39. A. W. Schlegel (1846).

40. Quoted from A. Nicoll (1962) 17.

41. See G. F. Reynolds (1931) and V. Klotz (1976). There are also a number of important studies on the relationship between the play and audience in

Shakespeare: see A. C. Sprague (1935), E. P. Nasser (1970) and I. Schabert, 'Gesamtkonzeption: Zuschauerbezug' in the volume edited by I. Schabert (1972) 260–72. See also, with particular reference to distancing techniques, D. B. Chaim (1984).

42. For an assessment of the significance of the audience and the ways it affects theatre performance see P. Brook (1968) 128–40.

43. For a discussion of the increased level of audience participation in modern experimental theatre, see R. Schechner (1973).

3. Sending and receiving information

1. For a discussion of the use of the theatre as a central metaphor in drama see A. Righter (1967) and K. Elam (1980) ch. 1.

2. This aspect of advance information has been analysed by T. F. van Laan (1970) 72f., though his analysis of characterisation techniques is rather one-sided. In this section we have chosen an example taken from the category of works that refer back to mythical events. The analogous problem of historical advance information has been discussed in exemplary fashion by E. Schanzer (1963) 10–70, on the basis of Shakespeare's *Julius Caesar*.

3. A. Dihle (1967) 171.

4. See M. Pfister (1974b) and for a discussion of intertextuality in general, see U. Broich and M. Pfister (1985).

5. J. L. Styan (1975) 59, speaks analogously of 'two kinds of energy, that created by (i) a fusion of impressions and (ii) an opposition of impressions, a fission which precedes the final fusion'.

6. S. Beckett (1963) 30.

7. H. Ibsen (1981) 3.

8. G. B. Shaw (1960) 100.

9. See A. Schöne (1964) 184–93.

10. S. Beckett (1965) 12, 54 and 94.

11. F. Dürrenmatt (1976) 75.

12. B. Evans (1960) viii–ix. See also M. Doran (1962), and for a discussion of figures awareness, see E. Lefèvre (1971).

13. G. E. Lessing (1969a) II, 533f. Similarly, S. T. Coleridge has emphasised that one of the positive and characteristic features of Shakespeare's dramas is the way they tend to offer 'expectation in preference to surprise' (1969) 115.

14. Letter of 2.10.1797, in Goethe and Schiller *Briefwechsel* (1970) 370.

15.. A. Lesky (1968) 146.

16. P. Szondi (1956) 23f.

17. For a discussion of Ibsen's analytical technique see P. Szondi (1956) 24f.

18. B. Evans (1960) viii.

19. G. G. Sedgewick (1948), A. R. Thompson (1948), R. B. Sharpe (1959) viii, B. O. States (1971) 23ff.

20. Discussed for the first time in C. Thirlwall (1833).

21. Our analysis of perspective structure overlaps in essence, if not terminologi-cally, with H. Schmid's (1973) investigation into the 'personal' and 'authorial context'. Schmid's terminology is derived from the literary theories of Czech structuralism. For an analysis of perspective in drama see E. Groff (1959/60), K. Seelig (1964), W. Görler (1974), M. Pfister (1974a) and H. Spittler (1979).

22. See the summary of research in M. Pfister (1974a) 15–18. The following

section contains a concise and, in part, differently accentuated summary of the methodological preliminaries (14–45) to this historical study.

23. F. Fergusson (1949) 115.
24. B. Brecht (1976a) 237.
25. See M. Doran (1954) and R. Levin (1971).
26. C. Brooks and R. B. Heilman (1945) 48f.
27. A more detailed analysis of this is contained in M. Pfister (1974a), 104–60.
28. W. Iser (1970) 15.
29. A. Chekhov (1956) 29 (transl. from German edn). In M. Pfister (1974a) 161–208, I analysed Shakespeare's *Tempest* as a close approximation of the ideal type of open perspective structure.
30. G. B. Shaw (1970–4) II, 517.
31. The most important contributions to this debate have been collected in the volume edited by R. Grimm (1970).
32. *Briefwechsel* (1970) 284ff., 403ff. and 969f.
33. B. Brecht (1963) IV, 142. (Translator's note: the translation in *Brecht on the Theatre* is wrong, hence my own version from the German.)
34. See P. Pütz (1970) 15. See below, 3.7.4.2.
35. F. Spielhagen (1883) 279f. and 286; (1898), 227ff. See also R. Grimm 'Naturalismus und episches Theater' in R. Grimm (ed.) (1970) 21–4.
36. B. Brecht (1964) 46. In this context see also H. Arntzen (1969).
37. A. Chekhov (1954) 333. See also H. Schmid (1973) 396f.
38. J. Littlewood and others (1965) 106–9.
39. See B. Balász (1949) 116ff. L. H. Eisner and H. Friedrich (eds.) (1958) 67–70, W. Dadek (1968) 205ff. and U. Broich (1971).
40. J. Littlewood and others (1965) 15–17.
41. For a more general discussion of the chorus see P. Pütz (1970) 142f.
42. F. Schiller (1965) II, 822.
43. F. Schiller (1965) II, 821.
44. Th. Wilder (1962) 40, 60, 32, 22, 50, 68, 25.
45. Aristotle, *Poetics*, ch. 18.
46. Horace, *Ars Poetica*, 193–5. English translation: 'Let the chorus sustain the part and strenuous duty of an actor and sing nothing between acts which does not advance and fitly blend into the plot.'
47. B. Brecht (1976b) 426.
48. B. Brecht (1979a) 64–5.
49. B. Brecht (1964) 44–5.
50. B. Brecht (1961) 319–21.
51. See G. E. Duckworth (1952) 132–8.
52. Plautus, *Miles Gloriosus*, 19–23.
53. Plautus, *Poenulus*, 550–4.
54. P. Weiss (1961) is correct to conclude that the illusion is not actually broken but simply replaced by another illusion on a different level: 'When an actor addresses an audience with an aside or even when he sits with it, he is still apart from it. He is in the play addressing or joining not that particular audience, but a play-audience, conceived of as looking at the rest of the play' (p. 195).
55. In this context see W. Clemen (1972) 96–123 and K. Schlüter (1958).
56. Lessing drew attention to this in his critique of the topos of the *ut pictura poesis* in his *Laokoon*.

57. An important manifesto of this particular school of analysis is the essay 'On the principles of Shakespeare interpretation' in G. W. Knight (1930) ch. 1. For a discussion of the interaction of the 'spatial' and 'temporal dimensions' see T. van Laan (1970) 283ff. and for the significance of the 'spatial dimension' in modern drama see M. Rosenberg (1958). R. Weimann (1962) contains a critique of this analytical perspective.

58. More recent works on exposition are those by T. M. Campbell (1922), D. Dibelius (1935), A. C. Sprague (1935), J. Gollwitzer (1937), D. E. Fields (1938), R. Petsch (1945) 97ff., J. Scherer (1959) 51–61, H. G. Bickert (1969), E. Lefèvre (1969) and P. Pütz (1970) 165–202.

59. E. T. Sehrt (1960).

60. G. Freytag (1968).

61. Our own differentiation criteria were already inherent in Marmontel's view that expositions could be divided into those that are presented 'tout d'un coup' and those that occur 'successivement'. Quoted from J. Scherer (1959) 54.

62. The following section is based on the theories of P. Pütz (1970).

63. E. Ionesco (1954) 11.

64. Goethe to Schiller, 22.4.1797; in *Briefwechsel* (1970) 288.

65. Quoted from G. E. Duckworth (1952) 108, which also contains an analysis of protatic figures in Plautus and Terence.

66. According to Donatus. See also G. E. Duckworth (1952) 108.

67. See R. Fieguth (1973) 191ff.

68. See J. Scherer's series of types (1959) 59f. – exposition by the chorus in a prologue, exposition by a soliloquy of the hero, expository dialogue between the hero and his confidant, expository dialogue between two confidants, and expository dialogue between two heroes. This pattern is adhered to in French classical drama (tragedies and comedies) alone and should therefore not be assumed to be a general rule. For discussions of the confidant see J. A. Fermaud (1940) and H. W. Lawton (1943).

69. H. v. Hofmannsthal (1963) 637 and 639.

70. P. Pütz (1970) 188.

71. *Poetics*, chs. 11 and 16.

72. See J. Scherer (1959) 125–46. The endings of classical Greek or Roman tragedies have been discussed in G. Kremer (1971), Latin theory and practice by M. F. Smith (1940), the theories of the later Latin grammarians and the Renaissance by M. T. Herrick (1964) 122ff. See also the chapter entitled 'Der Abschluß der Tragödie' in O. Mann (1958) 147–52, and P. Pütz (1970) 225–9.

73. See A. Spira (1957) and W. Schmidt (1963).

74. See also the comments on 'open ending' in P. Pütz (1970) 227–9.

75. B. Brecht (1966) 109.

76. T. Stoppard (1972) 81.

77. For a discussion of the relationship between suspense and conflict see B. Tomashevski (1965) and for one of the relationship between suspense and finality see E. Staiger (1946) 157–72 and P. Pütz (1970). K. Büchler (1908) discusses suspense as a general aesthetic problem.

78. This particular interpretation of suspense coincides with more recent developments in information theory. See I. and J. Fónagy (1971) and G. Wienold (1972) 88–95.

79. P. Pütz (1970) 62–154 has provided a systematic analysis of this kind of future-orientated information transmission under the heading 'Vorgriffe' ('anticipations'), but he does not make it clear enough that their function is to heighten the suspense. This last aspect has been emphasised in W. Clemen (1953) and (1972) 1–95. See also P. W. Harsh (1935).
80. For a discussion of tempo as a further possible parameter for measuring the intensity of suspense see section 7.4.5.4.
81. I. and J. Fónagy (1971) 74.

4. Verbal communication

1. For a discussion of the as yet rather underdeveloped state of research into dramatic speech see A. K. Kennedy (1975) 237–43. For a comparison of dramatic dialogue and 'naturally occurring conversation', see D. Burton (1980).
2. J. Mukařovský (1977) 113. See also the chapter 'Von den Funktionen der Sprache im Theaterschauspiel' ('The functions of language in drama') in R. Ingarden (1960) 403–25 – especially p. 406 – and J. Levy (1969) 137–41.
3. F. X. Kroetz (1976) 66–7.
4. For a discussion of this polyfunctionality see J. L. Styan (1960) 12ff.
5. In this we have based our analysis on the triadic functional model put forward by K. Bühler (1934), which was then expanded to a model with four positions by R. Ingarden (1960).
6. B. Jonson (1925–52) VIII, 625.
7. Goethe (1963) IV, 170.
8. A more detailed analysis of the various guises this expressive function might take is contained in 4.4.2.
9. G. E. Lessing (1969b) 101–2.
10. S. Beckett (1965) 75. In this context see W. Iser (1961).
11. P. Nichols (1970) 68f.
12. For a discussion of this in the context of modern drama see J. Vannier (1963). For a discussion of metalanguage in Shakespeare, see M. Pfister (1978/79).
13. G. E. Lessing (1972) 93.
14. M. Van Doren *Shakespeare* (New York, 1939) 89.
15. Our arguments are similar to those in P. Ure's 'Introduction' to *King Richard II*, 5th edn. (London, 1961), lxix–lxxi.
16. See M. Pfister (1978).
17. Wherever this happens, such as in Jaques' 'Nay then, God be wi'you, an you talk in blank verse' in Shakespeare's *As You Like It* (IV,i,28), the illusion is broken as the figures violate the internal communication system and thus comically alienate the dramatic form.
18. A. Hübler (1973) 10.
19. See S. K. Langer (1953) 315: 'In drama speech is an act, an utterance, motivated by visible and invisible other acts, and like them shaping the oncoming Future.' See also S. E. Fish (1976), J. A. Porter (1979), R. Schmachtenberg (1982) and M. Pfister (1985).
20. For an analysis of the structure of conversation see J. Mukařovský (1977).
21. V. Klotz (1969) 72.
22. Quoted from A. K. Kennedy (1975) 172.

23. Shaw (1958) 53. See also the section entitled 'The inevitable flatteries of tragedy in the 'Preface' to *Saint Joan*'; Shaw (1970–4) IV, 72–4.
24. See L. L. Schücking (1919).
25. Some of the important historically orientated studies of the soliloquy are F. Düsel (1897), R. Franz (1904), F. Leo (1908), M. L. Arnold (1911), E. E. Roessler (1915), J. D. Bickford (1922), W. Schadewaldt (1926), E. Vollmann (1934), U. Ellis-Fermor (1945) 96–126, J. Hürsch (1947), M. Braun (1962), W. Clemen (1964 and 1985), B. Denzler (1968), H. M. Meltzer (1974) and W. G. Müller (1982).
26. *Dictionary of World Literature*, ed. J. T. Shipley (Totowa, N.J. 1968) 272f. See also P. Pavis (1980) 260–2 and 376f.
27. See the chapter entitled 'Dialogue and monologue' in J. Mukařovský (1977).
28. See also H. C. Angermeyer (1971) 118–26 and R. Harweg (1971).
29. M. Maeterlinck (1915) 71–2.
30. For a discussion of the functions of the soliloquy see also P. Pütz (1970) 84–6. It should not be forgotten that it can also have the function of bridging a gap in time: a monologue or soliloquy may be inserted to create time for a change of clothes or role. For a typological survey of monologues and soliloquies classified according to their position, see H. W. Prescott (1939 and 1942).
31. Letter of 26.6.1869; H. Ibsen (1905) 174.
32. A. Strindberg (1979) 112.
33. For an analysis of the Elizabethan conventions associated with the soliloquy, see M. C. Bradbrook (1935) 125–36.
34. G. Büchner (1979) 26.
35. Our analysis of the two contrasting types of soliloquy reaches virtually the same conclusions as V. Klotz's description of the soliloquy in open and closed dramas (1969) 178–82.
36. Examples of this are included in M. C. Bradbrook (1935) 131.
37. The aside is only dealt with in a few historical studies; see, above all, W. Riehle (1964).
38. Calderón, *La dama duende* (*The Enchanted Lady*).
39. W. Riehle (1964) 42–5 uses this example to show what he means by 'secret direct form of address' or 'blind aside'. For a discussion of this special type see also W. Smith (1949).
40. An example of this is contained in Shakespeare's *Richard III* III,i, 79–81. Like the conventional soliloquy, the conventional monological aside has managed to survive being rejected by the naturalists. To take two extreme examples, E. O'Neill, in *Strange Interlude* (1928), used this convention as a medium for presenting inner monologue in drama, thereby expanding it both quantitatively and qualitatively as a dramatic category – for a discussion of this see M. Biese (1963) and E. Törnqvist (1968) – whilst Jean Tardieu has written a one-act play the whole of whose primary text is delivered as a series of asides, and the very title of which, *Oswalt et Zenaïde ou Les apartés*, is enough to reveal the author's intention of exposing the conventionality of the aside.
41. For discussions of the eavesdropping situation see V. E. Hiatt (1946) and W. Habicht (1968).
42. Hegel (1971) II, 527. See also A. W. Schlegel's essay 'Über den dramatischen Dialog' in (1962) II, 107–22. This normative and prescriptive view of dialogue also explains the large number of studies that have been written on the

subject of dialogue – though most of them are written from a historical rather than a systematically typological perspective: P. Gerhardt (1939/40), H. Krapp (1958), R. Ingarden (1960) 403–25, H. G. Coenen (1961), H. Brinkmann (1965), J. R. Brown (1965), W. Habicht (1967), A. Hillach (1967), J. Mukařovský (1967) 108–53, K. Hamburger (1968), W. H. Sokel (1968), G. Bauer (1969), A. Kaplan (1969), J. Müller (1970), R. Cohn (1971), T. Klammer (1973), H. Schmid (1973) 51–95, K. L. Berghahn (1970), A. K. Kennedy (1983).

43. See the more recent studies of stichomythia in W. Jens (1955), E. R. Schwinge (1968), B. Seidensticker (1968 and 1971). The borderline dividing stichomythia and longer forms of dialogical speech is at around five or six lines. See B. Mannsperger (1971) in this context.

44. J. Kaiser (1961) 73–5 is exemplary in this respect.

45. S. Beckett (1965) 75.

46. In this context see W. Habicht (1967), L. Kane (1984) and P. C. McGuire (1985).

47. F. X. Kroetz (1970) 6.

48. P. Handke (1973) 43f.

49. V. Klotz (1969) 86–9 and 162–78 has paraphrased this difference with the contrast between 'uniform sentence perspective' and 'polyperspective' and has provided examples of it.

50. A. Strindberg (1979) 111.

51. A complete repertoire, which would have to be derived from some form of linguistic pragmatics does not yet exist. However, a point of departure might be J. L. Austin's list of those verbs that make the illocutionary role of an utterance explicit. See J. L. Austin (1962) 150–63; also S. E. Fish (1976), J. A. Porter (1979), R. Schmachtenberg (1982) and M. Pfister (1985).

52. H. G. Coenen (1961).

53. R. C. Stalnaker (1973) 397.

54. E. Ionesco (1954) 16.

55. K. L. Berghahn (1970) 56.

56. More recent rhetorical analyses of the 'great speeches' in Elizabethan drama are those by M. B. Kennedy (1942), M. Joseph (1947), W. Clemen (1961), E. Kurka (1968) and W. G. Müller (1979).

57. Representative for this particular school of thought is C. F. E. Spurgeon (1935).

58. G. W. Knight (1930) led the way in this respect. His book included an enthusiastic introduction by T. S. Eliot, who welcomed this attempt to research into the 'pattern below the level of "plot" and "character"' (p. xviii). See also R. Weimann's justified criticisms of this in (1962). See above 3.7.1.

59. It was W. Clemen (1936 and 1951) who provided the decisive impetus in this respect. U. Ellis-Fermor (1945) in her chapter 'The functions of imagery in drama' (pp. 77–95) and A. S. Downer (1949) have taken a more general look at the function of figurative speech in drama.

60. The distinction between the 'vehicle' and 'tenor' has been derived from I. A. Richards The Philosophy of Rhetoric (London, 1936).

61. See M. M. Morozow (1949).

62. U. Ellis-Fermor (1945) 80–3.

63. V. Klotz (1969) 104–6.

64. O. Wilde (1948) 537 and 542.

5. Dramatis personae and dramatic figure

1. See F. Martini (1971) and J. Müller (1971).
2. According to T. van Laan (1970) 72, a dramatic figure is not a 'separate entity with autonomous existence'. This was already the view held by S. T. Coleridge against the 'real-life approach' of contemporary romantic theorists. See B. Hardy (1958).
3. This example is, of course, borrowed from A. C. Bradley (1904).
4. K. Hamburger (1968) 165f.
5. Th. Mann (1968) I,11. H. v. Hofmannsthal's 'Balzac' expresses similar sentiments in the dialogue 'Über Charaktere im Roman und Drama' (1902) in H. v. Hofmannsthal (1957) II, 352–6, esp. 356.
6. See U. Ellis-Fermor (1945).
7. F. Dürrenmatt (1976) 75.
8. We have based this on the interpretation of figure developed by J. M. Lotman (1972) 340–68.
9. The model we have suggested has been derived from the linguistic models in the areas of phonology and structural semantics in which the individual units of investigation are also presented as a set of distinctive features.
10. See H. Schlaffer (1972) 12. Of course, the function of a collective dramatis personae need not be restricted to defining the locale; it may also be one of a commentator or even a protagonist or antagonist. For a discussion of the collective figure, see also H. Müller (1970).
11. The function of the doubling of parts in pre-Shakespearean drama has been examined by D. M. Bevington (1962). See also Aristotle's *Poetics* (ch. 4) for the development in Greek tragedy from a single actor to two in Aeschylus and three in Sophocles.
12. J. Scherer (1965) 50 examines the dramatis personae of Molière's *Tartuffe* with exactly this parameter in mind.
13. S. Jansen (1968) has divided up the figures into a hierarchical pattern classified according to 1) figures that appear more than once but which do not need to be present with any other particular figures, 2) figures that appear more than once but which are never alone, 3) figures that appear more than once but which are always with another particular figure and 4) figures that only appear once. This typology is defined operationally, but is not sophisticated enough. See below, 5.3.3. – also A. van Kesteren in A. van Kesteren and H. Schmid (1975).
14. See N. Frye (1957) 163–85 ('The myth of spring: comedy').
15. The universal relevance of these differential features is shown in the fact that folklore research has demonstrated that the triad made up of sex, age and status are fundamental features of each person in folk narrative. In this context see E. K. and P. Maranda (1973) 135.
16. It originally appeared in Leningrad in 1928, see V. Propp (1968).
17. E. Souriau (1950) 57ff.
18. S. Marcus (1973) 287–370 ('Mathematical methods in the study of drama'). For a discussion of Marcus see B. Brainerd and V. Neufeldt (1974). See also the works by M. Dinu (1968, 1970 and 1974). J. Link (1974) 232–55 and (1975) uses the term 'configuration' to describe the structure of the dramatis personae.

19. S. Marcus (1973) 366.
20. J. Scherer (1959) 141.
21. S. Marcus (1973) 293f.
22. S. Marcus (1973) 300.
23. S. Marcus (1973) 292f. refers to the same parameter as 'population density'.
24. It is this aspect in particular that M. Dinu has concentrated on in his own studies. However, since his formula for calculating the probability of a certain configuration included the parameter relating to the relative frequency of each figure's appearances, he does not assume that all possible configurations are equally probable. He therefore classifies them according to the probability of their being realised. In this way he has been able to achieve a more refined yardstick for measuring the informational value of each individual configuration.
25. B. Beckermann (1970) 214–17. In addition to the chapters on 'characters' and characterisation in most theories of drama, see also N. Brooke (1964). Apart from that there is also a large number of historically based studies, such as those on Shakespeare by J. I. M. Stewart (1949), R. Fricker (1951), M. Doran (1954) ch. 9, L. Kirschbaum (1962), J. Dollimore (1984), C. Belsey (1985).
26. See J. M. Lotman (1972).
27. F. Hebbel (1961) II, 646.
28. E. M. Forster (1962) 75–85.
29. The majority of these stock figures have already been examined in a whole series of monographs, such as D. C. Boughner's (1954) study of the *miles gloriosus*.
30. E. Bentley (1965) 68f.
31. K. Ziegler (1957–62), column 2011. For a discussion of mono- and pluridimensionality see also the relevant chapters in V. Klotz (1969) 59–66 and 136–48.
32. V. Klotz (1969) 64.
33. Our opposition of 'explicit' and 'implicit' corresponds exactly to the contrast drawn by S. K. Langer (1942) ch. 4 between discursive and presentative modes of communication. An analogous distinction has also been made by P. Watzlawick and others (1967), chapter 2.5.
34. J. Dryden (1970) 62. For a discussion of this and perspectival figural commentary see M. Pfister (1974a) 120–5.
35. See S. T. Coleridge (1969) 212 on *Macbeth* I,v: 'Macbeth is described by Lady Macbeth so as at the same time to describe her own character.'
36. G. E. Lessing (1969a) II, 368f. O. Mann (1958) 117 investigates the relationship between characterisation by means of speech content (explicit) and by means of 'behaviour' (implicit) from a historical perspective and comes to the conclusion that Lessing's *Emilia Galotti* was the first German play in which 'behaviour' began to predominate over speech content.
37. F. Hebbel (1961) II, 766.
38. N. Luhmann (1970) 100.
39. See also J. L. Styan (1975) 37–47.
40. H. Ibsen (1980a) 9.
41. T. F. van Laan (1970) 76f.

6. Story and plot

1. Exemplary in this respect are the anthropological works of Claude Lévi-Strauss, especially his *Anthropologie structurale* (1958), the studies of folk-lore by E. K. and P. Maranda (1973) and the sketches by the French *récit* theorists such as C. Bremond (1964 and 1966), R. Barthes (1966) and T. Todorov (1968).
2. B. V. Tomashevski, *Teoria literatury* (1925), quoted from J. M. Lotman (1972) 330.
3. E. M. Forster (1962) 93. For a discussion of plot see also E. Dipple (1970) and U. Ellis-Fermor (1960).
4. *Poetics*, chs. 7–9. See also J. G. Barry (1970) 157–73. Barry's central category of a 'Basic pattern of event' (pp. 25–39), which as the 'root pattern of experience' (p. 31) underlies the foregrounded *mythos* or plot, is unfortunately too vague to be dealt with here. We are equally unable to discuss the archetypical structures of the *mythos* that were presented by N. Frye (1957). For concise discussions of 'action' see K. Elam (1980) 120–6 and L. Pikulik (1982); see also the monograph by S. Giles (1981).
5. M. Frisch (1972) 87f. For a discussion of the historical variability of the concept of causality see B. Beckermann (1970) 175f. In *La cantatrice chauve* Ionesco negated the Aristotelian premises of unity and coherence of plot even more radically and for different reasons than Brecht or Frisch.
6. However, see E. Lämmert (1955) 24 and, more recently, K. Stierle (1975). The French equivalent of *histoire* as a contrast to *discours* has been analysed in *récit* theory in the same way as we have done here. For an analysis of the English *story* see above, 6.1.1.2.
7. A. Hübler (1973) 20.
8. C. Bremond (1964).
9. T. Todorov (1968).
10. J. M. Lotman (1972) 332. See 7.3.1. below for a discussion of the semantic interpretation of space.
11. A. Hübler (1973) 14f.
12. These restrictions and the attempts to overcome them have been analysed by U. Ellis-Fermor (1945).
13. In this context see Aristotle, *Poetics* ch. 7: 'As then creatures and other organic structures must have a certain magnitude and yet be easily taken in by the eye, so too with plots: they must have length but must be easily taken in by the memory.'
14. Thus, in classical drama fights or armed combat were presented verbally from a teichoscopic perspective, whereas Shakespeare tried to solve the problem synecdochically by presenting a few combatants on stage representing whole armies.
15. H. Ibsen (1980b) 161–2.
16. Horace, *Ars Poetica* 185–8.
17. For a discussion of psychological distance see E. Bullough (1957) 91ff. and, in the same vein, U. Rapp (1973) 56–61.
18. V. Klotz (1969) 30–4 and P. Pütz (1970) 212–18 analyse hidden action in some detail.
19. Horace, *Ars Poetica* 179 and 180–2.

20. B. Beckermann (1970) 171ff. has provided us with a short historical sketch.
21. V. Klotz (1969) 32.
22. P. Pütz (1970) 213.
23. Schiller, *Mary Stuart*, lines 3839–75.
24. This represents a variation of the teichoscopic perspective. It shares with it the simultaneity of off-stage events and narrative report, but differs from it by the reduction of the reporter's ability to observe the events to a few acoustic impressions.
25. For a discussion of the report and the messenger's report see K. Schlüter (1958) and J. Scherer (1959) 229–44.
26. See A. Natew (1971) 82ff.
27. P. Pütz (1970) 216f.
28. F. Hebbel (1961) I, 270f.
29. R. Levin (1971) 5–20 has suggested a systematic typology for the various possibilities of combination.
30. See R. Petsch (1945) 171ff., N. Rabkin (1959), G. Reichert (1966) and R. Levin (1971).
31. See J. A. Barish (1953).
32. Examples of this are contained in G. Reichert (1966). M. Doran (1954) ch. 2 has derived this practice convincingly from contemporary studies of rhetoric and poetics.
33. See G. Reichert (1966) 42–5.
34. For a discussion of comic relief see H. Hadow (1915) and A. P. Rossiter (1961) 274–92.
35. S. T. Coleridge (1969) 205 and 208.
36. T. De Quincey (1916) 336.
37. F. Schlegel (1906) II 245. It was E. Schanzer (1969) 103 who drew our attention to this passage. Schanzer's concept of the plot-echo does not refer to situative or thematic equivalences between coordinated sequences alone but also to those between situations in one and the same sequence. This also applies to M. W. Black (1962).
38. For an analysis of the concept of 'reflection' in drama see H. T. Price (1948) and P. Pütz (1970) 147–51.
39. We have attempted to demonstrate this in more detail on the basis of *Twelfth Night*. See M. Pfister (1974a) 146–58.
40. A. W. Schlegel (1846) 412.
41. A. C. Bradley (1965) 214. See also E. Schanzer's detailed analysis of the correspondences and contrasts between the two plot sequences (1969) 105–9.
42. P. Pütz (1970) 103–5 restricts himself to this.
43. This mode of presentation is used in the transitions from the 'real' dramatic level to the level of the dream insets in Christopher Fry's *A Sleep of Prisoners* (1951), for example. For a discussion of the dream inset see J. Voigt (1954) 36–40 and W. Kayser (1963) 196.
44. A. Schnitzler (1962) I, 718.
45. For a different interpretation see P. Szondi (1956) 50–4.
46. A. Strindberg (1963) 521. Our interpretation is confirmed by the additional preliminary remark: 'But a single consciousness holds sway over them all – that of the dreamer.'
47. F. Grillparzer (1960–5) II, 28.

48. J. Voigt (1954) 169 defines the play-within-the-play as 'an insert in a drama which has its own autonomous chronology, space and action to the extent that two different chronological and spatial contexts, that of the play-within-the-play and the drama proper, exist side by side'. See also F. S. Boas (1927), R. J. Nelson (1958), D. Mehl (1961), W. Iser (1962), D. Mehl (1965) and M. Schmeling (1977).
49. L. Tieck (1964) 60.
50. Quoted from *Spectaculum VI* (1963) 364.
51. J. Voigt (1954) 51ff.
52. See V. O. Freeburg (1915) and J. V. Curry (1955).
53. See V. E. Hiatt (1946) and W. Habicht (1968) 161ff.
54. For a discussion of the theatre metaphor and its connection with the play-within-the-play see A. Righter (1967).
55. For an analysis of this kind of symmetry see C. Steinweg (1909).
56. We have omitted several coordinated secondary sequences such as Theseus' adventures whilst he was away (III,v).
57. We are not trying to claim that this three-phase structure is a universally applicable structural principle, but simply that it applies to this specific example. For this very reason the three phases that have been identified here differ from the classical triad made up of *protasis – epitasis – katastrophe*, or, to use the French terminology, *exposition – noeud – dénouement*.
58. J. Scherer (1959) 200.
59. For an analysis of the endings in French classical drama see J. Scherer (1959) 206–8.
60. P. Pütz (1970) 92–5 has rightly emphasised the 'futuric intention of the act endings' (p. 92). V. Klotz (1969) 67, on the other hand, is blinded by his antithetical perspective and fails to recognise the intention behind dividing a play into acts. He writes: 'Every act has a certain unity and autonomy of content. For each new act coincides with a new phase in the pragmatic and inner development.'
61. In this we have followed J. Scherer (1959) 205. See also D. and D. Kaisersgruber and others (1972) and C. Mauron (1968).
62. W. Kayser's analysis (1963) 170–3 suffers from his confusing these two aspects.
63. As such we agree with P. H. Levitt (1971) 9, who describes this unit of segmentation as 'the basic unit of construction', and also with S. Jansen (1971) 401, though he rather confuses the issue by describing it as a 'situation'. See also M. Dinu (1972).
64. J. Scherer (1959) 211–13.
65. K. Aichele (1971).
66. For a discussion of the dumb shows see D. Mehl (1975) and for the 'Rey(h)en' H. Steinberg (1914) and A. Schöne (1964).
67. B. A. Uspenskij (1975) 157–85 has analysed the aesthetic problems posed by the all-embracing or the segmenting frame in general terms.
68. In this context see J. Scherer (1959) 214–24. Scherer demonstrates that even French classical drama did not always and consistently mark *every single* change of configuration with a new *scène*. However, this is a problem that is irrelevant as far as the multimedial text is concerned.
69. See P. Pütz (1970) 27–31. See also F. Dürrenmatt (1966) 193f. in the seventh

of his '21 points on *The Physicists*': 'In a dramatic action chance consists of who met whom by chance, where and when'.

70. For a discussion of the entrances and exits in classical Graeco-Roman comedy see K. S. Bennett (1932) and M. Johnston (1933).
71. See J. Scherer (1959) 266–84.
72. Spanish classical plays and Portuguese dramas from the beginnings to the present tend to be divided into three acts, whereas French, English and German plays – especially the more serious variety – are normally structured around five acts, though in many modern texts dramatists do without subdivisions altogether or have one at the most. However, both the three-act and five-act systems can claim to have been derived from a classical source. The former may be said to derive from the writings of Donatus, the author of a commentary on Terence, who structured plays using a tripartite system of *protasis – epitasis – katastrophe*, whilst the latter is derived from Horace's *Ars Poetica* which called for 'neve minor neu sit quinto productior actus fabula'. In this context see W. Kayser (1963) 171f. For analyses of the problems posed by dividing plays into acts in antiquity see H. Holzapfel (1914), G. E. Duckworth (1952) 98–101 and K. Aichele (1971) 48–54. There is still no comprehensive study of the division of plays into acts. Space prevents us from including one here.
73. The most important recent contributions are those by T. W. Baldwin (1947), G. Heuser (1956), C. Leech (1957), W. T. Jewkes (1958), T. W. Baldwin (1965) and E. Jones (1971).
74. G. Freytag (1968).
75. We have quoted throughout from the 4th edition of 1969.
76. For a discussion of the history of this kind of disposition pattern see H. G. Bickert (1969) 22–39.
77. V. Klotz (1969) 25–38, 67–71, 99–112 and 149–56. B. Beckermann (1970) 186ff. has developed a similar kind of ideal-type opposition. He distinguishes between 'intensive' and 'extensive modes'. The first is represented by the Greek and French tradition and the dramas of Ibsen, the second by the plays of Shakespeare.
78. M. Kommerell (1957) 150.
79. G. Freytag (1968) 114–15.
80. Quoted from *Deutsche Dramaturgie der sechziger Jahre* (1974) 55.
81. V. Klotz (1969) 101–9.
82. V. Klotz (1969) 108.

7. Structures of time and space

1. See B. A. Uspenskij (1975) 90–4 for an analysis of the various degrees of specificity in time and space in the fine arts, literature and in drama and film.
2. See K. Hamburger's reflections (1968) 169–74 on the 'problem of the relationship between the real time–space context of the auditorium and the fictional and yet at the same time 'genuine' time–space context of the stage'.
3. P. Handke (1972) 22; for time, see also p. 28.
4. For an analysis of the concept of 'metatheatre' or 'metadrama' see L. Abel (1963), J. L. Calderwood (1969) and M. Pfister (1978–9).
5. In this context see J. E. Robinson (1959).

6. Aristotle, *Poetics* ch. 5.
7. B. Weinberg (1957) 160–5. For a discussion of the theory and practice of the unity of time and space in the dramas of French classicism, see J. Scherer (1959) 110–24 and 181–95.
8. In 1674 B. N. Boileau felt that he was bound to these rules by reason; see his *L'art poétique* III, lines 38–46.
9. G. E. Lessing (1969a) II, 520 and 522.
10. See T. M. Raysor (1927).
11. G. E. Lessing (1969a) II, 54.
12. *Dr Johnson on Shakespeare* (1969) 69 and 70. For a survey of Johnson's assessment of classicising theories of drama see R. D. Stock (1973). This discussion was continued and refined by Coleridge.
13. See the chapter entitled 'Narrowness and existentialism' in P. Szondi (1956) 95–104. The differing functions that closed structures of time and space fulfilled, depending on whether they were used in classical or naturalist drama, have already been discussed by E. Hirt (1927) 106ff.
14. E. Burns (1972) 71f. sees this shift in locale from the public to the private sphere as a direct correspondence with an analogous shift of emphasis in social reality.
15. *Theorie des Naturalismus* (1973) 168.
16. We shall return to discuss the ways time can be condensed later on (see below, 7.4.3.2.). P. Szondi (1956) 146–54 has analysed the time–space structures in this play in some detail.
17. H. Hoppe (1971) 17. Among the more recent works on the subject of space in drama are M. Dietrich (1965), D. Steinbach (1966), C. Leech (1969), J. Hintze (1969), W. Flemming (1970) and A. Ubersfeld (1981) 52–124.
18. Quoted from H. Hoppe (1971) 65.
19. J. M. Lotman (1972) 330.
20. For an analysis of the 'visual meaning' (N. Coghill) of the spatial groupings of figures in Shakespeare see R. Fricker (1956).
21. P. A. Jorgensen (1948) has analysed this vertical opposition in *Richard II* in some detail.
22. See G. Bachelard (1974).
23. For a discussion of the functions of off-stage noises see F. A. Shirley (1963).
24. For the following I am largely indebted to the studies by N. Frye (1949) and C. L. Barber (1959).
25. R. Hochhuth (1970) 127.
26. J. Dingel (1971) 352f.
27. See K. Ziegler (1954) and V. Klotz (1969) 45–59.
28. A. Strindberg (1979) 117.
29. A. Strindberg (1979) 113–14. Rooms with a similar amount of precise detail were also popular in the lyric dramas of the *fin-de-siècle*. See P. Szondi's analysis in (1975) 162f. See also P. Goetsch (1977) 123–61.
30. See V. Kotz (1969) 120–36.
31. Strindberg wrote in detail on the subject, see (1966) 104.
32. H. Hoppe (1971) 95–178.
33. See W. Habicht (1970) and E. Burns (1972) 91.
34. F. N. Mennemeier (1973) 72f. has analysed an example of this from Arnolt Bronnen's *Die Geburt der Jugend*.

35. A. Müller-Bellinghausen (1953), R. Stamm (1954).
36. H. Kindermann (1965).
37. See the chapter entitled 'Die perspektivische Darstellung des Schauplatzes' in M. Pfister (1974a) 168–78.
38. H. Oppel (1954) 209.
39. We would like to refer in passing to the verbal pinpointing of the locale by means of locality boards on stage. These were occasionally used on the Elizabethan stage.
40. For a discussion of the function of the off-stage area in Greek tragedy see K. Joerden (1960 and 1971).
41. Some of the more recent studies of props are J. Veltruský (1964), D. Steinbach (1966), J. Dingel (1971), H. Conway (1959), H. Hoppe (1971) and H.-G. Schwarz (1974). The function of letters as props has been discussed by V. Klotz (1972) 3–51.
42. See J. L. Styan (1975) 43f.
43. The following section is indebted to P. Pütz (1970) 113–25.
44. Even Aristotle discussed the role of the properties in the moment of recognition (*anagnorisis*; see ch. 16 of *The Poetics*). He felt, however, that the use of objects rather than memory, logical deduction or a new turn of events to bring about a dénouement was to be avoided. Nonetheless, in Western drama objects – or properties – continue to play an important part in the dénouement.
45. Quoted from *Playwrights on Playwriting* (1960) 114.
46. As far as drama is concerned, the two closely related questions of tense and the relationship between the fictional present of the play and the real presence of the performance have not been given adequate coverage in the literature on the subject. In this context see L. Sinclair (1956), J. Morgenstern (1960), I. Leimberg (1961), H. Oppel (1963), J. de Romilly (1968), P. Pütz (1970), Z. Stříbný (1974), M. Winkgens (1975), F. H. Link (1977) and A. Ubersfeld (1981) 230–51.
47. Herder (1964) II, 256.
48. S. K. Langer (1953) 306.
49. P. Pütz (1970) 11.
50. F. Dürrenmatt (1955) 24.
51. See B. A. Uspenskij (1975) 203.
52. See the stage directions in E. O'Neill (1969) 162f.
53. A. Holz and J. Schlaf (1966) 6.
54. See F. H. Link (1975) 121–9.
55. See N. Frye (1957) 163–239.
56. The average length of Elizabethan plays in performance is generally around three hours – or approximately twenty lines of verse per minute. See D. Klein (1967) and J. Smith (1969).
57. P. H. Levitt (1971) 24–34. The term was coined by W. Archer (1912).
58. Our own analysis goes some way beyond A. Hübler's distinction between 'played' (= primary) time and 'treated' (= tertiary) time; see (1973) 62.
59. P. Corneille (1963) 124–6 and 137–43. In making such concessions Corneille's intention is to make it easier to adhere to the unities of time and space.
60. Nonetheless, this is possible in view of the highly developed state of stage technology – for example by using unrealistically fast changes of lighting to

indicate the change from day to night. An example of this is the end of the first act in Beckett's *Waiting for Godot*.

61. See P. Szondi's chapter 'Spiel von der Zeit' in (1956) 146–54 for an analysis of the way time is compressed in modern drama.
62. See A. C. Bradley (1965) 360–5 and 419f., and Z. Stříbný (1969).
63. Goethe (1919); conversation of 18.4.1827.
64. See J. L. Halio (1962).
65. For a discussion of both contexts see A. Mendilow (1952).
66. For a discussion of the use of time in the modern one-act play see D. Schnetz (1967) 135–50.
67. In this context see the not particularly fruitful attempts in J. L. Styan (1960) 141–62 and P. Pütz (1970) 50–61.
68. See J. W. Draper (1957) and P. Pütz (1970) 60f. For a more general analysis of the inset, see F. Berry (1965).
69. See K. George (1980), P. Pavis (1980) 351–3, M. Pfister (1983) and P. Pavis (1985) 297–307.

Bibliography

I. Abbreviations

CE	College English
CL	Comparative Literature
CLTA	Cahiers de linguistique théorique et appliquée
CPh	Classical Philology
CQ	Critical Quarterly
DA	Dissertation Abstracts
DS	Drama Survey
DU	Der Deutschunterricht
DVjs	Deutsche Vierteljahresschrift für Literaturwissenschaft und Geistesgeschichte
EC	Essays in Criticism
E & S	Essays and Studies
Euph.	Euphorion. Zeitschrift für Literaturgeschichte
GRM	Germanisch-Romanische Monatsschrift
JAAC	Journal of Aesthetics and Art Criticism
KZfSS	Kölner Zeitschrift für Soziologie und Sozialpsychologie
LiLi	Zeitschrift für Literaturwissenschaft und Linguistik
MD	Modern Drama
MLN	Modern Language Notes
MLR	Modern Language Review
MPh	Modern Philology
MuK	Maske und Kothurn
NSp	Die Neueren Sprachen
SAB	Shakespeare Association Bulletin
SaS	Slovo a slovesnost
SEL	Studies in English Literature, 1500–1900
ShJb	Shakespeare-Jahrbuch
ShS	Shakespeare Survey
SPh	Studies in Philology
SQ	Shakespeare Quarterly
Stud. Gen.	Studium Generale
StZ	Sprache im technischen Zeitalter
tdr	Tulane Drama Review/The Drama Review
TQ	Theatre Quarterly
WW	Wirkendes Wort
ZfSL	Zeitschrift für französische Sprache und Literatur

II. Texts

Where possible foreign works are given here in English translated editions.

Aischylus 2 vols., ed. by H. W. Smyth, Loeb Classical Library (London, 1922–6).
Appia, A. *L'oeuvre d'art vivant* (Geneva, 1921).
Aristotle *The Poetics*, ed. by W. Hamilton Fyfe, Loeb Classical Library (London, 1927).
Artaud, A. *The Theatre and its Double*, transl. by V. Corti (London, 1970).
Ayckbourn, A. *The Norman Conquests* (London, 1975).
  Three Plays (London, 1977).
Bachelard, G., *The Poetics of Space*, transl. by M. Joles (New York, 1964).
Beaumont, F. and Fletcher, J. *The Knight of the Burning Pestle*, ed. by W. T. Williams (London, 1966).
Beckett, S. *Happy Days* (London, 1963).
  Waiting for Godot, 2nd edn (London, 1965).
  Collected shorter plays (London, 1984).
Boileau-Déspreaux, N. *L'art poétique*, ed. by D. N. Smith (Cambridge, 1919).
Brecht, B. *Schriften zum Theater*, 7 vols. (Frankfurt, 1963/4).
  Gesammelte Werke, 20 vols. (Frankfurt, 1967).
  Seven Plays by Bertolt Brecht, ed. and with introd. by E. Bentley (New York, 1961).
  Brecht on the Theatre, transl. with notes by J. Willett (London, 1964).
  The Good Woman of Setzuan, transl. by E. Bentley and M. Apelman (New York, 1957).
  (see also: *The Good Person of Szechwan*, transl. by J. Willett (London, 1965).
  Collected Plays, vol. II,ii, transl. and ed. by J. Willett and R. Manheim (London, 1979) and vol. VII, transl. by J. and T. Stern with W. H. Auden, and ed. by J. Willett and R. Manheim (London, 1976a).
  Poems: 1913–1956, transl. by J. Willett and R. Manheim (London, 1976b).
Brook, P. *The Empty Space* (London, 1968).
Büchner, G. *Woyzeck*, transl. by J. MacKendrick (London, 1979).
Calderón de la Barca, P. *Comédias*, facsimile edn (Farnborough, 1973).
Chekhov, A. *The Cherry Orchard*, in: *Plays*, transl. and with introd. by E. Feu (Harmondsworth, 1954).
  Dramatische Werke, transl. into German by S. v. Radecki (Zurich, 1968).
  (see also under Tschechow)
Coleridge on Shakespeare ed. by T. Hawkes (Harmondsworth, 1969).
Congreve, W. *The Way of the World*, ed. by L. Kronenberger (New York, 1959).
Corneille, P. and Th. *Théatre*, 2 vols. (Paris, 1894).
Corneille, P. *Trois discours sur le poème dramatique*, ed. by L. Forestier (Paris, 1963).
  The Cid. Cinna. The Theatrical Illusion, transl. by J. Cairncross (Harmondsworth, 1975).
De Quincey, T. 'On the knocking at the gate in *Macbeth*', in: *Shakespeare Criticism 1623–1840*, ed. by D. N. Smith (London, 1916 and often thereafter) 331–6.
Deutsche Dramaturgie der sechziger Jahre ed. by H. Kreuzer and P. Seibert (Tübingen, 1974).

Diderot, D. *The Paradox of Acting* (New York, 1957).

Dryden, J. *Selected Criticism*, ed. by J. Kinsley and G. Parfitt (Oxford, 1970).

Dürrenmatt, F. *Theaterprobleme* (Zurich, 1955).

Theater – Schriften und Reden (Zurich, 1966).

Writings on Theatre and Drama, transl. and with introd. by H. M. Waidson (London, 1976).

Einakter des Naturalismus, ed. by W. Rothe (Stuttgart, 1973).

Etherege, G. *The Man of Mode*, ed. by W. B. Carnochan (London, 1967).

Euripides *Medea*, in *Euripides in Four Volumes*, vol. IV, transl. by A. S. Way (London, 1964).

European Theories of the Drama ed. by B. H. Clark, rev. by H. Popkin (New York, 1965).

Frisch, M. *Tagebuch, 1966–1971* (Frankfurt, 1972).

Sketchbook 1946–1949, transl. by G. Skelton (New York and London, 1977).

Fry, Ch., *A Sleep of Prisoners* (London, 1951).

A Phoenix too Frequent, in: *Four Modern Verse Plays*, ed. by E. M. Browne (Harmondsworth, 1957).

Goethe, J. W. v. *Goethe on the Theatre. Selections from the Conversations with Eckermann*, transl. by J. Oxenford (New York, 1919).

Goethes Werke 14 vols., ed. by E. Trunz, 5th edn (Hamburg, 1963).

Goethe, J. W. v. and Schiller, F. v. *Briefwechsel*, ed. by P. Stapf (Berlin, 1970).

Goll, Y. *Methusalem oder der ewige Bürger*, ed. by R. Grimm and V. Žmegač, Komedia 12 (Berlin, 1966).

Gottsched, J. Ch. *Versuch einer Critischen Dichtkunst*, (repr. Darmstadt, 1973).

Griffiths, T. *Comedians* (London, 1976).

Grillparzer, F. *Werke* 4 vols., ed. by P. Frank and K. Pörnbacher (Munich, 1960–5).

Handke, P. *Stücke 1* (Frankfurt, 1972).

Stücke 2 (Frankfurt, 1973).

Hauptmann, G. *Rose Bernd*, ed. by H. Razinger (Berlin, 1968).

Gespräche mit G. Hauptmann ed. by J. Chapiro (Berlin, 1932).

Hebbel, F. *Sämtliche Werke*, 2 vols., ed. H. Geiger (Berlin, 1961).

Hegel, G. W. F. *Ästhetik* (Frankfurt, 1966).

Vorlesungen über die Ästhetik, 2 vols., ed. by R. Bubner (Stuttgart, 1971).

Herders Werke 5 vols., ed. W. Dobbek, 3rd edn (East Berlin, 1964).

Hochhuth, R. *Soldaten. Nekrolog auf Genf. Tragödie* (Reinbek, 1970).

Hölderlin, F. *Werke, Briefe, Dokumente*, ed. by P. Bertaux (Munich, 1963).

Hofmannsthal, H. v. *Gesammelte Werke*, 15 vols., ed. by H. Steiner (Frankfurt, 1952–9).

Ausgewählte Werke, 2 vols., ed. by R. Hirsch (Frankfurt, 1957).

The Difficult Man, in: *Selected Plays and Libretti*, ed. and with introd. by M. Hamburger (London, 1963).

Holz, A. and Schlaf, J. *Die Familie Selicke*, ed. by F. Martini (Stuttgart, 1966).

Horace *Satires, Epistles and Ars Poetica*, ed. by R. Fairclough, Loeb Classical Library (London, 1926).

The Correspondence of Henrik Ibsen, transl. by M. Morison (London, 1905).

Ibsen, H. *The Wild Duck*, transl. by C. Hampton (London, 1980a).

Peer Gynt, transl. by R. Fjelde, 2nd edn (Minneapolis, 1980b).

A Doll's House, in: *Four Major Plays*, transl. by J. Macfarlane (Oxford, 1981).

Ionesco, E. *La cantatrice chauve* (Paris, 1954).
   Notes et contre-notes (Paris, 1962).
   Dr Johnson on Shakespeare ed. by W. K. Wimsatt (Harmondsworth, 1969).
Jonson, B. *Volpone, or The Fox*, ed. by Ph. Brockbank (London, 1968).
   Timber, or Discoveries, in: *The Works of Ben Jonson*, vol. VIII, ed. by C. H.
      Herford and P. and E. Simpson (Oxford, 1925–52).
   The Alchemist, ed. by D. Brown (London, 1966).
Kaiser, G. *Stücke, Erzählungen, Aufsätze, Gedichte*, ed. by W. Huder (Cologne,
      1966).
Kleist, H. v. *Sämtliche Werke*, ed. by E. Laaths (Munich, no date).
Kroetz, F. X. *Heimarbeit. Hartnäckig. Männersache* (Frankfurt, 1970).
   Oberösterreich. Dolomitenstadt Lienz. Maria Magdalena. Münchner Kindl
      (Frankfurt, 1972).
   Michi's Blood, in: *Farmyard and Four Other Plays*, transl. by M. Roloff and D.
      Gordon (New York, 1976).
Lenz, J. M. R. *Werke und Schriften*, 2 vols., ed. by B. Titel and H. Haug (Stuttgart,
      1966/7).
Lessing, G. E. *Gesammelte Werke*, 2 vols., ed. by W. Stammler (Munich, 1969a).
   Emilia Galotti, in: *Five German Tragedies*, transl. and with introd. by F. J.
      Lamport (Harmondsworth, 1969b).
   Minna von Barnhelm, transl. and with introd. by K. J. Northcott (Chicago,
      1972).
Littlewood, J. and others *Oh! What a Lovely War* (London, 1965).
Lorca, F. G. *Collected Plays*, transl. by J. Graham-Luján and R. L. O'Connell
      (London, 1976).
Maeterlinck, M. *Interior*, in: *Three Little Dramas* (London, 1915).
Mann, Th. 'Versuch über das Theater', in: *Schriften und Reden zur Literatur,
      Kunst und Philosophie*, 3 vols., ed. by H. Bürgin (Frankfurt, 1968) I, 7–36.
Marlowe, Ch. *Doctor Faustus*, ed. by R. Gill (London, 1965).
Menander *The Principal Fragments*, ed. by F. G. Allinson, Loeb Classical Library,
      2nd edn (London, 1930).
   (but see also the new edition: vol. 1, ed. by W. G. Arnott, Loeb Classical Library
      (Cambridge, Mass., 1979), vols. 2 and 3 forthcoming).
Molière *Le Tartuffe*, ed. by R. Bernex (Paris, 1966).
   The Plays of Jean Baptiste Poquelin Molière, 8 vols., transl. by A. R. Waller
      (Edinburgh, 1907).
Mukařovský, J. *The Word and Verbal Art. Selected Essays*, transl. and ed. by J.
      Burbank and P. Steiner (New Haven and London, 1977).
Nestroys Werke 2 vols., ed. by P. Reimann and H. Böhm, 3rd edn (East Berlin,
      1969).
Nichols, P. *The National Health or 'Nurse Norton's Affair'* (London, 1970).
O'Neill, E. *Strange Interlude* (New York, 1928).
   The Emperor Jones. The Straw. Diff'rent (London, 1969).
Osborne, J. *Look Back in Anger* (London, 1957).
Pirandello, L. *Three Plays*, transl. by R. Rietly and others (London, 1985).
Plato *The Republic*, 2 vols., ed. by Shorey, Loeb Classical Library (London, 1937).
Plautus 5 vols., ed. by P. Nixon, Loeb Classical Library (London, 1916–38).
Playwrights on Playwriting, ed. by T. Cole (New York, 1960).
Priestley, J. B. *Time and the Conways and Other Plays* (Harmondsworth, 1969).

Racine, J. *Selected Plays*, transl. by J. Cairncross (Harmondsworth, 1968).

Schiller, F. v. *Sämtliche Werke*, 5 vols., ed. by G. Fricke et al., 4th edn (Munich, 1965).

Mary Stuart, in: *Five German Tragedies*, transl. and with introd. by F. J. Lamport (Harmondsworth, 1969).

Wallenstein's Death, in: *The Robbers, Wallenstein*, transl. and with introd. by F. J. Lamport (Harmondsworth, 1979).

Schlegel, A. W. *A Course of Lectures on Dramatic Art and Literature*, transl. by J. Black (London, 1846).

Sprache und Poetik, ed. by E. Lohner (Stuttgart, 1962).

Schlegel, F. 'Vom ästhetischen Werthe der griechischen Komödie', in: *Friedrich Schlegels sämmtliche Werke*, vol. IV (Vienna, 1822).

Jugendschriften, ed. by J. Minor (Vienna, 1906).

Schlegel, J. E. *Die stumme Schönheit*, ed. by W. Hecht (Berlin, 1962).

Schnitzler, A. *La Ronde*, adapted by J. Barton (Harmondsworth, 1962).

Scholz, W. v. *Gedanken zum Drama* (Munich, 1905).

Shakespeare, W. *The Complete Works*, ed. by P. Alexander (London, 1951).

Shaw, G. B. *Major Barbara* (Harmondsworth, 1960).

Collected Plays with their Prefaces (London, 1970–4).

Shaw on Theatre, ed. by E. J. West (London, 1958).

Sheridan, R. *The Rivals*, ed. by J. Lavin (New York, 1980).

Simpson, N. F. *One Way Pendulum* (London, 1960).

Sophocles, 2 vols., ed. by F. Storr, Loeb Classical Library (London, 1912).

Spectaculum VI. Sieben moderne Theaterstücke (Frankfurt, 1963).

Stanislavsky on the Art of the Stage, transl. and with introd. by D. Magarshack (London, 1950).

Stoppard, T. *Jumpers* (London, 1972).

Straßentheater ed. by A. Hüfner (Frankfurt, 1973).

Strindberg, A. *Twelve Plays*, transl. by E. Sprigge (London, 1963).

Über Drama und Theater, ed. by M. Kesting and V. Arpe (Cologne, 1966).

Miss Julia, in: *Eight Best Plays*, transl. by E. Björkman and N. Erichsen (reissue London, 1979).

Tardieu J. *Théâtre de chambre I* (Paris, 1955).

Terence 2 vols., ed. by J. Sargeaunt, Loeb Classical Library (London, 1912).

Theorie des Naturalismus ed. by Th. Meyer (Stuttgart, 1973).

Tieck, L. *Die verkehrte Welt*, ed. by K. Pestalozzi, Komedia 7 (Berlin, 1964).

Puss in Boots, transl. and ed. by G. Gillespie (Edinburgh, 1974).

Tschechow, A. *Nachlese* (Berlin, 1956).

Werner, Z. *Der vierundzwanzigste Februar*, ed. by J. Krogoll (Stuttgart, 1967).

The Works of Oscar Wilde, ed. by G. F. Maine (London, 1948).

Wilder, Th. *The Long Christmas Dinner and Other Plays in One Act* (London, 1931).

Our Town. The Skin of Our Teeth. The Matchmaker (Harmondsworth, 1962).

Wycherley, W. *The Country Wife*, ed. by D. Cook and J. Swannell (London, 1975).

III. Theory and criticism

* Titles prefixed by an asterisk are general works on theory of drama.

Abel, L. *Metatheatre* (New York, 1963).
Aichele, K. 'Das Epeisodion', in: W. Jens, ed. (1971) 47–83.
Angermeyer, H. C. *Zuschauer im Drama. Brecht – Dürrenmatt – Handke* (Frankfurt, 1971).
* Archer, W. *Playmaking* (Boston, 1912; repr. New York, 1960).
Arnold, M. L. *The Soliloquies of Shakespeare. A Study in Technique* (New York, 1911; repr. 1965).
Arntzen, H. 'Komödie und episches Theater', *DU* 21 (1969) 67–77.
* Asmuth, B. *Einführung in die Dramenanalyse* (Stuttgart, 1980).
Auerbach, E. *Mimesis. Dargestellte Wirklichkeit in der abendländischen Literatur*, 3rd edn (Berne, 1964); Engl. transl. by W. R. Task (Princeton, 1953).
Austin, J. L. *How to Do Things With Words* (Oxford, 1962).
Bab, J. *Das Theater im Lichte der Soziologie* (Leipzig, 1931).
Bachelard, G. *La poétique de l'espace*, 8th edn (Paris, 1974).
* Baker, G. P. *Dramatic Technique* (Boston, 1919).
Balázs, B. *Der Film. Wesen und Werden einer neuen Kunst* (Vienna, 1949).
Baldwin, T. W. *Shakespeare's Five-Act Structure* (Urbana, Ill., 1947).
   On Act and Scene Division in Shakespeare's First Folio (Carbondale, 1965).
Barber, C. L. *Shakespeare's Festive Comedy* (Princeton, 1959).
Barbu, Z. 'The sociology of drama', *New Society* 9 (1967) 161–4.
Barish, J. A. 'The double plot in *Volpone*', *MPh* 51 (1953) 83–92.
* Barry, J. G. *Dramatic Structure. The Shaping of Experience* (Berkeley, 1970).
Barthes, R. 'Introduction à l'analyse structurale des récits', *Communications* 8 (1966) 1–27.
Bassnett-McGuire, S. 'An introduction to theatre semiotics', *TQ* 38 (1980) 47–53.
Bauer, G. *Zur Poetik des Dialogs* (Darmstadt, 1969).
Baumol, W. J. and Bowen, W. G. *Performing Arts: The Economic Dilemma* (Cambridge, Mass., 1966).
* Beckermann, B. *Dynamics of Drama. Theory and Method of Analysis* (New York, 1970).
Beiss, A. *Das Drama als soziologisches Phänomen* (Braunschweig, 1954).
Belsey, C. *The Subject of Tragedy. Identity and Difference in Renaissance Drama* (London, 1985).
Bennett, K. S. *The Motivation of Exits in Greek and Latin Comedies* (Ann Arbor, 1932).
* Bentley, E. *The Life of the Drama* (New York, 1947; repr. London, 1965).
   ed. *The Theory of the Modern Stage* (Harmondsworth, 1968).
Berghahn, K. L. *Formen der Dialogführung in Schillers klassischen Dramen. Ein Beitrag zur Poetik des Dramas* (Münster, 1970).
Berry, F. *The Shakespearean Inset: Word and Picture* (London, 1965).
Bevington, D. M. *From Mankind to Marlowe* (London, 1962).
   Action is Eloquence. Shakespeare's Language of Gestures (Cambridge, Mass., 1984).

Bickert, H. G. *Studien zum Problem der Exposition im Drama der tektonischen Bauform* (Marburg, 1969).

Bickford, J. D. *Soliloquy in Ancient Comedy* (Princeton, 1922).

Biddle, B. J. and Thomas, E. J., eds. *Role Theory: Concepts and Research* (New York, 1966).

Biese, M. *Eugene O'Neill's 'Strange Interlude' and the Linguistic Presentation of the Interior Monologue* (Helsinki, 1963).

Black, M. W. 'Repeated Situations in Shakespeare's Plays', in: *Essays on Shakespeare and the Elizabethan Drama in Honor of Hardin Craig*, ed. by R. Hosley (Columbia, 1962) 247–59.

Boas, F. S. 'The play within the play', in: *The Shakespeare Association 1925–26* (London, 1927) 134–56.

Bogatyrev, P. 'Les signes du théâtre', *Poétique* 2 (1971) 517–30.

Boughner, D. C. *The Braggart in Renaissance Comedy* (Minneapolis, 1954).

* Boulton, M. *The Anatomy of Drama* (London, 1960).

Bourdieu, P. *Zur Soziologie der symbolischen Formen* (Frankfurt, 1970).

Bradbrook, M. C. *Themes and Conventions of Elizabethan Tragedy* (Cambridge, 1935).

English Dramatic Form (London, 1965).

Bradley, A. C. *Shakespearean Tragedy* (London, 1904; repr. 1965).

Brainerd, B. and Neufeldt, V. 'On Marcus' method for the analysis of the strategy of a play', *Poetics* 10 (1974) 31–4.

Braun, M. *Symbolismus and Illusionismus im englischen Drama vor 1620 . . . unter besonderer Berücksichtigung des Monologs und des Aside* (Diss. Munich, 1962).

Bremond, C. 'Le message narratif', *Communications* 4 (1964) 4–32; German translation in J. Ihwe, ed. (1971) III, 218–38.

'La logique des possibles narratifs', *Communications* 8 (1966) 60–76.

Brinkmann, H. 'Die Konstituierung der Rede', *WW* 5 (1965) 157–72.

Broich, U. 'Montage und Collage in Shakespeare–Bearbeitungen der Gegenwart', *Poetica* 4 (1971) 333–60.

Broich, U. and Pfister, M. eds. *Intertextualität* (Tübingen, 1985).

Brooke, N. 'The characters of drama', *CQ* 6 (1964) 72–82.

Brooks, C. *The Well Wrought Urn* (New York, 1947).

Brooks, C. and Heilman, R. B. *Understanding Drama* (New York, 1945).

Brown, J. R. 'Dialogue in Pinter and others', *CQ* 7 (1965) 225–43.

Shakespeare's Plays in Performance (London, 1966).

* *Drama* (London, 1968).

* ed. *Drama and the Theatre* (London, 1971).

Theatre Language (London, 1972).

Bruford, W. H. *Theatre, Drama and Audience in Goethe's Germany* (London, 1950).

Büchler, K. 'Die ästhetische Bedeutung der Spannung', *Zeitschrift für Ästhetik und allgemeine Kunstwissenschaft* 3 (1908) 207–54.

Bühler, K. *Sprachtheorie* (Jena, 1934).

Bullough, E. *Aesthetics* (London, 1957).

Burke, K. 'Dramatic Form – And: Tracking Down Implications', *tdr* 10 (1966) 54–63.

Burns, E.   *Theatricality. A Study of Convention in the Theatre and in Social Life* (London, 1972).

Burns, E. and T. eds.   *Sociology of Literature and Drama* (Harmondsworth, 1973).

Burton, D.   *Dialogue and Discourse. A sociolinguistic approach to modern drama dialogue and naturally occurring conversation* (London, 1980).

Butcher, S. H.   *Aristotle's Theory of Poetry and Fine Arts* 4th edn (New York, 1951).

Calderwood, J. L.   *Shakespearean Metadrama* (Minneapolis, 1969).

* Calderwood, J. L. and Toliver, H. E. eds.   *Perspectives on Drama* (New York, 1968).

Cameron, K. M. and Hoffmann, T.   *A Guide to Theatre Study* 2nd edn. (New York, 1974).

Campbell, T. M.   *Hebbel, Ibsen and the Analytic Exposition* (Heidelberg, 1922).

Chaim, D. B. *Distance in the Theatre. The Aesthetics of Audience Response* (Ann Arbor, 1984).

* Champigny, R.   *Le genre dramatique* (Monte Carlo, 1965).

Clemen, W.   *Shakespeares Bilder. Ihre Entwicklung und ihre Funktionen im dramatischen Werk* (Bonn 1936); Engl.: *The Development of Shakespeare's Imagery* (London, 1951).

'Anticipation and foreboding in Shakespeare's early histories', *ShS* 6 (1953) 25–35.

Die Tragödie vor Shakespeare (Heidelberg, 1955); Engl.: *English Tragedy before Shakespeare* (London, 1961).

* *Kommentar zu Shakespeares 'Richard III'* (Göttingen, 1957; 2nd edn 1969); Engl.: *A Commentary on Shakespeare's 'Richard III'* (London, 1968).

Shakespeares Monologe (Göttingen, 1964); 2nd edn (Munich, 1985); Engl.: *Shakespeare's Soliloquies* (Cambridge, 1964).

Shakespeare's Dramatic Art (London, 1972).

Coenen, H. G.   *Elemente der Racineschen Dialogtechnik* (Münster, 1961).

Coggin, P. A.   *The Uses of Drama: A Historical Survey of Drama and Education from Ancient Greece to the Present Day* (New York, 1956).

Cohn, R.   *Dialogue in American Drama* (Bloomington, Ind., 1971).

Cole, D.   *The Theatrical Event* (Middletown, 1975).

Conway, H.   *Stage Properties* (London, 1959).

Cook, A. S.   'Language and action in the drama', *CE* 28 (1966) 15–25.

Cornfeld, F. M.   *The Origin of Attic Comedy*, ed. Th. H. Gaster (Garden City, 1961).

* Corrigan, R. W. and Rosenberg, J. L. eds.   *The Context and Craft of Drama. Critical Essays on the Nature of Drama and Theatre* (San Francisco, 1964).

Corvin, M.   'Approche sémiologique d'un texte dramatique', *Littérature* 9 (1973) 86–100.

Crane, R. S.   *Critics and Criticism: Ancient and Modern* (Chicago, 1952; abridged edition Chicago, 1957).

Cube, F. v. and Reichert, W.   'Das Drama als Forschungsobjekt der Kybernetik', in: Kreuzer, H. and Gunzenhäuser, R. eds. *Mathematik und Dichtung*, 3rd edn (Munich, 1969) 333–45.

Curry, J. V.   *Deception in Elizabethan Comedy* (Chicago, 1955).

Curtius, E. R.   *Europäische Literatur und lateinisches Mittelalter* 3rd edn (Berne, 1961).

Dadek, W.   *Das Filmmedium. Zur Begründung einer allgemeinen Filmtheorie* (Munich, 1968).

Darlington, W. A.   *The Actor and his Audience* (London, 1949).

* Dawson, S. W.   *Drama and the Dramatic* (London, 1970).

Degrés 13 (1978) (Special issue on the semiology of theatre).

Démarcy, R.   *Eléments d'une sociologie du spectacle* (Paris, 1973).

Denzler, B.   *Der Monolog bei Terenz* (Diss. Zurich, 1968).

Descotes, M.   *Le public de théâtre et son histoire* (Paris, 1964).

Dibelius, D.   *Die Exposition im deutschen naturalistischen Drama* (Diss. Heidelberg, 1935).

Dietrich, M.   'Der Mensch und der szenische Raum', *MuK* 11 (1965) 193–206.

Dihle, A.   *Griechische Literaturgeschichte* (Stuttgart, 1967).

Dingel, J.   'Requisit und szenisches Bild', in: Jens (1971) 347–67.

Dinu, M.   'Structures linguistiques probabilistes issue de l'étude du théâtre', *CLTA* 5 (1968) 29–44.

  'Contributions à l'étude mathématique du théâtre', *Revue roumaine de mathématiques pures et appliquées* 15 (1970) 521–43.

  'L'interdépendance syntagmatique des scènes dans une pièce de théâtre', *CLTA* 9 (1972) 55–70.

  'La stratégie des personnages dramatiques à la lumière du calcul propositionnel bivalent', *Poetics* 10 (1974) 147–59.

Dipple, E.   *Plot* (London, 1970).

Dollimore, J.   *Radical Tragedy. Religion, Ideology and Power in the Drama of Shakespeare and his Contemporaries* (Brighton, 1984).

Doran, M.   *Endeavors of Art: A Study of Form in Elizabethan Drama* (Madison, 1954).

  '"Discrepant awareness" in Shakespeare's Comedies', *MPh* 60 (1962) 51–5.

Dort, B.   *Théâtre en jeu* (Paris, 1979).

Downer, A. S.   'The life of our design: the function of imagery in the poetic drama', *Hudson Review* 2 (1949) 242–63.

Draper, J. W.   *The Tempo-Patterns of Shakespeare's Plays* (Heidelberg, 1957).

Dubois, J. et alii   *Allgemeine Rhetorik* (Munich, 1974); translation of *Rhétorique générale* (Paris, 1970).

Duckworth, G. E.   *The Nature of Roman Comedy* (Princeton, 1952).

Düsel, F.   *Der dramatische Monolog in der Poetik des 17. und 18. Jahrhunderts und in den Dramen Lessings* (Hamburg, 1897).

Dukore, B.   *Dramatic Theory and Criticism. Greeks to Grotowski* (New York, 1974).

Duvignaud, J.   *Sociologie du théâtre* (Paris, 1963).

  L'Acteur (Paris, 1965).

  Spectacle et Société (Paris, 1970).

Eco, U.   'Paramètres de la sémiologie théâtrale', in: A. Helbo et alii (1975) 33–41.

Ehrenberg, V.   *The People of Aristophanes. A Sociology of Old Attic Comedy* (Oxford, 1951).

Eiden, E.   *Figur – Begebenheit – Situation* (Pfaffenweiler, 1986).

Eisner, L. H. and Friedrich, H. eds. *Film – Rundfunk – Fernsehen*, Fischer Lexikon (Frankfurt, 1958).

* Elam, K. *The Semiotics of Theatre and Drama* (London, 1980).

Ellis-Fermor, U. *The Frontiers of Drama* (London, 1945).

'The nature of plot in drama', *E&S*, N.S. 13 (1960) 65–81.

Else, G. F. *Aristotle's Poetics: The Argument* (Cambridge, Mass., 1957).

Eschbach, A. *Pragmasemiotik und Theater*, Kodikas-Suppl. 3 (Tübingen, 1979).

* Esslin, M. *An Anatomy of Drama* (New York, 1976).

Evans, B. *Shakespeare's Comedies* (Oxford, 1960).

* Fergusson, F. *The Idea of a Theater. The Art of Drama in Changing Perspective* (Princeton, 1949).

Fermaud, J. A. 'Défense du confident', *Romantic Review* (1940) 334–40.

Fieguth, R. 'Zur Rezeptionslenkung bei narrativen und dramatischen Werken', *StZ* 43 (1973) 186–201.

Fields, D. E. *The Technique of Exposition in Roman Comedy* (Chicago, 1938).

Findlater, R. *Banned: A Review of Theatrical Censorship in Britain* (London, 1967).

* Fischer-Lichte, E. *Semiotik des Theaters*, 3 vols. (Tübingen, 1983).

ed. *Das Drama und seine Inszenierung* (Tübingen, 1985).

Fish, S. E. 'How to do things with Austin and Searle: Speech-act theory and literary criticism', *MLN* 91 (1976) 983–1028.

* Flemming, W. *Epik und Dramatik. Versuch ihrer Wesensdeutung* (Berne, 1955).

'Betrachtungen zur Seinsweise von Theater, Drama und Buch', in: Fuchs, A. and Motekat, H. eds. *Stoffe, Formen, Strukturen, Borcherdt Festschrift* (Munich, 1962) 33–42.

'Funktionstypen des dramatischen Raumes', *GRM* 20 (1970) 55–62.

Fónagy, I. and J. 'Ein Meßwert der dramatischen Spannung', *Lili* 4 (1971) 73–98.

Forster, E. M. *Aspects of the Novel* (Harmondsworth, 1962; first edn 1927).

Franz, R. *Der Monolog und Ibsen* (Halle, 1904).

Freeburg, V. O. *Disguise Plots in Elizabethan Drama: A Study in Stage Tradition* (New York, 1915).

Frey, D. 'Zuschauer und Bühne. Eine Untersuchung über das Realitätsproblem des Schauspiels', *Kunstwissenschaftliche Grundfragen* (Vienna, 1946; repr. Darmstadt, 1972) 151–223.

* Freytag, G. *Die Technik des Dramas* 13th edn (repr. Darmstadt, 1965); Engl.: *Technique of Drama. An Exposition of Dramatic Composition and Art*, authorised translation from the 6th German edn by MacEwan, E. J. (reissue New York and London, 1968).

Fricker, R. *Kontrast und Polarität in den Charakterbildern Shakespeares* (Berne, 1951).

'Das szenische Bild bei Shakespeare', *Annales Universitatis Saraviensis* 5 (1956) 227–40.

Frye, N. 'The Argument of Comedy', in *English Institute Essays 1948*, Robertson, D. A. ed. (New York, 1949) 58–73.

Anatomy of Criticism (Princeton, 1957).

Gassner, J. ed. *Directions in Modern Theater and Drama* (New York, 1965).

Gaster, Th. H. *Thespis: Ritual, Myth and Drama in the Ancient Near East* (New York, 1966).

* Geiger, H. and Haarmann, H. *Aspekte des Dramas* (Wiesbaden, 1978).
George, K. *Rhythm in Drama* (Pittsburgh, Pa., 1980).
Giles, S. *The Problem of Action in Modern European Drama* (Stuttgart, 1981).
Goetsch, P. *Bauformen des modernen englischen und amerikanischen Dramas* (Darmstadt, 1977).
Goffman, E. *The Presentation of Self in Everyday Life* (New York, 1959).
Goldmann, L. *Le Dieu caché* (Paris, 1955).
Soziologie des Romans (Neuwied, 1970).
Towards a Sociology of the Novel, transl. by A. Sheridan (London, 1975).
Gollwitzer, J. *Die Prolog- und Expositionstechnik der griechischen Tragödie* (Munich, 1937).
Goodlad, J. S. R. *A Sociology of Popular Drama* (London, 1971).
Görler, W. '"Undramatische" Elemente in der griechisch-römanischen Komödie. Überlegungen zum Erzählerstandpunkt im Drama', *Poetica* 6 (1974) 259–84.
* Gouhier, H. *L'œuvre théâtrale* (Paris, 1958).
Granville-Barker, H. *The Uses of Drama* (Princeton, 1945).
* Greiner, N., Hasler, J., Kurzenberger, H. and Pikulik, L. *Einführung ins Drama* 2 vols. (Munich, 1982).
Grimm, R. ed. *Episches Theater* 2nd edn (Cologne, 1970).
Deutsche Dramentheorie, 2 vols. (Frankfurt, 1971).
Groff, E. 'Point of view in modern drama', *Modern Drama* 2 (1959/60) 268–82.
Gurvitch, G. 'Sociologie du théâtre', *Les Lettres Nouvelles* 35 (1956) 196–210.
Habicht, W. 'Der Dialog und das Schweigen im "Theater des Absurden"', *NSp* 66 (1967) 53–66.
Studien zur Dramenform vor Shakespeare (Heidelberg, 1968).
'Becketts Baum und Shakespeares Wälder', *ShJb (West)* (1970) 77–98.
Hadow, H. *The Uses of Comic Episodes in Tragedy*, English Association Pamphlet, 31 (London, 1915).
Halio, J. L. '"No clock in the forest": time in *As You Like It*', *SEL* 2 (1962) 197–207.
Hamburger, K. 'Versuch einer Typologie des Dramas', *Poetica* 1 (1967) 145–53.
* 'Die dramatische Fiktion', *Die Logik der Dichtung* 2nd edn (Stuttgart, 1968) 154–76.
Harbage, A. *Shakespeare's Audience* (New York, 1941).
Hardy, B. '"I have a smack of Hamlet": Coleridge and Shakespeare's Characters', *EC* 8 (1958) 238–55.
Harris, M. and Montgomery, E. *Theatre Props* (London, 1975).
Harrison, J. E. *Ancient Art and Ritual* (New York, 1913).
Harsh, P. W. *Studies in 'Preparation' in Roman Comedy* (Chicago, 1935).
Harweg, R. 'Quelques aspects de la constitution monologique et dialogique des textes', *Semiotica* 4 (1971) 127–48.
Hasler, J. *Shakespeare's Theatrical Notation: The Comedies* (Berne, 1974).
Häuseroth, A. 'Über die Notwendigkeit und Wege einer empirischen Soziologie des Theaters', *KZfSS* 21 (1969) 550–9.
Hayman, R. *The Set-Up. An Anatomy of the English Theatre Today* (London, 1973).
Head, S. W. 'Content analysis of television drama programs', *Quarterly of Film, Radio and Television* 9 (1954) 175–94.

Heffner, H. C.   'Towards a definition of form in drama', in: *Classical Drama and Its Influence. Essays Presented to H. D. F. Kitto* (London, 1965) 137–54.

Helbo, A.   'Le code théâtrale', in A. Helbo et alii (1975) 12–27.

* *Les mots et les gestes. Essai sur le théâtre* (Lille, 1983).

Helbo, A. *et alii*, eds.   *Sémiologie de la representátion. Théâtre, télévision, bande dessinée* (Brussels, 1975).

Hempfer, K. W.   *Gattungstheorie* (Munich, 1973).

Herrick, M. T.   *Comic Theory in the Sixteenth Century* (Urbana, Ill., 1964).

Hess-Lüttich, E. W. B. ed.   *Multimedial Communication*, vol. II: *Theatre Semiotics*, Kodikas/Code Supplement 8 (Tübingen, 1982).

Heuser, G.   *Die aktlose Dramaturgie Shakespeares* (Diss. Marburg, 1956).

Hiatt, V. E.   *Eavesdropping in Roman Comedy* (Chicago, 1946).

Hillach, A.   *Die Dramatisierung des komischen Dialogs. Figur und Rolle bei Nestroy* (Munich, 1967).

Hintze, J.   *Das Raumproblem im modernen deutschen Drama und Theater* (Marburg, 1969).

* Hirt, E.   *Das Formgesetz der epischen, dramatischen und lyrischen Dichtung* (Leipzig, 1927).

Hodgson, J. ed.   *The Uses of Drama* (London, 1972).

Holzapfel, H.   *Kennt die griechische Tragödie eine Akteinteilung?* (Diss. Gießen, 1914).

Honzl, J.   'Herecká postava', *SaS* 4 (1938) 145–50.

'Pohyb divadelníko znaku', *SaS* 6 (1940) 177–88.

'Die Hierarchie der Theatermittel', in: A. van Kesteren and H. Schmid (1975) 133–42.

Hoppe, H.   *Das Theater der Gegenstände. Neue Formen szenischer Aktion* (Bensberg, 1971).

Hornby, R.   *Script into Performance. A Structuralist View of Play Production* (Austin, Texas, 1977).

* Hübler, A.   *Drama in der Vermittlung von Handlung, Sprache und Szene* (Bonn, 1973).

* Hürlimann, M., ed.   *Das Atlantisbuch des Theaters* (Zurich, 1966).

Hürsch, J.   *Der Monolog im deutschen Drama von Lessing bis Hebbel* (Diss. Zurich, 1947).

Ihwe, J. ed.   *Literaturwissenschaft und Linguistik. Eine Auswahl. Texte zur Theorie der Literaturwissenschaft*, 3 vols. (see also 1973 edn in 2 vols), (Frankfurt, 1971).

Ingarden, R.   *Das literarische Kunstwerk*, 2nd edn (Tübingen, 1960).

The Literary Work of Art: An Investigation of the Borderlines of Ontology, Logic and Theory of Literature. With an Appendix on the Functions of Language in the Theatre, transl. by G. G. Grabowicz (Evanston, Ill., 1973).

Iser, W.   'Das Spiel im Spiel', *Archiv* 198 (1962) 209–26.

Die Appellstruktur der Texte. Unbestimmtheit als Wirkungsbedingung literarischer Prosa (Konstanz, 1970).

Jakobson, R.   'Linguistics and Poetics', in: Th. A. Sebeok, ed. *Style in Language* (Cambridge, Mass., 1960) 350–77.

* Jansen, S.   'Esquisse d'une théorie de la forme dramatique', *Langages* 12 (1968) 71–93.

'Qu'est-ce qu'une situation dramatique?' *Orbis Litterarum* 28 (1973) 235–92.

* Jean, G. *Le Théâtre* (Paris, 1976).

Jens, W. *Die Stichomythie in der frühen griechischen Tragödie* (Munich, 1955).

ed., *Die Bauformen der griechischen Tragödie* (Munich, 1971).

Jewkes, W. T. *Act Division in Elizabethan and Jacobean Plays, 1583–1616* (Hamden, Conn., 1958).

Joerden, K. *Hinterszenischer Raum und außerszenische Zeit. Untersuchungen zur dramatischen Technik der griechischen Tragödie* (Diss. Tübingen, 1960).

'Zur Bedeutung des Außer- und Hinterszenischen', in: W. Jens (1971) 369–412.

Johnston, M. *Exits and Entrances in Roman Comedy* (New York, 1933).

Jones, D. B. 'Quantitative analysis of motion picture content', *Public Opinion Quarterly* 14 (1950) 554–8.

Jones, E. *Scenic Form in Shakespeare* (Oxford, 1971).

Jorgensen, P. A. 'Vertical patterns in *Richard II*', *SAB* 23 (1948) 119–34.

Joseph, M. *Shakespeare and the Arts of Language* (New York, 1947).

Kaemmerling, E. 'Theaterbezogene Lektüre und pragma-semantische Dramen-analyse', *StZ* (1979) 171–87.

Kaiser, J. *Grillparzers dramatischer Stil* (Munich, 1961).

Kaisersgruber, D. and D. and Lempert, J. *Phèdre. Pour une sémiotique de la représentation classique* (Paris, 1972).

Kane, L. *The Language of Silence. On the Unspoken and the Unspeakable in Modern Drama* (Rutherford, 1984).

Kaplan, A. 'The life of dialogue', in J. D. Roslansky, ed. *Communication* (Amsterdam, 1969) 87–106.

Kayser, W. *Das sprachliche Kunstwerk* 9th edn (Berne, 1963).

* Keller, W., ed. *Beiträge zur Poetik des Dramas* (Darmstadt, 1976).

Kennedy, A. K. *Six Dramatists in Search of a Language. Studies in Dramatic Language* (Cambridge, 1975).

Dramatic Dialogue. The duologue of personal encounter (Cambridge, 1983).

Kennedy, M. B. *The Oration in Shakespeare* (Chapel Hill, 1942).

Kindermann, H. *Bühne und Zuschauerraum. Ihre Zueinanderordnung seit der griechischen Antike* (Vienna, 1963).

'Der gesprochene Raum', *MuK* 11 (1965) 207–32.

Kirschbaum, L. *Character and Characterization in Shakespeare* (Detroit, 1962).

* Kitto, H. D. F. *Form and Meaning in Drama* (London, 1957).

Klammer, T. 'Foundations for a theory of dialogue structure', *Poetica* 9 (1973) 27–64.

Klein, D. 'Time allotted for an Elizabethan performance', *SQ* 18 (1967) 434–8.

* Klotz, V. *Geschlossene und offene Form im Drama*, 4th edn (Munich, 1969); 7th edn (Munich, 1975).

Bühnen-Briefe, Kritiken und Essays zum Theater (Wiesbaden, 1972).

Dramaturgie des Publikums (Munich, 1976).

Knauf, D. M. ed. *Papers in Dramatic Theory and Criticism* (Iowa City, 1968).

Knight, G. W. *The Wheel of Fire* (London, 1930).

Koch, W. A. 'Le texte normal, le théâtre et le film', *Linguistics* 48 (1969) 40–67.

'Absurdes Theater als Axiomatik einer strukturellen Dramentheorie', *Varia Semiotica* (Hildesheim, 1971) 417–31.

Kommerell, M. *Lessing und Aristoteles. Untersuchung über die Theorie der Tragödie*, 2nd edn (Frankfurt, 1957).

Kowzan, T. 'Le signe au théâtre. Introduction à la sémiologie de l'art du spectacle', *Diogène* 61 (1968) 35–59; also in T. Kowzan, *Littérature et spectacle dans leurs rapports esthétiques, thématiques et sémiologiques* (Warsaw, 1970) 133–83.

'Le texte et le spectacle. Rapports entre la mise en scène et la parole', *Cahiers de l'association internationale des études françaises* 81 (1969) 63–72.

* *Analyse sémiologique du spectacle théâtrale* (Lyons, 1976).

Krapp, H.   *Der Dialog bei Büchner* (Berlin, 1958).

Kremer, G.   'Die Struktur des Tragödienschlusses', in: W. Jens (1971) 117–41.

Kroll, W. and Flaker, A. eds.   *Literaturtheoretische Modelle und kommunikatives System* (Kronberg, 1974).

Kurka, E.   'Zur Darstellung von Redner und Rede in Shakespeares Dramen', *ShJb (Ost)* 104 (1968) 175–91.

Lämmert, E.   *Bauformen des Erzählens* (Stuttgart, 1955).

Langer, S. K.   *Philosophy in a New Key. A Study in the Symbolism of Reason, Rite and Art* (New York, 1942).

'The dramatic illusion', *Feeling and Form. A Theory of Art* (New York, 1953) 306–25.

Larthomas, P.   *Le langage dramatique* (Paris, 1972).

Lawton, H. W.   'The confidant in and before French classical tragedy', *MLR* 38 (1943) 18–31.

Leacroft, R. and H.   *Theatre and Playhouses* (London, 1984).

Leech, C.   'Shakespeare's use of a five-act structure', *NSp* n.s. 6 (1957) 246–69.

'The function of locality in the plays of Shakespeare and his contemporaries', in: D. Galloway, ed. *The Elizabethan Theatre* (Oshawa, 1969) 103–16.

Lefèvre, E.   *Die Expositionstechnik in den Komödien des Terenz* (Darmstadt, 1969).

'Das Wissen der Bühnenpersonen bei Menander und Terenz am Beispiel der *Andria*', *Museum Helveticum* 28 (1971) 21–48.

Leimberg, I.   *Untersuchungen zu Shakespeares Zeitvorstellung als ein Beitrag zur Interpretation der Tragödien* (Cologne, 1961).

Leo, F.   *Der Monolog im Drama: Ein Beitrag zur griechisch-römischen Poetik* (Berlin, 1908).

Lesky, A.   *Die griechische Tragödie*, 4th edn (Stuttgart, 1968).

Levin, R.   *The Multiple Plot in English Renaissance Drama* (Chicago, 1971).

* Levitt, P. H.   *A Structural Approach to the Analysis of Drama* (The Hague, 1971).

Levy, J.   *Die literarische Übersetzung* (Frankfurt, 1969) 128–59.

Lévi-Strauss, C.   *Anthropologie structurale* (Paris, 1958).

Link, F. H.   'Die Zeit in Shakespeares *Midsummer Night's Dream* und *The Merchant of Venice*', *ShJb (West)* (1975) 121–36.

Dramaturgie der Zeit (Freiburg, 1977).

Link, J.   *Literaturwissenschaftliche Grundbegriffe. Eine programmierte Einführung* (Munich, 1974) 311–33.

'Zur Theorie der Matrizierbarkeit dramatischer Konfigurationen', in: A. van Kesteren and H. Schmid (1975) 193–219.

Lioure, M.   *Le drame* (Paris, 1963).

Lotman, J. M.   *Die Struktur literarischer Texte*, transl. into German by R.-D. Keil (Munich, 1972).

Luhmann, N.   *Soziologische Aufklärung* (Cologne, 1970).

Lukács, G. 'Zur Soziologie des modernen Dramas', in: *Literatursoziologie*, ed. by P. Ludz (Neuwied, 1961) 261–95.

McGranahan, D. V. and Wayne, J. 'German and American traits reflected in popular drama', *Human Relations* 1 (1947) 429–55.

McGuire, P. C. *Speechless Dialect. Shakespeare's Open Silences* (California UP, 1985).

* Mann, O. *Poetik der Tragödie* (Berne, 1958).

Mannsperger, B. 'Die Rhesis', in: W. Jens (1971) 143–81.

Maranda, E. K. and P. 'Strukturelle Modelle in der Folklore', in: J. Ihwe (1973) II, 127–214.

Marcus, S. 'Ein mathematisch-linguistisches Dramenmodell', *LiLi* 1 (1971) 139–52.

  Mathematische Poetik, transl. into German by E. Mândroiu (Frankfurt, 1973).

  'Stratégie des personnages dramatiques', in: A. Helbo et alii, (1975) 73–95.

Martini, F. 'Die Poetik des Dramas im Sturm und Drang', in: R. Grimm (1971) I, 123–66.

Matejka, L. and Titunik, J. R. eds. *Semiotics of Art. Prague School Contributions* (Cambridge, Mass., 1976).

Mauron, C. *Phèdre* (Paris, 1968).

Mehl, D. 'Zur Entwicklung des Spiels im Spiel im elisabethanischen Drama', *ShJb* 97 (1961) 134–52.

  Die Pantomime im Drama der Shakespearezeit. Ein Beitrag zur Geschichte der 'Dumb Show' (Heidelberg, 1964); Engl. transl.: *The Elizabethan Dumb Show: The History of a Dramatic Convention* (London, 1975).

  'Forms and functions of the play within the play', *Renaissance Drama* 7 (1965) 41–62.

Meltzer, H. M. *Der Monolog in der frühen Stuart-Zeit* (Berne, 1974).

Mendilow, A. *Time and the Novel* (London, 1952).

Mennemeier, F. N. *Modernes Deutsches Drama I* (Munich, 1973).

* Millett, F. B. *The Art of Drama* (New York, 1935).

Monod, R. *Les textes du théâtre* (Paris, 1977).

Morgenstern, J. *The Drama and Its Timing* (New York, 1960).

Morozow, M. M. 'The individualization of Shakespeare's characters through imagery', *ShS* 2 (1949) 83–106.

Mounin, G. 'La communication théâtrale', *Introduction à la sémiologie* (Paris, 1970) 87–94.

Mukařovský, J. *Kapitel aus der Poetik*, transl. into German by W. Schamschula (Frankfurt, 1967).

  'Zum heutigen Stand einer Theorie des Theaters', in: A. van Kesteren and H. Schmid (1975) 76–95.

  The Word and Verbal Art. Selected Essays, transl. and ed. by J. Burbank and P. Steiner (New Haven/London, 1977).

Müller, G. *Dramaturgie des Theaters, des Hörspiels und des Films* (Würzburg, 1955).

Müller, H. 'Die Gestaltung des Volkes in Shakespeares Historiendramen', *ShJb (Ost)* 106 (1970) 127–75.

Müller, J. 'Zu Dialogstruktur und Sprachfiguration in Lessings *Nathan*-Drama', *Sprachkunst* 1,1/2 (1970) 42–69.

  'Goethes Dramentheorie', in: R. Grimm (1971) I, 167–213.

Müller, W. G.   *Die politische Rede bei Shakespeare* (Tübingen, 1979).
'Das Ich im Dialog mit sich selbst: Bemerkungen zur Struktur des dramatischen Monologs von Shakespeare bis zu Samuel Beckett', *DVjs* 56 (1982) 314–33.
Müller-Bellinghausen, A.   *Die Wortkulisse bei Shakespeare* (Diss. Freiburg, 1953).
Murray, G.   'The ritual forms preserved in Greek tragedy', in: J. E. Harrison (1912).
Nasser, E. P.   'Shakespeare's games with his audience', *The Rape of Cinderella* (Bloomington, Ind., 1970) 100–19.
* Natew, A.   *Das Dramatische und das Drama* (Velber, 1971).
Nelson, R. J.   *Play within a Play. The Dramatist's Conception of His Art: Shakespeare to Anouilh* (New Haven, 1958).
* Nicoll, A.   *The Theory of Drama* (New York, 1937).
* *The Theatre and Dramatic Theory* (London, 1962).
Ogibenin, B. L.   'Mask in the light of semiotics: A functional approach', *Semiotica* 13 (1975) 1–9.
* Olson, E.   *Tragedy and the Theory of Drama* (Detroit, 1961).
Oppel, H.   'Die Gonzalo-Utopie in Shakespeares *Sturm*', *DVjs* 28 (1954) 194–220.
'Die Zeit-Gestaltung im *Hamlet*', *Shakespeare-Studien zum Werk und zur Welt des Dichters* (Heidelberg, 1963) 107–32.
'Wortkulisse und Bühnenbild', *ShJb (West)* (1969) 50–60.
Orrell, J.   *The Quest for Shakespeare's Globe* (Cambridge, 1983).
Pagnini, M.   'Per una semiologica del teatro classico', *Strumenti critici* 12 (1970) 121–40.
Pavis, P.   *Problèmes de sémiologie théâtrale* (Montreal, 1976).
* *Dictionnaire du théâtre* (Paris, 1980).
Voix et images de la scène. Vers une sémiologie de la réception, 2nd, enlarged edn (Lille, 1985).
Peacock, R.   *The Poet in the Theatre* (London, 1946).
* *The Art of Drama*, 2nd edn (London, 1960).
* Petsch, R.   *Wesen und Formen des Dramas. Allgemeine Dramaturgie* (Halle, 1945).
Pfister, M.   *Studien zum Wandel der Perspektivenstruktur in elisabethanischen und jakobäischen Komödien* (Munich, 1974a).
'Vor- und Nachgeschichte der Tragödie Eduards II. von Marlowe über Brecht und Feuchtwanger bis zu Jhering und Kerr. Wirkungsästhetische Untersuchungen zur Klassikerrezeption in den zwanziger Jahren', in: *Großbritannien und Deutschland, Festschrift J. W. Bourke* ed. by O. Kuhn (Munich, 1974b) 372–403.
'Zur Theorie der Sympathielenkung im Drama', in: *Sympathielenkung in den Dramen Shakespeares*, eds. W. Habicht and I. Schabert (Munich, 1978).
'Kommentar, Metasprache und Metakommunikation im *Hamlet*', *ShJb (West)* (1978/9) 132–51.
'"Proportion kept": Zum dramatischen Rhythmus in *Richard II*', *ShJb (West)* (1983) 61–72.
'"Eloquence is Action": Shakespeare und die Sprechakttheorie' *Kodikas/Code. An International Journal of Semiotics* 8 (1985) 195–216.
Pikulik, L.   'Handlung', in: N. Greiner et alii (1982) I, 11–18.

* Platz-Waury, E. *Drama und Theater. Eine Einführung* (Tübingen, 1978).

Poetica 8 (1976) 'Dramentheorie–Handlungstheorie', 321–450.

Poetics 6 (1977) 203–382 (Special issue on mathematical analyses of drama, ed. S. Marcus).

Polti, G. *Les 36 situations dramatiques* (Paris, 1895).

Porter, J. A. *The Drama of Speech Acts. Shakespeare's Lancastrian Tetralogy* (California UP, 1979).

Pratt, N. J. Jr. *Dramatic Suspense in Seneca and in His Greek Precursors* (Princeton, 1939).

Prescott, H. W. 'Link Monologues in Roman Comedy', *CPh* 34 (1939) 1–23. 'Exit Monologues in Roman Comedy', *CPh* 37 (1942) 1–21.

Price, H. T. 'Mirror Scenes in Shakespeare', in: *J. Q. Adams Memorial Studies* ed. J. G. McManaway (Washington, 1948) 101–13.

Propp, V. *Morphology of the Folktale*, 2nd edn, rev. and ed. by Louis A. Wagner (London and Austin, Texas, 1968).

* Pütz, P. *Die Zeit im Drama. Zur Technik dramatischer Spannung* (Göttingen, 1970).

Rabkin, N. *The Double Plot in Elizabethan Drama* (Cambridge, Mass., 1959).

Rapp, U. *Handeln und Zuschauen. Untersuchungen über den theatersoziologischen Aspekt in der menschlichen Interaktion* (Neuwied, 1973).

Raysor, T. M. 'The downfall of the three unities', *MLN* 42 (1927) 1–9.

Reichert, G. *Die Entwicklung und Funktion der Nebenhandlung in der Tragödie vor Shakespeare* (Tübingen, 1966).

Reynolds, G. F. 'Literature for an audience', *SPh* 28 (1931) 273–87.

Riehle, W. *Das Beiseitesprechen bei Shakespeare* (Diss. Munich, 1964).

Righter, A. *Shakespeare and the Idea of the Play* (Harmondsworth, 1967).

* Roberts, V. M. *The Nature of Drama* (New York, 1971).

Robinson, J. E. *The Dramatic Unities in the Renaissance* (Diss. Illinois, 1959).

Roessler, E. E. *The Soliloquy in German Drama* (New York, 1915; repr. 1966).

Romilly, J. de *Time in Greek Tragedy* (Ithaca, 1968).

Rosenberg, M. 'A metaphor for dramatic form', *JAAC* 17 (1958) 174–80; also in J. Gassner (1965).

Rossiter, A. P. 'Comic relief', *Angel with Horns* (London, 1961) 274–92.

* Ruffini, F. *Semiotica del testo: l'esempio teatro* (Rome, 1978).

* Sanders, Th. *The Discovery of Drama* (Glenview, Ill., 1968).

Savona, J. ed. *Théâtre et théâtralité* (Montreal, 1981).

Schabert, I. ed. *Shakespeare-Handbuch* (Stuttgart, 1972; 2nd edn 1978). 'Gesamtkomposition: Zuschauerbezug', in: I. Schabert (1972) 260–72.

Schadewaldt, W. *Monolog und Selbstgespräch. Untersuchungen zur Formgeschichte der griechischen Tragödie* (Berlin, 1926).

Schäfer, M. *Die Kunst der außersprachlichen, sogenannten 'mimischen' Mittel im Spätwerk Hofmannsthals* (Diss. Saarbrücken, 1960).

Schanzer, E. *Shakespeare's Problem Plays* (London, 1963). 'Plot-echoes in Shakespeare's plays', *ShJb (West)* (1969) 103–21.

Schechner, R. 'Approaches to theory/criticism', *tdr* 10, 4 (1966) 20–53. 'Drama, script, theater, performance', *tdr* 15, 3 (1971) 73–89. 'Audience participation', *tdr* 17,3 (1973) 3–36. *Essay on Performance Theory. 1970–1976.* (New York, 1977).

Scherer, J. *La dramaturgie classique en France*, 2nd edn (Paris, 1959).

Tartuffe. Histoire et structure (Paris, 1965).

Scherer, K. *Non-verbale Kommunikation* (Hamburg, 1970).

Schlaffer, H. *Dramenform und Klassenstruktur. Eine Analyse der dramatis persona 'Volk'* (Stuttgart, 1972).

Schlüter, K. *Shakespeares dramatische Erzählkunst* (Heidelberg, 1958).

Schmachtenberg, R. *Sprechakttheorie und dramatischer Dialog. Ein Methodenansatz zur Drameninterpretation* (Tübingen, 1982).

Schmeling, M. *Das Spiel im Spiel. Ein Beitrag zur vergleichenden Literaturkritik* (Rheinfelden, 1977).

* Schmid, H. *Strukturalistische Dramentheorie. Semantische Analyse von Čechovs 'Ivanov' und 'Der Kirschgarten'* (Kronberg, 1973). ·

'Entwicklungsschritte zu einer modernen Dramentheorie im russischen Formalismus und im tschechischen Strukturalismus', in: A. van Kesteren and H. Schmid (1975) 7–40.

'Ist die Handlung die Konstruktionsdominante des Dramas?' *Poetica* 8 (1976) 177–207.

* Schmid, H. and van Kesteren, A. eds. *Semiotics of Drama and Theatre. New Perspectives in the Theory of Drama and the Theatre* (Amsterdam, 1985).

Schmidt, W. *Der Deus ex machina* (Diss. Tübingen, 1963).

Schnetz, D. *Der moderne Einakter. Eine poetologische Untersuchung* (Berne, 1967).

Scholes, R. 'The dramatic situations of Etienne Souriau', *Structuralism in Literature. An Introduction* (New Haven, 1974) 50–8.

* Scholz, W. v. *Das Drama. Wesen. Werden. Darstellung der dramatischen Kunst* (Tübingen, 1956).

Schöne, A. *Emblematik und Drama im Zeitalter des Barock* (Munich, 1964).

Schraud, P. *Theater als Information, Kommunikation und Ästhetik* (Diss. Vienna, 1966).

Schücking, L. L. *Die Charakterprobleme bei Shakespeare* (Leipzig, 1919).

Schwanitz, D. *Die Wirklichkeit der Inszenierung und die Inszenierung der Wirklichkeit* (Meisenheim, 1977).

Schwarz, H.-G. *Das stumme Zeichen. Der symbolische Gebrauch von Requisiten* (Bonn, 1974).

Schwinge, E. R. *Die Verwendung der Stichomythie in den Dramen des Euripides* (Heidelberg, 1968).

Sedgewick, G. G. *Of Irony, Especially in Drama* (Toronto, 1948).

Seelig, K. 'Zu den objektiven und subjektiven Voraussetzungen für die Darstellung der Perspektive und ihrer Gestaltung in der dramatischen Kunst', *Wissenschaftliche Zeitschrift der Universität Leipzig* 13 (1964) 854–62.

Sehrt, E.Th. *Der dramatische Auftakt in der elisabethanischen Tragödie* (Göttingen, 1960).

Seidensticker, B. *Die Gesprächsverdichtung in den Tragödien Senecas* (Hamburg, 1968).

'Die Stichomythie', in: W. Jens (1971) 183–220.

* Serpieri, A. et alii *Come communica il teatro: dal testo alla scena* (Milan, 1978).

Sharpe, R. B. *Irony in the Drama. An Essay on Impersonation, Shock and Catharsis* (Chapel Hill, 1959).

Shirley, F. A. *Shakespeare's Use of Off-Stage Sounds* (Lincoln, Nebr., 1963).

* Shroyer, F. B. and Gardemal, L. G. *Types of Drama* (Glenview, Ill., 1970).

Silbermann, A. 'Theater und Gesellschaft', in: M. Hürlimann (1966).

Sinclair, L. 'Time and the drama', *Explorations* 6 (1956) 68–78.

Sinfield, A. *Dramatic Monologue* (London, 1977).

Skwarczýnska, S. 'Anmerkungen zur Semantik der theatralischen Gestik', in: W. Kroll and A. Flaker (1974) 328–70.

Smith, J. 'Dramatic time versus clock time in Shakespeare', *SQ* 20 (1969) 65–9.

Smith, M. F. *The Technique of Solution in Roman Comedy* (Chicago, 1940).

Smith, W. 'The third type of aside', *MLN* 62 (1949) 510–13.

Sokel, W. H. 'Dialogführung und Dialog im expressionistischen Drama', in: *Aspekte des Expressionismus*, ed. W. Paulsen (Heidelberg, 1968).

Souriau, E. *Les deux cent mille situations dramatiques* (Paris, 1950).

* *Les grands problèmes de l'esthétique théâtrale* (Paris, 1960).

Southern, R. *The Seven Ages of the Theatre* (London, 1962).

Spielhagen, F. *Beiträge zur Theorie und Technik des Romans* (Leipzig, 1883).

Neue Beiträge zur Theorie und Technik der Epik und Dramatik (Leipzig, 1898).

Spira, A. *Untersuchungen zum Deus ex machina bei Sophokles und Euripides* (Diss. Frankfurt, 1957).

Spittler, H. *Darstellungsperspektiven im Drama* (Frankfurt, 1979).

Spitzer, L. '*Situation* as a term in literary criticism again', *MLN* 72 (1957) 124–8.

Sprague, A. C. *Shakespeare and the Audience. A Study in the Technique of Exposition* (Cambridge, Mass., 1935).

Spurgeon, C. F. E. *Shakespeare's Imagery and What It Tells Us* (Cambridge, 1935).

Staiger, E. *Grundbegriffe der Poetik* (Zurich, 1946).

Stalnaker, R. C. 'Pragmatics', in: *Präsuppositionen in Philosophie und Linguistik*, eds. J. S. Petöfi/D. Franck (Frankfurt, 1973) 389–408.

Stamm, R. *Shakespeare's Word-Scenery* (Zurich, 1954).

Stanzel, F. *Typische Formen des Romans* (Göttingen, 1964).

States, B. O. *Irony and Drama. A Poetics* (Ithaca, 1971).

Steidle, W. *Studien zum antiken Drama. Unter besonderer Berücksichtigung des Bühnenspiels* (Munich, 1968).

Steinbach, D. 'Die szenische Funktion des Bühnenraums und der Requisiten im modernen Theater', *DU* 18,1 (1966) 7–14.

Steinbeck, D. *Einleitung in die Theorie und Systematik der Theaterwissenschaft* (Berlin, 1970).

Steinberg, H. *Die Reyen in den Trauerspielen des Gryphius* (Diss. Göttingen, 1914).

Steinweg, C. *Racine. Kompositionsstudien* (Halle, 1909).

Stewart, J. I. M. *Character and Motive in Shakespeare* (London, 1949).

Stierle, K. 'Geschehen, Geschichte, Text der Geschichte', *Text als Handlung* (Munich, 1975) 49–55.

Stock, R. D. *Samuel Johnson and Neoclassical Dramatic Theory* (Lincoln, Nebr., 1973).

Stříbný, Z. 'The genesis of double time in pre-Shakespearean and Shakespearean drama', *Prague Studies in English* 13 (1969) 77–95.

'The idea and image of time in Shakespeare's early histories', *ShJb (Ost)* 110 (1974), 129–38.

Striedter, J. ed. *Russischer Formalismus* (Munich, 1969).
* Styan, J. L. *The Elements of Drama* (Cambridge, 1960).
* *The Dramatic Experience* (London, 1964).
'The play as a complex event', *Genre* 1 (1968) 38–54.
* *Drama, Stage and Audience* (Cambridge, 1975).
Szondi, P. *Theorie des modernen Dramas* (Frankfurt, 1956).
Das lyrische Drama des Fin de siècle, ed. H. Beese (Frankfurt, 1975).
Taylor, J. R. *The Penguin Dictionary of the Theatre*, 2nd edn (Harmondsworth, 1970).
tdr 84 (1979) 67–120 [special issue on the semiotics of drama].
Thirwall, C. 'On the irony of Sophocles', *Philological Museum* 2 (1833) 483–537.
* Thompson, A. R. *The Anatomy of Drama*, 2nd edn (Berkeley, 1946).
The Dry Mock. A Study of Irony in Drama (Berkeley, 1948).
Todorov, T. 'La grammaire du récit', *Langages* 12 (1968) 94–102; German translation, in: *Strukturalismus als interpretatives Verfahren* ed. H. Gallas (Neuwied, 1972) 57–72.
Tomashevski, B. 'Thématique', in: *Théorie de la littérature*, ed. T. Todorov (Paris, 1965) 263–307.
Törnqvist, E. *A Drama of Souls: Studies in O'Neill's Super-Naturalistic Technique* (Uppsala, 1968).
Turk, H. 'Die Gesprächsformen des Dramas', in: *Dialektischer Dialog* (Göttingen, 1975) 181–257.
* Ubersfeld, A. *Lire le théâtre* (Paris, 1977).
* *L'objet théâtrale* (Paris, 1980).
* *L'école du spectateur* (Paris, 1981).
Uspenskij, B. *Poetik der Komposition, Struktur des künstlerischen Textes und Typologie der Kompositionsformen*, transl. into German by G. Mayer, ed. K. Eimermacher (Frankfurt, 1975).
* van Kesteren, A. and Schmid, H. eds. *Moderne Dramentheorie* (Kronberg, 1975).
* van Laan, T. F. *The Idiom of Drama* (Ithaca, 1970).
Vannier, J. 'A theatre of language', *tdr* 7,3 (1963) 180–6.
Veinstein, A. *La mise en scène théâtrale et sa condition esthétique* (Paris, 1955).
Veltruský, J. 'Dramatický tekst jako součást divadle', *SaS* 4 (1938) 138–49.
'Man and object in the theater', in *A Prague School Reader on Esthetics, Literary Structure and Style*, ed. P. L. Garvin (Washington, 1964) 83–91.
'Das Drama als literarisches Werk', in: A. van Kesteren and H. Schmid (1975) 96–132.
Drama as Literature (Lisse, 1977).
Versus 21 (1978) (special issue on theatre and semiotics).
Villiers, A. *Théâtre et collectivité* (Paris, 1953).
Voigt, J. *Das Spiel im Spiel* (Diss. Göttingen, 1954).
Vollmann, E. *Ursprung und Entwicklung des Monologs bis zur Entfaltung bei Shakespeare* (Bonn, 1934).
Vowles, R. B. *Drama theory: A bibliography* (New York, 1956).
Watzlawick, P., Beavin, J. H. and Jackson, D. J. *Pragmatics of Human Communication* (New York, 1967).

Weimann, R.   *New Criticism und die Entwicklung der bürgerlichen Literaturwissenschaft* (Halle, 1962).

Shakespeare und die Tradition des Volkstheaters. Soziologie, Dramaturgie, Gestaltung (Berlin-Ost, 1967); English translation: *Shakespeare and the Popular Tradition in the Theatre* (Baltimore, 1978).

Theater und Gesellschaft in der Shakespeare-Kritik (Berlin-Ost, 1970).

Weinberg, B.   'From Aristotle to Pseudo-Aristotle', *CL* 5 (1953) 97–104.

'Castelvetro's theory of poetics', in: R. S. Crane (1957) 146–68.

Weiss, P.   *Nine Basic Arts* (Carbondale, 1961) ch. 11.

Wekwerth, M.   *Theater und Wissenschaft. Überlegungen für das Theater von heute und morgen* (Munich, 1974).

* Wells, S.   *Literature and Drama* (London, 1970).

Wendt, E.   *Moderne Dramaturgie* (Frankfurt, 1974).

Whitaker, T. R.   *Fields of Play in Modern Drama* (Princeton, 1977).

Wienold, G.   *Semiotik der Literatur* (Frankfurt, 1972).

* Williams, R.   *Drama in Performance* 2nd edn (New York, 1968).

Wilner, O. L.   'Contrast and repetition in the technique of character portrayal in Roman comedy', *CPh* 26 (1931) 264–83.

'The technical device of direct description of character in Roman comedy', *CPh* 33 (1938) 20–36.

Winkgens, M.   *Das Zeitproblem in Samuel Becketts Dramen* (Berne, 1975).

Wittkowski, W.   'Zur Ästhetik und Interpretation des Dramas', *DU* 6, Supplement (1963).

Wurmbach, H.   *Strukturbeschreibung und Interpretation in den Tamburlaine-Dramen von Christopher Marlowe* (Heidelberg, 1983).

Wuttke, B.   *Nichtsprachliche Darstellungsmittel des Theaters. Kommunikations- und zeichentheoretische Studien unter besonderer Berücksichtigung des satirischen Theaters* (Diss. Münster, 1973).

Yates, F.   *The Theatre of the World* (London, 1969).

Ziegler, K.   'Das deutsche Drama der Neuzeit', in: *Deutsche Philologie im Aufriß*, ed. W. Stammler, 2nd edn (Berlin, 1957–62), cols. 1997–2398.

'Zur Raum- und Bühnengestaltung des klassischen Dramentyps', *WW* 2nd Sonderheft (1954) 45–54.

Index of authors

Printed in the United Kingdom
by Lightning Source UK Ltd.
182